PRACTICAL SQL

PRACTICAL SQL

A Beginner's Guide to Storytelling with Data

by Anthony DeBarros

**no starch
press**

San Francisco

Printed in USA

First printing

22 21 20 19 18   1 2 3 4 5 6 7 8 9

ISBN-10: 1-59327-827-6
ISBN-13: 978-1-59327-827-4

Publisher: William Pollock
Production Editor: Janelle Ludowise
Cover Illustration: Josh Ellingson
Interior Design: Octopod Studios
Developmental Editors: Liz Chadwick and Annie Choi
Technical Reviewer: Josh Berkus
Copyeditor: Anne Marie Walker
Compositor: Janelle Ludowise
Proofreader: James Fraleigh

For information on distribution, translations, or bulk sales, please contact No Starch Press, Inc. directly:
No Starch Press, Inc.
245 8th Street, San Francisco, CA 94103
phone: 1.415.863.9900; info@nostarch.com
www.nostarch.com

Library of Congress Cataloging-in-Publication Data

Names: DeBarros, Anthony, author.
Title: Practical SQL : a beginner's guide to storytelling with data / Anthony
    DeBarros.
Description: San Francisco : No Starch Press, 2018. | Includes index.
Identifiers: LCCN 2018000030 (print) | LCCN 2017043947 (ebook) | ISBN
    9781593278458 (epub) | ISBN 1593278454 (epub) | ISBN 9781593278274
    (paperback) | ISBN 1593278276 (paperback) | ISBN 9781593278458 (ebook)
Subjects: LCSH: SQL (Computer program language) | Database design. | BISAC:
    COMPUTERS / Programming Languages / SQL. | COMPUTERS / Database Management
    / General. | COMPUTERS / Database Management / Data Mining.
Classification: LCC QA76.73.S67 (print) | LCC QA76.73.S67 D44 2018 (ebook) |
    DDC 005.75/6--dc23
LC record available at https://lccn.loc.gov/2018000030

About the Author

Anthony DeBarros is an award-winning journalist who has combined avid interests in data analysis, coding, and storytelling for much of his career. He spent more than 25 years with the Gannett company, including the *Poughkeepsie Journal*, *USA TODAY*, and Gannett Digital. He is currently senior vice president for content and product development for a publishing and events firm and lives and works in the Washington, D.C., area.

About the Technical Reviewer

Josh Berkus is a "hacker emeritus" for the PostgreSQL Project, where he served on the Core Team for 13 years. He was also a database consultant for 15 years, working with PostgreSQL, MySQL, CitusDB, Redis, CouchDB, Hadoop, and Microsoft SQL Server. Josh currently works as a Kubernetes community manager at Red Hat, Inc.

BRIEF CONTENTS

Foreword by Sarah Frostenson. xvii

Acknowledgments xxi

Introduction. xxiii

Chapter 1: Creating Your First Database and Table 1

Chapter 2: Beginning Data Exploration with SELECT 11

Chapter 3: Understanding Data Types 23

Chapter 4: Importing and Exporting Data 39

Chapter 5: Basic Math and Stats with SQL 55

Chapter 6: Joining Tables in a Relational Database 73

Chapter 7: Table Design That Works for You 93

Chapter 8: Extracting Information by Grouping and Summarizing 113

Chapter 9: Inspecting and Modifying Data 129

Chapter 10: Statistical Functions in SQL 155

Chapter 11: Working with Dates and Times 171

Chapter 12: Advanced Query Techniques 191

Chapter 13: Mining Text to Find Meaningful Data 211

Chapter 14: Analyzing Spatial Data with PostGIS 241

Chapter 15: Saving Time with Views, Functions, and Triggers. 267

Chapter 16: Using PostgreSQL from the Command Line 291

Chapter 17: Maintaining Your Database 313

Chapter 18: Identifying and Telling the Story Behind Your Data. 325

Appendix: Additional PostgreSQL Resources 333

Index 337

CONTENTS IN DETAIL

FOREWORD by Sarah Frostenson   xvii

ACKNOWLEDGMENTS   xxi

INTRODUCTION   xxiii
What Is SQL? xxiv
Why Use SQL? xxiv
About This Book xxv
Using the Book's Code Examples xxvii
Using PostgreSQL xxviii
        Installing PostgreSQL xxviii
        Working with pgAdmin xxxi
        Alternatives to pgAdmin xxxiii
Wrapping Up xxxiii

1
CREATING YOUR FIRST DATABASE AND TABLE   1
Creating a Database 3
        Executing SQL in pgAdmin 3
        Connecting to the Analysis Database 5
Creating a Table 5
        The CREATE TABLE Statement 6
        Making the teachers Table 7
Inserting Rows into a Table 8
        The INSERT Statement 8
        Viewing the Data 9
When Code Goes Bad 9
Formatting SQL for Readability 10
Wrapping Up 10
Try It Yourself 10

2
BEGINNING DATA EXPLORATION WITH SELECT   11
Basic SELECT Syntax 12
        Querying a Subset of Columns 13
        Using DISTINCT to Find Unique Values 14
Sorting Data with ORDER BY 15
Filtering Rows with WHERE 17
        Using LIKE and ILIKE with WHERE 19
        Combining Operators with AND and OR 20
Putting It All Together 21
Wrapping Up 21
Try It Yourself 22

3
UNDERSTANDING DATA TYPES
23

Characters 24
Numbers. 26
    Integers 27
    Auto-Incrementing Integers 27
    Decimal Numbers 28
    Choosing Your Number Data Type 31
Dates and Times 32
Using the Interval Data Type in Calculations 34
Miscellaneous Types. 35
Transforming Values from One Type to Another with CAST 35
CAST Shortcut Notation 36
Wrapping Up 36
Try It Yourself. 37

4
IMPORTING AND EXPORTING DATA
39

Working with Delimited Text Files 40
    Quoting Columns that Contain Delimiters. 41
    Handling Header Rows 41
Using COPY to Import Data. 42
Importing Census Data Describing Counties 43
    Creating the us_counties_2010 Table 44
    Census Columns and Data Types 45
    Performing the Census Import with COPY 47
Importing a Subset of Columns with COPY 49
Adding a Default Value to a Column During Import 50
Using COPY to Export Data. 51
    Exporting All Data. 51
    Exporting Particular Columns 52
    Exporting Query Results. 52
Importing and Exporting Through pgAdmin. 52
Wrapping Up 53
Try It Yourself. 54

5
BASIC MATH AND STATS WITH SQL
55

Math Operators. 56
    Math and Data Types 56
    Adding, Subtracting, and Multiplying 57
    Division and Modulo. 57
    Exponents, Roots, and Factorials. 58
    Minding the Order of Operations 59
Doing Math Across Census Table Columns 60
    Adding and Subtracting Columns 60
    Finding Percentages of the Whole. 62
    Tracking Percent Change 63
Aggregate Functions for Averages and Sums. 64

Finding the Median 65
    Finding the Median with Percentile Functions 66
    Median and Percentiles with Census Data 67
    Finding other Quantiles with Percentile Functions 67
    Creating a median() Function 69
Finding the Mode. 70
Wrapping Up 71
Try It Yourself. 71

6
JOINING TABLES IN A RELATIONAL DATABASE   73

Linking Tables Using JOIN 74
Relating Tables with Key Columns 74
Querying Multiple Tables Using JOIN. 77
JOIN Types 78
    JOIN. 80
    LEFT JOIN and RIGHT JOIN 80
    FULL OUTER JOIN. 82
    CROSS JOIN 82
Using NULL to Find Rows with Missing Values 83
Three Types of Table Relationships. 84
    One-to-One Relationship 84
    One-to-Many Relationship 84
    Many-to-Many Relationship 85
Selecting Specific Columns in a Join. 85
Simplifying JOIN Syntax with Table Aliases. 86
Joining Multiple Tables 87
Performing Math on Joined Table Columns 88
Wrapping Up 90
Try It Yourself. 91

7
TABLE DESIGN THAT WORKS FOR YOU   93

Naming Tables, Columns, and Other Identifiers. 94
    Using Quotes Around Identifiers to Enable Mixed Case 94
    Pitfalls with Quoting Identifiers 95
    Guidelines for Naming Identifiers 96
Controlling Column Values with Constraints. 96
    Primary Keys: Natural vs. Surrogate 97
    Foreign Keys 102
    Automatically Deleting Related Records with CASCADE. 104
    The CHECK Constraint 104
    The UNIQUE Constraint. 105
    The NOT NULL Constraint 106
    Removing Constraints or Adding Them Later. 107
Speeding Up Queries with Indexes. 108
    B-Tree: PostgreSQL's Default Index 108
    Considerations When Using Indexes 111
Wrapping Up 111
Try It Yourself. 112

8
EXTRACTING INFORMATION BY
GROUPING AND SUMMARIZING   **113**

Creating the Library Survey Tables. 114
    Creating the 2014 Library Data Table. 114
    Creating the 2009 Library Data Table. 116
Exploring the Library Data Using Aggregate Functions 117
    Counting Rows and Values Using count() 117
    Finding Maximum and Minimum Values Using max() and min() 119
    Aggregating Data Using GROUP BY. 120
Wrapping Up 128
Try It Yourself. 128

9
INSPECTING AND MODIFYING DATA   **129**

Importing Data on Meat, Poultry, and Egg Producers 130
Interviewing the Data Set 131
    Checking for Missing Values 132
    Checking for Inconsistent Data Values 134
    Checking for Malformed Values Using length() 135
Modifying Tables, Columns, and Data 136
    Modifying Tables with ALTER TABLE 137
    Modifying Values with UPDATE 138
    Creating Backup Tables. 139
    Restoring Missing Column Values 140
    Updating Values for Consistency. 142
    Repairing ZIP Codes Using Concatenation 143
    Updating Values Across Tables. 145
Deleting Unnecessary Data 147
    Deleting Rows from a Table 147
    Deleting a Column from a Table 148
    Deleting a Table from a Database. 148
Using Transaction Blocks to Save or Revert Changes 149
Improving Performance When Updating Large Tables 151
Wrapping Up 152
Try It Yourself. 152

10
STATISTICAL FUNCTIONS IN SQL   **155**

Creating a Census Stats Table. 156
    Measuring Correlation with corr(Y, X) 157
    Checking Additional Correlations 159
    Predicting Values with Regression Analysis. 160
    Finding the Effect of an Independent Variable with r-squared 163
Creating Rankings with SQL 164
    Ranking with rank() and dense_rank() 164
    Ranking Within Subgroups with PARTITION BY 165
Calculating Rates for Meaningful Comparisons 167

Wrapping Up 169
Try It Yourself. 169

11
WORKING WITH DATES AND TIMES   171

Data Types and Functions for Dates and Times 172
Manipulating Dates and Times 172
    Extracting the Components of a timestamp Value 173
    Creating Datetime Values from timestamp Components 174
    Retrieving the Current Date and Time 175
Working with Time Zones. 177
    Finding Your Time Zone Setting 177
    Setting the Time Zone 178
Calculations with Dates and Times 180
    Finding Patterns in New York City Taxi Data 180
    Finding Patterns in Amtrak Data 186
Wrapping Up 189
Try It Yourself. 190

12
ADVANCED QUERY TECHNIQUES   191

Using Subqueries. 192
    Filtering with Subqueries in a WHERE Clause. 192
    Creating Derived Tables with Subqueries 194
    Joining Derived Tables. 195
    Generating Columns with Subqueries 197
    Subquery Expressions 198
Common Table Expressions 200
Cross Tabulations. 203
    Installing the crosstab() Function 203
    Tabulating Survey Results 203
    Tabulating City Temperature Readings. 205
Reclassifying Values with CASE 207
Using CASE in a Common Table Expression 209
Wrapping Up 210
Try It Yourself. 210

13
MINING TEXT TO FIND MEANINGFUL DATA   211

Formatting Text Using String Functions 212
    Case Formatting 212
    Character Information 212
    Removing Characters 213
    Extracting and Replacing Characters. 213
Matching Text Patterns with Regular Expressions 214
    Regular Expression Notation 214
    Turning Text to Data with Regular Expression Functions 216
    Using Regular Expressions with WHERE. 228
    Additional Regular Expression Functions 230

Full Text Search in PostgreSQL. 231
    Text Search Data Types 231
    Creating a Table for Full Text Search. 233
    Searching Speech Text 234
    Ranking Query Matches by Relevance. 237
Wrapping Up 239
Try It Yourself. 239

14
ANALYZING SPATIAL DATA WITH POSTGIS   241

Installing PostGIS and Creating a Spatial Database 242
The Building Blocks of Spatial Data 243
Two-Dimensional Geometries. 243
    Well-Known Text Formats. 244
    A Note on Coordinate Systems. 245
    Spatial Reference System Identifier 246
PostGIS Data Types 247
Creating Spatial Objects with PostGIS Functions 247
    Creating a Geometry Type from Well-Known Text. 247
    Creating a Geography Type from Well-Known Text 248
    Point Functions 249
    LineString Functions. 249
    Polygon Functions 250
Analyzing Farmers' Markets Data 250
    Creating and Filling a Geography Column. 251
    Adding a GiST Index. 252
    Finding Geographies Within a Given Distance 253
    Finding the Distance Between Geographies 254
Working with Census Shapefiles 256
    Contents of a Shapefile 256
    Loading Shapefiles via the GUI Tool 257
    Exploring the Census 2010 Counties Shapefile. 259
Performing Spatial Joins 262
    Exploring Roads and Waterways Data 262
    Joining the Census Roads and Water Tables 263
    Finding the Location Where Objects Intersect 264
Wrapping Up 265
Try It Yourself. 265

15
SAVING TIME WITH VIEWS, FUNCTIONS, AND TRIGGERS   267

Using Views to Simplify Queries 268
    Creating and Querying Views 269
    Inserting, Updating, and Deleting Data Using a View 271
Programming Your Own Functions 275
    Creating the percent_change() Function 276
    Using the percent_change() Function 277
    Updating Data with a Function 278
    Using the Python Language in a Function 281

Automating Database Actions with Triggers 282
    Logging Grade Updates to a Table 282
    Automatically Classifying Temperatures 286
Wrapping Up 289
Try It Yourself 289

16
USING POSTGRESQL FROM THE COMMAND LINE   291

Setting Up the Command Line for psql 292
    Windows psql Setup 292
    macOS psql Setup 296
    Linux psql Setup 299
Working with psql 299
    Launching psql and Connecting to a Database 299
    Getting Help 300
    Changing the User and Database Connection 300
    Running SQL Queries on psql 301
    Navigating and Formatting Results 303
    Meta-Commands for Database Information 306
    Importing, Exporting, and Using Files 307
Additional Command Line Utilities to Expedite Tasks 310
    Adding a Database with createdb 310
    Loading Shapefiles with shp2pgsql 311
Wrapping Up 311
Try It Yourself 312

17
MAINTAINING YOUR DATABASE   313

Recovering Unused Space with VACUUM 314
    Tracking Table Size 314
    Monitoring the autovacuum Process 316
    Running VACUUM Manually 318
    Reducing Table Size with VACUUM FULL 318
Changing Server Settings 318
    Locating and Editing postgresql.conf 319
    Reloading Settings with pg_ctl 321
Backing Up and Restoring Your Database 321
    Using pg_dump to Back Up a Database or Table 321
    Restoring a Database Backup with pg_restore 322
    Additional Backup and Restore Options 323
Wrapping Up 323
Try It Yourself 323

18
IDENTIFYING AND TELLING THE STORY BEHIND YOUR DATA   325

Start with a Question 326
Document Your Process 326
Gather Your Data 326
No Data? Build Your Own Database 327

Assess the Data's Origins 328
Interview the Data with Queries 328
Consult the Data's Owner 328
Identify Key Indicators and Trends over Time 329
Ask Why. 331
Communicate Your Findings 331
Wrapping Up 332
Try It Yourself. 332

APPENDIX
ADDITIONAL POSTGRESQL RESOURCES   333

PostgreSQL Development Environments. 333
PostgreSQL Utilities, Tools, and Extensions 334
PostgreSQL News 335
Documentation. 335

INDEX   337

FOREWORD

When people ask which programming language I learned first, I often absent-mindedly reply, "Python," forgetting that it was actually with SQL that I first learned to write code. This is probably because learning SQL felt so intuitive after spending years running formulas in Excel spreadsheets. I didn't have a technical background, but I found SQL's syntax, unlike that of many other programming languages, straightforward and easy to implement. For example, you run SELECT * on a SQL table to make every row and column appear. You simply use the JOIN keyword to return rows of data from different related tables, which you can then further group, sort, and analyze.

I'm a graphics editor, and I've worked as a developer and journalist at a number of publications, including *POLITICO*, *Vox*, and *USA TODAY*. My daily responsibilities involve analyzing data and creating visualizations from what I find. I first used SQL when I worked at *The Chronicle of Higher Education* and its sister publication, *The Chronicle of Philanthropy*. Our team analyzed data ranging from nonprofit financials to faculty salaries at colleges and universities. Many of our projects included as much as 20 years' worth of data, and one of my main tasks was to import all that data into a SQL database and analyze it. I had to calculate the percent change in fundraising dollars at a nonprofit or find the median endowment size at a university to measure an institution's performance.

I discovered SQL to be a powerful language, one that fundamentally shaped my understanding of what you can—and can't—do with data. SQL excels at bringing order to messy, large data sets and helps you discover how different data sets are related. Plus, its queries and functions are easy to reuse within the same project or even in a different database.

This leads me to *Practical SQL*. Looking back, I wish I'd read Chapter 4 on "Importing and Exporting Data" so I could have understood the power of bulk imports instead of writing long, cumbersome INSERT statements when filling a table. The statistical capabilities of PostgreSQL, covered in Chapters 5 and 10 in this book, are also something I wish I had grasped earlier, as my data analysis often involves calculating the percent change or finding the average or median values. I'm embarrassed to say that I didn't know how percentile_cont(), covered in Chapter 5, could be used to easily calculate a median in PostgresSQL—with the added bonus that it also finds your data's natural breaks or quantiles.

But at that stage in my career, I was only scratching the surface of SQL's capabilities. It wasn't until 2014, when I became a data developer at Gannett Digital on a team led by Anthony DeBarros, that I learned to use PostgreSQL. I began to understand just how enormously powerful SQL was for creating a reproducible and sustainable workflow.

When I met Anthony, he had been working at *USA TODAY* and other Gannett properties for more than 20 years, where he had led teams that built databases and published award-winning investigations. Anthony was able to show me the ins and outs of our team's databases in addition to teaching me how to properly build and maintain my own. It was through working with Anthony that I truly learned how to code.

One of the first projects Anthony and I collaborated on was the 2014 U.S. midterm elections. We helped build an election forecast data visualization to show *USA TODAY* readers the latest polling averages, campaign finance data, and biographical information for more than 1,300 candidates in more than 500 congressional and gubernatorial races. Building our data infrastructure was a complex, multistep process powered by a PostgreSQL database at its heart.

Anthony taught me how to write code that funneled all the data from our sources into a half-dozen tables in PostgreSQL. From there, we could query the data into a format that would power the maps, charts, and front-end presentation of our election forecast.

Around this time, I also learned one of my favorite things about PostgreSQL—its powerful suite of geographic functions (Chapter 14 in this book). By adding the PostGIS extension to the database, you can create spatial data that you can then export as GeoJSON or as a shapefile, a format that is easy to map. You can also perform complex spatial analysis, like calculating the distance between two points or finding the density of schools or, as Anthony shows in the chapter, all the farmers' markets in a given radius.

It's a skill I've used repeatedly in my career. For example, I used it to build a data set of lead exposure risk at the census-tract level while at *Vox*, which I consider one of my crowning PostGIS achievements. Using this database, I was able to create a data set of every U.S. Census tract and its corresponding lead exposure risk in a spatial format that could be easily mapped at the national level.

With so many different programming languages available—more than 200, if you can believe it—it's truly overwhelming to know where to begin. One of the best pieces of advice I received when first starting to code was to find an inefficiency in my workflow that could be improved by coding. In my case, it was building a database to easily query a project's data. Maybe you're in a similar boat or maybe you just want to know how to analyze large data sets.

Regardless, you're probably looking for a no-nonsense guide that skips the programming jargon and delves into SQL in an easy-to-understand manner that is both practical and, more importantly, applicable. And that's exactly what *Practical SQL* does. It gets away from programming theory and focuses on teaching SQL by example, using real data sets you'll likely encounter. It also doesn't shy away from showing you how to deal with annoying messy data pitfalls: misspelled names, missing values, and columns with unsuitable data types. This is important because, as you'll quickly learn, there's no such thing as clean data.

Over the years, my role as a data journalist has evolved. I build fewer databases now and build more maps. I also report more. But the core requirement of my job, and what I learned when first learning SQL, remains the same: know thy data and to thine own data be true. In other words, the most important aspect of working with data is being able to understand what's in it.

You can't expect to ask the right questions of your data or tell a compelling story if you don't understand how to best analyze it. Fortunately, that's where *Practical SQL* comes in. It'll teach you the fundamentals of working with data so that you can discover your own stories and insights.

Sarah Frostenson
Graphics Editor at *POLITICO*

ACKNOWLEDGMENTS

Practical SQL is the work of many hands. My thanks, first, go to the team at No Starch Press. Thanks to Bill Pollock and Tyler Ortman for capturing the vision and sharpening the initial concept; to developmental editors Annie Choi and Liz Chadwick for refining each chapter; to copyeditor Anne Marie Walker for polishing the final drafts with an eagle eye; and to production editor Janelle Ludowise for laying out the book and keeping the process well organized.

Josh Berkus, Kubernetes community manager for Red Hat, Inc., served as our technical reviewer. To work with Josh was to receive a master class in SQL and PostgreSQL. Thank you, Josh, for your patience and high standards.

Thank you to Investigative Reporters and Editors (IRE) and its members and staff past and present for training journalists to find great stories in data. IRE is where I got my start with SQL and data journalism.

During my years at *USA TODAY*, many colleagues either taught me SQL or imparted memorable lessons on data analysis. Special thanks to

Paul Overberg for sharing his vast knowledge of demographics and the U.S. Census, to Lou Schilling for many technical lessons, to Christopher Schnaars for his SQL expertise, and to Sarah Frostenson for graciously agreeing to write the book's foreword.

My deepest appreciation goes to my dear wife, Elizabeth, and our sons. Thank you for making every day brighter and warmer, for your love, and for bearing with me as I completed this book.

INTRODUCTION

Shortly after joining the staff of *USA TODAY* I received a data set I would analyze almost every week for the next decade. It was the weekly Best-Selling Books list, which ranked the nation's top-selling books based on confidential sales data. The list not only produced an endless stream of story ideas to pitch, but it also captured the zeitgeist of America in a singular way.

For example, did you know that cookbooks sell a bit more during the week of Mother's Day, or that Oprah Winfrey turned many obscure writers into number one best-selling authors just by having them on her show? Week after week, the book list editor and I pored over the sales figures and book genres, ranking the data in search of the next headline. Rarely did we come up empty: we chronicled everything from the rocket-rise of the blockbuster *Harry Potter* series to the fact that *Oh, the Places You'll Go!* by Dr. Seuss has become a perennial gift for new graduates.

My technical companion during this time was the database programming language *SQL* (for *Structured Query Language*). Early on, I convinced *USA TODAY*'s IT department to grant me access to the SQL-based database system that powered our book list application. Using SQL, I was able to unlock the stories hidden in the database, which contained titles, authors, genres, and various codes that defined the publishing world. Analyzing data with SQL to discover interesting stories is exactly what you'll learn to do using this book.

What Is SQL?

SQL is a widely used programming language that allows you to define and query databases. Whether you're a marketing analyst, a journalist, or a researcher mapping neurons in the brain of a fruit fly, you'll benefit from using SQL to manage database objects as well as create, modify, explore, and summarize data.

Because SQL is a mature language that has been around for decades, it's deeply ingrained in many modern systems. A pair of IBM researchers first outlined the syntax for SQL (then called SEQUEL) in a 1974 paper, building on the theoretical work of the British computer scientist Edgar F. Codd. In 1979, a precursor to the database company Oracle (then called Relational Software) became the first to use the language in a commercial product. Today, it continues to rank as one of the most-used computer languages in the world, and that's unlikely to change soon.

SQL comes in several variants, which are generally tied to specific database systems. The American National Standards Institute (ANSI) and International Organization for Standardization (ISO), which set standards for products and technologies, provide standards for the language and shepherd revisions to it. The good news is that the variants don't stray far from the standard, so once you learn the SQL conventions for one database, you can transfer that knowledge to other systems.

Why Use SQL?

So why should you use SQL? After all, SQL is not usually the first tool people choose when they're learning to analyze data. In fact, many people start with Microsoft Excel spreadsheets and their assortment of analytic functions. After working with Excel, they might graduate to Access, the database system built into Microsoft Office, which has a graphical query interface that makes it easy to get work done, making SQL skills optional.

But as you might know, Excel and Access have their limits. Excel currently allows 1,048,576 rows maximum per worksheet, and Access limits database size to two gigabytes and limits columns to 255 per table. It's not uncommon for data sets to surpass those limits, particularly when you're working with data dumped from government systems. The last obstacle you want to discover while facing a deadline is that your database system doesn't have the capacity to get the job done.

Using a robust SQL database system allows you to work with terabytes of data, multiple related tables, and thousands of columns. It gives you improved programmatic control over the structure of your data, leading to efficiency, speed, and—most important—accuracy.

SQL is also an excellent adjunct to programming languages used in the data sciences, such as R and Python. If you use either language, you can connect to SQL databases and, in some cases, even incorporate SQL syntax directly into the language. For people with no background in programming languages, SQL often serves as an easy-to-understand introduction into concepts related to data structures and programming logic.

Additionally, knowing SQL can help you beyond data analysis. If you delve into building online applications, you'll find that databases provide the backend power for many common web frameworks, interactive maps, and content management systems. When you need to dig beneath the surface of these applications, SQL's capability to manipulate data and databases will come in very handy.

About This Book

Practical SQL is for people who encounter data in their everyday lives and want to learn how to analyze and transform it. To this end, I discuss real-world data and scenarios, such as U.S. Census demographics, crime statistics, and data about taxi rides in New York City. Along with information about databases and code, you'll also learn tips on how to analyze and acquire data as well as other valuable insights I've accumulated throughout my career. I won't focus on setting up servers or other tasks typically handled by a database administrator, but the SQL and PostgreSQL fundamentals you learn in this book will serve you well if you intend to go that route.

I've designed the exercises for beginner SQL coders but will assume that you know your way around your computer, including how to install programs, navigate your hard drive, and download files from the internet. Although many chapters in this book can stand alone, you should work through the book sequentially to build on the fundamentals. Some data sets used in early chapters reappear later in the book, so following the book in order will help you stay on track.

Practical SQL starts with the basics of databases, queries, tables, and data that are common to SQL across many database systems. Chapters 13 to 17 cover topics more specific to PostgreSQL, such as full text search and GIS. The following table of contents provides more detail about the topics discussed in each chapter:

Chapter 1: Creating Your First Database and Table introduces PostgreSQL, the pgAdmin user interface, and the code for loading a simple data set about teachers into a new database.

Chapter 2: Beginning Data Exploration with SELECT explores basic SQL query syntax, including how to sort and filter data.

Chapter 3: Understanding Data Types explains the definitions for setting columns in a table to hold specific types of data, from text to dates to various forms of numbers.

Chapter 4: Importing and Exporting Data explains how to use SQL commands to load data from external files and then export it. You'll load a table of U.S. Census population data that you'll use throughout the book.

Chapter 5: Basic Math and Stats with SQL covers arithmetic operations and introduces aggregate functions for finding sums, averages, and medians.

Chapter 6: Joining Tables in a Relational Database explains how to query multiple, related tables by joining them on key columns. You'll learn how and when to use different types of joins.

Chapter 7: Table Design that Works for You covers how to set up tables to improve the organization and integrity of your data as well as how to speed up queries using indexes.

Chapter 8: Extracting Information by Grouping and Summarizing explains how to use aggregate functions to find trends in U.S. library use based on annual surveys.

Chapter 9: Inspecting and Modifying Data explores how to find and fix incomplete or inaccurate data using a collection of records about meat, egg, and poultry producers as an example.

Chapter 10: Statistical Functions in SQL introduces correlation, regression, and ranking functions in SQL to help you derive more meaning from data sets.

Chapter 11: Working with Dates and Times explains how to create, manipulate, and query dates and times in your database, including working with time zones, using data on New York City taxi trips and Amtrak train schedules.

Chapter 12: Advanced Query Techniques explains how to use more complex SQL operations, such as subqueries and cross tabulations, and the CASE statement to reclassify values in a data set on temperature readings.

Chapter 13: Mining Text to Find Meaningful Data covers how to use PostgreSQL's full text search engine and regular expressions to extract data from unstructured text, using a collection of speeches by U.S. presidents as an example.

Chapter 14: Analyzing Spatial Data with PostGIS introduces data types and queries related to spatial objects, which will let you analyze geographical features like states, roads, and rivers.

Chapter 15: Saving Time with Views, Functions, and Triggers explains how to automate database tasks so you can avoid repeating routine work.

Chapter 16: Using PostgreSQL from the Command Line covers how to use text commands at your computer's command prompt to connect to your database and run queries.

Chapter 17: Maintaining Your Database provides tips and procedures for tracking the size of your database, customizing settings, and backing up data.

Chapter 18: Identifying and Telling the Story Behind Your Data provides guidelines for generating ideas for analysis, vetting data, drawing sound conclusions, and presenting your findings clearly.

Appendix: Additional PostgreSQL Resources lists software and documentation to help you grow your skills.

Each chapter ends with a "Try It Yourself" section that contains exercises to help you reinforce the topics you learned.

Using the Book's Code Examples

Each chapter includes code examples, and most use data sets I've already compiled. All the code and sample data in the book is available to download at *https://www.nostarch.com/practicalSQL/*. Click the **Download the code from GitHub** link to go to the GitHub repository that holds this material. At GitHub, you should see a "Clone or Download" button that gives you the option to download a ZIP file with all the materials. Save the file to your computer in a location where you can easily find it, such as your desktop.

Inside the ZIP file is a folder for each chapter. Each folder contains a file named *Chapter_XX* (*XX* is the chapter number) that ends with a *.sql* extension. You can open those files with a text editor or with the PostgreSQL administrative tool you'll install. You can copy and paste code when the book instructs you to run it. Note that in the book, several code examples are truncated to save space, but you'll need the full listing from the *.sql* file to complete the exercise. You'll know an example is truncated when you see --*snip*-- inside the listing.

Also in the *.sql* files, you'll see lines that begin with two hyphens (--) and a space. These are comments that provide the code's listing number and additional context, but they're not part of the code. These comments also note when the file has additional examples that aren't in the book.

> **NOTE** *After downloading data, Windows users might need to provide permission for the database to read files. To do so, right-click the folder containing the code and data, select Properties, and click the Security tab. Click **Edit**, then **Add**. Type the name **Everyone** into the object names box and click **OK**. Highlight Everyone in the user list, select all boxes under Allow, and then click **Apply** and **OK**.*

Using PostgreSQL

In this book, I'll teach you SQL using the open source PostgreSQL database system. PostgreSQL, or simply Postgres, is a robust database system that can handle very large amounts of data. Here are some reasons PostgreSQL is a great choice to use with this book:

- It's free.
- It's available for Windows, macOS, and Linux operating systems.
- Its SQL implementation closely follows ANSI standards.
- It's widely used for analytics and data mining, so finding help online from peers is easy.
- Its geospatial extension, PostGIS, lets you analyze geometric data and perform mapping functions.
- It's available in several variants, such as Amazon Redshift and Greenplum, which focus on processing huge data sets.
- It's a common choice for web applications, including those powered by the popular web frameworks Django and Ruby on Rails.

Of course, you can also use another database system, such as Microsoft SQL Server or MySQL; many code examples in this book translate easily to either SQL implementation. However, some examples, especially later in the book, do not, and you'll need to search online for equivalent solutions. Where appropriate, I'll note whether an example code follows the ANSI SQL standard and may be portable to other systems or whether it's specific to PostgreSQL.

Installing PostgreSQL

You'll start by installing the PostgreSQL database and the graphical administrative tool pgAdmin, which is software that makes it easy to manage your database, import and export data, and write queries.

One great benefit of working with PostgreSQL is that regardless of whether you work on Windows, macOS, or Linux, the open source community has made it easy to get PostgreSQL up and running. The following sections outline installation for all three operating systems as of this writing, but options might change as new versions are released. Check the documentation noted in each section as well as the GitHub repository with the book's resources; I'll maintain the files with updates and answers to frequently asked questions.

NOTE *Always install the latest available version of PostgreSQL for your operating system to ensure that it's up to date on security patches and new features. For this book, I'll assume you're using version 10.0 or later.*

Windows Installation

For Windows, I recommend using the installer provided by the company EnterpriseDB, which offers support and services for PostgreSQL users. EnterpriseDB's package bundles PostgreSQL with pgAdmin and the company's own Stack Builder, which also installs the spatial database extension PostGIS and programming language support, among other tools. To get the software, visit *https://www.enterprisedb.com/* and create a free account. Then go to the downloads page at *https://www.enterprisedb.com/software-downloads-postgres/*.

Select the latest available 64-bit Windows version of EDB Postgres Standard unless you're using an older PC with 32-bit Windows. After you download the installer, follow these steps:

1. Right-click the installer and select **Run as administrator**. Answer **Yes** to the question about allowing the program to make changes to your computer. The program will perform a setup task and then present an initial welcome screen. Click through it.

2. Choose your installation directory, accepting the default.

3. On the Select Components screen, select the boxes to install PostgreSQL Server, the pgAdmin tool, Stack Builder, and Command Line Tools.

4. Choose the location to store data. You can choose the default, which is in a "data" subdirectory in the PostgreSQL directory.

5. Choose a password. PostgreSQL is robust with security and permissions. This password is for the initial database superuser account, which is called postgres.

6. Select a port number where the server will listen. Unless you have another database or application using it, the default of 5432 should be fine. If you have another version of PostgreSQL already installed or some other application is using that default, the value might be 5433 or another number, which is also okay.

7. Select your locale. Using the default is fine. Then click through the summary screen to begin the installation, which will take several minutes.

8. When the installation is done, you'll be asked whether you want to launch EnterpriseDB's Stack Builder to obtain additional packages. Select the box and click **Finish**.

9. When Stack Builder launches, choose the PostgreSQL installation on the drop-down menu and click **Next**. A list of additional applications should download.

10. Expand the **Spatial Extensions** menu and select either the 32-bit or 64-bit version of PostGIS Bundle for the version of Postgres you installed. Also, expand the **Add-ons, tools and utilities** menu and select EDB Language Pack, which installs support for programming languages including Python. Click through several times; you'll need to wait while the installer downloads the additional components.

11. When installation files have been downloaded, click **Next** to install both components. For PostGIS, you'll need to agree to the license terms; click through until you're asked to Choose Components. Make sure PostGIS and Create spatial database are selected. Click **Next**, accept the default database location, and click **Next** again.

12. Enter your database password when prompted and continue through the prompts to finish installing PostGIS.

13. Answer **Yes** when asked to register GDAL. Also, answer **Yes** to the questions about setting POSTGIS_ENABLED_DRIVERS and enabling the POSTGIS_ENABLE_OUTDB_RASTERS environment variable.

When finished, a PostgreSQL folder that contains shortcuts and links to documentation should be on your Windows Start menu.

If you experience any hiccups installing PostgreSQL, refer to the "Troubleshooting" section of the EDB guide at *https://www.enterprisedb.com/resources/product-documentation/*. If you're unable to install PostGIS via Stack Builder, try downloading a separate installer from the PostGIS site at *http://postgis.net/windows_downloads/* and consult the guides at *http://postgis.net/documentation/*.

macOS Installation

For macOS users, I recommend obtaining Postgres.app, an open source macOS application that includes PostgreSQL as well as the PostGIS extension and a few other goodies:

1. Visit *http://postgresapp.com/* and download the app's Disk Image file that ends in *.dmg*.

2. Double-click the *.dmg* file to open it, and then drag and drop the app icon into your *Applications* folder.

3. Double-click the app icon. When Postgres.app opens, click **Initialize** to create and start a PostgreSQL database.

A small elephant icon in your menu bar indicates that you now have a database running. To use included PostgreSQL command line tools, you'll need to open your Terminal application and run the following code at the prompt (you can copy the code as a single line from the Postgres.app site at *https://postgresapp.com/documentation/install.html*):

```
sudo mkdir -p /etc/paths.d &&
echo /Applications/Postgres.app/Contents/Versions/latest/bin | sudo tee /etc/paths.d/
postgresapp
```

Next, because Postgres.app doesn't include pgAdmin, you'll need to follow these steps to download and run pgAdmin:

1. Visit the pgAdmin site's page for macOS downloads at *https://www.pgadmin.org/download/pgadmin-4-macos/*.

2. Select the latest version and download the installer (look for a Disk Image file that ends in *.dmg*).

3. Double-click the *.dmg* file, click through the prompt to accept the terms, and then drag pgAdmin's elephant app icon into your *Applications* folder.

4. Double-click the app icon to launch pgAdmin.

NOTE *On macOS, when you launch pgAdmin the first time, a dialog might appear that displays "pgAdmin4.app can't be opened because it is from an unidentified developer." Right-click the icon and select **Open**. The next dialog should give you the option to open the app; going forward, your Mac will remember you've granted this permission.*

Installation on macOS is relatively simple, but if you encounter any issues, review the documentation for Postgres.app at *https://postgresapp.com/documentation/* and for pgAdmin at *https://www.pgadmin.org/docs/*.

Linux Installation

If you're a Linux user, installing PostgreSQL becomes simultaneously easy and difficult, which in my experience is very much the way it is in the Linux universe. Most popular Linux distributions—including Ubuntu, Debian, and CentOS—bundle PostgreSQL in their standard package. However, some distributions stay on top of updates more than others. The best path is to consult your distribution's documentation for the best way to install PostgreSQL if it's not already included or if you want to upgrade to a more recent version.

Alternatively, the PostgreSQL project maintains complete up-to-date package repositories for Red Hat variants, Debian, and Ubuntu. Visit *https://yum.postgresql.org/* and *https://wiki.postgresql.org/wiki/Apt* for details. The packages you'll want to install include the client and server for PostgreSQL, pgAdmin (if available), PostGIS, and PL/Python. The exact names of these packages will vary according to your Linux distribution. You might also need to manually start the PostgreSQL database server.

pgAdmin is rarely part of Linux distributions. To install it, refer to the pgAdmin site at *https://www.pgadmin.org/download/* for the latest instructions and to see whether your platform is supported. If you're feeling adventurous, you can find instructions on building the app from source code at *https://www.pgadmin.org/download/pgadmin-4-source-code/*.

Working with pgAdmin

Before you can start writing code, you'll need to become familiar with pgAdmin, which is the administration and management tool for PostgreSQL. It's free, but don't underestimate its performance. In fact, pgAdmin is a full-featured tool similar to tools for purchase, such as Microsoft's SQL Server Management Studio, in its capability to let you control multiple aspects of server operations. It includes a graphical interface for configuring and administrating your PostgreSQL server and databases, and—most appropriately for this book—offers a SQL query tool for writing, testing, and saving queries.

If you're using Windows, pgAdmin should come with the PostgreSQL package you downloaded from EnterpriseDB. On the Start menu, select

PostgreSQL ▸ **pgAdmin 4** (the version number of Postgres should also appear in the menu). If you're using macOS and have installed pgAdmin separately, click the pgAdmin icon in your *Applications* folder, making sure you've also launched Postgres.app.

When you open pgAdmin, it should look similar to Figure 1.

Figure 1: The macOS version of the pgAdmin opening screen

The left vertical pane displays an object browser where you can view available servers, databases, users, and other objects. Across the top of the screen is a collection of menu items, and below those are tabs to display various aspects of database objects and performance.

Next, use the following steps to connect to the default database:

1. In the object browser, expand the plus sign (+) to the left of the Servers node to show the default server. Depending on your operating system, the default server name could be *localhost* or *PostgreSQL x*, where *x* is the Postgres version number.

2. Double-click the server name. Enter the password you chose during installation if prompted. A brief message appears while pgAdmin is establishing a connection. When you're connected, several new object items should display under the server name.

3. Expand *Databases* and then expand the default database postgres.

4. Under postgres, expand the *Schemas* object, and then expand *public*.

Your object browser pane should look similar to Figure 2.

NOTE *If pgAdmin doesn't show a default under Servers, you'll need to add it. Right-click Servers, and choose the Create Server option. In the dialog, type a name for your server in the General tab. On the Connection tab, in the Host name/address box, type* localhost. *Click **Save**, and you should see your server listed.*

This collection of objects defines every feature of your database server. There's a lot here, but for now we'll focus on the location of tables. To view a table's structure or perform actions on it with pgAdmin, this is where you can access the table. In Chapter 1, you'll use this browser to create a new database and leave the default postgres as is.

In addition, pgAdmin includes a *Query Tool*, which is where you write and execute code. To open the Query Tool, in pgAdmin's object browser, click once on any database to highlight it. For example, click the postgres database and then select **Tools ▸ Query Tool**. The Query Tool has two panes: one for writing queries and one for output.

It's possible to open multiple tabs to connect to and write queries for different databases or just to organize your code the way you would like. To open another tab, click another database in the object browser and open the Query Tool again via the menu.

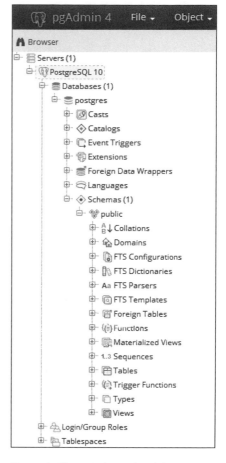

Figure 2: The pgAdmin object browser

Alternatives to pgAdmin

Although pgAdmin is great for beginners, you're not required to use it. If you prefer another administrative tool that works with PostgreSQL, feel free to use it. If you want to use your system's command line for all the exercises in this book, Chapter 16 provides instructions on using the PostgreSQL command line tool psql. (The Appendix lists PostgreSQL resources you can explore to find additional administrative tools.)

Wrapping Up

Now that you've installed PostgreSQL and pgAdmin, you're ready to start learning SQL and use it to discover valuable insights into your data!

In Chapter 1, you'll learn how to create a database and a table, and then you'll load some data to explore its contents. Let's get started!

1

CREATING YOUR FIRST DATABASE AND TABLE

SQL is more than just a means for extracting knowledge from data. It's also a language for *defining* the structures that hold data so we can organize *relationships* in the data. Chief among those structures is the table.

A table is a grid of rows and columns that store data. Each row holds a collection of columns, and each column contains data of a specified type: most commonly, numbers, characters, and dates. We use SQL to define the structure of a table and how each table might relate to other tables in the database. We also use SQL to extract, or *query*, data from tables.

Understanding tables is fundamental to understanding the data in your database. Whenever I start working with a fresh database, the first thing I do is look at the tables within. I look for clues in the table names and their column structure. Do the tables contain text, numbers, or both? How many rows are in each table?

Next, I look at how many tables are in the database. The simplest database might have a single table. A full-bore application that handles customer data or tracks air travel might have dozens or hundreds. The number of tables tells me not only how much data I'll need to analyze, but also hints that I should explore relationships among the data in each table.

Before you dig into SQL, let's look at an example of what the contents of tables might look like. We'll use a hypothetical database for managing a school's class enrollment; within that database are several tables that track students and their classes. The first table, called student_enrollment, shows the students that are signed up for each class section:

student_id	class_id	class_section	semester
CHRISPA004	COMPSCI101	3	Fall 2017
DAVISHE010	COMPSCI101	3	Fall 2017
ABRILDA002	ENG101	40	Fall 2017
DAVISHE010	ENG101	40	Fall 2017
RILEYPH002	ENG101	40	Fall 2017

This table shows that two students have signed up for COMPSCI101, and three have signed up for ENG101. But where are the details about each student and class? In this example, these details are stored in separate tables called students and classes, and each table relates to this one. This is where the power of a *relational database* begins to show itself.

The first several rows of the students table include the following:

student_id	first_name	last_name	dob
ABRILDA002	Abril	Davis	1999-01-10
CHRISPA004	Chris	Park	1996-04-10
DAVISHE010	Davis	Hernandez	1987-09-14
RILEYPH002	Riley	Phelps	1996-06-15

The students table contains details on each student, using the value in the student_id column to identify each one. That value acts as a unique *key* that connects both tables, giving you the ability to create rows such as the following with the class_id column from student_enrollment and the first_name and last_name columns from students:

class_id	first_name	last_name
COMPSCI101	Davis	Hernandez
COMPSCI101	Chris	Park
ENG101	Abril	Davis
ENG101	Davis	Hernandez
ENG101	Riley	Phelps

The classes table would work the same way, with a class_id column and several columns of detail about the class. Database builders prefer to organize data using separate tables for each main *entity* the database manages in order to reduce redundant data. In the example, we store each student's name and date of birth just once. Even if the student signs up for multiple classes—as Davis Hernandez did—we don't waste database space entering his name next to each class in the student_enrollment table. We just include his student ID.

Given that tables are a core building block of every database, in this chapter you'll start your SQL coding adventure by creating a table inside a new database. Then you'll load data into the table and view the completed table.

Creating a Database

The PostgreSQL program you downloaded in the Introduction is a *database management system*, a software package that allows you to define, manage, and query databases. When you installed PostgreSQL, it created a *database server*—an instance of the application running on your computer—that includes a default database called postgres. The database is a collection of objects that includes tables, functions, user roles, and much more. According to the PostgreSQL documentation, the default database is "meant for use by users, utilities and third party applications" (see *https://www.postgresql.org/docs/current/static/app-initdb.html*). In the exercises in this chapter, we'll leave the default as is and instead create a new one. We'll do this to keep objects related to a particular topic or application organized together.

To create a database, you use just one line of SQL, shown in Listing 1-1. This code, along with all the examples in this book, is available for download via the resources at *https://www.nostarch.com/practicalSQL/*.

```
CREATE DATABASE analysis;
```

Listing 1-1: Creating a database named analysis

This statement creates a database on your server named analysis using default PostgreSQL settings. Note that the code consists of two keywords—CREATE and DATABASE—followed by the name of the new database. The statement ends with a semicolon, which signals the end of the command. The semicolon ends all PostgreSQL statements and is part of the ANSI SQL standard. Sometimes you can omit the semicolon, but not always, and particularly not when running multiple statements in the admin. So, using the semicolon is a good habit to form.

Executing SQL in pgAdmin

As part of the Introduction to this book, you also installed the graphical administrative tool pgAdmin (if you didn't, go ahead and do that now). For much of our work, you'll use pgAdmin to run (or execute) the SQL statements we write. Later in the book in Chapter 16, I'll show you how to run SQL statements in a terminal window using the PostgreSQL command line program psql, but getting started is a bit easier with a graphical interface.

We'll use pgAdmin to run the SQL statement in Listing 1-1 that creates the database. Then, we'll connect to the new database and create a table. Follow these steps:

1. Run PostgreSQL. If you're using Windows, the installer set PostgreSQL to launch every time you boot up. On macOS, you must double-click *Postgres.app* in your Applications folder.

2. Launch pgAdmin. As you did in the Introduction, in the left vertical pane (the object browser) expand the plus sign to the left of the Servers node to show the default server. Depending on how you installed PostgreSQL, the default server may be named *localhost* or *PostgreSQL x*, where *x* is the version of the application.

3. Double-click the server name. If you supplied a password during installation, enter it at the prompt. You'll see a brief message that pgAdmin is establishing a connection.

4. In pgAdmin's object browser, expand **Databases** and click once on the postgres database to highlight it, as shown in Figure 1-1.

5. Open the Query Tool by choosing **Tools ▸ Query Tool**.

6. In the SQL Editor pane (the top horizontal pane), type or copy the code from Listing 1-1.

7. Click the lightning bolt icon to execute the statement. PostgreSQL creates the database, and in the Output pane in the Query Tool under Messages you'll see a notice indicating the query returned successfully, as shown in Figure 1-2.

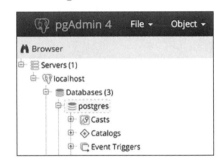

Figure 1-1: Connecting to the default postgres database

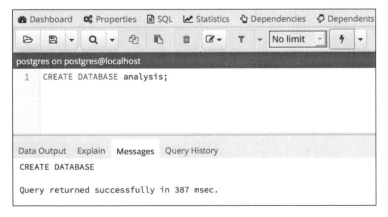

Figure 1-2: Creating the analysis database

8. To see your new database, right-click **Databases** in the object browser. From the pop-up menu, select **Refresh**, and the analysis database will appear in the list, as shown in Figure 1-3.

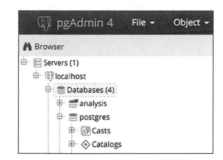

Good work! You now have a database called analysis, which you can use for the majority of the exercises in this book. In your own work, it's generally a best practice to create a new database for each project to keep tables with related data together.

Figure 1-3: The analysis database displayed in the object browser

Connecting to the Analysis Database

Before you create a table, you must ensure that pgAdmin is connected to the analysis database rather than to the default postgres database.

To do that, follow these steps:

1. Close the Query Tool by clicking the **X** at the top right of the tool. You don't need to save the file when prompted.
2. In the object browser, click once on the analysis database.
3. Reopen the Query Tool by choosing **Tools ▸ Query Tool**.
4. You should now see the label analysis on postgres@localhost at the top of the Query Tool window. (Again, instead of localhost, your version may show PostgreSQL.)

Now, any code you execute will apply to the analysis database.

Creating a Table

As I mentioned earlier, tables are where data lives and its relationships are defined. When you create a table, you assign a name to each *column* (sometimes referred to as a *field* or *attribute*) and assign it a *data type*. These are the values the column will accept—such as text, integers, decimals, and dates—and the definition of the data type is one way SQL enforces the integrity of data. For example, a column defined as date will take data in one of several standard formats, such as YYYY-MM-DD. If you try to enter characters not in a date format, for instance, the word peach, you'll receive an error.

Data stored in a table can be accessed and analyzed, or queried, with SQL statements. You can sort, edit, and view the data, and easily alter the table later if your needs change.

Let's make a table in the analysis database.

The CREATE TABLE Statement

For this exercise, we'll use an often-discussed piece of data: teacher salaries. Listing 1-2 shows the SQL statement to create a table called teachers:

```
❶ CREATE TABLE teachers (
    ❷ id bigserial,
    ❸ first_name varchar(25),
       last_name varchar(50),
       school varchar(50),
    ❹ hire_date date,
    ❺ salary numeric
❻ );
```

Listing 1-2: Creating a table named teachers with six columns

This table definition is far from comprehensive. For example, it's missing several *constraints* that would ensure that columns that must be filled do indeed have data or that we're not inadvertently entering duplicate values. I cover constraints in detail in Chapter 7, but in these early chapters I'm omitting them to focus on getting you started on exploring data.

The code begins with the two SQL keywords ❶ CREATE and TABLE that, together with the name teachers, signal PostgreSQL that the next bit of code describes a table to add to the database. Following an opening parenthesis, the statement includes a comma-separated list of column names along with their data types. For style purposes, each new line of code is on its own line and indented four spaces, which isn't required, but it makes the code more readable.

Each column name represents one discrete data element defined by a data type. The id column ❷ is of data type bigserial, a special integer type that auto-increments every time you add a row to the table. The first row receives the value of 1 in the id column, the second row 2, and so on. The bigserial data type and other serial types are PostgreSQL-specific implementations, but most database systems have a similar feature.

Next, we create columns for the teacher's first and last name, and the school where they teach ❸. Each is of the data type varchar, a text column with a maximum length specified by the number in parentheses. We're assuming that no one in the database will have a last name of more than 50 characters. Although this is a safe assumption, you'll discover over time that exceptions will always surprise you.

The teacher's hire_date ❹ is set to the data type date, and the salary column ❺ is a numeric. I'll cover data types more thoroughly in Chapter 3, but this table shows some common examples of data types. The code block wraps up ❻ with a closing parenthesis and a semicolon.

Now that you have a sense of how SQL looks, let's run this code in pgAdmin.

Making the teachers Table

You have your code and you're connected to the database, so you can make the table using the same steps we did when we created the database:

1. Open the pgAdmin Query Tool (if it's not open, click once on the analysis database in pgAdmin's object browser, and then choose **Tools ▸ Query Tool**).
2. Copy the CREATE TABLE script from Listing 1-2 into the SQL Editor.
3. Execute the script by clicking the lightning bolt icon.

If all goes well, you'll see a message in the pgAdmin Query Tool's bottom output pane that reads, Query returned successfully with no result in 84 msec. Of course, the number of milliseconds will vary depending on your system.

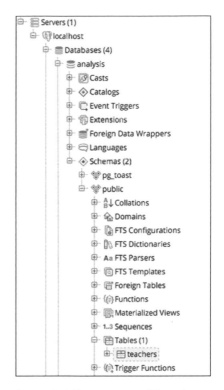

Now, find the table you created. Go back to the main pgAdmin window and, in the object browser, right-click the analysis database and choose **Refresh**. Choose **Schemas ▸ public ▸ Tables** to see your new table, as shown in Figure 1-4.

Expand the teachers table node by clicking the plus sign to the left of its name. This reveals more details about the table, including the column names, as shown in Figure 1-5. Other information appears as well, such as indexes, triggers, and constraints, but I'll cover those in later chapters. Clicking on the table name and then selecting the **SQL** menu in the pgAdmin workspace will display the SQL statement used to make the teachers table.

Congratulations! So far, you've built a database and added a table to it. The next step is to add data to the table so you can write your first query.

Figure 1-4: The teachers table in the object browser

Figure 1-5: Table details for teachers

Inserting Rows into a Table

You can add data to a PostgreSQL table in several ways. Often, you'll work with a large number of rows, so the easiest method is to import data from a text file or another database directly into a table. But just to get started, we'll add a few rows using an INSERT INTO ... VALUES statement that specifies the target columns and the data values. Then we'll view the data in its new home.

The INSERT Statement

To insert some data into the table, you first need to erase the CREATE TABLE statement you just ran. Then, following the same steps as you did to create the database and table, copy the code in Listing 1-3 into your pgAdmin Query Tool:

```
❶ INSERT INTO teachers (first_name, last_name, school, hire_date, salary)
❷ VALUES ('Janet', 'Smith', 'F.D. Roosevelt HS', '2011-10-30', 36200),
         ('Lee', 'Reynolds', 'F.D. Roosevelt HS', '1993-05-22', 65000),
         ('Samuel', 'Cole', 'Myers Middle School', '2005-08-01', 43500),
         ('Samantha', 'Bush', 'Myers Middle School', '2011-10-30', 36200),
         ('Betty', 'Diaz', 'Myers Middle School', '2005-08-30', 43500),
         ('Kathleen', 'Roush', 'F.D. Roosevelt HS', '2010-10-22', 38500);❸
```

Listing 1-3: Inserting data into the teachers table

This code block inserts names and data for six teachers. Here, the PostgreSQL syntax follows the ANSI SQL standard: after the INSERT INTO keywords is the name of the table, and in parentheses are the columns to be filled ❶. In the next row is the VALUES keyword and the data to insert into each column in each row ❷. You need to enclose the data for each row in a set of parentheses, and inside each set of parentheses, use a comma to separate each column value. The order of the values must also match the order of the columns specified after the table name. Each row of data ends with a comma, and the last row ends the entire statement with a semicolon ❸.

Notice that certain values that we're inserting are enclosed in single quotes, but some are not. This is a standard SQL requirement. Text and dates require quotes; numbers, including integers and decimals, don't require quotes. I'll highlight this requirement as it comes up in examples. Also, note the date format we're using: a four-digit year is followed by the month and date, and each part is joined by a hyphen. This is the international standard for date formats; using it will help you avoid confusion. (Why is it best to use the format *YYYY-MM-DD*? Check out *https://xkcd.com/1179/* to see a great comic about it.) PostgreSQL supports many additional date formats, and I'll use several in examples.

You might be wondering about the id column, which is the first column in the table. When you created the table, your script specified that column to be the bigserial data type. So as PostgreSQL inserts each row, it automatically fills the id column with an auto-incrementing integer. I'll cover that in detail in Chapter 3 when I discuss data types.

Now, run the code. This time the message in the Query Tool should include the words `Query returned successfully: 6 rows affected`.

Viewing the Data

You can take a quick look at the data you just loaded into the teachers table using pgAdmin. In the object browser, locate the table and right-click. In the pop-up menu, choose **View/Edit Data ▶ All Rows**. As Figure 1-6 shows, you'll see the six rows of data in the table with each column filled by the values in the SQL statement.

Data Output	Explain	Messages	Query History			
	id bigint	first_name character var}	last_name character var}	school character varying	hire_date date	salary numeric
1	1	Janet	Smith	F.D. Roosevelt ...	2011-10-30	36200
2	2	Lee	Reynolds	F.D. Roosevelt ...	1993-05-22	65000
3	3	Samuel	Cole	Myers Middle S...	2005-08-01	43500
4	4	Samantha	Bush	Myers Middle S...	2011-10-30	36200
5	5	Betty	Diaz	Myers Middle S...	2005-08-30	43500
6	6	Kathleen	Roush	F.D. Roosevelt ...	2010-10-22	38500

Figure 1-6: Viewing table data directly in pgAdmin

Notice that even though you didn't insert a value for the id column, each teacher has an ID number assigned.

You can view data using the pgAdmin interface in a few ways, but we'll focus on writing SQL to handle those tasks.

When Code Goes Bad

There may be a universe where code always works, but unfortunately, we haven't invented a machine capable of transporting us there. Errors happen. Whether you make a typo or mix up the order of operations, computer languages are unforgiving about syntax. For example, if you forget a comma in the code in Listing 1-3, PostgreSQL squawks back an error:

```
ERROR:  syntax error at or near "("
LINE 5:    ('Samuel', 'Cole', 'Myers Middle School', '2005-08-01', 43...
           ^
********** Error **********
```

Fortunately, the error message hints at what's wrong and where: a syntax error is near an open parenthesis on line 5. But sometimes error messages can be more obscure. In that case, you do what the best coders do: a quick internet search for the error message. Most likely, someone else has experienced the same issue and might know the answer.

Formatting SQL for Readability

SQL requires no special formatting to run, so you're free to use your own psychedelic style of uppercase, lowercase, and random indentations. But that won't win you any friends when others need to work with your code (and sooner or later someone will). For the sake of readability and being a good coder, it's best to follow these conventions:

- Uppercase SQL keywords, such as SELECT. Some SQL coders also upper-case the names of data types, such as TEXT and INTEGER. I use lowercase characters for data types in this book to separate them in your mind from keywords, but you can uppercase them if desired.

- Avoid camel case and instead use lowercase_and_underscores for object names, such as tables and column names (see more details about case in Chapter 7).

- Indent clauses and code blocks for readability using either two or four spaces. Some coders prefer tabs to spaces; use whichever works best for you or your organization.

We'll explore other SQL coding conventions as we go through the book, but these are the basics.

Wrapping Up

You accomplished quite a bit in this first chapter: you created a database and a table, and then loaded data into it. You're on your way to adding SQL to your data analysis toolkit! In the next chapter, you'll use this set of teacher data to learn the basics of querying a table using SELECT.

TRY IT YOURSELF

Here are two exercises to help you explore concepts related to databases, tables, and data relationships:

1. Imagine you're building a database to catalog all the animals at your local zoo. You want one table to track the kinds of animals in the collection and another table to track the specifics on each animal. Write CREATE TABLE statements for each table that include some of the columns you need. Why did you include the columns you chose?

2. Now create INSERT statements to load sample data into the tables. How can you view the data via the pgAdmin tool? Create an additional INSERT statement for one of your tables. Purposely omit one of the required commas separating the entries in the VALUES clause of the query. What is the error message? Would it help you find the error in the code?

2

BEGINNING DATA
EXPLORATION WITH SELECT

For me, the best part of digging into data isn't the prerequisites of gathering, loading, or cleaning the data, but when I actually get to *interview* the data. Those are the moments when I discover whether the data is clean or dirty, whether it's complete, and most of all, what story the data can tell. Think of interviewing data as a process akin to interviewing a person applying for a job. You want to ask questions that reveal whether the reality of their expertise matches their resume.

Interviewing is exciting because you discover truths. For example, you might find that half the respondents forgot to fill out the email field in the questionnaire, or the mayor hasn't paid property taxes for the past five years. Or you might learn that your data is dirty: names are spelled inconsistently, dates are incorrect, or numbers don't jibe with your expectations. Your findings become part of the data's story.

In SQL, interviewing data starts with the SELECT keyword, which retrieves rows and columns from one or more of the tables in a database.

A SELECT statement can be simple, retrieving everything in a single table, or it can be complex enough to link dozens of tables while handling multiple calculations and filtering by exact criteria.

We'll start with simple SELECT statements.

Basic SELECT Syntax

Here's a SELECT statement that fetches every row and column in a table called my_table:

```
SELECT * FROM my_table;
```

This single line of code shows the most basic form of a SQL query. The asterisk following the SELECT keyword is a *wildcard*. A wildcard is like a stand-in for a value: it doesn't represent anything in particular and instead represents everything that value could possibly be. Here, it's shorthand for "select all columns." If you had given a column name instead of the wildcard, this command would select the values in that column. The FROM keyword indicates you want the query to return data from a particular table. The semicolon after the table name tells PostgreSQL it's the end of the query statement.

Let's use this SELECT statement with the asterisk wildcard on the teachers table you created in Chapter 1. Once again, open pgAdmin, select the analysis database, and open the Query Tool. Then execute the statement shown in Listing 2-1:

```
SELECT * FROM teachers;
```

Listing 2-1: Querying all rows and columns from the teachers table

The result set in the Query Tool's output pane contains all the rows and columns you inserted into the teachers table in Chapter 1. The rows may not always appear in this order, but that's okay.

id	first_name	last_name	school	hire_date	salary
1	Janet	Smith	F.D. Roosevelt HS	2011-10-30	36200
2	Lee	Reynolds	F.D. Roosevelt HS	1993-05-22	65000
3	Samuel	Cole	Myers Middle School	2005-08-01	43500
4	Samantha	Bush	Myers Middle School	2011-10-30	36200
5	Betty	Diaz	Myers Middle School	2005-08-30	43500
6	Kathleen	Roush	F.D. Roosevelt HS	2010-10-22	38500

Note that the id column (of type bigserial) automatically fills with sequential integers, even though you didn't explicitly insert them. Very handy. This auto-incrementing integer acts as a unique identifier, or key, that not only ensures each row in the table is unique, but also will later give us a way to connect this table to other tables in the database.

Let's move on to refining this query.

Querying a Subset of Columns

Using the asterisk wildcard is helpful for discovering the entire contents of a table. But often it's more practical to limit the columns the query retrieves, especially with large databases. You can do this by naming columns, separated by commas, right after the SELECT keyword. For example:

```
SELECT some_column, another_column, amazing_column FROM table_name;
```

With that syntax, the query will retrieve all rows from just those three columns.

Let's apply this to the teachers table. Perhaps in your analysis you want to focus on teachers' names and salaries, not the school where they work or when they were hired. In that case, you might select only a few columns from the table instead of using the asterisk wildcard. Enter the statement shown in Listing 2-2. Notice that the order of the columns in the query is different than the order in the table: you're able to retrieve columns in any order you'd like.

```
SELECT last_name, first_name, salary FROM teachers;
```

Listing 2-2: Querying a subset of columns

Now, in the result set, you've limited the columns to three:

```
last_name    first_name    salary
---------    ----------    ------
Smith        Janet         36200
Reynolds     Lee           65000
Cole         Samuel        43500
Bush         Samantha      36200
Diaz         Betty         43500
Roush        Kathleen      38500
```

Although these examples are basic, they illustrate a good strategy for beginning your interview of a data set. Generally, it's wise to start your analysis by checking whether your data is present and in the format you expect. Are dates in a complete month-date-year format, or are they entered (as I once ruefully observed) as text with the month and year only? Does every row have a value? Are there mysteriously no last names starting with letters beyond "M"? All these issues indicate potential hazards ranging from missing data to shoddy recordkeeping somewhere in the workflow.

We're only working with a table of six rows, but when you're facing a table of thousands or even millions of rows, it's essential to get a quick read on your data quality and the range of values it contains. To do this, let's dig deeper and add several SQL keywords.

Using DISTINCT to Find Unique Values

In a table, it's not unusual for a column to contain rows with duplicate values. In the teachers table, for example, the school column lists the same school names multiple times because each school employs many teachers.

To understand the range of values in a column, we can use the DISTINCT keyword as part of a query that eliminates duplicates and shows only unique values. Use the DISTINCT keyword immediately after SELECT, as shown in Listing 2-3:

```
SELECT DISTINCT school
FROM teachers;
```

Listing 2-3: Querying distinct values in the school column

The result is as follows:

```
school
-------------------
F.D. Roosevelt HS
Myers Middle School
```

Even though six rows are in the table, the output shows just the two unique school names in the school column. This is a helpful first step toward assessing data quality. For example, if a school name is spelled more than one way, those spelling variations will be easy to spot and correct. When you're working with dates or numbers, DISTINCT will help highlight inconsistent or broken formatting. For example, you might inherit a data set in which dates were entered in a column formatted with a text data type. That practice (which you should avoid) allows malformed dates to exist:

```
date
---------
5/30/2019
6//2019
6/1/2019
6/2/2019
```

The DISTINCT keyword also works on more than one column at a time. If we add a column, the query returns each unique pair of values. Run the code in Listing 2-4:

```
SELECT DISTINCT school, salary
FROM teachers;
```

Listing 2-4: Querying distinct pairs of values in the school and salary columns

Now the query returns each unique (or distinct) salary earned at each school. Because two teachers at Myers Middle School earn $43,500, that pair is listed in just one row, and the query returns five rows rather than all six in the table:

school	salary
Myers Middle School	43500
Myers Middle School	36200
F.D. Roosevelt HS	65000
F.D. Roosevelt HS	38500
F.D. Roosevelt HS	36200

This technique gives us the ability to ask, "For each x in the table, what are all the y values?" For each factory, what are all the chemicals it produces? For each election district, who are all the candidates running for office? For each concert hall, who are the artists playing this month?

SQL offers more sophisticated techniques with aggregate functions that let us count, sum, and find minimum and maximum values. I'll cover those in detail in Chapter 5 and Chapter 8.

Sorting Data with ORDER BY

Data can make more sense, and may reveal patterns more readily, when it's arranged in order rather than jumbled randomly.

In SQL, we order the results of a query using a clause containing the keywords ORDER BY followed by the name of the column or columns to sort. Applying this clause doesn't change the original table, only the result of the query. Listing 2-5 shows an example using the teachers table:

```
SELECT first_name, last_name, salary
FROM teachers
ORDER BY salary DESC;
```

Listing 2-5: Sorting a column with ORDER BY

By default, ORDER BY sorts values in ascending order, but here I sort in descending order by adding the DESC keyword. (The optional ASC keyword specifies sorting in ascending order.) Now, by ordering the salary column from highest to lowest, I can determine which teachers earn the most:

first_name	last_name	salary
Lee	Reynolds	65000
Samuel	Cole	43500
Betty	Diaz	43500
Kathleen	Roush	38500
Janet	Smith	36200
Samantha	Bush	36200

SORTING TEXT MAY SURPRISE YOU

Sorting a column of numbers in PostgreSQL yields what you might expect: the data ranked from largest value to smallest or vice versa depending on whether or not you use the DESC keyword. But sorting a column with letters or other characters may return surprising results, especially if it has a mix of uppercase and lowercase characters, punctuation, or numbers that are treated as text.

During PostgreSQL installation, the server is assigned a particular *locale* for *collation*, or ordering of text, as well as a *character set*. Both are based either on settings in the computer's operating system or custom options supplied during installation. (You can read more about collation in the official PostgreSQL documentation at *https://www.postgresql.org/docs/current/static/collation.html*.) For example, on my Mac, my PostgreSQL install is set to the locale en_US, or U.S. English, and the character set UTF-8. You can view your server's collation setting by executing the statement SHOW ALL; and viewing the value of the parameter lc_collate.

In a character set, each character gets a numerical value, and the sorting order depends on the order of those values. Based on UTF-8, PostgreSQL sorts characters in this order:

1. Punctuation marks, including quotes, parentheses, and math operators

2. Numbers 0 to 9

3. Additional punctuation, including the question mark

4. Capital letters from A to Z

5. More punctuation, including brackets and underscore

6. Lowercase letters a to z

7. Additional punctuation, special characters, and the extended alphabet

Normally, the sorting order won't be an issue because character columns usually just contain names, places, descriptions, and other straightforward text. But if you're wondering why the word *Ladybug* appears before *ladybug* in your sort, you now have an explanation.

The ability to sort in our queries gives us great flexibility in how we view and present data. For example, we're not limited to sorting on just one column. Enter the statement in Listing 2-6:

```
SELECT last_name, school, hire_date
FROM teachers
❶ ORDER BY school ASC, hire_date DESC;
```

Listing 2-6: Sorting multiple columns with ORDER BY

In this case, we're retrieving the last names of teachers, their school, and the date they were hired. By sorting the school column in ascending order and hire_date in descending order ❶, we create a listing of teachers grouped by school with the most recently hired teachers listed first. This shows us who the newest teachers are at each school. The result set should look like this:

```
last_name    school              hire_date
---------    ------------------  ----------
Smith        F.D. Roosevelt HS   2011-10-30
Roush        F.D. Roosevelt HS   2010-10-22
Reynolds     F.D. Roosevelt HS   1993-05-22
Bush         Myers Middle School 2011-10-30
Diaz         Myers Middle School 2005-08-30
Cole         Myers Middle School 2005-08-01
```

You can use ORDER BY on more than two columns, but you'll soon reach a point of diminishing returns where the effect will be hardly noticeable. Imagine if you added columns about teachers' highest college degree attained, the grade level taught, and birthdate to the ORDER BY clause. It would be difficult to understand the various sort directions in the output all at once, much less communicate that to others. Digesting data happens most easily when the result focuses on answering a specific question; therefore, a better strategy is to limit the number of columns in your query to only the most important, and then run several queries to answer each question you have.

Filtering Rows with WHERE

Sometimes, you'll want to limit the rows a query returns to only those in which one or more columns meet certain criteria. Using teachers as an example, you might want to find all teachers hired before a particular year or all teachers making more than $75,000 at elementary schools. For these tasks, we use the WHERE clause.

The WHERE keyword allows you to find rows that match a specific value, a range of values, or multiple values based on criteria supplied via an *operator*. You also can exclude rows based on criteria.

Listing 2-7 shows a basic example. Note that in standard SQL syntax, the WHERE clause follows the FROM keyword and the name of the table or tables being queried:

```
SELECT last_name, school, hire_date
FROM teachers
WHERE school = 'Myers Middle School';
```

Listing 2-7: Filtering rows using WHERE

The result set shows just the teachers assigned to Myers Middle School:

```
last_name    school              hire_date
---------    ------------------  ----------
Cole         Myers Middle School 2005-08-01
Bush         Myers Middle School 2011-10-30
Diaz         Myers Middle School 2005-08-30
```

Here, I'm using the equals comparison operator to find rows that exactly match a value, but of course you can use other operators with WHERE to customize your filter criteria. Table 2-1 provides a summary of the most commonly used comparison operators. Depending on your database system, many more might be available.

Table 2-1: Comparison and Matching Operators in PostgreSQL

Operator	Function	Example
=	Equal to	WHERE school = 'Baker Middle'
<> or !=	Not equal to[*]	WHERE school <> 'Baker Middle'
>	Greater than	WHERE salary > 20000
<	Less than	WHERE salary < 60500
>=	Greater than or equal to	WHERE salary >= 20000
<=	Less than or equal to	WHERE salary <= 60500
BETWEEN	Within a range	WHERE salary BETWEEN 20000 AND 40000
IN	Match one of a set of values	WHERE last_name IN ('Bush', 'Roush')
LIKE	Match a pattern (case sensitive)	WHERE first_name LIKE 'Sam%'
ILIKE	Match a pattern (case insensitive)	WHERE first_name ILIKE 'sam%'
NOT	Negates a condition	WHERE first_name NOT ILIKE 'sam%'

[*] The != operator is not part of standard ANSI SQL but is available in PostgreSQL and several other database systems.

The following examples show comparison operators in action. First, we use the equals operator to find teachers whose first name is Janet:

```
SELECT first_name, last_name, school
FROM teachers
WHERE first_name = 'Janet';
```

Next, we list all school names in the table but exclude F.D. Roosevelt HS using the not equal operator:

```
SELECT school
FROM teachers
WHERE school != 'F.D. Roosevelt HS';
```

Here we use the less than operator to list teachers hired before January 1, 2000 (using the date format *YYYY-MM-DD*):

```
SELECT first_name, last_name, hire_date
FROM teachers
WHERE hire_date < '2000-01-01';
```

Then we find teachers who earn $43,500 or more using the >= operator:

```
SELECT first_name, last_name, salary
FROM teachers
WHERE salary >= 43500;
```

The next query uses the BETWEEN operator to find teachers who earn between $40,000 and $65,000. Note that BETWEEN is *inclusive*, meaning the result will include values matching the start and end ranges specified.

```
SELECT first_name, last_name, school, salary
FROM teachers
WHERE salary BETWEEN 40000 AND 65000;
```

We'll return to these operators throughout the book, because they'll play a key role in helping us ferret out the data and answers we want to find.

Using LIKE and ILIKE with WHERE

Comparison operators are fairly straightforward, but LIKE and ILIKE deserve additional explanation. First, both let you search for patterns in strings by using two special characters:

Percent sign (%)   A wildcard matching one or more characters

Underscore (_)   A wildcard matching just one character

For example, if you're trying to find the word baker, the following LIKE patterns will match it:

```
LIKE 'b%'
LIKE '%ak%'
LIKE '_aker'
LIKE 'ba_er'
```

The difference? The LIKE operator, which is part of the ANSI SQL standard, is case sensitive. The ILIKE operator, which is a PostgreSQL-only implementation, is case insensitive. Listing 2-8 shows how the two keywords give you different results. The first WHERE clause uses LIKE ❶ to find names that start with the characters sam, and because it's case sensitive, it will return zero results. The second, using the case-insensitive ILIKE ❷, will return Samuel and Samantha from the table:

```
  SELECT first_name
  FROM teachers
❶ WHERE first_name LIKE 'sam%';

  SELECT first_name
  FROM teachers
❷ WHERE first_name ILIKE 'sam%';
```

Listing 2-8: Filtering with LIKE and ILIKE

Over the years, I've gravitated toward using ILIKE and wildcard operators in searches to make sure I'm not inadvertently excluding results from searches. I don't assume that whoever typed the names of people, places, products, or other proper nouns always remembered to capitalize them. And if one of the goals of interviewing data is to understand its quality, using a case-insensitive search will help you find variations.

Because LIKE and ILIKE search for patterns, performance on large databases can be slow. We can improve performance using indexes, which I'll cover in "Speeding Up Queries with Indexes" on page 108.

Combining Operators with AND and OR

Comparison operators become even more useful when we combine them. To do this, we connect them using keywords AND and OR along with, if needed, parentheses.

The statements in Listing 2-9 show three examples that combine operators this way:

```
  SELECT *
  FROM teachers
❶ WHERE school = 'Myers Middle School'
        AND salary < 40000;

  SELECT *
  FROM teachers
❷ WHERE last_name = 'Cole'
        OR last_name = 'Bush';

  SELECT *
  FROM teachers
❸ WHERE school = 'F.D. Roosevelt HS'
        AND (salary < 38000 OR salary > 40000);
```

Listing 2-9: Combining operators using AND and OR

The first query uses AND in the WHERE clause ❶ to find teachers who work at Myers Middle School and have a salary less than $40,000. Because we connect the two conditions using AND, both must be true for a row to meet the criteria in the WHERE clause and be returned in the query results.

The second example uses OR ❷ to search for any teacher whose last name matches Cole or Bush. When we connect conditions using OR, only one of the conditions must be true for a row to meet the criteria of the WHERE clause.

The final example looks for teachers at Roosevelt whose salaries are either less than $38,000 or greater than $40,000 ❸. When we place statements inside parentheses, those are evaluated as a group before being combined with other criteria. In this case, the school name must be exactly F.D. Roosevelt HS and the salary must be either less or higher than specified for a row to meet the criteria of the WHERE clause.

Putting It All Together

You can begin to see how even the previous simple queries allow us to delve into our data with flexibility and precision to find what we're looking for. You can combine comparison operator statements using the AND and OR keywords to provide multiple criteria for filtering, and you can include an ORDER BY clause to rank the results.

With the preceding information in mind, let's combine the concepts in this chapter into one statement to show how they fit together. SQL is particular about the order of keywords, so follow this convention:

```
SELECT column_names
FROM table_name
WHERE criteria
ORDER BY column_names;
```

Listing 2-10 shows a query against the teachers table that includes all the aforementioned pieces:

```
SELECT first_name, last_name, school, hire_date, salary
FROM teachers
WHERE school LIKE '%Roos%'
ORDER BY hire_date DESC;
```

Listing 2-10: A SELECT statement including WHERE and ORDER BY

This listing returns teachers at Roosevelt High School, ordered from newest hire to earliest. We can see a clear correlation between a teacher's hire date at the school and his or her current salary level:

first_name	last_name	school	hire_date	salary
Janet	Smith	F.D. Roosevelt HS	2011-10-30	36200
Kathleen	Roush	F.D. Roosevelt HS	2010-10-22	38500
Lee	Reynolds	F.D. Roosevelt HS	1993-05-22	65000

Wrapping Up

Now that you've learned the basic structure of a few different SQL queries, you've acquired the foundation for many of the additional skills I'll cover in later chapters. Sorting, filtering, and choosing only the most important columns from a table can yield a surprising amount of information from your data and help you find the story it tells.

In the next chapter, you'll learn about another foundational aspect of SQL: data types.

TRY IT YOURSELF

Explore basic queries with these exercises:

1. The school district superintendent asks for a list of teachers in each school. Write a query that lists the schools in alphabetical order along with teachers ordered by last name A–Z.

2. Write a query that finds the one teacher whose first name starts with the letter S and who earns more than $40,000.

3. Rank teachers hired since January 1, 2010, ordered by highest paid to lowest.

3

UNDERSTANDING DATA TYPES

Whenever I dig into a new database, I check the *data type* specified for each column in each table. If I'm lucky, I can get my hands on a *data dictionary*: a document that lists each column; specifies whether it's a number, character, or other type; and explains the column values. Unfortunately, many organizations don't create and maintain good documentation, so it's not unusual to hear, "We don't have a data dictionary." In that case, I try to learn by inspecting the table structures in pgAdmin.

It's important to understand data types because storing data in the appropriate format is fundamental to building usable databases and performing accurate analysis. In addition, a data type is a programming concept applicable to more than just SQL. The concepts you'll explore in this chapter will transfer well to additional languages you may want to learn.

In a SQL database, each column in a table can hold one and only one data type, which is defined in the CREATE TABLE statement. You declare the data type after naming the column. Here's a simple example that includes two columns, one a date and the other an integer:

```
CREATE TABLE eagle_watch (
    observed_date date,
    eagles_seen integer
);
```

In this table named eagle_watch (for an annual inventory of bald eagles), the observed_date column is declared to hold date values by adding the date type declaration after its name. Similarly, eagles_seen is set to hold whole numbers with the integer type declaration.

These data types are among the three categories you'll encounter most:

Characters   Any character or symbol

Numbers   Includes whole numbers and fractions

Dates and times   Types holding temporal information

Let's look at each data type in depth; I'll note whether they're part of standard ANSI SQL or specific to PostgreSQL.

Characters

Character string types are general-purpose types suitable for any combination of text, numbers, and symbols. Character types include:

char(*n*)
A fixed-length column where the character length is specified by *n*. A column set at char(20) stores 20 characters per row regardless of how many characters you insert. If you insert fewer than 20 characters in any row, PostgreSQL pads the rest of that column with spaces. This type, which is part of standard SQL, also can be specified with the longer name character(*n*). Nowadays, char(*n*) is used infrequently and is mainly a remnant of legacy computer systems.

varchar(*n*)
A variable-length column where the *maximum* length is specified by *n*. If you insert fewer characters than the maximum, PostgreSQL will not store extra spaces. For example, the string blue will take four spaces, whereas the string 123 will take three. In large databases, this practice saves considerable space. This type, included in standard SQL, also can be specified using the longer name character varying(*n*).

text
> A variable-length column of unlimited length. (According to the PostgreSQL documentation, the longest possible character string you can store is about 1 gigabyte.) The text type is not part of the SQL standard, but you'll find similar implementations in other database systems, including Microsoft SQL Server and MySQL.

According to PostgreSQL documentation at *https://www.postgresql.org/docs/current/static/datatype-character.html*, there is no substantial difference in performance among the three types. That may differ if you're using another database manager, so it's wise to check the docs. The flexibility and potential space savings of varchar and text seem to give them an advantage. But if you search discussions online, some users suggest that defining a column that will always have the same number of characters with char is a good way to signal what data it should contain. For instance, you might use char(2) for U.S. state postal abbreviations.

To see these three character types in action, run the script in Listing 3-1. This script will build and load a simple table and then export the data to a text file on your computer.

```
CREATE TABLE char_data_types (
❶  varchar_column varchar(10),
    char_column char(10),
    text_column text
);

❷ INSERT INTO char_data_types
VALUES
    ('abc', 'abc', 'abc'),
    ('defghi', 'defghi', 'defghi');

❸ COPY char_data_types TO 'C:\YourDirectory\typetest.txt'
❹ WITH (FORMAT CSV, HEADER, DELIMITER '|');
```

Listing 3-1: Character data types in action

The script defines three character columns ❶ of different types and inserts two rows of the same string into each ❷. Unlike the INSERT INTO statement you learned in Chapter 1, here we're not specifying the names of the columns. If the VALUES statements match the number of columns in the table, the database will assume you're inserting values in the order the column definitions were specified in the table.

Next, the script uses the PostgreSQL COPY keyword ❸ to export the data to a text file named typetest.txt in a directory you specify. You'll need to replace *C:\YourDirectory* with the full path to the directory on your computer where you want to save the file. The examples in this book use Windows format and a path to a directory called *YourDirectory* on the C: drive. Linux and macOS file paths have a different format. On my Mac, the path to a file on the desktop is */Users/anthony/Desktop/*. On Linux, my desktop is located at */home/anthony/Desktop/*. The directory must exist already; PostgreSQL won't create it for you.

In PostgreSQL, `COPY` *table_name* `FROM` is the import function and `COPY` *table_name* `TO` is the export function. I'll cover them in depth in Chapter 4; for now, all you need to know is that the `WITH` keyword options ❹ will format the data in the file with each column separated by a *pipe* character (|). That way, you can easily see where spaces fill out the unused portions of the char column.

To see the output, open *typetest.txt* using a plain text editor (not Word or Excel, or another spreadsheet application). The contents should look like this:

```
varchar_column|char_column|text_column
abc|abc       |abc
defghi|defghi    |defghi
```

Even though you specified 10 characters for both the `varchar` and `char` columns, only the `char` column outputs 10 characters every time, padding unused characters with spaces. The `varchar` and `text` columns store only the characters you inserted.

Again, there's no real performance difference among the three types, although this example shows that `char` can potentially consume more storage space than needed. A few unused spaces in each column might seem negligible, but multiply that over millions of rows in dozens of tables and you'll soon wish you had been more economical.

Typically, using `varchar` with an *n* value sufficient to handle outliers is a solid strategy.

Numbers

Number columns hold various types of (you guessed it) numbers, but that's not all: they also allow you to perform calculations on those numbers. That's an important distinction from numbers you store as strings in a character column, which can't be added, multiplied, divided, or perform any other math operation. Also, as I discussed in Chapter 2, numbers stored as characters sort differently than numbers stored as numbers, arranging in text rather than numerical order. So, if you're doing math or the numeric order is important, use number types.

The SQL number types include:

Integers   Whole numbers, both positive and negative

Fixed-point and floating-point   Two formats of fractions of whole numbers

We'll look at each type separately.

Integers

The integer data types are the most common number types you'll find when exploring data in a SQL database. Think of all the places integers appear in life: your street or apartment number, the serial number on your refrigerator, the number on a raffle ticket. These are *whole numbers*, both positive and negative, including zero.

The SQL standard provides three integer types: smallint, integer, and bigint. The difference between the three types is the maximum size of the numbers they can hold. Table 3-1 shows the upper and lower limits of each, as well as how much storage each requires in bytes.

Table 3-1: Integer Data Types

Data type	Storage size	Range
smallint	2 bytes	−32768 to +32767
integer	4 bytes	−2147483648 to +2147483647
bigint	8 bytes	−9223372036854775808 to +9223372036854775807

Even though it eats up the most storage, bigint will cover just about any requirement you'll ever have with a number column. Its use is a must if you're working with numbers larger than about 2.1 billion, but you can easily make it your go-to default and never worry. On the other hand, if you're confident numbers will remain within the integer limit, that type is a good choice because it doesn't consume as much space as bigint (a concern when dealing with millions of data rows).

When the data values will remain constrained, smallint makes sense: days of the month or years are good examples. The smallint type will use half the storage as integer, so it's a smart database design decision if the column values will always fit within its range.

If you try to insert a number into any of these columns that is outside its range, the database will stop the operation and return an out of range error.

Auto-Incrementing Integers

In Chapter 1, when you made the teachers table, you created an id column with the declaration of bigserial: this and its siblings smallserial and serial are not so much true data types as a special *implementation* of the corresponding smallint, integer, and bigint types. When you add a column with a serial type, PostgreSQL will *auto-increment* the value in the column each time you insert a row, starting with 1, up to the maximum of each integer type.

The serial types are implementations of the ANSI SQL standard for auto-numbered *identity columns*. Each database manager implements these in its own way. For example, Microsoft SQL Server uses an IDENTITY keyword to set a column to auto-increment.

To use a serial type on a column, declare it in the CREATE TABLE statement as you would an integer type. For example, you could create a table called people that has an id column in each row:

```
CREATE TABLE people (
    id serial,
    person_name varchar(100)
);
```

Every time a new person_name is added to the table, the id column will increment by 1.

Table 3-2 shows the serial types and the ranges they cover.

Table 3-2: Serial Data Types

Data type	Storage size	Range
smallserial	2 bytes	1 to 32767
serial	4 bytes	1 to 2147483647
bigserial	8 bytes	1 to 9223372036854775807

As with this example and in teachers in Chapter 1, makers of databases often employ a serial type to create a unique ID number, also known as a key, for each row in the table. Each row then has its own ID that other tables in the database can reference. I'll cover this concept of relating tables in Chapter 6. Because the column is auto-incrementing, you don't need to insert a number into that column when adding data; PostgreSQL handles that for you.

NOTE *Even though a column with a serial type auto-increments each time a row is added, some scenarios will create gaps in the sequence of numbers in the column. If a row is deleted, for example, the value in that row is never replaced. Or, if a row insert is aborted, the sequence for the column will still be incremented.*

Decimal Numbers

As opposed to integers, *decimals* represent a whole number plus a fraction of a whole number; the fraction is represented by digits following a *decimal point*. In a SQL database, they're handled by *fixed-point* and *floating-point* data types. For example, the distance from my house to the nearest grocery store is 6.7 miles; I could insert 6.7 into either a fixed-point or floating-point column with no complaint from PostgreSQL. The only difference is how the computer stores the data. In a moment, you'll see that has important implications.

Fixed-Point Numbers

The fixed-point type, also called the *arbitrary precision* type, is numeric(*precision,scale*). You give the argument precision as the maximum number of digits to the left and right of the decimal point, and the argument scale as the number of digits allowable on the right of the decimal point. Alternately, you can specify this type using decimal(*precision,scale*). Both are part of the ANSI SQL standard. If you omit specifying a scale value, the scale will be set to zero; in effect, that creates an integer. If you omit specifying the precision and the scale, the database will store values of any precision and scale up to the maximum allowed. (That's up to 131,072 digits before the decimal point and 16,383 digits after the decimal point, according to the PostgreSQL documentation at *https://www.postgresql.org/docs/current/static/datatype-numeric.html*.)

For example, let's say you're collecting rainfall totals from several local airports—not an unlikely data analysis task. The U.S. National Weather Service provides this data with rainfall typically measured to two decimal places. (And, if you're like me, you have a distant memory of your third-grade math teacher explaining that two digits after a decimal is the hundredths place.)

To record rainfall in the database using five digits total (the precision) and two digits maximum to the right of the decimal (the scale), you'd specify it as numeric(5,2). The database will always return two digits to the right of the decimal point, even if you don't enter a number that contains two digits. For example, 1.47, 1.00, and 121.50.

Floating-Point Types

The two floating-point types are real and double precision. The difference between the two is how much data they store. The real type allows precision to six decimal digits, and double precision to 15 decimal points of precision, both of which include the number of digits on both sides of the point. These floating-point types are also called *variable-precision* types. The database stores the number in parts representing the digits and an exponent—the location where the decimal point belongs. So, unlike numeric, where we specify fixed precision and scale, the decimal point in a given column can "float" depending on the number.

Using Fixed- and Floating-Point Types

Each type has differing limits on the number of total digits, or precision, it can hold, as shown in Table 3-3.

Table 3-3: Fixed-Point and Floating-Point Data Types

Data type	Storage size	Storage type	Range
numeric, decimal	variable	Fixed-point	Up to 131072 digits before the decimal point; up to 16383 digits after the decimal point
real	4 bytes	Floating-point	6 decimal digits precision
double precision	8 bytes	Floating-point	15 decimal digits precision

To see how each of the three data types handles the same numbers, create a small table and insert a variety of test cases, as shown in Listing 3-2:

```
CREATE TABLE number_data_types (
 ❶ numeric_column numeric(20,5),
    real_column real,
    double_column double precision
);

❷ INSERT INTO number_data_types
VALUES
    (.7, .7, .7),
    (2.13579, 2.13579, 2.13579),
    (2.1357987654, 2.1357987654, 2.1357987654);

SELECT * FROM number_data_types;
```

Listing 3-2: Number data types in action

We've created a table with one column for each of the fractional data types ❶ and loaded three rows into the table ❷. Each row repeats the same number across all three columns. When the last line of the script runs and we select everything from the table, we get the following:

numeric_column	real_column	double_column
0.70000	0.7	0.7
2.13579	2.13579	2.13579
2.13580	2.1358	2.1357987654

Notice what happened. The numeric column, set with a scale of five, stores five digits after the decimal point whether or not you inserted that many. If fewer than five, it pads the rest with zeros. If more than five, it rounds them— as with the third-row number with 10 digits after the decimal.

The real and double precision columns store only the number of digits present with no padding. Again on the third row, the number is rounded when inserted into the real column because that type has a maximum of six digits of precision. The double precision column can hold up to 15 digits, so it stores the entire number.

Trouble with Floating-Point Math

If you're thinking, "Well, numbers stored as a floating-point look just like numbers stored as fixed," tread cautiously. The way computers store floating-point numbers can lead to unintended mathematical errors. Look at what happens when we do some calculations on these numbers. Run the script in Listing 3-3.

```
SELECT
 ❶ numeric_column * 10000000 AS "Fixed",
    real_column   * 10000000 AS "Float"
```

```
  FROM number_data_types
❷ WHERE numeric_column = .7;
```

Listing 3-3: Rounding issues with float columns

Here, we multiply the `numeric_column` and the `real_column` by 10 million ❶ and use a `WHERE` clause to filter out just the first row ❷. We should get the same result for both calculations, right? Here's what the query returns:

Fixed	Float
7000000.00000	6999999.88079071

Hello! No wonder floating-point types are referred to as "inexact." It's a good thing I'm not using this math to launch a mission to Mars or calculate the federal budget deficit.

The reason floating-point math produces such errors is that the computer attempts to squeeze lots of information into a finite number of bits. The topic is the subject of a lot of writings and is beyond the scope of this book, but if you're interested, you'll find the link to a good synopsis at *https://www.nostarch.com/practicalSQL/*.

The storage required by the `numeric` data type is variable, and depending on the precision and scale specified, `numeric` can consume considerably more space than the floating-point types. If you're working with millions of rows, it's worth considering whether you can live with relatively inexact floating-point math.

Choosing Your Number Data Type

For now, here are three guidelines to consider when you're dealing with number data types:

1. Use integers when possible. Unless your data uses decimals, stick with integer types.
2. If you're working with decimal data and need calculations to be exact (dealing with money, for example), choose `numeric` or its equivalent, `decimal`. Float types will save space, but the inexactness of floating-point math won't pass muster in many applications. Use them only when exactness is not as important.
3. Choose a big enough number type. Unless you're designing a database to hold millions of rows, err on the side of bigger. When using `numeric` or `decimal`, set the precision large enough to accommodate the number of digits on both sides of the decimal point. With whole numbers, use bigint unless you're absolutely sure column values will be constrained to fit into the smaller `integer` or `smallint` types.

Dates and Times

Whenever you enter a date into a search form, you're reaping the benefit of databases having an awareness of the current time (received from the server) plus the ability to handle formats for dates, times, and the nuances of the calendar, such as leap years and time zones. This is essential for story-telling with data, because the issue of *when* something occurred is usually as valuable a question as who, what, or how many were involved.

PostgreSQL's date and time support includes the four major data types shown in Table 3-4.

Table 3-4: Date and Time Data Types

Data type	Storage size	Description	Range
timestamp	8 bytes	Date and time	4713 BC to 294276 AD
date	4 bytes	Date (no time)	4713 BC to 5874897 AD
time	8 bytes	Time (no date)	00:00:00 to 24:00:00
interval	16 bytes	Time interval	+/– 178,000,000 years

Here's a rundown of data types for times and dates in PostgreSQL:

timestamp   Records date and time, which are useful for a range of situations you might track: departures and arrivals of passenger flights, a schedule of Major League Baseball games, or incidents along a time-line. Typically, you'll want to add the keywords with time zone to ensure that the time recorded for an event includes the time zone where it occurred. Otherwise, times recorded in various places around the globe become impossible to compare. The format timestamp with time zone is part of the SQL standard; with PostgreSQL you can specify the same data type using timestamptz.

date   Records just the date.

time   Records just the time. Again, you'll want to add the with time zone keywords.

interval   Holds a value representing a unit of time expressed in the format *quantity unit*. It doesn't record the start or end of a time period, only its length. Examples include 12 days or 8 hours. (The PostgreSQL documentation at *https://www.postgresql.org/docs/current/static/datatype-datetime.html* lists unit values ranging from microsecond to millennium.) You'll typically use this type for calculations or filtering on other date and time columns.

Let's focus on the timestamp with time zone and interval types. To see these in action, run the script in Listing 3-4.

```
❶ CREATE TABLE date_time_types (
    timestamp_column timestamp with time zone,
    interval_column interval
);
```

```
❷ INSERT INTO date_time_types
  VALUES
      ('2018-12-31 01:00 EST','2 days'),
      ('2018-12-31 01:00 -8','1 month'),
      ('2018-12-31 01:00 Australia/Melbourne','1 century'),
   ❸ (now(),'1 week');

  SELECT * FROM date_time_types;
```

Listing 3-4: The timestamp *and* interval *types in action*

Here, we create a table with a column for both types ❶ and insert four
rows ❷. For the first three rows, our insert for the timestamp_column uses the
same date and time (December 31, 2018 at 1 AM) using the International
Organization for Standardization (ISO) format for dates and times: *YYYY
-MM-DD HH:MM:SS*. SQL supports additional date formats (such as *MM/DD/YYYY*),
but ISO is recommended for portability worldwide.

Following the time, we specify a time zone but use a different format
in each of the first three rows: in the first row, we use the abbreviation EST,
which is Eastern Standard Time in the United States.

In the second row, we set the time zone with the value -8. That represents the number of hours difference, or *offset*, from Coordinated Universal
Time (UTC). UTC refers to an overall world time standard as well as the
value of UTC +/− 00:00, the time zone that covers the United Kingdom and
Western Africa. (For a map of UTC time zones, see *https://en.wikipedia.org/
wiki/Coordinated_Universal_Time#/media/File:Standard_World_Time_Zones.png*.)
Using a value of -8 specifies a time zone eight hours behind UTC, which is
the Pacific time zone in the United States and Canada.

For the third row, we specify the time zone using the name of an area
and location: Australia/Melbourne. That format uses values found in a standard time zone database often employed in computer programming. You
can learn more about the time zone database at *https://en.wikipedia.org/wiki/
Tz_database*.

In the fourth row, instead of specifying dates, times, and time zones,
the script uses PostgreSQL's now() function ❸, which captures the current
transaction time from your hardware.

After the script runs, the output should look similar to (but not exactly
like) this:

```
timestamp_column                   interval_column
-----------------------------      ---------------
2018-12-31 01:00:00-05             2 days
2018-12-31 04:00:00-05             1 mon
2018-12-30 09:00:00-05             100 years
2019-01-25 21:31:15.716063-05      7 days
```

Even though we supplied the same date and time in the first three
rows on the timestamp_column, each row's output differs. The reason is that
pgAdmin reports the date and time relative to my time zone, which in the

results shown is indicated by the UTC offset of -05 at the end of each time-stamp. A UTC offset of -05 means five hours behind UTC time, equivalent to the U.S. Eastern time zone, where I live. If you live in a different time zone, you'll likely see a different offset; the times and dates also may differ from what's shown here. We can change how PostgreSQL reports these time-stamp values, and I'll cover how to do that plus other tips for wrangling dates and times in Chapter 11.

Finally, the interval_column shows the values you entered. PostgreSQL changed 1 century to 100 years and 1 week to 7 days because of its preferred default settings for interval display. Read the "Interval Input" section of the PostgreSQL documentation at *https://www.postgresql.org/docs/current/static/datatype-datetime.html* to learn more about options related to intervals.

Using the interval Data Type in Calculations

The interval data type is useful for easy-to-understand calculations on date and time data. For example, let's say you have a column that holds the date a client signed a contract. Using interval data, you can add 90 days to each contract date to determine when to follow up with the client.

To see how the interval data type works, we'll use the date_time_types table we just created, as shown in Listing 3-5:

```
SELECT
    timestamp_column,
    interval_column,
  ❶ timestamp_column - interval_column AS new_date
FROM date_time_types;
```

Listing 3-5: Using the interval data type

This is a typical SELECT statement except we'll compute a column called new_date ❶ that contains the result of timestamp_column minus interval_column. (Computed columns are called *expressions*; we'll use this technique often.) In each row, we subtract the unit of time indicated by the interval data type from the date. This produces the following result:

timestamp_column	interval_column	new_date
2018-12-31 01:00:00-05	2 days	2018-12-29 01:00:00-05
2018-12-31 04:00:00-05	1 mon	2018-11-30 04:00:00-05
2018-12-30 09:00:00-05	100 years	1918-12-30 09:00:00-05
2019-01-25 21:31:15.716063-05	7 days	2019-01-18 21:31:15.716063-05

Note that the new_date column by default is formatted as type timestamp with time zone, allowing for the display of time values as well as dates if the interval value uses them. Again, your output may be different based on your time zone.

Miscellaneous Types

The character, number, and date/time types you've learned so far will likely comprise the bulk of the work you do with SQL. But PostgreSQL supports many additional types, including but not limited to:

- A Boolean type that stores a value of true or false
- Geometric types that include points, lines, circles, and other two-dimensional objects
- Network address types, such as IP or MAC addresses
- A Universally Unique Identifier (UUID) type, sometimes used as a unique key value in tables
- XML and JSON data types that store information in those structured formats

I'll cover these types as required throughout the book.

Transforming Values from One Type to Another with CAST

Occasionally, you may need to transform a value from its stored data type to another type; for example, when you retrieve a number as a character so you can combine it with text or when you must treat a date stored as characters as an actual date type so you can sort it in date order or perform interval calculations. You can perform these conversions using the CAST() function.

The CAST() function only succeeds when the target data type can accommodate the original value. Casting an integer as text is possible, because the character types can include numbers. Casting text with letters of the alphabet as a number is not.

Listing 3-6 has three examples using the three data type tables we just created. The first two examples work, but the third will try to perform an invalid type conversion so you can see what a type casting error looks like.

```
❶ SELECT timestamp_column, CAST(timestamp_column AS varchar(10))
FROM date_time_types;

❷ SELECT numeric_column,
        CAST(numeric_column AS integer),
        CAST(numeric_column AS varchar(6))
FROM number_data_types;

❸ SELECT CAST(char_column AS integer) FROM char_data_types;
```

Listing 3-6: Three CAST() examples

The first SELECT statement ❶ returns the timestamp_column value as a varchar, which you'll recall is a variable-length character column. In this case, I've set the character length to 10, which means when converted to a character string, only the first 10 characters are kept. That's handy in this case, because that just gives us the date segment of the column and excludes the time. Of course, there are better ways to remove the time from a timestamp, and I'll cover those in "Extracting the Components of a timestamp Value" on page 173.

The second SELECT statement ❷ returns the numeric_column three times: in its original form and then as an integer and as a character. Upon conversion to an integer, PostgreSQL rounds the value to a whole number. But with the varchar conversion, no rounding occurs: the value is simply sliced at the sixth character.

The final SELECT doesn't work ❸: it returns an error of invalid input syntax for integer because letters can't become integers!

CAST Shortcut Notation

It's always best to write SQL that can be read by another person who might pick it up later, and the way CAST() is written makes what you intended when you used it fairly obvious. However, PostgreSQL also offers a less-obvious shortcut notation that takes less space: the *double colon*.

Insert the double colon in between the name of the column and the data type you want to convert it to. For example, these two statements cast timestamp_column as a varchar:

```
SELECT timestamp_column, CAST(timestamp_column AS varchar(10))
FROM date_time_types;

SELECT timestamp_column::varchar(10)
FROM date_time_types;
```

Use whichever suits you, but be aware that the double colon is a PostgreSQL-only implementation not found in other SQL variants.

Wrapping Up

You're now equipped to better understand the nuances of the data formats you encounter while digging into databases. If you come across monetary values stored as floating-point numbers, you'll be sure to convert them to decimals before performing any math. And you'll know how to use the right kind of text column to keep your database from growing too big.

Next, I'll continue with SQL foundations and show you how to import external data into your database.

Continue exploring data types with these exercises:

1. Your company delivers fruit and vegetables to local grocery stores, and you need to track the mileage driven by each driver each day to a tenth of a mile. Assuming no driver would ever travel more than 999 miles in a day, what would be an appropriate data type for the mileage column in your table? Why?

2. In the table listing each driver in your company, what are appropriate data types for the drivers' first and last names? Why is it a good idea to separate first and last names into two columns rather than having one larger name column?

3. Assume you have a text column that includes strings formatted as dates. One of the strings is written as `'4//2017'`. What will happen when you try to convert that string to the `timestamp` data type?

4

IMPORTING AND EXPORTING DATA

So far, you've learned how to add a handful of rows to a table using SQL INSERT statements. A row-by-row insert is useful for making quick test tables or adding a few rows to an existing table. But it's more likely you'll need to load hundreds, thousands, or even millions of rows, and no one wants to write separate INSERT statements in those situations. Fortunately, you don't have to.

If your data exists in a *delimited* text file (with one table row per line of text and each column value separated by a comma or other character) PostgreSQL can import the data in bulk via its COPY command. This command is a PostgreSQL-specific implementation with options for including or excluding columns and handling various delimited text types.

In the opposite direction, COPY will also *export* data from PostgreSQL tables or from the result of a query to a delimited text file. This technique is handy when you want to share data with colleagues or move it into another format, such as an Excel file.

I briefly touched on COPY for export in "Characters" on page 24, but in this chapter I'll discuss import and export in more depth. For importing, I'll start by introducing you to one of my favorite data sets: the Decennial U.S. Census population tally by county.

Three steps form the outline of most of the imports you'll do:

1. Prep the source data in the form of a delimited text file.
2. Create a table to store the data.
3. Write a COPY script to perform the import.

After the import is done, we'll check the data and look at additional options for importing and exporting.

A delimited text file is the most common file format that's portable across proprietary and open source systems, so we'll focus on that file type. If you want to transfer data from another database program's proprietary format directly to PostgreSQL, such as Microsoft Access or MySQL, you'll need to use a third-party tool. Check the PostgreSQL wiki at *https://wiki.postgresql.org/wiki/* and search for "Converting from other Databases to PostgreSQL" for a list of tools.

If you're using SQL with another database manager, check the other database's documentation for how it handles bulk imports. The MySQL database, for example, has a LOAD DATA INFILE statement, and Microsoft's SQL Server has its own BULK INSERT command.

Working with Delimited Text Files

Many software applications store data in a unique format, and translating one data format to another is about as easy as a person trying to read the Cyrillic alphabet if they understand only English. Fortunately, most software can import from and export to a delimited text file, which is a common data format that serves as a middle ground.

A delimited text file contains rows of data, and each row represents one row in a table. In each row, a character separates, or delimits, each data column. I've seen all kinds of characters used as delimiters, from ampersands to pipes, but the comma is most commonly used; hence the name of a file type you'll see often: *comma-separated values (CSV)*. The terms *CSV* and *comma-delimited* are interchangeable.

Here's a typical data row you might see in a comma-delimited file:

John,Doe,123 Main St.,Hyde Park,NY,845-555-1212

Notice that a comma separates each piece of data—first name, last name, street, town, state, and phone—without any spaces. The commas tell the software to treat each item as a separate column, either upon import or export. Simple enough.

Quoting Columns that Contain Delimiters

Using commas as a column delimiter leads to a potential dilemma: what if the value in a column includes a comma? For example, sometimes people combine an apartment number with a street address, as in 123 Main St., Apartment 200. Unless the system for delimiting accounts for that extra comma, during import the line will appear to have an extra column and cause the import to fail.

To handle such cases, delimited files wrap columns that contain a delimiter character with an arbitrary character called a *text qualifier* that tells SQL to ignore the delimiter character held within. Most of the time in comma-delimited files the text qualifier used is the double quote. Here's the example data row again, but with the street name surrounded by double quotes:

```
John,Doe,"123 Main St., Apartment 200",Hyde Park,NY,845-555-1212
```

On import, the database will recognize that double quotes signify one column regardless of whether it finds a delimiter within the quotes. When importing CSV files, PostgreSQL by default ignores delimiters inside double-quoted columns, but you can specify a different text qualifier if your import requires it. (And, given the sometimes odd choices made by IT professionals, you may indeed need to employ a different character.)

Handling Header Rows

Another feature you'll often find inside a delimited text file is the *header row*. As the name implies, it's a single row at the top, or head, of the file that lists the name of each data field. Usually, a header is created during the export of data from a database. Here's an example with the delimited row I've been using:

```
FIRSTNAME,LASTNAME,STREET,CITY,STATE,PHONE
John,Doe,"123 Main St., Apartment 200",Hyde Park,NY,845-555-1212
```

Header rows serve a few purposes. For one, the values in the header row identify the data in each column, which is particularly useful when you're deciphering a file's contents. Second, some database managers (although not PostgreSQL) use the header row to map columns in the delimited file to the correct columns in the import table. Because PostgreSQL doesn't use the header row, we don't want that row imported to a table, so we'll use a HEADER option in the COPY command to exclude it. I'll cover this with all COPY options in the next section.

Using COPY to Import Data

To import data from an external file into our database, first we need to check out a source CSV file and build the table in PostgreSQL to hold the data. Thereafter, the SQL statement for the import is relatively simple. All you need are the three lines of code in Listing 4-1:

```
❶ COPY table_name
❷ FROM 'C:\YourDirectory\your_file.csv'
❸ WITH (FORMAT CSV, HEADER);
```

Listing 4-1: Using COPY for data import

The block of code starts with the COPY keyword ❶ followed by the name of the target table, which must already exist in your database. Think of this syntax as meaning, "Copy data to my table called *table_name*."

The FROM keyword ❷ identifies the full path to the source file, including its name. The way you designate the path depends on your operating system. For Windows, begin with the drive letter, colon, backslash, and directory names. For example, to import a file located on my Windows desktop, the FROM line would read:

```
FROM 'C:\Users\Anthony\Desktop\my_file.csv'
```

On macOS or Linux, start at the system root directory with a forward slash and proceed from there. Here's what the FROM line might look like when importing a file located on my Mac desktop:

```
FROM '/Users/anthony/Desktop/my_file.csv'
```

Note that in both cases the full path and filename are surrounded by single quotes. For the examples in the book, I use the Windows-style path `C:\YourDirectory\` as a placeholder. Replace that with the path where you stored the file.

The WITH keyword ❸ lets you specify options, surrounded by parentheses, that you can tailor to your input or output file. Here we specify that the external file should be comma-delimited, and that we should exclude the file's header row in the import. It's worth examining all the options in the official PostgreSQL documentation at *https://www.postgresql.org/docs/current/static/sql-copy.html*, but here is a list of the options you'll commonly use:

Input and output file format

Use the FORMAT *format_name* option to specify the type of file you're reading or writing. Format names are CSV, TEXT, or BINARY. Unless you're deep into building technical systems, you'll rarely encounter a need to work with BINARY, where data is stored as a sequence of bytes. More often, you'll work with standard CSV files. In the TEXT format, a *tab* character is the delimiter by default (although you can specify another character) and backslash characters such as \r are recognized as their ASCII equivalents—in this case, a carriage return. The TEXT format is used mainly by PostgreSQL's built-in backup programs.

Presence of a header row

On import, use HEADER to specify that the source file has a header row. You can also specify it longhand as HEADER ON, which tells the database to start importing with the second line of the file, preventing the unwanted import of the header. You don't want the column names in the header to become part of the data in the table. On export, using HEADER tells the database to include the column names as a header row in the output file, which is usually helpful to do.

Delimiter

The DELIMITER '*character*' option lets you specify which character your import or export file uses as a delimiter. The delimiter must be a single character and cannot be a carriage return. If you use FORMAT CSV, the assumed delimiter is a comma. I include DELIMITER here to show that you have the option to specify a different delimiter if that's how your data arrived. For example, if you received pipe-delimited data, you would treat the option this way: DELIMITER '|'.

Quote character

Earlier, you learned that in a CSV, commas inside a single column value will mess up your import unless the column value is surrounded by a character that serves as a text qualifier, telling the database to handle the value within as one column. By default, PostgreSQL uses the double quote, but if the CSV you're importing uses a different character, you can specify it with the QUOTE '*quote_character*' option.

Now that you better understand delimited files, you're ready to import one.

Importing Census Data Describing Counties

The data set you'll work with in this import exercise is considerably larger than the teachers table you made in Chapter 1. It contains census data about every county in the United States and is 3,143 rows deep and 91 columns wide.

To understand the data, it helps to know a little about the U.S. Census. Every 10 years, the government conducts a full count of the population—one of several ongoing programs by the Census Bureau to collect demographic data. Each household in America receives a questionnaire about each person in it—their age, gender, race, and whether they are Hispanic or not. The U.S. Constitution mandates the count to determine how many members from each state make up the U.S. House of Representatives. Based on the 2010 Census, for example, Texas gained four seats in the House while New York and Ohio lost two seats each. Although apportioning House seats is the count's main purpose, the data's also a boon for trend trackers studying the population. A good synopsis of the 2010 count's findings is available at *https://www.census.gov/prod/cen2010/briefs/c2010br-01.pdf*.

The Census Bureau reports overall population totals and counts by race and ethnicity for various geographies including states, counties, cities, places, and school districts. For this exercise, I compiled a select collection of columns for the 2010 Census county-level counts into a file named *us_counties_2010.csv*. Download the *us_counties_2010.csv* file from *https://www.nostarch.com/practicalSQL/* and save it to a folder on your computer.

Open the file with a plain text editor. You should see a header row that begins with these columns:

```
NAME,STUSAB,SUMLEV,REGION,DIVISION,STATE,COUNTY --snip--
```

Let's explore some of the columns by examining the code for creating the import table.

Creating the us_counties_2010 Table

The code in Listing 4-2 shows only an abbreviated version of the CREATE TABLE script; many of the columns have been omitted. The full version is available (and annotated) along with all the code examples in the book's resources. To import it properly, you'll need to download the full table definition.

```
CREATE TABLE us_counties_2010 (
❶ geo_name varchar(90),
❷ state_us_abbreviation varchar(2),
❸ summary_level varchar(3),
❹ region smallint,
   division smallint,
   state_fips varchar(2),
   county_fips varchar(3),
❺ area_land bigint,
   area_water bigint,
❻ population_count_100_percent integer,
   housing_unit_count_100_percent integer,
❼ internal_point_lat numeric(10,7),
   internal_point_lon numeric(10,7),
❽ p0010001 integer,
   p0010002 integer,
   p0010003 integer,
   p0010004 integer,
   p0010005 integer,
   --snip--
   p0040049 integer,
   p0040065 integer,
```

```
    p0040072 integer,
    h0010001 integer,
    h0010002 integer,
    h0010003 integer
);
```

Listing 4-2: A CREATE TABLE statement for census county data

To create the table, in pgAdmin click the analysis database that you created in Chapter 1. (It's best to store the data in this book in analysis because we'll reuse some of it in later chapters.) From the pgAdmin menu bar, select **Tools ▸ Query Tool**. Paste the script into the window and run it.

Return to the main pgAdmin window, and in the object browser, right-click and refresh the analysis database. Choose **Schemas ▸ public ▸ Tables** to see the new table. Although it's empty, you can see the structure by running a basic SELECT query in pgAdmin's Query Tool:

```
SELECT * from us_counties_2010;
```

When you run the SELECT query, you'll see the columns in the table you created. No data rows exist yet.

Census Columns and Data Types

Before we import the CSV file into the table, let's walk through several of the columns and the data types I chose in Listing 4-2. As my guide, I used the official census data dictionary for this data set found at *http://www.census.gov/ prod/cen2010/doc/pl94-171.pdf*, although I give some columns more readable names in the table definition. Relying on a data dictionary when possible is good practice, because it helps you avoid misconfiguring columns or potentially losing data. Always ask if one is available, or do an online search if the data is public.

In this set of census data, and thus the table you just made, each row describes the demographics of one county, starting with its geo_name ❶ and its two-character state abbreviation, the state_us_abbreviation ❷. Because both are text, we store them as varchar. The data dictionary indicates that the maximum length of the geo_name field is 90 characters, but because most names are shorter, using varchar will conserve space if we fill the field with a shorter name, such as Lee County, while allowing us to specify the maximum 90 characters.

The geography, or summary level, represented by each row is described by summary_level ❸. We're working only with county-level data, so the code is the same for each row: 050. Even though that code resembles a number, we're treating it as text by again using varchar. If we used an integer type, that leading 0 would be stripped on import, leaving 50. We don't want to do that because 050 is the complete summary level code, and we'd be altering the meaning of the data if the leading 0 were lost. Also, we won't be doing any math with this value.

Numbers from 0 to 9 in `region` and `division` ❹ represent the location of a county in the United States, such as the Northeast, Midwest, or South Atlantic. No number is higher than 9, so we define the columns with type `smallint`. We again use `varchar` for `state_fips` and `county_fips`, which are the standard federal codes for those entities, because those codes contain leading zeros that should not be stripped. It's always important to distinguish codes from numbers; these state and county values are actually labels as opposed to numbers used for math.

The number of square meters for land and water in the county are recorded in `area_land` and `area_water` ❺, respectively. In certain places—such as Alaska, where there's lots of land to go with all that snow—some values easily surpass the `integer` type's maximum of 2,147,483,648. For that reason, we're using `bigint`, which will handle the 376,855,656,455 square meters in the Yukon-Koyukuk Census Area with room to spare.

Next, `population_count_100_percent` and `housing_unit_count_100_percent` ❻ are the total counts of population and housing units in the geography. In 2010, the United States had 308.7 million people and 131.7 million housing units. The population and housing units for any county fits well within the `integer` data type's limits, so we use that for both.

The latitude and longitude of a point near the center of the county, called an *internal point*, are specified in `internal_point_lat` and `internal _point_lon` ❼, respectively. The Census Bureau—along with many mapping systems—expresses latitude and longitude coordinates using a *decimal degrees* system. *Latitude* represents positions north and south on the globe, with the equator at 0 degrees, the North Pole at 90 degrees, and the South Pole at −90 degrees.

Longitude represents locations east and west, with the *Prime Meridian* that passes through Greenwich in London at 0 degrees longitude. From there, longitude increases both east and west (positive numbers to the east and negative to the west) until they meet at 180 degrees on the opposite side of the globe. The location there, known as the *antimeridian*, is used as the basis for the *International Date Line*.

When reporting interior points, the Census Bureau uses up to seven decimal places. With a value up to 180 to the left of the decimal, we need to account for a maximum of 10 digits total. So, we're using `numeric` with a precision of `10` and a scale of `7`.

NOTE   *PostgreSQL, through the PostGIS extension, can store geometric data, which includes points that represent latitude and longitude in a single column. We'll explore geometric data when we cover geographical queries in Chapter 14.*

Finally, we reach a series of columns ❽ that contain iterations of the population counts by race and ethnicity for the county as well as housing unit counts. The full set of 2010 Census data contains 291 of these columns. I've pared that down to 78 for this exercise, omitting many of the columns to make the data set more compact for these exercises.

I won't discuss all the columns now, but Table 4-1 shows a small sample.

Table 4-1: Census Population-Count Columns

Column name	Description
p0010001	Total population
p0010002	Population of one race
p0010003	Population of one race: White alone
p0010004	Population of one race: Black or African American alone
p0010005	Population of one race: American Indian and Alaska Native alone
p0010006	Population of one race: Asian alone
p0010007	Population of one race: Native Hawaiian and Other Pacific Islander alone
p0010008	Population of one race: Some Other Race alone

You'll explore this data more in the next chapter when we look at math with SQL. For now, let's run the import.

Performing the Census Import with COPY

Now you're ready to bring the census data into the table. Run the code in Listing 4-3, remembering to change the path to the file to match the location of the data on your computer:

```
COPY us_counties_2010
FROM 'C:\YourDirectory\us_counties_2010.csv'
WITH (FORMAT CSV, HEADER);
```

Listing 4-3: Importing census data using COPY

When the code executes, you should see the following message in pgAdmin:

```
Query returned successfully: 3143 rows affected
```

That's good news: the import CSV has the same number of rows. If you have an issue with the source CSV or your import statement, the database will throw an error. For example, if one of the rows in the CSV had more columns than in the target table, you'd see an error message that provides a hint as to how to fix it:

```
ERROR: extra data after last expected column
SQL state: 22P04
Context: COPY us_counties_2010, line 2: "Autauga County,AL,050,3,6,01,001 ..."
```

Even if no errors are reported, it's always a good idea to visually scan the data you just imported to ensure everything looks as expected. Start with a SELECT query of all columns and rows:

```
SELECT * FROM us_counties_2010;
```

There should be 3,143 rows displayed in pgAdmin, and as you scroll left and right through the result set, each field should have the expected values. Let's review some columns that we took particular care to define with the appropriate data types. For example, run the following query to show the counties with the largest area_land values. We'll use a LIMIT clause, which will cause the query to only return the number of rows we want; here, we'll ask for three:

```
SELECT geo_name, state_us_abbreviation, area_land
FROM us_counties_2010
ORDER BY area_land DESC
LIMIT 3;
```

This query ranks county-level geographies from largest land area to smallest in square meters. We defined area_land as bigint because the largest values in the field are bigger than the upper range provided by regular integer. As you might expect, big Alaskan geographies are at the top:

geo_name	state_us_abbreviation	area_land
Yukon-Koyukuk Census Area	AK	376855656455
North Slope Borough	AK	229720054439
Bethel Census Area	AK	105075822708

Next, check the latitude and longitude columns of internal_point_lat and internal_point_lon, which we defined with numeric(10,7). This code sorts the counties by longitude from the greatest to smallest value. This time, we'll use LIMIT to retrieve five rows:

```
SELECT geo_name, state_us_abbreviation, internal_point_lon
FROM us_counties_2010
ORDER BY internal_point_lon DESC
LIMIT 5;
```

Longitude measures locations from east to west, with locations west of the Prime Meridian in England represented as negative numbers starting with –1, –2, –3, and so on the farther west you go. We sorted in descending order, so we'd expect the easternmost counties of the United States to show at the top of the query result. Instead—surprise!—there's a lone Alaska geography at the top:

geo_name	state_us_abbreviation	internal_point_lon
Aleutians West Census Area	AK	178.3388130
Washington County	ME	-67.6093542
Hancock County	ME	-68.3707034
Aroostook County	ME	-68.6494098
Penobscot County	ME	-68.6574869

Here's why: the Alaskan Aleutian Islands extend so far west (farther west than Hawaii) that they cross the antimeridian at 180 degrees longitude by less than 2 degrees. Once past the antimeridian, longitude turns positive, counting back down to 0. Fortunately, it's not a mistake in the data; however, it's a fact you can tuck away for your next trivia team competition.

Congratulations! You have a legitimate set of government demographic data in your database. I'll use it to demonstrate exporting data with COPY later in this chapter, and then you'll use it to learn math functions in Chapter 5. Before we move on to exporting data, let's examine a few additional importing techniques.

Importing a Subset of Columns with COPY

If a CSV file doesn't have data for all the columns in your target database table, you can still import the data you have by specifying which columns are present in the data. Consider this scenario: you're researching the salaries of all town supervisors in your state so you can analyze government spending trends by geography. To get started, you create a table called supervisor_salaries with the code in Listing 4-4:

```
CREATE TABLE supervisor_salaries (
    town varchar(30),
    county varchar(30),
    supervisor varchar(30),
    start_date date,
    salary money,
    benefits money
);
```

Listing 4-4: Creating a table to track supervisor salaries

You want columns for the town and county, the supervisor's name, the date he or she started, and salary and benefits (assuming you just care about current levels). However, the first county clerk you contact says, "Sorry, we only have town, supervisor, and salary. You'll need to get the rest from elsewhere." You tell them to send a CSV anyway. You'll import what you can.

I've included such a sample CSV you can download in the book's resources at *https://www.nostarch.com/practicalSQL/*, called *supervisor_salaries .csv*. You could try to import it using this basic COPY syntax:

```
COPY supervisor_salaries
FROM 'C:\YourDirectory\supervisor_salaries.csv'
WITH (FORMAT CSV, HEADER);
```

But if you do, PostgreSQL will return an error:

```
********* Error *********
ERROR: missing data for column "start_date"
SQL state: 22P04
Context: COPY supervisor_salaries, line 2: "Anytown,Jones,27000"
```

The database complains that when it got to the fourth column of the table, start_date, it couldn't find any data in the CSV. The workaround for this situation is to tell the database which columns in the table are present in the CSV, as shown in Listing 4-5:

```
COPY supervisor_salaries ❶(town, supervisor, salary)
FROM 'C:\YourDirectory\supervisor_salaries.csv'
WITH (FORMAT CSV, HEADER);
```

Listing 4-5: Importing salaries data from CSV to three table columns

By noting in parentheses ❶ the three present columns after the table name, we tell PostgreSQL to only look for data to fill those columns when it reads the CSV. Now, if you select the first couple of rows from the table, you'll see only those columns filled:

town	county	supervisor	start_date	salary	benefits
Anytown		Jones		$27,000.00	
Bumblyburg		Baker		$24,999.00	

Adding a Default Value to a Column During Import

What if you want to populate the county column during the import, even though the value is missing from the CSV file? You can do so by using a *temporary table*. Temporary tables exist only until you end your database session. When you reopen the database (or lose your connection), those tables disappear. They're handy for performing intermediary operations on data as part of your processing pipeline; we'll use one to add a county name to the supervisor_salaries table as we import the CSV.

Start by clearing the data you already imported into supervisor_salaries using a DELETE query:

```
DELETE FROM supervisor_salaries;
```

When that query finishes, run the code in Listing 4-6:

```
❶ CREATE TEMPORARY TABLE supervisor_salaries_temp (LIKE supervisor_salaries);

❷ COPY supervisor_salaries_temp (town, supervisor, salary)
  FROM 'C:\YourDirectory\supervisor_salaries.csv'
  WITH (FORMAT CSV, HEADER);

❸ INSERT INTO supervisor_salaries (town, county, supervisor, salary)
  SELECT town, 'Some County', supervisor, salary
  FROM supervisor_salaries_temp;

❹ DROP TABLE supervisor_salaries_temp;
```

Listing 4-6: Using a temporary table to add a default value to a column during import

This script performs four tasks. First, we create a temporary table called supervisor_salaries_temp ❶ based on the original supervisor_salaries table by passing as an argument the LIKE keyword (covered in "Using LIKE and ILIKE with WHERE" on page 19) followed by the parent table to copy. Then we import the *supervisor_salaries.csv* file ❷ into the temporary table using the now-familiar COPY syntax.

Next, we use an INSERT statement to fill the salaries table ❸. Instead of specifying values, we employ a SELECT statement to query the temporary table. That query specifies the value for the second column, not as a column name, but as a string inside single quotes.

Finally, we use DROP TABLE to erase the temporary table ❹. The temporary table will automatically disappear when you disconnect from the PostgreSQL session, but this removes it now in case we want to run the query again against another CSV.

After you run the query, run a SELECT statement on the first couple of rows to see the effect:

town	county	supervisor	start_date	salary	benefits
Anytown	Some County	Jones		$27,000.00	
Bumblyburg	Some County	Baker		$24,999.00	

Now you've filled the county field with a value. The path to this import might seem laborious, but it's instructive to see how data processing can require multiple steps to get the desired results. The good news is that this temporary table demo is an apt indicator of the flexibility SQL offers to control data handling.

Using COPY to Export Data

The main difference between exporting and importing data with COPY is that rather than using FROM to identify the source data, you use TO for the path and name of the output file. You control how much data to export— an entire table, just a few columns, or to fine-tune it even more, the results of a query.

Let's look at three quick examples.

Exporting All Data

The simplest export sends everything in a table to a file. Earlier, you created the table us_counties_2010 with 91 columns and 3,143 rows of census data. The SQL statement in Listing 4-7 exports all the data to a text file named *us_counties_export.txt*. The WITH keyword option tells PostgreSQL to include a header row and use the pipe symbol instead of a comma for a delimiter. I've used the *.txt* file extension here for two reasons. First, it demonstrates that you can export to any text file format; second, we're using a pipe for a delimiter, not a comma. I like to avoid calling files *.csv* unless they truly have commas as a separator.

Remember to change the output directory to your preferred location.

```
COPY us_counties_2010
TO 'C:\YourDirectory\us_counties_export.txt'
WITH (FORMAT CSV, HEADER, DELIMITER '|');
```

Listing 4-7: Exporting an entire table with COPY

Exporting Particular Columns

You don't always need (or want) to export all your data: you might have sensitive information, such as Social Security numbers or birthdates, that need to remain private. Or, in the case of the census county data, maybe you're working with a mapping program and only need the county name and its geographic coordinates to plot the locations. We can export only these three columns by listing them in parentheses after the table name, as shown in Listing 4-8. Of course, you must enter these column names precisely as they're listed in the data for PostgreSQL to recognize them.

```
COPY us_counties_2010 (geo_name, internal_point_lat, internal_point_lon)
TO 'C:\YourDirectory\us_counties_latlon_export.txt'
WITH (FORMAT CSV, HEADER, DELIMITER '|');
```

Listing 4-8: Exporting selected columns from a table with COPY

Exporting Query Results

Additionally, you can add a query to COPY to fine-tune your output. In Listing 4-9 we export the name and state abbreviation of only those counties whose name contains the letters mill in either uppercase or lowercase by using the case-insensitive ILIKE and the % wildcard character we covered in "Using LIKE and ILIKE with WHERE" on page 19.

```
COPY (
    SELECT geo_name, state_us_abbreviation
    FROM us_counties_2010
    WHERE geo_name ILIKE '%mill%'
    )
TO 'C:\YourDirectory\us_counties_mill_export.txt'
WITH (FORMAT CSV, HEADER, DELIMITER '|');
```

Listing 4-9: Exporting query results with COPY

After running the code, your output file should have nine rows with county names including Miller, Roger Mills, and Vermillion.

Importing and Exporting Through pgAdmin

At times, the SQL COPY commands won't be able to handle certain imports and exports, typically when you're connected to a PostgreSQL instance running on a computer other than yours, perhaps elsewhere on a network. When that happens, you might not have access to that computer's filesystem, which makes setting the path in the FROM or TO clause difficult.

One workaround is to use pgAdmin's built-in import/export wizard. In pgAdmin's object browser (the left vertical pane), locate the list of tables in your analysis database by choosing **Databases ▸ analysis ▸ Schemas ▸ public ▸ Tables**.

Next, right-click on the table you want to import to or export from, and select **Import/Export**. A dialog appears that lets you choose either to import or export from that table, as shown in Figure 4-1.

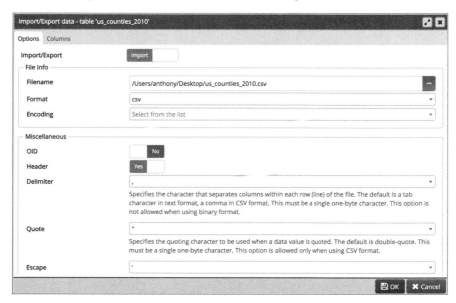

Figure 4-1: The pgAdmin Import/Export dialog

To import, move the Import/Export slider to **Import**. Then click the three dots to the right of the **Filename** box to locate your CSV file. From the Format drop-down list, choose **csv**. Then adjust the header, delimiter, quoting, and other options as needed. Click **OK** to import the data.

To export, use the same dialog and follow similar steps.

Wrapping Up

Now that you've learned how to bring external data into your database, you can start digging into a myriad of data sets, whether you want to explore one of the thousands of publicly available data sets, or data related to your own career or studies. Plenty of data is available in CSV format or a format easily convertible to CSV. Look for data dictionaries to help you understand the data and choose the right data type for each field.

The census data you imported as part of this chapter's exercises will play a starring role in the next chapter in which we explore math functions with SQL.

TRY IT YOURSELF

Continue your exploration of data import and export with these exercises. Remember to consult the PostgreSQL documentation at *https://www.postgresql .org/docs/current/static/sql-copy.html* for hints:

1. Write a WITH statement to include with COPY to handle the import of an imaginary text file whose first couple of rows look like this:

```
id:movie:actor
50:#Mission: Impossible#:Tom Cruise
```

2. Using the table us_counties_2010 you created and filled in this chapter, export to a CSV file the 20 counties in the United States that have the most housing units. Make sure you export only each county's name, state, and number of housing units. (Hint: Housing units are totaled for each county in the column housing_unit_count_100_percent.)

3. Imagine you're importing a file that contains a column with these values:

```
17519.668
20084.461
18976.335
```

   Will a column in your target table with data type numeric(3,8) work for these values? Why or why not?

5

BASIC MATH AND STATS WITH SQL

If your data includes any of the number data types we explored in Chapter 3—integers, decimals, or floating points—sooner or later your analysis will include some calculations. For example, you might want to know the average of all the dollar values in a column, or add values in two columns to produce a total for each row. SQL handles calculations ranging from basic math through advanced statistics.

In this chapter, I'll start with the basics and progress to math functions and beginning statistics. I'll also discuss calculations related to percentages and percent change. For several of the exercises, we'll use the 2010 Decennial Census data you imported in Chapter 4.

Math Operators

Let's start with the basic math you learned in grade school (and all's forgiven if you've forgotten some of it). Table 5-1 shows nine math operators you'll use most often in your calculations. The first four (addition, subtraction, multiplication, and division) are part of the ANSI SQL standard that are implemented in all database systems. The others are PostgreSQL-specific operators, although if you're using another database, it likely has functions or operators to perform those operations. For example, the modulo operator (%) works in Microsoft SQL Server and MySQL as well as with PostgreSQL. If you're using another database system, check its documentation.

Table 5-1: Basic Math Operators

Operator	Description
+	Addition
-	Subtraction
*	Multiplication
/	Division (returns the quotient only, no remainder)
%	Modulo (returns just the remainder)
^	Exponentiation
|/	Square root
||/	Cube root
!	Factorial

We'll step through each of these operators by executing simple SQL queries on plain numbers rather than operating on a table or another database object. You can either enter the statements separately into the pgAdmin query tool and execute them one at a time, or if you copied the code for this chapter from the resources at *https://www.nostarch.com/practicalSQL/*, you can highlight each line before executing it.

Math and Data Types

As you work through the examples, note the data type of each result, which is listed beneath each column name in the pgAdmin results grid. The type returned for a calculation will vary depending on the operation and the data type of the input numbers.

In calculations with an operator between two numbers—addition, subtraction, multiplication, and division—the data type returned follows this pattern:

- Two integers return an integer.
- A numeric on either side of the operator returns a numeric.
- Anything with a floating-point number returns a floating-point number of type double precision.

However, the exponentiation, root, and factorial functions are different. Each takes one number either before or after the operator and returns numeric and floating-point types, even when the input is an integer.

Sometimes the result's data type will suit your needs; other times, you may need to use CAST to change the data type, as mentioned in "Transforming Values from One Type to Another with CAST" on page 35, such as if you need to feed the result into a function that takes a certain type. I'll note those times as we work through the book.

Adding, Subtracting, and Multiplying

Let's start with simple integer addition, subtraction, and multiplication. Listing 5-1 shows three examples, each with the SELECT keyword followed by the math formula. Since Chapter 2, we've used SELECT for its main purpose: to retrieve data from a table. But with PostgreSQL, Microsoft's SQL Server, MySQL, and some other database management systems, it's possible to omit the table name for math and string operations while testing, as we do here. For readability's sake, I recommend you use a single space before and after the math operator; although using spaces isn't strictly necessary for your code to work, it is good practice.

```
❶ SELECT 2 + 2;
❷ SELECT 9 - 1;
❸ SELECT 3 * 4;
```

Listing 5-1: Basic addition, subtraction, and multiplication with SQL

None of these statements are rocket science, so you shouldn't be surprised that running SELECT 2 + 2; ❶ in the query tool shows a result of 4. Similarly, the examples for subtraction ❷ and multiplication ❸ yield what you'd expect: 8 and 12. The output displays in a column, as with any query result. But because we're not querying a table and specifying a column, the results appear beneath a ?column? name, signifying an unknown column:

```
?column?
--------
       4
```

That's okay. We're not affecting any data in a table, just displaying a result.

Division and Modulo

Division with SQL gets a little trickier because of the difference between math with integers and math with decimals, which was mentioned earlier. Add in *modulo*, an operator that returns just the *remainder* in a division operation, and the results can be confusing. So, to make it clear, Listing 5-2 shows four examples:

```
❶ SELECT 11 / 6;
❷ SELECT 11 % 6;
```

```
❸ SELECT 11.0 / 6;
❹ SELECT CAST (11 AS numeric(3,1)) / 6;
```

Listing 5-2: Integer and decimal division with SQL

The first statement uses the / operator ❶ to divide the integer 11 by another integer, 6. If you do that math in your head, you know the answer is 1 with a remainder of 5. However, running this query yields 1, which is how SQL handles division of one integer by another—by reporting only the integer *quotient*. If you want to retrieve the *remainder* as an integer, you must perform the same calculation using the modulo operator %, as in ❷. That statement returns just the remainder, in this case 5. No single operation will provide you with both the quotient and the remainder as integers.

Modulo is useful for more than just fetching a remainder: you can also use it as a test condition. For example, to check whether a number is even, you can test it using the % 2 operation. If the result is 0 with no remainder, the number is even.

If you want to divide two numbers and have the result return as a numeric type, you can do so in two ways: first, if one or both of the numbers is a numeric, the result will by default be expressed as a numeric. That's what happens when I divide 11.0 by 6 ❸. Execute that query, and the result is 1.83333. The number of decimal digits displayed may vary according to your PostgreSQL and system settings.

Second, if you're working with data stored only as integers and need to force decimal division, you can CAST one of the integers to a numeric type ❹. Executing this again returns 1.83333.

Exponents, Roots, and Factorials

Beyond the basics, PostgreSQL-flavored SQL also provides operators to square, cube, or otherwise raise a base number to an exponent, as well as find roots or the factorial of a number. Listing 5-3 shows these operations in action:

```
❶ SELECT 3 ^ 4;
❷ SELECT |/ 10;
  SELECT sqrt(10);
❸ SELECT ||/ 10;
❹ SELECT 4 !;
```

Listing 5-3: Exponents, roots, and factorials with SQL

The exponentiation operator (^) allows you to raise a given base number to an exponent, as in ❶, where 3 ^ 4 (colloquially, we'd call that three to the fourth power) returns 81.

You can find the square root of a number in two ways: using the |/ operator ❷ or the sqrt(*n*) function. For a cube root, use the ||/ operator ❸. Both are *prefix operators*, named because they come before a single value.

To find the *factorial* of a number, use the ! operator. It's a *suffix operator*, coming after a single value. You'll use factorials in many places in math, but perhaps the most common is to determine how many ways a number of items can be ordered. Say you have four photographs. How many ways could you order them next to each other on a wall? To find the answer, you'd calculate the factorial by starting with the number of items and multiplying all the smaller positive integers. So, at ❹, the factorial statement of 4 ! is equivalent to $4 \times 3 \times 2 \times 1$. That's 24 ways to order four photos. No wonder decorating takes so long sometimes!

Again, these operators are specific to PostgreSQL; they're not part of the SQL standard. If you're using another database application, check its documentation for how it implements these operations.

Minding the Order of Operations

Can you recall from your earliest math lessons what the order of operations, or *operator precedence*, is on a mathematical expression? When you string together several numbers and operators, which calculations does SQL execute first? Not surprisingly, SQL follows the established math standard. For the PostgreSQL operators discussed so far, the order is:

1. Exponents and roots
2. Multiplication, division, modulo
3. Addition and subtraction

Given these rules, you'll need to encase an operation in parentheses if you want to calculate it in a different order. For example, the following two expressions yield different results:

```
SELECT 7 + 8 * 9;
SELECT (7 + 8) * 9;
```

The first expression returns 79 because the multiplication operation receives precedence and is processed before the addition. The second returns 135 because the parentheses force the addition operation to occur first.

Here's a second example using exponents:

```
SELECT 3 ^ 3 - 1;
SELECT 3 ^ (3 - 1);
```

Exponent operations take precedence over subtraction, so without parentheses the entire expression is evaluated left to right and the operation to find 3 to the power of 3 happens first. Then 1 is subtracted, returning 26. In the second example, the parentheses force the subtraction to happen first, so the operation results in 9, which is 3 to the power of 2.

Keep operator precedence in mind to avoid having to correct your analysis later!

Doing Math Across Census Table Columns

Let's try to use the most frequently used SQL math operators on real data by digging into the 2010 Decennial Census population table, us_counties_2010, that you imported in Chapter 4. Instead of using numbers in queries, we'll use the names of the columns that contain the numbers. When we execute the query, the calculation will occur on each row of the table.

To refresh your memory about the data, run the script in Listing 5-4. It should return 3,143 rows showing the name and state of each county in the United States, and the number of people who identified with one of six race categories or a combination of two or more races.

The 2010 Census form received by each household—the so-called "short form"—allowed people to check either just one or multiple boxes under the question of race. (You can review the form at *https://www.census .gov/2010census/pdf/2010_Questionnaire_Info.pdf.*) People who checked one box were counted in categories such as "White Alone" or "Black or African American Alone." Respondents who selected more than one box were tabulated in the overall category of "Two or More Races," and the census data set breaks those down in detail.

```
SELECT geo_name,
       state_us_abbreviation AS "st",
       p0010001 AS❶ "Total Population",
       p0010003 AS "White Alone",
       p0010004 AS "Black or African American Alone",
       p0010005 AS "Am Indian/Alaska Native Alone",
       p0010006 AS "Asian Alone",
       p0010007 AS "Native Hawaiian and Other Pacific Islander Alone",
       p0010008 AS "Some Other Race Alone",
       p0010009 AS "Two or More Races"
FROM us_counties_2010;
```

Listing 5-4: Selecting census population columns by race with aliases

In us_counties_2010, each race and household data column contains a census code. For example, the "Asian Alone" column is reported as p0010006. Although those codes might be economical and compact, they make it difficult to understand which column is which when the query returns with just that code. In Listing 5-4, I employ a little trick to clarify the output by using the AS keyword ❶ to give each column a more readable alias in the result set. We could rename all the columns upon import, but with the census it's best to use the code to refer to the same column names in the documentation if needed.

Adding and Subtracting Columns

Now, let's try a simple calculation on two of the race columns in Listing 5-5, adding the number of people who identified as white alone or black alone in each county.

```
SELECT geo_name,
       state_us_abbreviation AS "st",
       p0010003 AS "White Alone",
       p0010004 AS "Black Alone",
❶     p0010003 + p0010004 AS "Total White and Black"
FROM us_counties_2010;
```

Listing 5-5: Adding two columns in us_counties_2010

Providing p0010003 + p0010004 ❶ as one of the columns in the SELECT statement handles the calculation. Again, I use the AS keyword to provide a readable alias for the column. If you don't provide an alias, PostgreSQL uses the label ?column?, which is far less than helpful.

Run the query to see the results. The first few rows should resemble this output:

geo_name	st	White Alone	Black Alone	Total White and Black
Autauga County	AL	42855	9643	52498
Baldwin County	AL	156153	17105	173258
Barbour County	AL	13180	12875	26055

A quick check with a calculator or pencil and paper confirms that the total column equals the sum of the columns you added. Excellent!

Now, let's build on this to test our data and validate that we imported columns correctly. The six race "Alone" columns plus the "Two or More Races" column should add up to the same number as the total population. The code in Listing 5-6 should show that it does:

```
SELECT geo_name,
       state_us_abbreviation AS "st",
❶     p0010001 AS "Total",
❷     p0010003 + p0010004 + p0010005 + p0010006 + p0010007
           + p0010008 + p0010009 AS "All Races",
❸     (p0010003 + p0010004 + p0010005 + p0010006 + p0010007
           + p0010008 + p0010009) - p0010001 AS "Difference"
FROM us_counties_2010
❹ ORDER BY "Difference" DESC;
```

Listing 5-6: Checking census data totals

This query includes the population total ❶, followed by a calculation adding the seven race columns as All Races ❷. The population total and the races total should be identical, but rather than manually check, we also add a column that subtracts the population total column from the sum of the race columns ❸. That column, named Difference, should contain a zero in each row if all the data is in the right place. To avoid having to scan all 3,143 rows, we add an ORDER BY clause ❹ on the named column. Any rows showing a difference should appear at the top or bottom of the query result.

Run the query; the first few rows should provide this result:

geo_name	st	Total	All Races	Difference
Autauga County	AL	54571	54571	0
Baldwin County	AL	182265	182265	0
Barbour County	AL	27457	27457	0

With the Difference column showing zeros, we can be confident that our import was clean. Whenever I encounter or import a new data set, I like to perform little tests like this. They help me better understand the data and head off any potential issues before I dig into analysis.

Finding Percentages of the Whole

Let's dig deeper into the census data to find meaningful differences in the population demographics of the counties. One way to do this (with any data set, in fact) is to calculate what percentage of the whole a particular variable represents. With the census data, we can learn a lot by comparing percentages from county to county and also by examining how percentages vary over time.

To figure out the percentage of the whole, divide the number in question by the total. For example, if you had a basket of 12 apples and used 9 in a pie, that would be 9 / 12 or .75—commonly expressed as 75 percent.

To try this on the census counties data, use the code in Listing 5-7, which calculates for each county the percentage of the population that reported their race as Asian:

```
SELECT geo_name,
       state_us_abbreviation AS "st",
       (CAST ❶(p0010006 AS numeric(8,1)) / p0010001) * 100 AS "pct_asian"
FROM us_counties_2010
ORDER BY "pct_asian" DESC;
```

Listing 5-7: Calculating the percentage of the population that is Asian by county

The key piece of this query divides p0010006, the column with the count of Asian alone, by p0010001, the column for total population ❶.

If we use the data as their original integer types, we won't get the fractional result we need: every row will display a result of 0, the quotient. Instead, we force decimal division by using CAST on one of the integers. The last part multiplies the result by 100 to present the result as a fraction of 100—the way most people understand percentages.

By sorting from highest to lowest percentage, the top of the output is as follows:

geo_name	st	pct_asian
Honolulu County	HI	43.8949776910996247400
Aleutians East Borough	AK	35.9758038841133397010
San Francisco County	CA	33.2716536166460722650

Santa Clara County	CA	32.02237037519322063600
Kauai County	HI	31.32461880132953749400
Aleutians West Census Area	AK	28.87969789606185937800

Tracking Percent Change

Another key indicator in data analysis is percent change: how much bigger, or smaller, is one number than another? Percent change calculations are often employed when analyzing change over time, and they're particularly useful for comparing change among similar items.

Some examples include:

- The year-over-year change in the number of vehicles sold by each automobile maker.
- The monthly change in subscriptions to each email list owned by a marketing firm.
- The annual increase or decrease in enrollment at schools across the nation.

The formula to calculate percent change can be expressed like this:

$$(\textit{new number} - \textit{old number}) \; / \; \textit{old number}$$

So, if you own a lemonade stand and sold 73 glasses of lemonade today and 59 glasses yesterday, you'd figure the day-to-day percent change like this:

$$(73 - 59) \; / \; 59 = .237 = 23.7\%$$

Let's try this with a small collection of test data related to spending in departments of a hypothetical local government. Listing 5-8 calculates which departments had the greatest percentage increase and loss:

```
❶ CREATE TABLE percent_change (
      department varchar(20),
      spend_2014 numeric(10,2),
      spend_2017 numeric(10,2)
  );

❷ INSERT INTO percent_change
  VALUES
      ('Building', 250000, 289000),
      ('Assessor', 178556, 179500),
      ('Library', 87777, 90001),
      ('Clerk', 451980, 650000),
      ('Police', 250000, 223000),
      ('Recreation', 199000, 195000);

  SELECT department,
         spend_2014,
         spend_2017,
```

```
❸ round( (spend_2017 - spend_2014) /
                spend_2014 * 100, 1) AS "pct_change"
FROM percent_change;
```

Listing 5-8: Calculating percent change

Listing 5-8 creates a small table called percent_change ❶ and inserts six rows ❷ with data on department spending for the years 2014 and 2017. The percent change formula ❸ subtracts spend_2014 from spend_2017 and then divides by spend_2014. We multiply by 100 to express the result as a portion of 100.

To simplify the output, this time I've added the round() function to remove all but one decimal place. The function takes two arguments: the column or expression to be rounded, and the number of decimal places to display. Because both numbers are type numeric, the result will also be a numeric.

The script creates this result:

```
department     spend_2014     spend_2017     pct_change
----------     ----------     ----------     ----------
Building       250000.00      289000.00            15.6
Assessor       178556.00      179500.00             0.5
Library         87777.00       90001.00             2.5
Clerk          451980.00      650000.00            43.8
Police         250000.00      223000.00           -10.8
Recreation     199000.00      195000.00            -2.0
```

Now, it's just a matter of finding out why the Clerk department's spending has outpaced others in the town.

Aggregate Functions for Averages and Sums

So far, we've performed math operations across columns in each row of a table. SQL also lets you calculate a result from values within the same column using *aggregate functions*. You can see a full list of PostgreSQL aggregates, which calculate a single result from multiple inputs, at *https://www .postgresql.org/docs/current/static/functions-aggregate.html*. Two of the most-used aggregate functions in data analysis are avg() and sum().

Returning to the us_counties_2010 census table, it's reasonable to want to calculate the total population of all counties plus the average population of all counties. Using avg() and sum() on column p0010001 (the total population) makes it easy, as shown in Listing 5-9. Again, we use the round() function to remove numbers after the decimal point in the average calculation.

```
SELECT sum(p0010001) AS "County Sum",
       round(avg(p0010001), 0) AS "County Average"
FROM us_counties_2010;
```

Listing 5-9: Using the sum() and avg() aggregate functions

This calculation produces the following result:

County Sum	County Average
308745538	98233

The population for all counties in the United States in 2010 added up to approximately 308.7 million, and the average county population was 98,233.

Finding the Median

The *median* value in a set of numbers is as important an indicator, if not more so, than the average. Here's the difference between median and average, and why median matters:

Average The sum of all the values divided by the number of values

Median The "middle" value in an ordered set of values

Why is median important for data analysis? Consider this example: let's say six kids, ages 10, 11, 10, 9, 13, and 12, go on a field trip. It's easy to add the ages and divide by six to get the group's average age:

$$(10 + 11 + 10 + 9 + 13 + 12) / 6 = 10.8$$

Because the ages are within a narrow range, the 10.8 average is a good representation of the group. But averages are less helpful when the values are bunched, or skewed, toward one end of the distribution, or if the group includes outliers.

For example, what if an older chaperone joins the field trip? With ages of 10, 11, 10, 9, 13, 12, and 46, the average age increases considerably:

$$(10 + 11 + 10 + 9 + 13 + 12 + 46) / 7 = 15.9$$

Now the average doesn't represent the group well because the outlier skews it, making it an unreliable indicator.

This is where medians shine. The median is the midpoint in an ordered list of values—the point at which half the values are more and half are less. Using the field trip, we order the attendees' ages from lowest to highest:

9, 10, 10, 11, 12, 13, 46

The middle (median) value is 11. Half the values are higher, and half are lower. Given this group, the median of 11 is a better picture of the typical age than the average of 15.9.

If the set of values is an even number, you average the two middle numbers to find the median. Let's add another student (age 12) to the field trip:

9, 10, 10, 11, 12, 12, 13, 46

Now, the two middle values are 11 and 12. To find the median, we average them: 11.5.

Medians are reported frequently in financial news. Reports on housing prices often use medians because a few sales of McMansions in a ZIP Code that is otherwise modest can make averages useless. The same goes for sports player salaries: one or two superstars can skew a team's average.

A good test is to calculate the average and the median for a group of values. If they're close, the group is probably normally distributed (the familiar bell curve), and the average is useful. If they're far apart, the values are not normally distributed and the median is the better representation.

Finding the Median with Percentile Functions

PostgreSQL (as with most relational databases) does not have a built-in median() function, similar to what you'd find in Excel or other spreadsheet programs. It's also not included in the ANSI SQL standard. But we can use a SQL *percentile* function to find the median as well as other *quantiles* or *cut points*, which are the points that divide a group of numbers into equal sizes. Percentile functions are part of standard ANSI SQL.

In statistics, percentiles indicate the point in an ordered set of data below which a certain percentage of the data is found. For example, a doctor might tell you that your height places you in the 60th percentile for an adult in your age group. That means 60 percent of people are your height or shorter.

The median is equivalent to the 50th percentile—again, half the values are below and half above. SQL's percentile functions allow us to calculate that easily, although we have to pay attention to a difference in how the two versions of the function—percentile_cont(*n*) and percentile_disc(*n*)—handle calculations. Both functions are part of the ANSI SQL standard and are present in PostgreSQL, Microsoft SQL Server, and other databases.

The percentile_cont(*n*) function calculates percentiles as *continuous* values. That is, the result does not have to be one of the numbers in the data set but can be a decimal value in between two of the numbers. This follows the methodology for calculating medians on an even number of values, where the median is the average of the two middle numbers. On the other hand, percentile_disc(*n*) returns only *discrete* values. That is, the result returned will be rounded to one of the numbers in the set.

To make this distinction clear, let's use Listing 5-10 to make a test table and fill in six numbers.

```
CREATE TABLE percentile_test (
    numbers integer
);

INSERT INTO percentile_test (numbers) VALUES
    (1), (2), (3), (4), (5), (6);

SELECT
 ❶ percentile_cont(.5)
    WITHIN GROUP (ORDER BY numbers),
 ❷ percentile_disc(.5)
```

```
    WITHIN GROUP (ORDER BY numbers)
FROM percentile_test;
```

Listing 5-10: Testing SQL percentile functions

In both the continuous ❶ and discrete ❷ percentile functions, we enter .5 to represent the 50th percentile, which is equivalent to the median. Running the code returns the following:

```
percentile_cont    percentile_disc
---------------    ---------------
          3.5                    3
```

The percentile_cont() function returned what we'd expect the median to be: 3.5. But because percentile_disc() calculates discrete values, it reports 3, the last value in the first 50 percent of the numbers. Because the accepted method of calculating medians is to average the two middle values in an even-numbered set, use percentile_cont(.5) to find a median.

Median and Percentiles with Census Data

Our census data can show how a median tells a different story than an average. Listing 5-11 adds percentile_cont() alongside the sum() and avg() aggregates we've used so far:

```
SELECT sum(p0010001) AS "County Sum",
       round(avg(p0010001), 0) AS "County Average",
       percentile_cont(.5)
       WITHIN GROUP (ORDER BY p0010001) AS "County Median"
FROM us_counties_2010;
```

Listing 5-11: Using sum(), avg(), and percentile_cont() aggregate functions

Your result should equal the following:

```
County Sum    County Average    County Median
----------    --------------    -------------
 308745538             98233            25857
```

The median and average are far apart, which shows that averages can mislead. As of 2010, half the counties in America had fewer than 25,857 people, whereas half had more. If you gave a presentation on U.S. demographics and told the audience that the "average county in America had 98,200 people," they'd walk away with a skewed picture of reality. Nearly 40 counties had a million or more people as of the 2010 Decennial Census, and Los Angeles County had close to 10 million. That pushes the average higher.

Finding Other Quantiles with Percentile Functions

You can also slice data into smaller equal groups. Most common are *quartiles* (four equal groups), *quintiles* (five groups), and *deciles* (10 groups). To find any individual value, you can just plug it into a percentile function. For example, to find the value marking the first quartile, or the lowest 25 percent of data, you'd use a value of .25:

```
percentile_cont(.25)
```

However, entering values one at a time is laborious if you want to generate multiple cut points. Instead, you can pass values into percentile_cont() using an *array*, a SQL data type that contains a list of items. Listing 5-12 shows how to calculate all four quartiles at once:

```
SELECT percentile_cont(❶array[.25,.5,.75])
       WITHIN GROUP (ORDER BY p0010001) AS "quartiles"
FROM us_counties_2010;
```

Listing 5-12: Passing an array of values to percentile_cont()

In this example, we create an array of cut points by enclosing values in a *constructor* ❶ called array[]. Inside the square brackets, we provide comma-separated values representing the three points at which to cut to create four quartiles. Run the query, and you should see this output:

```
quartiles
--------------------
{11104.5,25857,66699}
```

Because we passed in an array, PostgreSQL returns an array, denoted by curly brackets. Each quartile is separated by commas. The first quartile is 11,104.5, which means 25 percent of counties have a population that is equal to or lower than this value. The second quartile is the same as the median: 25,857. The third quartile is 66,699, meaning the largest 25 percent of counties have at least this large of a population.

Arrays come with a host of functions (noted for PostgreSQL at *https://www.postgresql.org/docs/current/static/functions-array.html*) that allow you to perform tasks such as adding or removing values or counting the elements. A handy function for working with the result returned in Listing 5-12 is unnest(), which makes the array easier to read by turning it into rows. Listing 5-13 shows the code:

```
SELECT unnest(
            percentile_cont(array[.25,.5,.75])
            WITHIN GROUP (ORDER BY p0010001)
            ) AS "quartiles"
FROM us_counties_2010;
```

Listing 5-13: Using unnest() to turn an array into rows

Now the output should be in rows:

```
quartiles
---------
  11104.5
    25857
    66699
```

If we were computing deciles, pulling them from the resulting array and displaying them in rows would be especially helpful.

Creating a median() Function

Although PostgreSQL does not have a built-in median() aggregate function, if you're adventurous, the PostgreSQL wiki at *http://wiki.postgresql.org/wiki/ Aggregate_Median* provides a script to create one. Listing 5-14 shows the script:

```
❶ CREATE OR REPLACE FUNCTION _final_median(anyarray)
     RETURNS float8 AS
  $$
    WITH q AS
    (
       SELECT val
       FROM unnest($1) val
       WHERE VAL IS NOT NULL
       ORDER BY 1
    ),
    cnt AS
    (
       SELECT COUNT(*) AS c FROM q
    )
    SELECT AVG(val)::float8
    FROM
    (
       SELECT val FROM q
       LIMIT  2 - MOD((SELECT c FROM cnt), 2)
       OFFSET GREATEST(CEIL((SELECT c FROM cnt) / 2.0) - 1,0)
    ) q2;
  $$
  LANGUAGE sql IMMUTABLE;

❷ CREATE AGGREGATE median(anyelement) (
    SFUNC=array_append,
    STYPE=anyarray,
    FINALFUNC=_final_median,
    INITCOND='{}'
  );
```

Listing 5-14: Creating a median() aggregate function in PostgreSQL

Given what you've learned so far, the code for making a median() aggregate function may look inscrutable. I'll cover functions in more depth later in the book, but for now note that the code contains two main blocks: one to make a function called _final_median ❶ that sorts the values in the column and finds the midpoint, and a second that serves as the callable aggregate function median() ❷ and passes values to _final_median. For now, you can skip reviewing the script line by line and simply execute the code.

Let's add the median() function to the census query and try it next to percentile_cont(), as shown in Listing 5-15:

```
SELECT sum(p0010001) AS "County Sum",
       round(AVG(p0010001), 0) AS "County Average",
       median(p0010001) AS "County Median",
       percentile_cont(.5)
       WITHIN GROUP (ORDER BY p0010001) AS "50th Percentile"
FROM us_counties_2010;
```

Listing 5-15: Using a median() aggregate function

The query results show that the median function and the percentile function return the same value:

County Sum	County Average	County Median	50th Percentile
308745538	98233	25857	25857

So when should you use median() instead of a percentile function? There is no simple answer. The median() syntax is easier to remember, albeit a chore to set up for each database, and it's specific to PostgreSQL. Also, in practice, median() executes more slowly and may perform poorly on large data sets or slow machines. On the other hand, percentile_cont() is portable across several SQL database managers, including Microsoft SQL Server, and allows you to find any percentile from 0 to 100. Ultimately, you can try both and decide.

Finding the Mode

Additionally, we can find the *mode*, the value that appears most often, using the PostgreSQL mode() function. The function is not part of standard SQL and has a syntax similar to the percentile functions. Listing 5-16 shows a mode() calculation on p0010001, the total population column:

```
SELECT mode() WITHIN GROUP (ORDER BY p0010001)
FROM us_counties_2010;
```

Listing 5-16: Finding the most frequent value with mode()

The result is 21720, a population count shared by counties in Mississippi, Oregon, and West Virginia.

Wrapping Up

Working with numbers is a key step in acquiring meaning from your data, and with the math skills covered in this chapter, you're ready to handle the foundations of numerical analysis with SQL. Later in the book, you'll learn about deeper statistical concepts including regression and correlation. At this point, you have the basics of sums, averages, and percentiles. You've also learned how a median can be a fairer assessment of a group of values than an average. That alone can help you avoid inaccurate conclusions.

In the next chapter, I'll introduce you to the power of joining data in two or more tables to increase your options for data analysis. We'll use the 2010 Census data you've already loaded into the analysis database and explore additional data sets.

TRY IT YOURSELF

Here are three exercises to test your SQL math skills:

1. Write a SQL statement for calculating the area of a circle whose radius is 5 inches. (If you don't remember the formula, it's an easy web search.) Do you need parentheses in your calculation? Why or why not?

2. Using the 2010 Census county data, find out which New York state county has the highest percentage of the population that identified as "American Indian/Alaska Native Alone." What can you learn about that county from online research that explains the relatively large proportion of American Indian population compared with other New York counties?

3. Was the 2010 median county population higher in California or New York?

6

JOINING TABLES IN A RELATIONAL DATABASE

In Chapter 1, I introduced the concept of a *relational database*, an application that supports data stored across multiple, related tables. In a relational model, each table typically holds data on one entity—such as students, cars, purchases, houses—and each row in the table describes one of those entities. A process known as a *table join* allows us to link rows in one table to rows in other tables.

The concept of relational databases came from the British computer scientist Edgar F. Codd. While working for IBM in 1970, he published a paper called "A Relational Model of Data for Large Shared Data Banks." His ideas revolutionized database design and led to the development of SQL. Using the relational model, you can build tables that eliminate duplicate data, are easier to maintain, and provide for increased flexibility in writing queries to get just the data you want.

Linking Tables Using JOIN

To connect tables in a query, we use a `JOIN ... ON` statement (or one of the other `JOIN` variants I'll cover in this chapter). The `JOIN` statement links one table to another in the database during a query, using matching values in columns we specify in both tables. The syntax takes this form:

```
SELECT *
FROM table_a JOIN table_b
ON table_a.key_column = table_b.foreign_key_column
```

This is similar to the basic `SELECT` syntax you've already learned, but instead of naming one table in the `FROM` clause, we name a table, give the `JOIN` keyword, and then name a second table. The `ON` keyword follows, where we specify the columns we want to use to match values. When the query runs, it examines both tables and then returns columns from both tables where the values match in the columns specified in the `ON` clause.

Matching based on equality between values is the most common use of the `ON` clause, but you can use any expression that evaluates to the *Boolean* results `true` or `false`. For example, you could match where values from one column are greater than or equal to values in the other:

```
ON table_a.key_column >= table_b.foreign_key_column
```

That's rare, but it's an option if your analysis requires it.

Relating Tables with Key Columns

Consider this example of relating tables with key columns: imagine you're a data analyst with the task of checking on a public agency's payroll spending by department. You file a Freedom of Information Act request for that agency's salary data, expecting to receive a simple spreadsheet listing each employee and their salary, arranged like this:

```
dept   location    first_name   last_name   salary
----   --------    ----------   ---------   ------
Tax    Atlanta     Nancy        Jones       62500
Tax    Atlanta     Lee          Smith       59300
IT     Boston      Soo          Nguyen      83000
IT     Boston      Janet        King        95000
```

But that's not what arrives. Instead, the agency sends you a data dump from its payroll system: a dozen CSV files, each representing one table in its database. You read the document explaining the data layout (be sure to always ask for it!) and start to make sense of the columns in each table. Two of the tables stand out: one named `employees` and another named `departments`.

Using the code in Listing 6-1, let's create versions of these tables, insert rows, and examine how to join the data in both tables. Using the analysis database you've created for these exercises, run all the code, and then look at the data either by using a basic SELECT statement or clicking the table name in pgAdmin and selecting **View/Edit Data ▶ All Rows**.

```
CREATE TABLE departments (
    dept_id bigserial,
    dept varchar(100),
    city varchar(100),
 ❶ CONSTRAINT dept_key PRIMARY KEY (dept_id),
 ❷ CONSTRAINT dept_city_unique UNIQUE (dept, city)
);

CREATE TABLE employees (
    emp_id bigserial,
    first_name varchar(100),
    last_name varchar(100),
    salary integer,
 ❸ dept_id integer REFERENCES departments (dept_id),
 ❹ CONSTRAINT emp_key PRIMARY KEY (emp_id),
 ❺ CONSTRAINT emp_dept_unique UNIQUE (emp_id, dept_id)
);

INSERT INTO departments (dept, city)
VALUES
    ('Tax', 'Atlanta'),
    ('IT', 'Boston');

INSERT INTO employees (first_name, last_name, salary, dept_id)
VALUES
    ('Nancy', 'Jones', 62500, 1),
    ('Lee', 'Smith', 59300, 1),
    ('Soo', 'Nguyen', 83000, 2),
    ('Janet', 'King', 95000, 2);
```

Listing 6-1: Creating the departments and employees tables

The two tables follow Codd's relational model in that each describes attributes about a single entity, in this case the agency's departments and employees. In the departments table, you should see the following contents:

dept_id	dept	city
1	Tax	Atlanta
2	IT	Boston

The dept_id column is the table's primary key. A *primary key* is a column or collection of columns whose values uniquely identify each row in a table. A valid primary key column enforces certain constraints:

- The column or collection of columns must have a unique value for each row.
- The column or collection of columns can't have missing values.

You define the primary key for departments ❶ and employees ❹ using a CONSTRAINT keyword, which I'll cover in depth with additional constraint types in Chapter 7. The dept_id column uniquely identifies the department, and although this example contains only a department name and city, such a table would likely include additional information, such as an address or contact information.

The employees table should have the following contents:

emp_id	first_name	last_name	salary	dept_id
1	Nancy	Jones	62500	1
2	Lee	Smith	59300	1
3	Soo	Nguyen	83000	2
4	Janet	King	95000	2

The emp_id column uniquely identifies each row in the employees table. For you to know which department each employee works in, the table includes a dept_id column. The values in this column refer to values in the departments table's primary key. We call this a *foreign key*, which you add as a constraint ❸ when creating the table. A foreign key constraint requires a value entered in a column to already exist in the primary key of the table it references. So, values in dept_id in the employees table must exist in dept_id in the departments table; otherwise, you can't add them. Unlike a primary key, a foreign key column can be empty, and it can contain duplicate values.

In this example, the dept_id associated with the employee Nancy Jones is 1; this refers to the value of 1 in the departments table's primary key, dept_id. That tells us that Nancy Jones is part of the Tax department located in Atlanta.

NOTE *Primary key values only need to be unique within a table. That's why it's okay for both the employees table and the departments table to have primary key values using the same numbers.*

Both tables also include a UNIQUE constraint, which I'll also discuss in more depth in "The UNIQUE Constraint" on page 105. Briefly, it guarantees that values in a column, or a combination of values in more than one column, are unique. In departments, it requires that each row have a unique pair of values for dept and city ❷. In employees, each row must have a unique pair of emp_id and dept_id ❺. You add these constraints to avoid duplicate data. For example, you can't have two tax departments in Atlanta.

You might ask: what is the advantage of breaking apart data into components like this? Well, consider what this sample of data would look like if you had received it the way you initially thought you would, all in one table:

dept	location	first_name	last_name	salary
Tax	Atlanta	Nancy	Jones	62500
Tax	Atlanta	Lee	Smith	59300
IT	Boston	Soo	Nguyen	83000
IT	Boston	Janet	King	95000

First, when you combine data from various entities in one table, inevitably you have to repeat information. This happens here: the department name and location is spelled out for each employee. This is fine when the table consists of four rows like this, or even 4,000. But when a table holds millions of rows, repeating lengthy strings is redundant and wastes precious space.

Second, cramming unrelated data into one table makes managing the data difficult. What if the Marketing department changes its name to Brand Marketing? Each row in the table would require an update. It's simpler to store department names and locations in just one table and update it only once.

Now that you know the basics of how tables can relate, let's look at how to join them in a query.

Querying Multiple Tables Using JOIN

When you join tables in a query, the database connects rows in both tables where the columns you specified for the join have matching values. The query results then include columns from both tables if you requested them as part of the query. You also can use columns from the joined tables to filter results using a WHERE clause.

Queries that join tables are similar in syntax to basic SELECT statements. The difference is that the query also specifies the following:

- The tables and columns to join, using a SQL JOIN ... ON statement
- The type of join to perform using variations of the JOIN keyword

Let's look at the overall JOIN ... ON syntax first and then explore various types of joins. To join the example employees and departments tables and see all related data from both, start by writing a query like the one in Listing 6-2:

```
❶ SELECT *
❷ FROM employees JOIN departments
❸ ON employees.dept_id = departments.dept_id;
```

Listing 6-2: Joining the employees and departments tables

In the example, you include an asterisk wildcard with the SELECT statement to choose all columns from both tables ❶. Next, the JOIN keyword ❷ goes between the two tables you want data from. Finally, you specify the columns to join the tables using the ON keyword ❸. For each table, you provide the table name, a period, and the column that contains the key values. An equal sign goes between the two table and column names.

When you run the query, the results include all values from both tables where values in the `dept_id` columns match. In fact, even the `dept_id` field appears twice because you selected all columns of both tables:

emp_id	first_name	last_name	salary	dept_id	dept_id	dept	city
1	Nancy	Jones	62500	1	1	Tax	Atlanta
2	Lee	Smith	59300	1	1	Tax	Atlanta
3	Soo	Nguyen	83000	2	2	IT	Boston
4	Janet	King	95000	2	2	IT	Boston

So, even though the data lives in two tables, each with a focused set of columns, you can query those tables to pull the relevant data back together. In "Selecting Specific Columns in a Join" on page 85, I'll show you how to retrieve only the columns you want from both tables.

JOIN Types

There's more than one way to join tables in SQL, and the type of join you'll use depends on how you want to retrieve data. The following list describes the different types of joins. While reviewing each, it's helpful to think of two tables side by side, one on the left of the JOIN keyword and the other on the right. A data-driven example of each join follows the list:

JOIN   Returns rows from both tables where matching values are found in the joined columns of both tables. Alternate syntax is INNER JOIN.

LEFT JOIN   Returns every row from the left table plus rows that match values in the joined column from the right table. When a left table row doesn't have a match in the right table, the result shows no values from the right table.

RIGHT JOIN   Returns every row from the right table plus rows that match the key values in the key column from the left table. When a right table row doesn't have a match in the left table, the result shows no values from the left table.

FULL OUTER JOIN   Returns every row from both tables and matches rows; then joins the rows where values in the joined columns match. If there's no match for a value in either the left or right table, the query result contains an empty row for the other table.

CROSS JOIN   Returns every possible combination of rows from both tables.

These join types are best illustrated with data. Say you have two simple tables that hold names of schools. To better visualize join types, let's call the tables `schools_left` and `schools_right`. There are four rows in `schools_left`:

```
id   left_school
--   ------------------------
1    Oak Street School
2    Roosevelt High School
```

```
5     Washington Middle School
6     Jefferson High School
```

There are five rows in schools_right:

```
id    right_school
--    --------------------
1     Oak Street School
2     Roosevelt High School
3     Morrison Elementary
4     Chase Magnet Academy
6     Jefferson High School
```

Notice that only schools with the id of 1, 2, and 6 match in both tables. Working with two tables of similar data is a common scenario for a data analyst, and a common task would be to identify which schools exist in both tables. Using different joins can help you find those schools, plus other details.

Again using your analysis database, run the code in Listing 6-3 to build and populate these two tables:

```
CREATE TABLE schools_left (
❶  id integer CONSTRAINT left_id_key PRIMARY KEY,
   left_school varchar(30)
);

CREATE TABLE schools_right (
❷  id integer CONSTRAINT right_id_key PRIMARY KEY,
   right_school varchar(30)
);

❸ INSERT INTO schools_left (id, left_school) VALUES
      (1, 'Oak Street School'),
      (2, 'Roosevelt High School'),
      (5, 'Washington Middle School'),
      (6, 'Jefferson High School');

INSERT INTO schools_right (id, right_school) VALUES
      (1, 'Oak Street School'),
      (2, 'Roosevelt High School'),
      (3, 'Morrison Elementary'),
      (4, 'Chase Magnet Academy'),
      (6, 'Jefferson High School');
```

Listing 6-3: Creating two tables to explore JOIN types

We create and fill two tables: the declarations for these should by now look familiar, but there's one new element: we add a primary key to each table. After the declaration for the schools_left id column ❶ and schools_right id column, ❷ the keywords CONSTRAINT key_name PRIMARY KEY indicate that those columns will serve as the primary key for their table.

That means for each row in both tables, the id column must be filled and contain a value that is unique for each row in that table. Finally, we use the familiar INSERT statements ❸ to add the data to the tables.

JOIN

We use JOIN, or INNER JOIN, when we want to return rows that have a match in the columns we used for the join. To see an example of this, run the code in Listing 6-4, which joins the two tables you just made:

```
SELECT *
FROM schools_left JOIN schools_right
ON schools_left.id = schools_right.id;
```

Listing 6-4: Using JOIN

Similar to the method we used in Listing 6-2, we specify the two tables to join around the JOIN keyword. Then we specify which columns we're joining on, in this case the id columns of both tables. Three school IDs match in both tables, so JOIN returns only the three rows of those IDs that match. Schools that exist only in one of the two tables don't appear in the result. Notice also that the columns from the left table display on the left of the result table:

id	left_school	id	right_school
1	Oak Street School	1	Oak Street School
2	Roosevelt High School	2	Roosevelt High School
6	Jefferson High School	6	Jefferson High School

When should you use JOIN? Typically, when you're working with well-structured, well-maintained data sets and only need to find rows that exist in all the tables you're joining. Because JOIN doesn't provide rows that exist in only one of the tables, if you want to see all the data in one or more of the tables, use one of the other join types.

LEFT JOIN and RIGHT JOIN

In contrast to JOIN, the LEFT JOIN and RIGHT JOIN keywords each return all rows from one table and display blank rows from the other table if no matching values are found in the joined columns. Let's look at LEFT JOIN in action first. Execute the code in Listing 6-5:

```
SELECT *
FROM schools_left LEFT JOIN schools_right
ON schools_left.id = schools_right.id;
```

Listing 6-5: Using LEFT JOIN

The result of the query shows all four rows from `schools_left` as well as the three rows in `schools_right` where the id fields matched. Because `schools_right` doesn't contain a value of 5 in its `right_id` column, there's no match, so `LEFT JOIN` shows an empty row on the right rather than omitting the entire row from the left table as with `JOIN`. The rows from `schools_right` that don't match any values in `schools_left` are omitted from the results:

```
id   left_school               id   right_school
--   ----------------------    --   --------------------
1    Oak Street School         1    Oak Street School
2    Roosevelt High School     2    Roosevelt High School
5    Washington Middle School
6    Jefferson High School     6    Jefferson High School
```

We see similar but opposite behavior by running `RIGHT JOIN`, as in Listing 6-6:

```sql
SELECT *
FROM schools_left RIGHT JOIN schools_right
ON schools_left.id = schools_right.id;
```

Listing 6-6: Using `RIGHT JOIN`

This time, the query returns all rows from `schools_right` plus rows from `schools_left` where the id columns have matching values, but the query doesn't return the rows of `schools_left` that don't have a match with `schools_right`:

```
id   left_school               id   right_school
--   --------------------      --   --------------------
1    Oak Street School         1    Oak Street School
2    Roosevelt High School     2    Roosevelt High School
                               3    Morrison Elementary
                               4    Chase Magnet Academy
6    Jefferson High School     6    Jefferson High School
```

You'd use either of these join types in a few circumstances:

- You want your query results to contain all the rows from one of the tables.
- You want to look for missing values in one of the tables; for example, when you're comparing data about an entity representing two different time periods.
- When you know some rows in a joined table won't have matching values.

FULL OUTER JOIN

When you want to see all rows from both tables in a join, regardless of whether any match, use the FULL OUTER JOIN option. To see it in action, run Listing 6-7:

```
SELECT *
FROM schools_left FULL OUTER JOIN schools_right
ON schools_left.id = schools_right.id;
```

Listing 6-7: Using FULL OUTER JOIN

The result gives every row from the left table, including matching rows and blanks for missing rows from the right table, followed by any leftover missing rows from the right table:

id	left_school	id	right_school
1	Oak Street School	1	Oak Street School
2	Roosevelt High School	2	Roosevelt High School
5	Washington Middle School		
6	Jefferson High School	6	Jefferson High School
		4	Chase Magnet Academy
		3	Morrison Elementary

A full outer join is admittedly less useful and used less often than inner and left or right joins. Still, you can use it for a couple of tasks: to merge two data sources that partially overlap or to visualize the degree to which the tables share matching values.

CROSS JOIN

In a CROSS JOIN query, the result (also known as a *Cartesian product*) lines up each row in the left table with each row in the right table to present all possible combinations of rows. Listing 6-8 shows the CROSS JOIN syntax; because the join doesn't need to find matches between key fields, there's no need to provide the clause using the ON keyword.

```
SELECT *
FROM schools_left CROSS JOIN schools_right;
```

Listing 6-8: Using CROSS JOIN

The result has 20 rows—the product of four rows in the left table times five rows in the right:

id	left_school	id	right_school
1	Oak Street School	1	Oak Street School
1	Oak Street School	2	Roosevelt High School
1	Oak Street School	3	Morrison Elementary
1	Oak Street School	4	Chase Magnet Academy

1	Oak Street School	6	Jefferson High School
2	Roosevelt High School	1	Oak Street School
2	Roosevelt High School	2	Roosevelt High School
2	Roosevelt High School	3	Morrison Elementary
2	Roosevelt High School	4	Chase Magnet Academy
2	Roosevelt High School	6	Jefferson High School
5	Washington Middle School	1	Oak Street School
5	Washington Middle School	2	Roosevelt High School
5	Washington Middle School	3	Morrison Elementary
5	Washington Middle School	4	Chase Magnet Academy
5	Washington Middle School	6	Jefferson High School
6	Jefferson High School	1	Oak Street School
6	Jefferson High School	2	Roosevelt High School
6	Jefferson High School	3	Morrison Elementary
6	Jefferson High School	4	Chase Magnet Academy
6	Jefferson High School	6	Jefferson High School

Unless you want to take an extra-long coffee break, I'd suggest avoiding a CROSS JOIN query on large tables. Two tables with 250,000 records each would produce a result set of 62.5 *billion* rows and tax even the hardiest server. A more practical use would be generating data to create a checklist, such as all colors you'd want to offer for each shirt style in a warehouse.

Using NULL to Find Rows with Missing Values

Being able to reveal missing data from one of the tables is valuable when you're digging through data. Any time you join tables, it's wise to vet the quality of the data and understand it better by discovering whether all key values in one table appear in another. There are many reasons why a discrepancy might exist, such as a clerical error, incomplete output from the database, or some change in the data over time. All this information is important context for making correct inferences about the data.

When you have only a handful of rows, eyeballing the data is an easy way to look for rows with missing data. For large tables, you need a better strategy: filtering to show all rows without a match. To do this, we employ the keyword NULL.

In SQL, NULL is a special value that represents a condition in which there's no data present or where the data is unknown because it wasn't included. For example, if a person filling out an address form skips the "Middle Initial" field, rather than storing an empty string in the database, we'd use NULL to represent the unknown value. It's important to keep in mind that NULL is different from 0 or an empty string that you'd place in a character field using two quotes (""). Both those values could have some unintended meaning that's open to misinterpretation, so you use NULL to show that the value is unknown. And unlike 0 or an empty string, you can use NULL across data types.

When a SQL join returns empty rows in one of the tables, those columns don't come back empty but instead come back with the value NULL. In

Listing 6-9, we'll find those rows by adding a WHERE clause to filter for NULL by using the phrase IS NULL on the right_id column. If we wanted to look for columns *with* data, we'd use IS NOT NULL.

```
SELECT *
FROM schools_left LEFT JOIN schools_right
ON schools_left.id = schools_right.id
WHERE schools_right.id IS NULL;
```

Listing 6-9: Filtering to show missing values with IS NULL

Now the result of the join shows only the one row from the left table that didn't have a match on the right side.

id	left_school	id	right_school
5	Washington Middle School		

Three Types of Table Relationships

Part of the science (or art, some may say) of joining tables involves understanding how the database designer intends for the tables to relate, also known as the database's *relational model*. The three types of table relationships are one to one, one to many, and many to many.

One-to-One Relationship

In our JOIN example in Listing 6-4, there is only one match for an id in each of the two tables. In addition, there are no duplicate id values in either table: only one row in the left table exists with an id of 1, and only one row in the right table has an id of 1. In database parlance, this is called a *one-to-one* relationship. Consider another example: joining two tables with state-by-state census data. One table might contain household income data and the other data on educational attainment. Both tables would have 51 rows (one for each state plus Washington, D.C.), and if we wanted to join them on a key such as state name, state abbreviation, or a standard geography code, we'd have only one match for each key value in each table.

One-to-Many Relationship

In a *one-to-many* relationship, a key value in the first table will have multiple matching values in the second table's joined column. Consider a database that tracks automobiles. One table would hold data on automobile manufacturers, with one row each for Ford, Honda, Kia, and so on. A second table with model names, such as Focus, Civic, Sedona, and Accord, would have several rows matching each row in the manufacturers' table.

Many-to-Many Relationship

In a *many-to-many* relationship, multiple rows in the first table will have multiple matching rows in the second table. As an example, a table of baseball players could be joined to a table of field positions. Each player can be assigned to multiple positions, and each position can be played by multiple people.

Understanding these relationships is essential because it helps us discern whether the results of queries accurately reflect the structure of the database.

Selecting Specific Columns in a Join

So far, we've used the asterisk wildcard to select all columns from both tables. That's okay for quick data checks, but more often you'll want to specify a subset of columns. You can focus on just the data you want and avoid inadvertently changing the query results if someone adds a new column to a table.

As you learned in single-table queries, to select particular columns you use the SELECT keyword followed by the desired column names. When joining tables, the syntax changes slightly: you must include the column as well as its table name. The reason is that more than one table can contain columns with the same name, which is certainly true of our joined tables so far.

Consider the following query, which tries to fetch an id column without naming the table:

```
SELECT id
FROM schools_left LEFT JOIN schools_right
ON schools_left.id = schools_right.id;
```

Because id exists in both schools_left and schools_right, the server throws an error that appears in pgAdmin's results pane: column reference "id" is ambiguous. It's not clear which table id belongs to.

To fix the error, we need to add the table name in front of each column we're querying, as we do in the ON clause. Listing 6-10 shows the syntax, specifying that we want the id column from schools_left. We're also fetching the school names from both tables.

```
SELECT schools_left.id,
       schools_left.left_school,
       schools_right.right_school
FROM schools_left LEFT JOIN schools_right
ON schools_left.id = schools_right.id;
```

Listing 6-10: Querying specific columns in a join

We simply prefix each column name with the table it comes from, and the rest of the query syntax is the same. The result returns the requested columns from each table:

```
id   left_school               right_school
--   -----------------------   ---------------------
1    Oak Street School         Oak Street School
2    Roosevelt High School     Roosevelt High School
5    Washington Middle School
6    Jefferson High School     Jefferson High School
```

We can also add the AS keyword we used previously with census data to make it clear in the results that the id column is from schools_left. The syntax would look like this:

```
SELECT schools_left.id AS left_id, ...
```

This would display the name of the schools_left id column as left_id. We could do this for all the other columns we select using the same syntax, but the next section describes another, better method we can use to rename multiple columns.

Simplifying JOIN Syntax with Table Aliases

Naming the table for a column is easy enough, but doing so for multiple columns clutters your code. One of the best ways to serve your colleagues is to write code that's readable, which should generally not involve making them wade through table names repeated for 25 columns! The way to write more concise code is to use a shorthand approach called *table aliases*.

To create a table alias, we place a character or two after the table name when we declare it in the FROM clause. (You can use more than a couple of characters for an alias, but if the goal is to simplify code, don't go overboard.) Those characters then serve as an alias we can use instead of the full table name anywhere we reference the table in the code. Listing 6-11 demonstrates how this works:

```
SELECT lt.id,
       lt.left_school,
       rt.right_school
❶ FROM schools_left AS lt LEFT JOIN schools_right AS rt
ON lt.id = rt.id;
```

Listing 6-11: Simplifying code with table aliases

In the FROM clause, we declare the alias lt to represent schools_left and the alias rt to represent schools_right ❶ using the AS keyword. Once that's in place, we can use the aliases instead of the full table names everywhere else in the code. Immediately, our SQL looks more compact, and that's ideal.

Joining Multiple Tables

Of course, SQL joins aren't limited to two tables. We can continue adding tables to the query as long as we have columns with matching values to join on. Let's say we obtain two more school-related tables and want to join them to schools_left in a three-table join. Here are the tables: schools_enrollment has the number of students per school:

id	enrollment
1	360
2	1001
5	450
6	927

The schools_grades table contains the grade levels housed in each building:

id	grades
1	K-3
2	9-12
5	6-8
6	9-12

To write the query, we'll use Listing 6-12 to create the tables and load the data:

```
CREATE TABLE schools_enrollment (
    id integer,
    enrollment integer
);

CREATE TABLE schools_grades (
    id integer,
    grades varchar(10)
);

INSERT INTO schools_enrollment (id, enrollment)
VALUES
    (1, 360),
    (2, 1001),
    (5, 450),
    (6, 927);

INSERT INTO schools_grades (id, grades)
VALUES
    (1, 'K-3'),
    (2, '9-12'),
    (5, '6-8'),
    (6, '9-12');
```

```
   SELECT lt.id, lt.left_school, en.enrollment, gr.grades
❶ FROM schools_left AS lt LEFT JOIN schools_enrollment AS en
       ON lt.id = en.id
❷ LEFT JOIN schools_grades AS gr
       ON lt.id = gr.id;
```

Listing 6-12: Joining multiple tables

After we run the CREATE TABLE and INSERT portions of the script, the results consist of schools_enrollment and schools_grades tables, each with records that relate to schools_left from earlier in the chapter. We then connect all three tables.

In the SELECT query, we join schools_left to schools_enrollment ❶ using the tables' id fields. We also declare table aliases to keep the code compact. Next, the query joins schools_left to school_grades again on the id fields ❷.

Our result now includes columns from all three tables:

```
id   left_school                enrollment   grades
--   ------------------------   ----------   ------
 1   Oak Street School                 360   K-3
 2   Roosevelt High School            1001   9-12
 5   Washington Middle School          450   6-8
 6   Jefferson High School             927   9-12
```

If you need to, you can add even more tables to the query using additional joins. You can also join on different columns, depending on the tables' relationships. Although there is no hard limit in SQL to the number of tables you can join in a single query, some database systems might impose one. Check the documentation.

Performing Math on Joined Table Columns

The math functions we explored in Chapter 5 are just as usable when working with joined tables. We just need to include the table name when referencing a column in an operation, as we did when selecting table columns. If you work with any data that has a new release at regular intervals, you'll find this concept useful for joining a newly released table to an older one and exploring how values have changed.

That's certainly what I and many journalists do each time a new set of census data is released. We'll load the new data and try to find patterns in the growth or decline of the population, income, education, and other indicators. Let's look at how to do this by revisiting the us_counties_2010 table we created in Chapter 4 and loading similar county data from the previous Decennial Census, in 2000, to a new table. Run the code in Listing 6-13, making sure you've saved the CSV file somewhere first:

```
❶ CREATE TABLE us_counties_2000 (
      geo_name varchar(90),
      state_us_abbreviation varchar(2),
      state_fips varchar(2),
```

```
      county_fips varchar(3),
      p0010001 integer,
      p0010002 integer,
      p0010003 integer,
      p0010004 integer,
      p0010005 integer,
      p0010006 integer,
      p0010007 integer,
      p0010008 integer,
      p0010009 integer,
      p0010010 integer,
      p0020002 integer,
      p0020003 integer
   );

❷ COPY us_counties_2000
   FROM 'C:\YourDirectory\us_counties_2000.csv'
   WITH (FORMAT CSV, HEADER);

❸ SELECT c2010.geo_name,
         c2010.state_us_abbreviation AS state,
         c2010.p0010001 AS pop_2010,
         c2000.p0010001 AS pop_2000,
         c2010.p0010001 - c2000.p0010001 AS raw_change,
      ❹ round( (CAST(c2010.p0010001 AS numeric(8,1)) - c2000.p0010001)
            / c2000.p0010001 * 100, 1 ) AS pct_change
   FROM us_counties_2010 c2010 INNER JOIN us_counties_2000 c2000
❺ ON c2010.state_fips = c2000.state_fips
      AND c2010.county_fips = c2000.county_fips
   ❻ AND c2010.p0010001 <> c2000.p0010001
❼ ORDER BY pct_change DESC;
```

Listing 6-13: Performing math on joined census tables

In this code, we're building on earlier foundations. We have the familiar CREATE TABLE statement ❶, which for this exercise includes state and county codes, a geo_name column with the full name of the state and county, and nine columns with population counts including total population and counts by race. The COPY statement ❷ imports a CSV file with the census data; you can find *us_counties_2000.csv* along with all of the book's resources at *https://www.nostarch.com/practicalSQL/*. After you've downloaded the file, you'll need to change the file path to the location where you saved it.

When you've finished the import, you should have a table named us_counties_2000 with 3,141 rows. As with the 2010 data, this table has a column named p0010001 that contains the total population for each county in the United States. Because both tables have the same column, it makes sense to calculate the percent change in population for each county between 2000 and 2010. Which counties have led the nation in growth? Which ones have a decline in population?

We'll use the percent change calculation we used in Chapter 5 to get the answer. The SELECT statement ❸ includes the county's name and state abbreviation from the 2010 table, which is aliased with c2010. Next are the p0010001 total population columns from the 2010 and 2000 tables, both renamed with unique names using AS to distinguish them in the results. To get the raw change in population, we subtract the 2000 population from the 2010 count, and to find the percent change, we employ a formula ❹ and round the results to one decimal point.

We join by matching values in two columns in both tables: state_fips and county_fips ❺. The reason to join on two columns instead of one is that in both tables, we need the combination of a state code and a county code to find a unique county. I've added a third condition ❻ to illustrate using an inequality. This limits the join to counties where the p0010001 population column has a different value. We combine all three conditions using the AND keyword. Using that syntax, a join happens when all three conditions are satisfied. Finally, the results are sorted in descending order by percent change ❼ so we can see the fastest growers at the top.

That's a lot of work, but it's worth it. Here's what the first five rows of the results indicate:

name	state	pop_2010	pop_2000	raw_change	pct_change
Kendall County	IL	114736	54544	60192	110.4
Pinal County	AZ	375770	179727	196043	109.1
Flagler County	FL	95696	49832	45864	92.0
Lincoln County	SD	44828	24131	20697	85.8
Loudoun County	VA	312311	169599	142712	84.1

Two counties, Kendall in Illinois and Pinal in Arizona, more than doubled their population in 10 years, with counties in Florida, South Dakota, and Virginia not far behind. That's a valuable story we've extracted from this analysis and a starting point for understanding national population trends. If you were to dig into the data further, you might find that many of the counties with the largest growth from 2000 to 2010 were suburban bedroom communities that benefited from the decade's housing boom, and that a more recent trend sees Americans leaving rural areas to move to cities. That could make for an interesting analysis following the 2020 Decennial Census.

Wrapping Up

Given that table relationships are foundational to database architecture, learning to join tables in queries allows you to handle many of the more complex data sets you'll encounter. Experimenting with the different types of joins on tables can tell you a great deal about how data have been gathered and reveal when there's a quality issue. Make trying various joins a routine part of your exploration of a new data set.

Moving forward, we'll continue building on these bigger concepts as we drill deeper into finding information in data sets and working with the finer nuances of handling data types and making sure we have quality data. But first, we'll look at one more foundational element: employing best practices to build reliable, speedy databases with SQL.

Continue your exploration of joins with these exercises:

1. The table us_counties_2010 contains 3,143 rows, and us_counties_2000 has 3,141. That reflects the ongoing adjustments to county-level geographies that typically result from government decision making. Using appropriate joins and the NULL value, identify which counties don't exist in both tables. For fun, search online to find out why they're missing.

2. Using either the median() or percentile_cont() functions in Chapter 5, determine the median of the percent change in county population.

3. Which county had the greatest percentage loss of population between 2000 and 2010? Do you have any idea why? (Hint: A major weather event happened in 2005.)

7

TABLE DESIGN THAT WORKS FOR YOU

Obsession with detail can be a good thing. When you're running out the door, it's reassuring to know your keys will be hanging on the hook where you *always* leave them. The same holds true for database design. When you need to excavate a nugget of information from dozens of tables and millions of rows, you'll appreciate a dose of that same detail obsession. When you organize data into a finely tuned, smartly named set of tables, the analysis experience becomes more manageable.

In this chapter, I'll build on Chapter 6 by introducing *best practices* for organizing and tuning SQL databases, whether they're yours or ones you inherit for analysis. You already know how to create basic tables and add columns with the appropriate data type and a primary key. Now, we'll dig deeper into table design by exploring naming rules and conventions, ways to maintain the integrity of your data, and how to add indexes to tables to speed up queries.

Naming Tables, Columns, and Other Identifiers

Developers tend to follow different SQL style patterns when naming tables, columns, and other objects (called *identifiers*). Some prefer to use *camel case*, as in berrySmoothie, where words are strung together and the first letter of each word is capitalized except for the first word. *Pascal case*, as in BerrySmoothie, follows a similar pattern but capitalizes the first letter of the first word too. With *snake case*, as in berry_smoothie, all the words are lowercase and separated by underscores. So far, I've been using snake case in most of the examples, such as in the table us_counties_2010.

You'll find passionate supporters of each naming convention, and some preferences are tied to individual database applications or programming languages. For example, Microsoft recommends Pascal case for its SQL Server users. Whichever convention you prefer, it's most important to choose a style and apply it consistently. Be sure to check whether your organization has a style guide or offer to collaborate on one, and then follow it religiously.

Mixing styles or following none generally leads to a mess. It will be difficult to know which table is the most current, which is the backup, or the difference between two similarly named tables. For example, imagine connecting to a database and finding the following collection of tables:

```
Customers

customers

custBackup

customer_analysis

customer_test2

customer_testMarch2012

customeranalysis
```

In addition, working without a consistent naming scheme makes it problematic for others to dive into your data and makes it challenging for you to pick up where you left off.

Let's explore considerations related to naming identifiers and suggestions for best practices.

Using Quotes Around Identifiers to Enable Mixed Case

Standard ANSI SQL and many database-specific variants of SQL treat identifiers as case-insensitive unless you provide a delimiter around them—typically double quotes. Consider these two hypothetical CREATE TABLE statements for PostgreSQL:

```
CREATE TABLE customers (
    customer_id serial,
    --snip--
);

CREATE TABLE Customers (
```

```
    customer_id serial,
    --snip--
);
```

When you execute these statements in order, the first CREATE TABLE command creates a table called customers. But rather than creating a second table called Customers, the second statement will throw an error: relation "customers" already exists. Because you didn't quote the identifier, PostgreSQL treats customers and Customers as the same identifier, disregarding the case. If you want to preserve the uppercase letter and create a separate table named Customers, you must surround the identifier with quotes, like this:

```
CREATE TABLE "Customers" (
    customer_id serial,
    --snip--
);
```

Now, PostgreSQL retains the uppercase C and creates Customers as well as customers. Later, to query Customers rather than customers, you'll have to quote its name in the SELECT statement:

```
SELECT * FROM "Customers";
```

Of course, you wouldn't want two tables with such similar names because of the high risk of a mix-up. This example simply illustrates the behavior of SQL in PostgreSQL.

Pitfalls with Quoting Identifiers

Using quotation marks also permits characters not otherwise allowed in an identifier, including spaces. But be aware of the negatives of using this method: for example, you might want to throw quotes around "trees planted" and use that as a column name in a reforestation database, but then all users will have to provide quotes on every subsequent reference to that column. Omit the quotes and the database will respond with an error, identifying trees and planted as separate columns missing a comma between them. A more readable and reliable option is to use snake case, as in trees_planted.

Another downside to quoting is that it lets you use SQL *reserved keywords*, such as TABLE, WHERE, or SELECT, as an identifier. Reserved keywords are words SQL designates as having special meaning in the language. Most database developers frown on using reserved keywords as identifiers. At a minimum it's confusing, and at worst neglecting or forgetting to quote that keyword later will result in an error because the database will interpret the word as a command instead of an identifier.

NOTE   *For PostgreSQL, you can find a list of keywords documented at* https://www
.postgresql.org/docs/current/static/sql-keywords-appendix.html. *In addition, many code editors and database tools, including pgAdmin, will automatically highlight keywords in a particular color.*

Guidelines for Naming Identifiers

Given the extra burden of quoting and its potential problems, it's best to keep your identifier names simple, unquoted, and consistent. Here are my recommendations:

- **Use snake case.** Snake case is readable and reliable, as shown in the earlier trees_planted example. It's used throughout the official PostgreSQL documentation and helps make multiword names easy to understand: video_on_demand makes more sense at a glance than videoondemand.

- **Make names easy to understand and avoid cryptic abbreviations.** If you're building a database related to travel, arrival_time is a better reminder of the content as a column name than arv_tm.

- **For table names, use plurals.** Tables hold rows, and each row represents one instance of an entity. So, use plural names for tables, such as teachers, vehicles, or departments.

- **Mind the length.** The maximum number of characters allowed for an identifier name varies by database application: the SQL standard is 128 characters, but PostgreSQL limits you to 63, and the Oracle system maximum is 30. If you're writing code that may get reused in another database system, lean toward shorter identifier names.

- **When making copies of tables, use names that will help you manage them later.** One method is to append a YYYY_MM_DD date to the table name when you create it, such as tire_sizes_2017_10_20. An additional benefit is that the table names will sort in date order.

Controlling Column Values with Constraints

A column's data type already broadly defines the kind of data it will accept: integers versus characters, for example. But SQL provides several additional constraints that let us further specify acceptable values for a column based on rules and logical tests. With constraints, we can avoid the "garbage in, garbage out" phenomenon, which is what happens when poor-quality data result in inaccurate or incomplete analysis. Constraints help maintain the quality of the data and ensure the integrity of the relationships among tables.

In Chapter 6, you learned about *primary* and *foreign keys*, which are two of the most commonly used constraints. Let's review them as well as the following additional constraint types:

CHECK   Evaluates whether the data falls within values we specify

UNIQUE   Ensures that values in a column or group of columns are unique in each row in the table

NOT NULL   Prevents NULL values in a column

We can add constraints in two ways: as a *column constraint* or as a *table constraint*. A column constraint only applies to that column. It's declared with the column name and data type in the CREATE TABLE statement, and it gets checked whenever a change is made to the column. With a table constraint, we can supply criteria that apply to one or more columns. We declare it in the CREATE TABLE statement immediately after defining all the table columns, and it gets checked whenever a change is made to a row in the table.

Let's explore these constraints, their syntax, and their usefulness in table design.

Primary Keys: Natural vs. Surrogate

In Chapter 6, you learned about giving a table a *primary key*: a column or collection of columns whose values uniquely identify each row in a table. A primary key is a constraint, and it imposes two rules on the column or columns that make up the key:

1. Each column in the key must have a unique value for each row.
2. No column in the key can have missing values.

Primary keys also provide a means of relating tables to each other and maintaining *referential integrity*, which is ensuring that rows in related tables have matching values when we expect them to. The simple primary key example in "Relating Tables with Key Columns" on page 74 had a single ID field that used an integer inserted by us, the user. However, as with most areas of SQL, you can implement primary keys in several ways. Often, the data will suggest the best path. But first we must assess whether to use a *natural key* or a *surrogate key* as the primary key.

Using Existing Columns for Natural Keys

You implement a natural key by using one or more of the table's existing columns rather than creating a column and filling it with artificial values to act as keys. If a column's values obey the primary key constraint—unique for every row and never empty—it can be used as a natural key. A value in the column can change as long as the new value doesn't cause a violation of the constraint.

An example of a natural key is a driver's license identification number issued by a local Department of Motor Vehicles. Within a governmental jurisdiction, such as a state in the United States, we'd reasonably expect that all drivers would receive a unique ID on their licenses. But if we were compiling a national driver's license database, we might not be able to make that assumption; several states could independently issue the same ID code. In that case, the driver_id column may not have unique values and cannot be used as the natural key unless it's combined with one or more additional columns. Regardless, as you build tables, you'll encounter many values suitable for natural keys: a part number, a serial number, or a book's ISBN are all good examples.

Introducing Columns for Surrogate Keys

Instead of relying on existing data, a surrogate key typically consists of a single column that you fill with artificial values. This might be a sequential number auto-generated by the database; for example, using a serial data type (covered in "Auto-Incrementing Integers" on page 27). Some developers like to use a *Universally Unique Identifier (UUID)*, which is a code comprised of 32 hexadecimal digits that identifies computer hardware or software. Here's an example:

```
2911d8a8-6dea-4a46-af23-d64175a08237
```

Pros and Cons of Key Types

As with most SQL debates, there are arguments for using either type of primary key. Reasons cited for using natural keys often include the following:

- The data already exists in the table, and you don't need to add a column to create a key.
- Because the natural key data has meaning, it can reduce the need to join tables when searching.

Alternatively, advocates of surrogate keys highlight these points in favor:

- Because a surrogate key doesn't have any meaning in itself and its values are independent of the data in the table, if your data changes later, you're not limited by the key structure.
- Natural keys tend to consume more storage than the integers typically used for surrogate keys.

A well-designed table should have one or more columns that can serve as a natural key. An example is a product table with a unique product code. But in a table of employees, it might be difficult to find any single column, or even multiple columns, that would be unique on a row-by-row basis to serve as a primary key. In that case, you can create a surrogate key, but you probably should reconsider the table structure.

Primary Key Syntax

In "JOIN Types" on page 78, you created primary keys on the schools_left and schools_right tables to try out JOIN types. In fact, these were surrogate keys: in both tables, you created columns called id to use as the key and used the keywords CONSTRAINT *key_name* PRIMARY KEY to declare them as primary keys. Let's work through several more primary key examples.

In Listing 7-1, we declare a primary key using the column constraint and table constraint methods on a table similar to the driver's license example mentioned earlier. Because we expect the driver's license IDs to always be unique, we'll use that column as a natural key.

```
CREATE TABLE natural_key_example (
❶ license_id varchar(10) CONSTRAINT license_key PRIMARY KEY,
   first_name varchar(50),
   last_name varchar(50)
);

❷ DROP TABLE natural_key_example;

CREATE TABLE natural_key_example (
   license_id varchar(10),
   first_name varchar(50),
   last_name varchar(50),
❸ CONSTRAINT license_key PRIMARY KEY (license_id)
);
```

Listing 7-1: Declaring a single-column natural key as a primary key

We first use the column constraint syntax to declare license_id as the primary key by adding the CONSTRAINT keyword ❶ followed by a name for the key and then the keywords PRIMARY KEY. An advantage of using this syntax is that it's easy to understand at a glance which column is designated as the primary key. Note that in the column constraint syntax you can omit the CONSTRAINT keyword and name for the key, and simply use PRIMARY KEY.

Next, we delete the table from the database by using the DROP TABLE command ❷ to prepare for the table constraint example.

To add the same primary key using the table constraint syntax, we declare the CONSTRAINT after listing the final column ❸ with the column we want to use as the key in parentheses. In this example, we end up with the same column for the primary key as we did with the column constraint syntax. However, you must use the table constraint syntax when you want to create a primary key using more than one column. In that case, you would list the columns in parentheses, separated by commas. We'll explore that in a moment.

First, let's look at how having a primary key protects you from ruining the integrity of your data. Listing 7-2 contains two INSERT statements:

```
INSERT INTO natural_key_example (license_id, first_name, last_name)
VALUES ('T229901', 'Lynn', 'Malero');

INSERT INTO natural_key_example (license_id, first_name, last_name)
VALUES ('T229901', 'Sam', 'Tracy');
```

Listing 7-2: An example of a primary key violation

When you execute the first INSERT statement on its own, the server loads a row into the natural_key_example table without any issue. When you attempt to execute the second, the server replies with an error:

```
ERROR:  duplicate key value violates unique constraint "license_key"
DETAIL:  Key (license_id)=(T229901) already exists.
```

Before adding the row, the server checked whether a `license_id` of T229901 was already present in the table. Because it was, and because a primary key by definition must be unique for each row, the server rejected the operation. The rules of the fictional DMV state that no two drivers can have the same license ID, so checking for and rejecting duplicate data is one way for the database to enforce that rule.

Creating a Composite Primary Key

If we want to create a natural key but a single column in the table isn't sufficient for meeting the primary key requirements for uniqueness, we may be able to create a suitable key from a combination of columns, which is called a *composite primary key*.

As a hypothetical example, let's use a table that tracks student school attendance. The combination of a student ID column and a date column would give us unique data for each row, tracking whether or not the student was in school each day during a school year. To create a composite primary key from two or more columns, you must declare it using the table constraint syntax mentioned earlier. Listing 7-3 creates an example table for the student attendance scenario. The school database would record each `student_id` only once per `school_day`, creating a unique value for the row. A present column of data type `boolean` indicates whether the student was there on that day.

```
CREATE TABLE natural_key_composite_example (
    student_id varchar(10),
    school_day date,
    present boolean,
    CONSTRAINT student_key PRIMARY KEY (student_id, school_day)
);
```

Listing 7-3: Declaring a composite primary key as a natural key

The syntax in Listing 7-3 follows the same table constraint format for adding a primary key for one column, but we pass two (or more) columns as arguments rather than one. Again, we can simulate a key violation by attempting to insert a row where the combination of values in the two key columns—`student_id` and `school_day`—is not unique to the table. Run the code in Listing 7-4:

```
INSERT INTO natural_key_composite_example (student_id, school_day, present)
VALUES(775, '1/22/2017', 'Y');

INSERT INTO natural_key_composite_example (student_id, school_day, present)
VALUES(775, '1/23/2017', 'Y');

INSERT INTO natural_key_composite_example (student_id, school_day, present)
VALUES(775, '1/23/2017', 'N');
```

Listing 7-4: Example of a composite primary key violation

The first two INSERT statements execute fine because there's no duplication of values in the combination of key columns. But the third statement causes an error because the student_id and school_day values it contains match a combination that already exists in the table:

```
ERROR:  duplicate key value violates unique constraint "student_key"
DETAIL:  Key (student_id, school_day)=(775, 2017-01-23) already exists.
```

You can create composite keys with more than two columns. The specific database you're using imposes the limit to the number of columns you can use.

Creating an Auto-Incrementing Surrogate Key

If a table you're creating has no columns suitable for a natural primary key, you may have a data integrity problem; in that case, it's best to reconsider how you're structuring the database. If you're inheriting data for analysis or feel strongly about using surrogate keys, you can create a column and fill it with unique values. Earlier, I mentioned that some developers use UUIDs for this; others rely on software to generate a unique code. For our purposes, an easy way to create a surrogate primary key is with an auto-incrementing integer using one of the serial data types discussed in "Auto-Incrementing Integers" on page 27.

Recall the three serial types: smallserial, serial, and bigserial. They correspond to the integer types smallint, integer, and bigint in terms of the range of values they handle and the amount of disk storage they consume. For a primary key, it may be tempting to try to save disk space by using serial, which handles numbers as large as 2,147,483,647. But many a database developer has received a late-night call from a user frantic to know why their application is broken, only to discover that the database is trying to generate a number one greater than the data type's maximum. For this reason, with PostgreSQL, it's generally wise to use bigserial, which accepts numbers as high as 9.2 *quintillion*. You can set it and forget it, as shown in the first column defined in Listing 7-5:

```
CREATE TABLE surrogate_key_example (
❶ order_number bigserial,
    product_name varchar(50),
    order_date date,
❷ CONSTRAINT order_key PRIMARY KEY (order_number)
);

❸ INSERT INTO surrogate_key_example (product_name, order_date)
VALUES ('Beachball Polish', '2015-03-17'),
       ('Wrinkle De-Atomizer', '2017-05-22'),
       ('Flux Capacitor', '1985-10-26');

SELECT * FROM surrogate_key_example;
```

Listing 7-5: Declaring a bigserial column as a surrogate key

Listing 7-5 shows how to declare the `bigserial` ❶ data type for an order_number column and set the column as the primary key ❷. When you insert data into the table ❸, you can omit the order_number column. With order_number set to `bigserial`, the database will create a new value for that column on each insert. The new value will be one greater than the largest already created for the column.

Run `SELECT * FROM surrogate_key_example;` to see how the column fills in automatically:

order_number	product_name	order_date
1	Beachball Polish	2015-03-17
2	Wrinkle De-Atomizer	2017-05-22
3	Flux Capacitor	1985-10-26

The database will add one to order_number each time a new row is inserted. But it won't fill any gaps in the sequence created after rows are deleted.

Foreign Keys

With the *foreign key* constraint, SQL very helpfully provides a way to ensure data in related tables doesn't end up unrelated, or orphaned. A foreign key is one or more columns in a table that match the primary key of another table. But a foreign key also imposes a constraint: values entered must already exist in the primary key or other unique key of the table it references. If not, the value is rejected. This constraint ensures that we don't end up with rows in one table that have no relation to rows in the other tables we can join them to.

To illustrate, Listing 7-6 shows two tables from a hypothetical database tracking motor vehicle activity:

```
CREATE TABLE licenses (
    license_id varchar(10),
    first_name varchar(50),
    last_name varchar(50),
 ❶ CONSTRAINT licenses_key PRIMARY KEY (license_id)
);

CREATE TABLE registrations (
    registration_id varchar(10),
    registration_date date,
 ❷ license_id varchar(10) REFERENCES licenses (license_id),
    CONSTRAINT registration_key PRIMARY KEY (registration_id, license_id)
);

❸ INSERT INTO licenses (license_id, first_name, last_name)
   VALUES ('T229901', 'Lynn', 'Malero');

❹ INSERT INTO registrations (registration_id, registration_date, license_id)
   VALUES ('A203391', '3/17/2017', 'T229901');
```

```
❺ INSERT INTO registrations (registration_id, registration_date, license_id)
  VALUES ('A75772', '3/17/2017', 'T000001');
```

Listing 7-6: A foreign key example

The first table, licenses, is similar to the natural_key_example table we made earlier and uses a driver's unique license_id ❶ as a natural primary key. The second table, registrations, is for tracking vehicle registrations. A single license ID might be connected to multiple vehicle registrations, because each licensed driver can register multiple vehicles over a number of years. Also, a single vehicle could be registered to multiple license holders, establishing, as you learned in Chapter 6, a many-to-many relationship.

Here's how that relationship is expressed via SQL: in the registrations table, we designate the column license_id as a foreign key by adding the REFERENCES keyword, followed by the table name and column for it to reference ❷.

Now, when we insert a row into registrations, the database will test whether the value inserted into license_id already exists in the license_id primary key column of the licenses table. If it doesn't, the database returns an error, which is important. If any rows in registrations didn't correspond to a row in licenses, we'd have no way to write a query to find the person who registered the vehicle.

To see this constraint in action, create the two tables and execute the INSERT statements one at a time. The first adds a row to licenses ❸ that includes the value T229901 for the license_id. The second adds a row to registrations ❹ where the foreign key contains the same value. So far, so good, because the value exists in both tables. But we encounter an error with the third insert, which tries to add a row to registrations ❺ with a value for license_id that's not in licenses:

```
ERROR:  insert or update on table "registrations" violates foreign key
constraint "registrations_license_id_fkey"
DETAIL:  Key (license_id)=(T000001) is not present in table "licenses".
```

The resulting error is good because it shows the database is keeping the data clean. But it also indicates a few practical implications: first, it affects the order we insert data. We cannot add data to a table that contains a foreign key before the other table referenced by the key has the related records, or we'll get an error. In this example, we'd have to create a driver's license record before inserting a related registration record (if you think about it, that's what your local department of motor vehicles probably does).

Second, the reverse applies when we delete data. To maintain referential integrity, the foreign key constraint prevents us from deleting a row from licenses before removing any related rows in registrations, because doing so would leave an orphaned record. We would have to delete the related row in registrations first, and then delete the row in licenses. However, ANSI SQL provides a way to handle this order of operations automatically using the ON DELETE CASCADE keywords, which I'll discuss next.

Automatically Deleting Related Records with CASCADE

To delete a row in licenses and have that action automatically delete any related rows in registrations, we can specify that behavior by adding ON DELETE CASCADE when defining the foreign key constraint.

When we create the registrations table, the keywords would go at the end of the definition of the license_id column, like this:

```
CREATE TABLE registrations (
    registration_id varchar(10),
    registration_date date,
    license_id varchar(10) REFERENCES licenses (license_id) ON DELETE CASCADE,
    CONSTRAINT registration_key PRIMARY KEY (registration_id, license_id)
);
```

Now, deleting a row in licenses should also delete all related rows in registrations. This allows us to delete a driver's license without first having to manually remove any registrations to it. It also maintains data integrity by ensuring deleting a license doesn't leave orphaned rows in registrations.

The CHECK Constraint

A CHECK constraint evaluates whether data added to a column meets the expected criteria, which we specify with a logical test. If the criteria aren't met, the database returns an error. The CHECK constraint is extremely valuable because it can prevent columns from getting loaded with nonsensical data. For example, a new employee's birthdate probably shouldn't be more than 120 years in the past, so you can set a cap on birthdates. Or, in most schools I know, Z isn't a valid letter grade for a course (although my barely passing algebra grade felt like it), so we might insert constraints that only accept the values A–F.

As with primary keys, we can implement a CHECK constraint as a column constraint or a table constraint. For a column constraint, declare it in the CREATE TABLE statement after the column name and data type: CHECK (*logical expression*). As a table constraint, use the syntax CONSTRAINT *constraint_name* CHECK (*logical expression*) after all columns are defined.

Listing 7-7 shows a CHECK constraint applied to two columns in a table we might use to track the user role and salary of employees within an organization. It uses the table constraint syntax for the primary key and the CHECK constraint.

```
CREATE TABLE check_constraint_example (
    user_id bigserial,
    user_role varchar(50),
    salary integer,
    CONSTRAINT user_id_key PRIMARY KEY (user_id),
  ❶ CONSTRAINT check_role_in_list CHECK (user_role IN('Admin', 'Staff')),
  ❷ CONSTRAINT check_salary_not_zero CHECK (salary > 0)
);
```

Listing 7-7: Examples of CHECK constraints

We create the table and set the `user_id` column as an auto-incrementing surrogate primary key. The first `CHECK` ❶ tests whether values entered into the `user_role` column match one of two predefined strings, `Admin` or `Staff`, by using the SQL `IN` operator. The second `CHECK` tests whether values entered in the `salary` column are greater than 0, because no one should be earning a negative amount ❷. Both tests are another example of a *Boolean expression*, a statement that evaluates as either true or false. If a value tested by the constraint evaluates as true, the check passes.

NOTE   *Developers may debate whether check logic belongs in the database, in the application in front of the database, such as a human resources system, or both. One advantage of checks in the database is that the database will maintain data integrity in the case of changes to the application, even if a new system gets built or users are given alternate ways to add data.*

When values are inserted or updated, the database checks them against the constraint. If the values in either column violate the constraint—or, for that matter, if the primary key constraint is violated—the database will reject the change.

If we use the table constraint syntax, we also can combine more than one test in a single `CHECK` statement. Say we have a table related to student achievement. We could add the following:

```
CONSTRAINT grad_check CHECK (credits >= 120 AND tuition = 'Paid')
```

Notice that we combine two logical tests by enclosing them in parentheses and connecting them with `AND`. Here, both Boolean expressions must evaluate as `true` for the entire check to pass. You can also test values across columns, as in the following example where we want to make sure an item's sale price is a discount on the original, assuming we have columns for both values:

```
CONSTRAINT sale_check CHECK (sale_price < retail_price)
```

Inside the parentheses, the logical expression checks that the sale price is less than the retail price.

The UNIQUE Constraint

We can also ensure that a column has a unique value in each row by using the `UNIQUE` constraint. If ensuring unique values sounds similar to the purpose of a primary key, it is. But `UNIQUE` has one important difference. In a primary key, no values can be `NULL`, but a `UNIQUE` constraint permits multiple `NULL` values in a column.

To show the usefulness of `UNIQUE`, look at the code in Listing 7-8, which is a table for tracking contact info:

```
CREATE TABLE unique_constraint_example (
    contact_id bigserial CONSTRAINT contact_id_key PRIMARY KEY,
```

```
        first_name varchar(50),
        last_name varchar(50),
        email varchar(200),
    ❶ CONSTRAINT email_unique UNIQUE (email)
);

INSERT INTO unique_constraint_example (first_name, last_name, email)
VALUES ('Samantha', 'Lee', 'slee@example.org');

INSERT INTO unique_constraint_example (first_name, last_name, email)
VALUES ('Betty', 'Diaz', 'bdiaz@example.org');

INSERT INTO unique_constraint_example (first_name, last_name, email)
❷ VALUES ('Sasha', 'Lee', 'slee@example.org');
```

Listing 7-8: A UNIQUE constraint example

In this table, contact_id serves as a surrogate primary key, uniquely identifying each row. But we also have an email column, the main point of contact with each person. We'd expect this column to contain only unique email addresses, but those addresses might change over time. So, we use UNIQUE ❶ to ensure that any time we add or update a contact's email we're not providing one that already exists. If we do try to insert an email that already exists ❷, the database will return an error:

```
ERROR:  duplicate key value violates unique constraint "email_unique"
DETAIL:  Key (email)=(slee@example.org) already exists.
```

Again, the error shows the database is working for us.

The NOT NULL Constraint

In Chapter 6, you learned about NULL, a special value in SQL that represents a condition where no data is present in a row in a column or the value is unknown. You've also learned that NULL values are not allowed in a primary key, because primary keys need to uniquely identify each row in a table. But there will be other columns besides primary keys where you don't want to allow empty values. For example, in a table listing each student in a school, it would be necessary for columns containing first and last names to be filled for each row. To require a value in a column, SQL provides the NOT NULL constraint, which simply prevents a column from accepting empty values.

Listing 7-9 demonstrates the NOT NULL syntax:

```
CREATE TABLE not_null_example (
    student_id bigserial,
    first_name varchar(50) NOT NULL,
    last_name varchar(50) NOT NULL,
    CONSTRAINT student_id_key PRIMARY KEY (student_id)
);
```

Listing 7-9: A NOT NULL constraint example

Here, we declare NOT NULL for the first_name and last_name columns because it's likely we'd require those pieces of information in a table tracking student information. If we attempt an INSERT on the table and don't include values for those columns, the database will notify us of the violation.

Removing Constraints or Adding Them Later

So far, we've been placing constraints on tables at the time of creation. You can also remove a constraint or later add one to an existing table using ALTER TABLE, the SQL command that makes changes to tables and columns. We'll work with ALTER TABLE more in Chapter 9, but for now we'll review the syntax for adding and removing constraints.

To remove a primary key, foreign key, or a UNIQUE constraint, you would write an ALTER TABLE statement in this format:

```
ALTER TABLE table_name DROP CONSTRAINT constraint_name;
```

To drop a NOT NULL constraint, the statement operates on the column, so you must use the additional ALTER COLUMN keywords, like so:

```
ALTER TABLE table_name ALTER COLUMN column_name DROP NOT NULL;
```

Let's use these statements to modify the not_null_example table you just made, as shown in Listing 7-10:

```
ALTER TABLE not_null_example DROP CONSTRAINT student_id_key;
ALTER TABLE not_null_example ADD CONSTRAINT student_id_key PRIMARY KEY (student_id);
ALTER TABLE not_null_example ALTER COLUMN first_name DROP NOT NULL;
ALTER TABLE not_null_example ALTER COLUMN first_name SET NOT NULL;
```

Listing 7-10: Dropping and adding a primary key and a NOT NULL constraint

Execute the statements one at a time to make changes to the table. Each time, you can view the changes to the table definition in pgAdmin by clicking the table name once, and then clicking the **SQL** tab above the query window. With the first ALTER TABLE statement, we use DROP CONSTRAINT to remove the primary key named student_id_key. We then add the primary key back using ADD CONSTRAINT. We'd use that same syntax to add a constraint to any existing table.

NOTE *You can only add a constraint to an existing table if the data in the target column obeys the limits of the constraint. For example, you can't place a primary key constraint on a column that has duplicate or empty values.*

In the third statement, ALTER COLUMN and DROP NOT NULL remove the NOT NULL constraint from the first_name column. Finally, SET NOT NULL adds the constraint.

Speeding Up Queries with Indexes

In the same way that a book's index helps you find information more quickly, you can speed up queries by adding an *index* to one or more columns. The database uses the index as a shortcut rather than scanning each row to find data. That's admittedly a simplistic picture of what, in SQL databases, is a nontrivial topic. I could write several chapters on SQL indexes and tuning databases for performance, but instead I'll offer general guidance on using indexes and a PostgreSQL-specific example that demonstrates their benefits.

B-Tree: PostgreSQL's Default Index

While following along in this book, you've already created several indexes, perhaps without knowing. Each time you add a primary key or UNIQUE constraint to a table, PostgreSQL (as well as most database systems) places an index on the column. Indexes are stored separately from the table data, but they're accessed automatically when you run a query and are updated every time a row is added or removed from the table.

In PostgreSQL, the default index type is the *B-Tree index*. It's created automatically on the columns designated for the primary key or a UNIQUE constraint, and it's also the type created by default when you execute a CREATE INDEX statement. B-Tree, short for *balanced tree*, is so named because the structure organizes the data in a way that when you search for a value, it looks from the top of the tree down through branches until it locates the data you want. (Of course, the process is a lot more complicated than that. A good start on understanding more about the B-Tree is the B-Tree Wikipedia entry.) A B-Tree index is useful for data that can be ordered and searched using equality and range operators, such as <, <=, =, >=, >, and BETWEEN.

PostgreSQL incorporates additional index types, including the *Generalized Inverted Index (GIN)* and the *Generalized Search Tree (GiST)*. Each has distinct uses, and I'll incorporate them in later chapters on full text search and queries using geometry types.

For now, let's see a B-Tree index speed a simple search query. For this exercise, we'll use a large data set comprising more than 900,000 New York City street addresses, compiled by the OpenAddresses project at *https://openaddresses.io/*. The file with the data, *city_of_new_york.csv*, is available for you to download along with all the resources for this book from *https://www.nostarch.com/practicalSQL/*.

After you've downloaded the file, use the code in Listing 7-11 to create a new_york_addresses table and import the address data. You're a pro at this by now, although the import will take longer than the tiny data sets you've loaded so far. The final, loaded table is 126MB, and on one of my systems, it took nearly a minute for the COPY command to complete.

```
CREATE TABLE new_york_addresses (
    longitude numeric(9,6),
    latitude numeric(9,6),
```

```
    street_number varchar(10),
    street varchar(32),
    unit varchar(7),
    postcode varchar(5),
    id integer CONSTRAINT new_york_key PRIMARY KEY
);

COPY new_york_addresses
FROM 'C:\YourDirectory\city_of_new_york.csv'
WITH (FORMAT CSV, HEADER);
```

Listing 7-11: Importing New York City address data

When the data loads, run a quick SELECT query to visually check that you have 940,374 rows and seven columns. A common use for this data might be to search for matches in the street column, so we'll use that example for exploring index performance.

Benchmarking Query Performance with EXPLAIN

We'll measure how well an index can improve query speed by checking the performance before and after adding one. To do this, we'll use PostgreSQL's EXPLAIN command, which is specific to PostgreSQL and not part of standard SQL. The EXPLAIN command provides output that lists the *query plan* for a specific database query. This might include how the database plans to scan the table, whether or not it will use indexes, and so on. If we add the ANALYZE keyword, EXPLAIN will carry out the query and show the actual execution time, which is what we want for the current exercise.

Recording Some Control Execution Times

Run each of the three queries in Listing 7-12 one at a time. We're using typical SELECT queries with a WHERE clause but with the keywords EXPLAIN ANALYZE included at the beginning. Instead of showing the query results, these keywords tell the database to execute the query and display statistics about the query process and how long it took to execute.

```
EXPLAIN ANALYZE SELECT * FROM new_york_addresses
WHERE street = 'BROADWAY';

EXPLAIN ANALYZE SELECT * FROM new_york_addresses
WHERE street = '52 STREET';

EXPLAIN ANALYZE SELECT * FROM new_york_addresses
WHERE street = 'ZWICKY AVENUE';
```

Listing 7-12: Benchmark queries for index performance

On my system, the first query returns these stats:

❶ Seq Scan on new_york_addresses (cost=0.00..20730.68 rows=3730 width=46)
   (actual time=0.055..289.426 rows=3336 loops=1)
     Filter: ((street)::text = 'BROADWAY'::text)

```
          Rows Removed by Filter: 937038
        Planning time: 0.617 ms
❷ Execution time: 289.838 ms
```

Not all the output is relevant here, so I won't decode it all, but two lines are pertinent. The first indicates that to find any rows where street = 'BROADWAY', the database will conduct a sequential scan ❶ of the table. That's a synonym for a full table scan: each row will be examined, and the database will remove any row that doesn't match BROADWAY. The execution time (on my computer about 290 milliseconds) ❷ is how long this will take. Your time will depend on factors including your computer hardware.

Run each query in Listing 7-12 and record the execution time for each.

Adding the Index

Now, let's see how adding an index changes the query's search method and how fast it works. Listing 7-13 shows the SQL statement for creating the index with PostgreSQL:

```
CREATE INDEX street_idx ON new_york_addresses (street);
```

Listing 7-13: Creating a B-Tree index on the new_york_addresses table

Notice that it's similar to the commands for creating constraints we've covered in the chapter already. (Other database systems have their own variants and options for creating indexes, and there is no ANSI standard.) We give the CREATE INDEX keywords followed by a name we choose for the index, in this case street_idx. Then ON is added, followed by the target table and column.

Execute the CREATE INDEX statement, and PostgreSQL will scan the values in the street column and build the index from them. We only need to create the index once. When the task finishes, rerun each of the three queries in Listing 7-12 and record the execution times reported by EXPLAIN ANALYZE. For example:

```
Bitmap Heap Scan on new_york_addresses  (cost=65.80..5962.17 rows=2758
width=46) (actual time=1.792..9.816 rows=3336 loops=1)
   Recheck Cond: ((street)::text = 'BROADWAY'::text)
   Heap Blocks: exact=2157
❶    -> Bitmap Index Scan on street_idx  (cost=0.00..65.11 rows=2758 width=0)
        (actual time=1.253..1.253 rows=3336 loops=1)
          Index Cond: ((street)::text = 'BROADWAY'::text)
Planning time: 0.163 ms
❷ Execution time: 5.887 ms
```

Do you notice a change? First, instead of a sequential scan, the EXPLAIN ANALYZE statistics for each query show that the database is now using an index scan on street_idx ❶ instead of visiting each row. Also, the query speed is now markedly faster ❷. Table 7-1 shows the execution times (rounded) from my computer before and after adding the index.

Table 7-1: Measuring Index Performance

Query Filter	Before Index	After Index
WHERE street = 'BROADWAY'	290 ms	6 ms
WHERE street = '52 STREET'	271 ms	6 ms
WHERE street = 'ZWICKY AVENUE'	306 ms	1 ms

The execution times are much, much better, effectively a quarter second faster or more per query. Is a quarter second that impressive? Well, whether you're seeking answers in data using repeated querying or creating a database system for thousands of users, the time savings adds up.

If you ever need to remove an index from a table—perhaps if you're testing the performance of several index types—use the DROP INDEX command followed by the name of the index to remove.

Considerations When Using Indexes

You've seen that indexes have significant performance benefits, so does that mean you should add an index to every column in a table? Not so fast! Indexes are valuable, but they're not always needed. In addition, they do enlarge the database and impose a maintenance cost on writing data. Here are a few tips for judging when to uses indexes:

- Consult the documentation for the database manager you're using to learn about the kinds of indexes available and which to use on particular data types. PostgreSQL, for example, has five more index types in addition to B-Tree. One, called GiST, is particularly suited to the geometry data types I'll discuss later in the book. Full text search, which you'll learn in Chapter 13, also benefits from indexing.

- Consider adding indexes to any columns you'll use in table joins. Primary keys are indexed by default in PostgreSQL, but foreign key columns in related tables are not and are a good target for indexes.

- Add indexes to columns that will frequently end up in a query WHERE clause. As you've seen, search performance is significantly improved via indexes.

- Use EXPLAIN ANALYZE to test performance under a variety of configurations if you're unsure. Optimization is a process!

Wrapping Up

With the tools you've added to your toolbox in this chapter, you're ready to ensure that the databases you build or inherit are best suited for your collection and exploration of data. Your queries will run faster, you can exclude unwanted values, and your database objects will have consistent organization. That's a boon for you and for others who share your data.

This chapter concludes the first part of the book, which focused on giving you the essentials to dig into SQL databases. I'll continue building on these foundations as we explore more complex queries and strategies for data analysis. In the next chapter, we'll use SQL aggregate functions to assess the quality of a data set and get usable information from it.

TRY IT YOURSELF

Are you ready to test yourself on the concepts covered in this chapter? Consider the following two tables from a database you're making to keep track of your vinyl LP collection. Start by reviewing these CREATE TABLE statements:

```
CREATE TABLE albums (
    album_id bigserial,
    album_catalog_code varchar(100),
    album_title text,
    album_artist text,
    album_release_date date,
    album_genre varchar(40),
    album_description text
);

CREATE TABLE songs (
    song_id bigserial,
    song_title text,
    song_artist text,
    album_id bigint
);
```

The albums table includes information specific to the overall collection of songs on the disc. The songs table catalogs each track on the album. Each song has a title and its own artist column, because each song might feature its own collection of artists.

Use the tables to answer these questions:

1. Modify these CREATE TABLE statements to include primary and foreign keys plus additional constraints on both tables. Explain why you made your choices.

2. Instead of using album_id as a surrogate key for your primary key, are there any columns in albums that could be useful as a natural key? What would you have to know to decide?

3. To speed up queries, which columns are good candidates for indexes?

8

EXTRACTING INFORMATION BY GROUPING AND SUMMARIZING

Every data set tells a story, and it's the data analyst's job to find out what that story is. In Chapter 2, you learned about interviewing data using SELECT statements, which included sorting columns, finding distinct values, and filtering results. You've also learned the fundamentals of SQL math, data types, table design, and joining tables. With all these tools under your belt, you're ready to summarize data using grouping and SQL functions.

Summarizing data allows us to identify useful information we wouldn't be able to see otherwise. In this chapter, we'll use the well-known institution of your local library as our example.

Despite changes in the way people consume information, libraries remain a vital part of communities worldwide. But the internet and advancements in library technology have changed how we use libraries. For example, ebooks and online access to digital materials now have a permanent place in libraries along with books and periodicals.

In the United States, the Institute of Museum and Library Services (IMLS) measures library activity as part of its annual Public Libraries Survey. The survey collects data from more than 9,000 library administrative entities, defined by the survey as agencies that provide library services to a particular locality. Some agencies are county library systems, and others are part of school districts. Data on each agency includes the number of branches, staff, books, hours open per year, and so on. The IMLS has been collecting data each year since 1988 and includes all public library agencies in the 50 states plus the District of Columbia and several territories, such as American Samoa. (Read more about the program at *https://www.imls.gov/ research-evaluation/data-collection/public-libraries-survey/.*)

For this exercise, we'll assume the role of an analyst who just received a fresh copy of the library data set to produce a report describing trends from the data. We'll need to create two tables, one with data from the 2014 survey and the second from the 2009 survey. Then we'll summarize the more interesting data in each table and join the tables to see the five-year trends. During the analysis, you'll learn SQL techniques for summarizing data using *aggregate functions* and *grouping*.

Creating the Library Survey Tables

Let's create the 2014 and 2009 library survey tables and import the data. We'll use appropriate data types for each column and add constraints and an index to each table to preserve data integrity and speed up queries.

Creating the 2014 Library Data Table

We'll start by creating the table for the 2014 library data. Using the CREATE TABLE statement, Listing 8-1 builds pls_fy2014_pupld14a, a table for the fiscal year 2014 Public Library Data File from the Public Libraries Survey. The Public Library Data File summarizes data at the agency level, counting activity at all agency outlets, which include central libraries, branch libraries, and bookmobiles. The annual survey generates two additional files we won't use: one summarizes data at the state level, and the other has data on individual outlets. For this exercise, those files are redundant, but you can read about the data they contain in the 2014 data dictionary, available from the IMLS at *https://www.imls.gov/sites/default/files/fy2014_pls_data_file_documentation.pdf.*

For convenience, I've created a naming scheme for the tables: pls refers to the survey title, fy2014 is the fiscal year the data covers, and pupld14a is the name of the particular file from the survey. For simplicity, I've selected just 72 of the more relevant columns from the 159 in the original survey file to fill the pls_fy2014_pupld14a table, excluding data like the codes that explain the source of individual responses. When a library didn't provide data, the agency derived the data using other means, but we don't need that information for this exercise.

Note that Listing 8-1 is abbreviated for convenience. The full data set and code for creating and loading this table is available for download with all the book's resources at *https://www.nostarch.com/practicalSQL/*.

```
CREATE TABLE pls_fy2014_pupld14a (
    stabr varchar(2) NOT NULL,
❶ fscskey varchar(6) CONSTRAINT fscskey2014_key PRIMARY KEY,
    libid varchar(20) NOT NULL,
    libname varchar(100) NOT NULL,
    obereg varchar(2) NOT NULL,
    rstatus integer NOT NULL,
    statstru varchar(2) NOT NULL,
    statname varchar(2) NOT NULL,
    stataddr varchar(2) NOT NULL,
    --snip--
    wifisess integer NOT NULL,
    yr_sub integer NOT NULL
);

❷ CREATE INDEX libname2014_idx ON pls_fy2014_pupld14a (libname);
   CREATE INDEX stabr2014_idx ON pls_fy2014_pupld14a (stabr);
   CREATE INDEX city2014_idx ON pls_fy2014_pupld14a (city);
   CREATE INDEX visits2014_idx ON pls_fy2014_pupld14a (visits);

❸ COPY pls_fy2014_pupld14a
   FROM 'C:\YourDirectory\pls_fy2014_pupld14a.csv'
   WITH (FORMAT CSV, HEADER);
```

Listing 8-1: Creating and filling the 2014 Public Libraries Survey table

After finding the code and data file for Listing 8-1, connect to your analysis database in pgAdmin and run it. Remember to change `C:\YourDirectory\` to the path where you saved the CSV file.

Here's what it does: first, the code makes the table via CREATE TABLE. We assign a primary key constraint to the column named fscskey ❶, a unique code the data dictionary says is assigned to each library. Because it's unique, present in each row, and unlikely to change, it can serve as a natural primary key.

The definition for each column includes the appropriate data type and NOT NULL constraints where the columns have no missing values. If you look carefully in the data dictionary, you'll notice that I changed the column named database in the CSV file to databases in the table. The reason is that database is a SQL reserved keyword, and it's unwise to use keywords as identifiers because it can lead to unintended consequences in queries or other functions.

The startdat and enddat columns contain dates, but we've set their data type to varchar(10) in the code because in the CSV file those columns include non-date values, and our import will fail if we try to use a date data type. In Chapter 9, you'll learn how to clean up cases like these. For now, those columns are fine as is.

After creating the table, we add indexes ❷ to columns we'll use for queries. This provides faster results when we search the column for a particular library. The COPY statement ❸ imports the data from a CSV file named *pls_fy2014_pupld14a.csv* using the file path you provide.

Creating the 2009 Library Data Table

Creating the table for the 2009 library data follows similar steps, as shown in Listing 8-2. Most ongoing surveys will have a handful of year-to-year changes because the makers of the survey either think of new questions or modify existing ones, so the included columns will be slightly different in this table. That's one reason the data providers create new tables instead of adding rows to a cumulative table. For example, the 2014 file has a wifisess column, which lists the annual number of Wi-Fi sessions the library provided, but this column doesn't exist in the 2009 data. The data dictionary for this survey year is at *https://www.imls.gov/sites/default/files/fy2009_pls _data_file_documentation.pdf*.

After you build this table, import the CSV file *pls_fy2009_pupld09a*. This file is also available to download along with all the book's resources at *https:// www.nostarch.com/practicalSQL/*. When you've saved the file and added the correct file path to the COPY statement, execute the code in Listing 8-2:

```
CREATE TABLE pls_fy2009_pupld09a (
    stabr varchar(2) NOT NULL,
  ❶ fscskey varchar(6) CONSTRAINT fscskey2009_key PRIMARY KEY,
    libid varchar(20) NOT NULL,
    libname varchar(100) NOT NULL,
    address varchar(35) NOT NULL,
    city varchar(20) NOT NULL,
    zip varchar(5) NOT NULL,
    zip4 varchar(4) NOT NULL,
    cnty varchar(20) NOT NULL,
    --snip--
    fipsst varchar(2) NOT NULL,
    fipsco varchar(3) NOT NULL
);

❷ CREATE INDEX libname2009_idx ON pls_fy2009_pupld09a (libname);
CREATE INDEX stabr2009_idx ON pls_fy2009_pupld09a (stabr);
CREATE INDEX city2009_idx ON pls_fy2009_pupld09a (city);
CREATE INDEX visits2009_idx ON pls_fy2009_pupld09a (visits);

COPY pls_fy2009_pupld09a
FROM 'C:\YourDirectory\pls_fy2009_pupld09a.csv'
WITH (FORMAT CSV, HEADER);
```

Listing 8-2: Creating and filling the 2009 Public Libraries Survey table

We use fscskey as the primary key again ❶, and we create an index on libname and other columns ❷. Now, let's mine the two tables of library data from 2014 and 2009 to discover their stories.

Exploring the Library Data Using Aggregate Functions

Aggregate functions combine values from multiple rows and return a single result based on an operation on those values. For example, you might return the average of values with the avg() function, as you learned in Chapter 5. That's just one of many aggregate functions in SQL. Some are part of the SQL standard, and others are specific to PostgreSQL and other database managers. Most of the aggregate functions used in this chapter are part of standard SQL (a full list of PostgreSQL aggregates is at *https://www.postgresql.org/docs/current/static/functions-aggregate.html*).

In this section, we'll work through the library data using aggregates on single and multiple columns, and then explore how you can expand their use by grouping the results they return with values from additional columns.

Counting Rows and Values Using count()

After importing a data set, a sensible first step is to make sure the table has the expected number of rows. For example, the IMLS documentation for the 2014 data says the file we imported has 9,305 rows, and the 2009 file has 9,299 rows. When we count the number of rows in those tables, the results should match those counts.

The count() aggregate function, which is part of the ANSI SQL standard, makes it easy to check the number of rows and perform other counting tasks. If we supply an asterisk as an input, such as count(*), the asterisk acts as a wildcard, so the function returns the number of table rows regardless of whether they include NULL values. We do this in both statements in Listing 8-3:

```
SELECT count(*)
FROM pls_fy2014_pupld14a;

SELECT count(*)
FROM pls_fy2009_pupld09a;
```

Listing 8-3: Using count() for table row counts

Run each of the commands in Listing 8-3 one at a time to see the table row counts. For pls_fy2014_pupld14a, the result should be:

```
count
-----
 9305
```

And for pls_fy2009_pupld09a, the result should be:

```
count
-----
 9299
```

Both results match the number of rows we expected.

*You can also check the row count using the pgAdmin interface, but it's clunky. Right-clicking the table name in pgAdmin's object browser and selecting **View/Edit Data ▸ All Rows** executes a SQL query for all rows. Then, a pop-up message in the results pane shows the row count, but it disappears after a few seconds.*

Comparing the number of table rows to what the documentation says is important because it will alert us to issues such as missing rows or cases where we might have imported the wrong file.

Counting Values Present in a Column

To return the number of rows in a specific column that contain values, we supply the name of a column as input to the count() function rather than an asterisk. For example, if you scan the CREATE TABLE statements for both library tables closely, you'll notice that we omitted the NOT NULL constraint for the salaries column plus several others. The reason is that not every library agency reported salaries, and some rows have NULL values.

To count the number of rows in the salaries column from 2014 that have values, run the count() function in Listing 8-4:

```
SELECT count(salaries)
FROM pls_fy2014_pupld14a;
```

Listing 8-4: Using count() for the number of values in a column

The result shows 5,983 rows have a value in salaries:

```
count
-----
 5983
```

This number is far lower than the number of rows that exist in the table. In the 2014 data, slightly less than two-thirds of the agencies reported salaries, and you'd want to note that fact when reporting any results of calculations performed on those columns. This check is important because the extent to which values are present in a column might influence your decision on whether to proceed with analysis at all. Checking with experts on the topic and digging deeper into the data is usually a good idea, and I recommend seeking expert advice as part of a broader analysis methodology (for more on this topic, see Chapter 18).

Counting Distinct Values in a Column

In Chapter 2, I covered the DISTINCT keyword, which is part of the SQL standard. When added after SELECT in a query, DISTINCT returns a list of unique values. We can use it to see unique values in one column, or we can see unique combinations of values from multiple columns. Another use of DISTINCT is to add it to the count() function, which causes the function to return a count of distinct values from a column.

Listing 8-5 shows two queries. The first counts all values in the 2014 table's libname column. The second does the same but includes DISTINCT in front of the column name. Run them both, one at a time.

```
SELECT count(libname)
FROM pls_fy2014_pupld14a;

SELECT count(DISTINCT libname)
FROM pls_fy2014_pupld14a;
```

Listing 8-5: Using count() for the number of distinct values in a column

The first query returns a row count that matches the number of rows in the table that we found using Listing 8-3:

```
count
-----
 9305
```

That's good. We expect to have the library agency name listed in every row. But the second query returns a smaller number:

```
count
-----
 8515
```

Using DISTINCT to remove duplicates reduces the number of library names to the 8,515 that are unique. My closer inspection of the data shows that 530 library agencies share their name with one or more other agencies. As one example, nine library agencies are named OXFORD PUBLIC LIBRARY in the table, each one in a city or town named Oxford in different states, including Alabama, Connecticut, Kansas, and Pennsylvania, among others. We'll write a query to see combinations of distinct values in "Aggregating Data Using GROUP BY" on page 120.

Finding Maximum and Minimum Values Using max() and min()

Knowing the largest and smallest numbers in a column is useful for a couple of reasons. First, it helps us get a sense of the scope of the values reported for a particular variable. Second, the functions used, max() and min(), can reveal unexpected issues with the data, as you'll see now with the libraries data.

Both max() and min() work the same way: you use a SELECT statement followed by the function with the name of a column supplied. Listing 8-6 uses max() and min() on the 2014 table with the visits column as input. The visits column records the number of annual visits to the library agency and all of its branches. Run the code, and then we'll review the output.

```
SELECT max(visits), min(visits)
FROM pls_fy2014_pupld14a;
```

Listing 8-6: Finding the most and fewest visits using max() and min()

The query returns the following results:

```
max        min
--------   ---
17729020    -3
```

Well, that's interesting. The maximum value of more than 17.7 million is reasonable for a large city library system, but -3 as the minimum? On the surface, that result seems like a mistake, but it turns out that the creators of the library survey are employing a problematic yet common convention in data collection: using a negative number or some artificially high value as an indicator.

In this case, the survey creators used negative numbers to indicate the following conditions:

1. A value of -1 indicates a "nonresponse" to that question.
2. A value of -3 indicates "not applicable" and is used when a library agency has closed either temporarily or permanently.

We'll need to account for and exclude negative values as we explore the data, because summing a column and including the negative values will result in an incorrect total. We can do this using a WHERE clause to filter them. It's a good thing we discovered this issue now rather than later after spending a lot of time on deeper analysis!

NOTE   *A better alternative for this negative value scenario is to use NULL in rows in the visits column where response data is absent, and then create a separate visits_flag column to hold codes explaining why. This technique separates number values from information about them.*

Aggregating Data Using GROUP BY

When you use the GROUP BY clause with aggregate functions, you can group results according to the values in one or more columns. This allows us to perform operations like sum() or count() for every state in our table or for every type of library agency.

Let's explore how using GROUP BY with aggregates works. On its own, GROUP BY, which is also part of standard ANSI SQL, eliminates duplicate values from the results, similar to DISTINCT. Listing 8-7 shows the GROUP BY clause in action:

```
  SELECT stabr
  FROM pls_fy2014_pupld14a
❶ GROUP BY stabr
  ORDER BY stabr;
```

Listing 8-7: Using GROUP BY on the stabr column

The GROUP BY clause ❶ follows the FROM clause and includes the column name to group. In this case, we're selecting stabr, which contains the state abbreviation, and grouping by that same column. We then use ORDER BY stabr as well so that the grouped results are in alphabetical order. This will yield a result with unique state abbreviations from the 2014 table. Here's a portion of the results:

```
stabr
-----
AK
AL
AR
AS
AZ
CA
--snip--
WV
WY
```

Notice that there are no duplicates in the 56 rows returned. These standard two-letter postal abbreviations include the 50 states plus Washington, D.C., and several U.S. territories, such as American Samoa and the U.S. Virgin Islands.

You're not limited to grouping just one column. In Listing 8-8, we use the GROUP BY clause on the 2014 data to specify the city and stabr columns for grouping:

```
SELECT city, stabr
FROM pls_fy2014_pupld14a
GROUP BY city, stabr
ORDER BY city, stabr;
```

Listing 8-8: Using GROUP BY on the city and stabr columns

The results get sorted by city and then by state, and the output shows unique combinations in that order:

```
city          stabr
----------    -----
ABBEVILLE     AL
ABBEVILLE     LA
ABBEVILLE     SC
ABBOTSFORD    WI
ABERDEEN      ID
ABERDEEN      SD
ABERNATHY     TX
--snip--
```

This grouping returns 9,088 rows, 217 fewer than the total table rows. The result indicates there are multiple occasions where the file includes more than one library agency for a particular city and state combination.

Combining GROUP BY with count()

If we combine GROUP BY with an aggregate function, such as count(), we can pull more descriptive information from our data. For example, we know 9,305 library agencies are in the 2014 table. We can get a count of agencies by state and sort them to see which states have the most. Listing 8-9 shows how:

```
❶ SELECT stabr, count(*)
   FROM pls_fy2014_pupld14a
❷ GROUP BY stabr
❸ ORDER BY count(*) DESC;
```

Listing 8-9: Using GROUP BY with count() on the stabr column

Unlike in earlier examples, we're now asking for the values in the stabr column and a count of those values. In the list of columns to query ❶, we specify stabr and the count() function with an asterisk as its input. As before, the asterisk causes count() to include NULL values. Also, when we select individual columns along with an aggregate function, we must include the columns in a GROUP BY clause ❷. If we don't, the database will return an error telling us to do so. The reason is that you can't group values by aggregating and have ungrouped column values in the same query.

To sort the results and have the state with the largest number of agencies at the top, we can ORDER BY the count() function ❸ in descending order using DESC.

Run the code in Listing 8-9. The results show New York, Illinois, and Texas as the states with the greatest number of library agencies in 2014:

```
stabr   count
-----   -----
NY       756
IL       625
TX       556
IA       543
PA       455
MI       389
WI       381
MA       370
--snip--
```

Remember that our table represents library agencies that serve a locality. Just because New York, Illinois, and Texas have the greatest number of library agencies doesn't mean they have the greatest number of outlets where you can walk in and peruse the shelves. An agency might have one central library only, or it might have no central libraries but 23 branches spread around a county. To count outlets, each row in the table also has values in the columns centlib and branlib, which record the number of central and branch libraries, respectively. To find totals, we would use the sum() aggregate function on both columns.

Using GROUP BY on Multiple Columns with count()

We can glean yet more information from our data by combining GROUP BY with the count() function and multiple columns. For example, the stataddr column in both tables contains a code indicating whether the agency's address changed in the last year. The values in stataddr are:

00 No change from last year

07 Moved to a new location

15 Minor address change

Listing 8-10 shows the code for counting the number of agencies in each state that moved, had a minor address change, or had no change using GROUP BY with stabr and stataddr and adding count():

```
❶ SELECT stabr, stataddr, count(*)
  FROM pls_fy2014_pupld14a
❷ GROUP BY stabr, stataddr
❸ ORDER BY stabr ASC, count(*) DESC;
```

Listing 8-10: Using GROUP BY with count() of the stabr and stataddr columns

The key sections of the query are the column names and the count() function after SELECT ❶, and making sure both columns are reflected in the GROUP BY clause ❷. The effect of grouping by two columns is that count() will show the number of unique combinations of stabr and stataddr.

To make the output easier to read, let's sort first by the state code in ascending order and then by the count in descending order ❸. Here are the results:

stabr	stataddr	count
AK	00	70
AK	15	10
AK	07	5
AL	00	221
AL	07	3
AR	00	58
AS	00	1
AZ	00	91
--snip--		

The first few rows of the results show that code 00 (no change in address) is the most common value for each state. We'd expect that because it's likely there are more library agencies that haven't changed address than those that have. The result helps assure us that we're analyzing the data in a sound way. If code 07 (moved to a new location) was the most frequent in each state, that would raise a question about whether we've written the query correctly or whether there's an issue with the data.

Revisiting sum() to Examine Library Visits

So far, we've combined grouping with aggregate functions, like count(), on columns within a single table to provide results grouped by a column's values. Now let's expand the technique to include grouping and aggregating across joined tables using the 2014 and 2009 libraries data. Our goal is to identify trends in library visits spanning that five-year period. To do this, we need to calculate totals using the sum() aggregate function.

Before we dig into these queries, let's address the issue of using the values -3 and -1 to indicate "not applicable" and "nonresponse." To prevent these negative numbers with no meaning as quantities from affecting the analysis, we'll filter them out using a WHERE clause to limit the queries to rows where values in visits are zero or greater.

Let's start by calculating the sum of annual visits to libraries from the individual 2014 and 2009 tables. Run each SELECT statement in Listing 8-11 separately:

```
SELECT sum(visits) AS visits_2014
FROM pls_fy2014_pupld14a
WHERE visits >= 0;

SELECT sum(visits) AS visits_2009
FROM pls_fy2009_pupld09a
WHERE visits >= 0;
```

Listing 8-11: Using the sum() aggregate function to total visits to libraries in 2014 and 2009

For 2014, visits totaled approximately 1.4 billion.

```
visits_2014
-----------
 1425930900
```

For 2009, visits totaled approximately 1.6 billion. We're onto something here, but it may not be good news. The trend seems to point downward with visits dropping about 10 percent from 2009 to 2014.

```
visits_2009
-----------
 1591799201
```

These queries sum overall visits. But from the row counts we ran earlier in the chapter, we know that each table contains a different number of library agencies: 9,305 in 2014 and 9,299 in 2009 due to agencies opening, closing, or merging. So, let's determine how the sum of visits will differ if we limit the analysis to library agencies that exist in both tables. We can do that by joining the tables, as shown in Listing 8-12:

```
❶ SELECT sum(pls14.visits) AS visits_2014,
         sum(pls09.visits) AS visits_2009
❷ FROM pls_fy2014_pupld14a pls14 JOIN pls_fy2009_pupld09a pls09
```

```
     ON pls14.fscskey = pls09.fscskey
❸ WHERE pls14.visits >= 0 AND pls09.visits >= 0;
```

Listing 8-12: Using the sum() aggregate function to total visits on joined 2014 and 2009 library tables

This query pulls together a few concepts we covered in earlier chapters, including table joins. At the top, we use the sum() aggregate function ❶ to total the visits columns from the 2014 and 2009 tables. When we join the tables on the tables' primary keys, we're declaring table aliases ❷ as we explored in Chapter 6. Here, we declare pls14 as the alias for the 2014 table and pls09 as the alias for the 2009 table to avoid having to write the lengthier full table names throughout the query.

Note that we use a standard JOIN, also known as an INNER JOIN. That means the query results will only include rows where the primary key values of both tables (the column fscskey) match.

Using the WHERE clause ❸, we return rows where both tables have a value of zero or greater in the visits column. As we did in Listing 8-11, we specify that the result should include only those rows where visits are greater than or equal to 0 in both tables. This will prevent the artificial negative values from impacting the sums.

Run the query. The results should look like this:

```
visits_2014    visits_2009
-----------    -----------
 1417299241     1585455205
```

The results are similar to what we found by querying the tables separately, although these totals are six to eight million smaller. The reason is that the query referenced only agencies with an fscskey in both tables. Still, the downward trend holds. We'll need to dig a little deeper to get the full story.

NOTE   *Although we joined the tables on fscskey, it's entirely possible that some library agencies that appear in both tables merged or split between 2009 and 2014. A call to the IMLS asking about caveats for working with this data is a good idea.*

Grouping Visit Sums by State

Now that we know library visits dropped for the United States as a whole between 2009 and 2014, you might ask yourself, "Did every part of the country see a decrease, or did the degree of the trend vary by region?" We can answer this question by modifying our preceding query to group by the state code. Let's also use a percent-change calculation to compare the trend by state. Listing 8-13 contains the full code:

```
❶ SELECT pls14.stabr,
        sum(pls14.visits) AS visits_2014,
        sum(pls09.visits) AS visits_2009,
        round( (CAST(sum(pls14.visits) AS decimal(10,1)) - sum(pls09.visits)) /
                  sum(pls09.visits) * 100, 2 ) AS pct_change❷
```

```
FROM pls_fy2014_pupld14a pls14 JOIN pls_fy2009_pupld09a pls09
ON pls14.fscskey = pls09.fscskey
WHERE pls14.visits >= 0 AND pls09.visits >= 0
❸ GROUP BY pls14.stabr
❹ ORDER BY pct_change DESC;
```

Listing 8-13: Using GROUP BY to track percent change in library visits by state

We follow the SELECT keyword with the stabr column ❶ from the 2014 table; that same column appears in the GROUP BY clause ❸. It doesn't matter which table's stabr column we use because we're only querying agencies that appear in both tables. After SELECT, we also include the now-familiar percent-change calculation you learned in Chapter 5, which gets the alias pct_change ❷ for readability. We end the query with an ORDER BY clause ❹, using the pct_change column alias.

When you run the query, the top of the results shows 10 states or territories with an increase in visits from 2009 to 2014. The rest of the results show a decline. Oklahoma, at the bottom of the ranking, had a 35 percent drop!

stabr	visits_2014	visits_2009	pct_change
GU	103593	60763	70.49
DC	4230790	2944774	43.67
LA	17242110	15591805	10.58
MT	4582604	4386504	4.47
AL	17113602	16933967	1.06
AR	10762521	10660058	0.96
KY	19256394	19113478	0.75
CO	32978245	32782247	0.60
SC	18178677	18105931	0.40
SD	3899554	3890392	0.24
MA	42011647	42237888	-0.54
AK	3486955	3525093	-1.08
ID	8730670	8847034	-1.32
NH	7508751	7675823	-2.18
WY	3666825	3756294	-2.38
--snip--			
RI	5259143	6612167	-20.46
NC	33952977	43111094	-21.24
PR	193279	257032	-24.80
GA	28891017	40922598	-29.40
OK	13678542	21171452	-35.39

This useful data should lead a data analyst to investigate what's driving the changes, particularly the largest ones. Data analysis can sometimes raise as many questions as it answers, but that's part of the process. It's always worth a phone call to a person with knowledge about the data to provide context for the results. Sometimes, they may have a very good explanation. Other times, an expert will say, "That doesn't sound right." That answer might send you back to the keeper of the data or the documentation to find out if you overlooked a code or a nuance with the data.

Filtering an Aggregate Query Using HAVING

We can refine our analysis by examining a subset of states and territories that share similar characteristics. With percent change in visits, it makes sense to separate large states from small states. In a small state like Rhode Island, one library closing could have a significant effect. A single closure in California might be scarcely noticed in a statewide count. To look at states with a similar volume in visits, we could sort the results by either of the visits columns, but it would be cleaner to get a smaller result set in our query.

To filter the results of aggregate functions, we need to use the HAVING clause that's part of standard ANSI SQL. You're already familiar with using WHERE for filtering, but aggregate functions, such as sum(), can't be used within a WHERE clause because they operate at the row level, and aggregate functions work across rows. The HAVING clause places conditions on groups created by aggregating. The code in Listing 8-14 modifies the query in Listing 8-13 by inserting the HAVING clause after GROUP BY:

```
SELECT pls14.stabr,
       sum(pls14.visits) AS visits_2014,
       sum(pls09.visits) AS visits_2009,
       round( (CAST(sum(pls14.visits) AS decimal(10,1)) - sum(pls09.visits)) /
                   sum(pls09.visits) * 100, 2 ) AS pct_change
FROM pls_fy2014_pupld14a pls14 JOIN pls_fy2009_pupld09a pls09
ON pls14.fscskey = pls09.fscskey
WHERE pls14.visits >= 0 AND pls09.visits >= 0
GROUP BY pls14.stabr
❶ HAVING sum(pls14.visits) > 50000000
ORDER BY pct_change DESC;
```

Listing 8-14: Using a HAVING clause to filter the results of an aggregate query

In this case, we've set our query results to include only rows with a sum of visits in 2014 greater than 50 million. That's an arbitrary value I chose to show only the very largest states. Adding the HAVING clause ❶ reduces the number of rows in the output to just six. In practice, you might experiment with various values. Here are the results:

stabr	visits_2014	visits_2009	pct_change
TX	72876601	78838400	-7.56
CA	162787836	182181408	-10.65
OH	82495138	92402369	-10.72
NY	106453546	119810969	-11.15
IL	72598213	82438755	-11.94
FL	73165352	87730886	-16.60

Each of the six states has experienced a decline in visits, but notice that the percent-change variation isn't as wide as in the full set of states and territories. Depending on what we learn from library experts, looking at the states with the most activity as a group might be helpful in describing trends, as would looking at other groupings. Think of a sentence or bullet point you might write that would say, "In the nation's largest states, visits decreased between 8 percent and 17 percent between 2009 and 2014." You could write similar sentences about medium-sized states and small states.

Wrapping Up

If this chapter has inspired you to visit your local library and check out a couple of books, ask a librarian whether their branch has seen a rise or drop in visits over the last few years. Chances are, you can guess the answer now. In this chapter, you learned how to use standard SQL techniques to summarize data in a table by grouping values and using a handful of aggregate functions. By joining data sets, you were able to identify some interesting five-year trends.

You also learned that data doesn't always come perfectly packaged. The use of negative values in columns as an indicator rather than as an actual numeric value forced us to filter out those rows. Unfortunately, data sets offer those kinds of challenges more often than not. In the next chapter, you'll learn techniques to clean up a data set that has a number of issues. In subsequent chapters, you'll also discover more aggregate functions to help you find the stories in your data.

TRY IT YOURSELF

Put your grouping and aggregating skills to the test with these challenges:

1. We saw that library visits have declined recently in most places. But what is the pattern in the use of technology in libraries? Both the 2014 and 2009 library survey tables contain the columns gpterms (the number of internet-connected computers used by the public) and pitusr (uses of public internet computers per year). Modify the code in Listing 8-13 to calculate the percent change in the sum of each column over time. Watch out for negative values!

2. Both library survey tables contain a column called obereg, a two-digit Bureau of Economic Analysis Code that classifies each library agency according to a region of the United States, such as New England, Rocky Mountains, and so on. Just as we calculated the percent change in visits grouped by state, do the same to group percent changes in visits by U.S. region using obereg. Consult the survey documentation to find the meaning of each region code. For a bonus challenge, create a table with the obereg code as the primary key and the region name as text, and join it to the summary query to group by the region name rather than the code.

3. Thinking back to the types of joins you learned in Chapter 6, which join type will show you all the rows in both tables, including those without a match? Write such a query and add an IS NULL filter in a WHERE clause to show agencies not included in one or the other table.

9

INSPECTING AND MODIFYING DATA

If you asked me to propose a toast to a newly minted class of data analysts, I'd probably raise my glass and say, "May your data always be free of errors and may it always arrive perfectly structured!" Life would be ideal if these sentiments were feasible. In reality, you'll sometimes receive data in such a sorry state that it's hard to analyze without modifying it in some way. This is called *dirty data*, which is a general label for data with errors, missing values, or poor organization that makes standard queries ineffective. When data is converted from one file type to another or when a column receives the wrong data type, information can be lost. Typos and spelling inconsistencies can also result in dirty data. Whatever the cause may be, dirty data is the bane of the data analyst.

In this chapter, you'll use SQL to clean up dirty data as well as perform other useful maintenance tasks. You'll learn how to examine data to assess its quality and how to modify data and tables to make analysis easier. But the techniques you'll learn will be useful for more than just cleaning data.

The ability to make changes to data and tables gives you options for updating or adding new information to your database as it becomes available, elevating your database from a static collection to a living record.

Let's begin by importing our data.

Importing Data on Meat, Poultry, and Egg Producers

For this example, we'll use a directory of U.S. meat, poultry, and egg producers. The Food Safety and Inspection Service (FSIS), an agency within the U.S. Department of Agriculture, compiles and updates this database every month. The FSIS is responsible for inspecting animals and food at more than 6,000 meat processing plants, slaughterhouses, farms, and the like. If inspectors find a problem, such as bacterial contamination or mislabeled food, the agency can issue a recall. Anyone interested in agriculture business, food supply chain, or outbreaks of foodborne illnesses will find the directory useful. Read more about the agency on its site at *https://www.fsis.usda.gov/*.

The file we'll use comes from the directory's page on *https://www.data .gov/*, a website run by the U.S. federal government that catalogs thousands of data sets from various federal agencies (*https://catalog.data.gov/dataset/ meat-poultry-and-egg-inspection-directory-by-establishment-name/*). We'll examine the original data as it was available for download, with the exception of the ZIP Codes column (I'll explain why later). You'll find the data in the file *MPI_Directory_by_Establishment_Name.csv* along with other resources for this book at *https://www.nostarch.com/practicalSQL/*.

To import the file into PostgreSQL, use the code in Listing 9-1 to create a table called meat_poultry_egg_inspect and use COPY to add the CSV file to the table. As in previous examples, use pgAdmin to connect to your analysis database, and then open the Query Tool to run the code. Remember to change the path in the COPY statement to reflect the location of your CSV file.

```
CREATE TABLE meat_poultry_egg_inspect (
❶ est_number varchar(50) CONSTRAINT est_number_key PRIMARY KEY,
    company varchar(100),
    street varchar(100),
    city varchar(30),
    st varchar(2),
    zip varchar(5),
    phone varchar(14),
    grant_date date,
❷ activities text,
    dbas text
);

❸ COPY meat_poultry_egg_inspect
   FROM 'C:\YourDirectory\MPI_Directory_by_Establishment_Name.csv'
   WITH (FORMAT CSV, HEADER, DELIMITER ',');

❹ CREATE INDEX company_idx ON meat_poultry_egg_inspect (company);
```

Listing 9-1: Importing the FSIS Meat, Poultry, and Egg Inspection Directory

The `meat_poultry_egg_inspect` table has 10 columns. We add a natural primary key constraint to the `est_number` column ❶, which contains a unique value for each row that identifies the establishment. Most of the remaining columns relate to the company's name and location. You'll use the activities column ❷, which describes activities at the company, in the "Try It Yourself" exercise at the end of this chapter. We set the `activities` and `dbas` columns to `text`, a data type that in PostgreSQL affords us up to 1GB of characters, because some of the strings in the columns are thousands of characters long. We import the CSV file ❸ and then create an index on the `company` column ❹ to speed up searches for particular companies.

For practice, let's use the `count()` aggregate function introduced in Chapter 8 to check how many rows are in the `meat_poultry_egg_inspect` table:

```
SELECT count(*) FROM meat_poultry_egg_inspect;
```

The result should show 6,287 rows. Now let's find out what the data contains and determine whether we can glean useful information from it as is, or if we need to modify it in some way.

Interviewing the Data Set

Interviewing data is my favorite part of analysis. We interview a data set to discover its details: what it holds, what questions it can answer, and how suitable it is for our purposes, the same way a job interview reveals whether a candidate has the skills required for the position.

The aggregate queries you learned in Chapter 8 are a useful interviewing tool because they often expose the limitations of a data set or raise questions you may want to ask before drawing conclusions in your analysis and assuming the validity of your findings.

For example, the `meat_poultry_egg_inspect` table's rows describe food producers. At first glance, we might assume that each company in each row operates at a distinct address. But it's never safe to assume in data analysis, so let's check using the code in Listing 9-2:

```
SELECT company,
       street,
       city,
       st,
       count(*) AS address_count
FROM meat_poultry_egg_inspect
GROUP BY company, street, city, st
HAVING count(*) > 1
ORDER BY company, street, city, st;
```

Listing 9-2: Finding multiple companies at the same address

Here, we group companies by unique combinations of the company, street, city, and st columns. Then we use count(*), which returns the number of rows for each combination of those columns and gives it the alias `address_count`. Using the `HAVING` clause introduced in Chapter 8, we filter the results to show only cases where more than one row has the same combination of values. This should return all duplicate addresses for a company.

The query returns 23 rows, which means there are close to two dozen cases where the same company is listed multiple times at the same address:

```
company                 street                  city        st   address_count
----------------------  ----------------------  ----------  --   -------------
Acre Station Meat Farm   17076 Hwy 32 N          Pinetown    NC               2
Beltex Corporation       3801 North Grove Street Fort Worth  TX               2
Cloverleaf Cold Storage  111 Imperial Drive      Sanford     NC               2
--snip--
```

This is not necessarily a problem. There may be valid reasons for a company to appear multiple times at the same address. For example, two types of processing plants could exist with the same name. On the other hand, we may have found data entry errors. Either way, it's sound practice to eliminate concerns about the validity of a data set before relying on it, and the result should prompt us to investigate individual cases before we draw conclusions. However, this data set has other issues that we need to look at before we can get meaningful information from it. Let's work through a few examples.

Checking for Missing Values

Let's start checking for missing values by asking a basic question: how many of the meat, poultry, and egg processing companies are in each state? Finding out whether we have values from all states and whether any rows are missing a state code will serve as another useful check on the data. We'll use the aggregate function `count()` along with `GROUP BY` to determine this, as shown in Listing 9-3:

```
SELECT st,
       count(*) AS st_count
FROM meat_poultry_egg_inspect
GROUP BY st
ORDER BY st;
```

Listing 9-3: Grouping and counting states

The query is a simple count similar to the examples in Chapter 8. When you run the query, it tallies the number of times each state postal code (st) appears in the table. Your result should include 57 rows, grouped by the state postal code in the column st. Why more than the 50 U.S. states? Because the data includes Puerto Rico and other unincorporated U.S. territories, such as

Guam and American Samoa. Alaska (AK) is at the top of the results with a count of 17 establishments:

```
st    st_count
--    --------
AK          17
AL          93
AR          87
AS           1
--snip--
WA         139
WI         184
WV          23
WY           1
             3
```

However, the row at the bottom of the list has a count of 3 and a NULL value in the st_count column. To find out what this means, let's query the rows where the st column has NULL values.

NOTE *Depending on the database implementation, NULL values will either appear first or last in a sorted column. In PostgreSQL, they appear last by default. The ANSI SQL standard doesn't specify one or the other, but it lets you add NULLS FIRST or NULLS LAST to an ORDER BY clause to specify a preference. For example, to make NULL values appear first in the preceding query, the clause would read ORDER BY st NULLS FIRST.*

In Listing 9-4, we use the technique covered in "Using NULL to Find Rows with Missing Values" on page 83, adding a WHERE clause with the st column and the IS NULL keywords to find which rows are missing a state code:

```
SELECT est_number,
       company,
       city,
       st,
       zip
FROM meat_poultry_egg_inspect
WHERE st IS NULL;
```

Listing 9-4: Using IS NULL to find missing values in the st column

This query returns three rows that don't have a value in the st column:

est_number	company	city	st	zip
V18677A	Atlas Inspection, Inc.	Blaine		55449
M45319+P45319	Hall-Namie Packing Company, Inc			36671
M263A+P263A+V263A	Jones Dairy Farm			53538

If we want an accurate count of establishments per state, these missing values would lead to an incorrect result. To find the source of this dirty data, it's worth making a quick visual check of the original file downloaded from *https://www.data.gov/*. Unless you're working with files in the gigabyte range, you can usually open a CSV file in a text editor and search for the row. If you're working with larger files, you might be able to examine the source data using utilities such as grep (on Linux and macOS) or findstr (on Windows). In this case, a visual check confirms that, indeed, there was no state listed in those rows in the CSV file, so the error is organic to the data, not one introduced during import.

In our interview of the data so far, we've discovered that we'll need to add missing values to the st column to clean up this table. Let's look at what other issues exist in our data set and make a list of cleanup tasks.

Checking for Inconsistent Data Values

Inconsistent data is another factor that can hamper our analysis. We can check for inconsistently entered data within a column by using GROUP BY with count(). When you scan the unduplicated values in the results, you might be able to spot variations in the spelling of names or other attributes.

For example, many of the 6,200 companies in our table are multiple locations owned by a few multinational food corporations, such as Cargill or Tyson Foods. To find out how many locations each company owns, we would try to count the values in the company column. Let's see what happens when we do, using the query in Listing 9-5:

```
SELECT company,
       count(*) AS company_count
FROM meat_poultry_egg_inspect
GROUP BY company
ORDER BY company ASC;
```

Listing 9-5: Using GROUP BY and count() to find inconsistent company names

Scrolling through the results reveals a number of cases in which a company's name is spelled several different ways. For example, notice the entries for the Armour-Eckrich brand:

```
company                           company_count
-------------------------         -------------
--snip--
Armour - Eckrich Meats, LLC                   1
Armour-Eckrich Meats LLC                      3
Armour-Eckrich Meats, Inc.                    1
Armour-Eckrich Meats, LLC                     2
--snip--
```

At least four different spellings are shown for seven establishments that are likely owned by the same company. If we later perform any aggregation by company, it would help to standardize the names so all of the items counted or summed are grouped properly. Let's add that to our list of items to fix.

Checking for Malformed Values Using length()

It's a good idea to check for unexpected values in a column that should be consistently formatted. For example, each entry in the zip column in the meat_poultry_egg_inspect table should be formatted in the style of U.S. ZIP Codes with five digits. However, that's not what is in our data set.

Solely for the purpose of this example, I replicated an error I've committed before. When I converted the original Excel file to a CSV file, I stored the ZIP Code in the "General" number format in the spreadsheet instead of as a text value. By doing so, any ZIP Code that begins with a zero, such as 07502 for Paterson, NJ, lost the leading zero because an integer can't start with a zero. As a result, 07502 appears in the table as 7502. You can make this error in a variety of ways, including by copying and pasting data into Excel columns set to "General." After being burned a few times, I learned to take extra caution with numbers that should be formatted as text.

My deliberate error appears when we run the code in Listing 9-6. The example introduces length(), a *string function* that counts the number of characters in a string. We combine length() with count() and GROUP BY to determine how many rows have five characters in the zip field and how many have a value other than five. To make it easy to scan the results, we use length() in the ORDER BY clause.

```
SELECT length(zip),
       count(*) AS length_count
FROM meat_poultry_egg_inspect
GROUP BY length(zip)
ORDER BY length(zip) ASC;
```

Listing 9-6: Using length() and count() to test the zip column

The results confirm the formatting error. As you can see, 496 of the ZIP Codes are four characters long, and 86 are three characters long, which means these numbers originally had two leading zeros that my conversion erroneously eliminated:

length	length_count
3	86
4	496
5	5705

Using the WHERE clause, we can check the details of the results to see which states these shortened ZIP Codes correspond to, as shown in Listing 9-7:

```
SELECT st,
       count(*) AS st_count
FROM meat_poultry_egg_inspect
❶ WHERE length(zip) < 5
```

```
GROUP BY st
ORDER BY st ASC;
```

Listing 9-7: Filtering with `length()` to find short zip values

The `length()` function inside the `WHERE` clause ❶ returns a count of rows where the ZIP Code is less than five characters for each state code. The result is what we would expect. The states are largely in the Northeast region of the United States where ZIP Codes often start with a zero:

st	st_count
CT	55
MA	101
ME	24
NH	18
NJ	244
PR	84
RI	27
VI	2
VT	27

Obviously, we don't want this error to persist, so we'll add it to our list of items to correct. So far, we need to correct the following issues in our data set:

- Missing values for three rows in the st column
- Inconsistent spelling of at least one company's name
- Inaccurate ZIP Codes due to file conversion

Next, we'll look at how to use SQL to fix these issues by modifying your data.

Modifying Tables, Columns, and Data

Almost nothing in a database, from tables to columns and the data types and values they contain, is set in concrete after it's created. As your needs change, you can add columns to a table, change data types on existing columns, and edit values. Fortunately, you can use SQL to modify, delete, or add to existing data and structures. Given the issues we discovered in the meat_poultry_egg _inspect table, being able to modify our database will come in handy.

To make changes to our database, we'll use two SQL commands: the first command, ALTER TABLE, is part of the ANSI SQL standard and provides options to ADD COLUMN, ALTER COLUMN, and DROP COLUMN, among others. Typically, PostgreSQL and other databases include implementation-specific extensions to ALTER TABLE that provide an array of options for managing database objects (see *https://www.postgresql.org/docs/current/static/sql-altertable.html*). For our exercises, we'll stick with the core options.

The second command, UPDATE, also included in the SQL standard, allows you to change values in a table's columns. You can supply criteria using the WHERE clause to choose which rows to update.

Let's explore the basic syntax and options for both commands, and then use them to fix the issues in our data set.

Modifying Tables with ALTER TABLE

We can use the `ALTER TABLE` statement to modify the structure of tables. The following examples show the syntax for common operations that are part of standard ANSI SQL. The code for adding a column to a table looks like this:

```
ALTER TABLE table ADD COLUMN column data_type;
```

Similarly, we can remove a column with the following syntax:

```
ALTER TABLE table DROP COLUMN column;
```

To change the data type of a column, we would use this code:

```
ALTER TABLE table ALTER COLUMN column SET DATA TYPE data_type;
```

Adding a `NOT NULL` constraint to a column will look like the following:

```
ALTER TABLE table ALTER COLUMN column SET NOT NULL;
```

Note that in PostgreSQL and some other systems, adding a constraint to the table causes all rows to be checked to see whether they comply with the constraint. If the table has millions of rows, this could take a while.

Removing the NOT NULL constraint looks like this:

```
ALTER TABLE table ALTER COLUMN column DROP NOT NULL;
```

When you execute an ALTER TABLE statement with the placeholders filled in, you should see a message that reads ALTER TABLE in the pgAdmin output screen. If an operation violates a constraint or if you attempt to change a column's data type and the existing values in the column won't conform to the new data type, PostgreSQL returns an error. But PostgreSQL won't give you any warning about deleting data when you drop a column, so use extra caution before dropping a column.

Modifying Values with UPDATE

The UPDATE statement modifies the data in a column in all rows or in a subset of rows that meet a condition. Its basic syntax, which would update the data in every row in a column, follows this form:

```
UPDATE table
SET column = value;
```

We first pass UPDATE the name of the table to update, and then pass the SET clause the column that contains the values to change. The new *value* to place in the column can be a string, number, the name of another column, or even a query or expression that generates a value. We can update values in multiple columns at a time by adding additional columns and source values, and separating each column and value statement with a comma:

```
UPDATE table
SET column_a = value,
    column_b = value;
```

To restrict the update to particular rows, we add a WHERE clause with some criteria that must be met before the update can happen:

```
UPDATE table
SET column = value
WHERE criteria;
```

We can also update one table with values from another table. Standard ANSI SQL requires that we use a *subquery*, a query inside a query, to specify which values and rows to update:

```
UPDATE table
SET column = (SELECT column
             FROM table_b
             WHERE table.column = table_b.column)
WHERE EXISTS (SELECT column
             FROM table_b
             WHERE table.column = table_b.column);
```

The value portion of the SET clause is a subquery, which is a SELECT statement inside parentheses that generates the values for the update. Similarly, the WHERE EXISTS clause uses a SELECT statement to generate values that serve as the filter for the update. If we didn't use this clause, we might inadvertently set some values to NULL without planning to. (If this syntax looks somewhat complicated, that's okay. I'll cover subqueries in detail in Chapter 12.)

Some database managers offer additional syntax for updating across tables. PostgreSQL supports the ANSI standard but also a simpler syntax using a FROM clause for updating values across tables:

```
UPDATE table
SET column = table_b.column
FROM table_b
WHERE table.column = table_b.column;
```

When you execute an UPDATE statement, PostgreSQL returns a message stating UPDATE along with the number of rows affected.

Creating Backup Tables

Before modifying a table, it's a good idea to make a copy for reference and backup in case you accidentally destroy some data. Listing 9-8 shows how to use a variation of the familiar CREATE TABLE statement to make a new table based on the existing data and structure of the table we want to duplicate:

```
CREATE TABLE meat_poultry_egg_inspect_backup AS
SELECT * FROM meat_poultry_egg_inspect;
```

Listing 9-8: Backing up a table

After running the CREATE TABLE statement, the result should be a pristine copy of your table with the new specified name. You can confirm this by counting the number of records in both tables with one query:

```
SELECT
    (SELECT count(*) FROM meat_poultry_egg_inspect) AS original,
    (SELECT count(*) FROM meat_poultry_egg_inspect_backup) AS backup;
```

The results should return a count of 6,287 from both tables, like this:

```
original    backup
--------    ------
    6287      6287
```

If the counts match, you can be sure your backup table is an exact copy of the structure and contents of the original table. As an added measure and for easy reference, we'll use ALTER TABLE to make copies of column data within the table we're updating.

NOTE *Indexes are not copied when creating a table backup using the CREATE TABLE statement. If you decide to run queries on the backup, be sure to create a separate index on that table.*

Restoring Missing Column Values

Earlier in this chapter, the query in Listing 9-4 revealed that three rows in the meat_poultry_egg_inspect table don't have a value in the st column:

```
est_number          company                         city    st  zip
----------------    ------------------------------  ------  --  -----
V18677A             Atlas Inspection, Inc.          Blaine      55449
M45319+P45319       Hall-Namie Packing Company, Inc             36671
M263A+P263A+V263A   Jones Dairy Farm                            53538
```

To get a complete count of establishments in each state, we need to fill those missing values using an UPDATE statement.

Creating a Column Copy

Even though we've backed up this table, let's take extra caution and make a copy of the st column within the table so we still have the original data if we make some dire error somewhere! Let's create the copy and fill it with the existing st column values using the SQL statements in Listing 9-9:

❶ ALTER TABLE meat_poultry_egg_inspect ADD COLUMN st_copy varchar(2);

UPDATE meat_poultry_egg_inspect
❷ SET st_copy = st;

Listing 9-9: Creating and filling the st_copy column with ALTER TABLE and UPDATE

The ALTER TABLE statement ❶ adds a column called st_copy using the same varchar data type as the original st column. Next, the UPDATE statement's SET clause ❷ fills our newly created st_copy column with the values in column st. Because we don't specify any criteria using a WHERE clause, values in every row are updated, and PostgreSQL returns the message UPDATE 6287. Again, it's worth noting that on a very large table, this operation could take some time and also substantially increase the table's size. Making a column copy in addition to a table backup isn't entirely necessary, but if you're the patient, cautious type, it can be worthwhile.

We can confirm the values were copied properly with a simple SELECT query on both columns, as in Listing 9-10:

```
SELECT st,
       st_copy
FROM meat_poultry_egg_inspect
ORDER BY st;
```

Listing 9-10: Checking values in the st and st_copy columns

The SELECT query returns 6,287 rows showing both columns holding values except the three rows with missing values:

```
st    st_copy
--    -------
AK    AK
AK    AK
AK    AK
AK    AK
--snip--
```

Now, with our original data safely stored in the st_copy column, we can update the three rows with missing state codes. This is now our in-table backup, so if something goes drastically wrong while we're updating the missing data in the original column, we can easily copy the original data back in. I'll show you how after we apply the first updates.

Updating Rows Where Values Are Missing

To update those rows missing values, we first find the values we need with a quick online search: Atlas Inspection is located in Minnesota; Hall-Namie Packing is in Alabama; and Jones Dairy is in Wisconsin. Add those states to the appropriate rows using the code in Listing 9-11:

```
UPDATE meat_poultry_egg_inspect
SET st = 'MN'
❶ WHERE est_number = 'V18677A';

UPDATE meat_poultry_egg_inspect
SET st = 'AL'
WHERE est_number = 'M45319+P45319';

UPDATE meat_poultry_egg_inspect
SET st = 'WI'
WHERE est_number = 'M263A+P263A+V263A';
```

Listing 9-11: Updating the st column for three establishments

Because we want each UPDATE statement to affect a single row, we include a WHERE clause ❶ for each that identifies the company's unique est_number, which is the table's primary key. When we run each query, PostgreSQL responds with the message UPDATE 1, showing that only one row was updated for each query.

If we rerun the code in Listing 9-4 to find rows where st is NULL, the query should return nothing. Success! Our count of establishments by state is now complete.

Restoring Original Values

What happens if we botch an update by providing the wrong values or updating the wrong rows? Because we've backed up the entire table and the st column within the table, we can easily copy the data back from either location. Listing 9-12 shows the two options.

❶ UPDATE meat_poultry_egg_inspect
SET st = st_copy;

❷ UPDATE meat_poultry_egg_inspect original
SET st = backup.st
FROM meat_poultry_egg_inspect_backup backup
WHERE original.est_number = backup.est_number;

Listing 9-12: Restoring original st column values

To restore the values from the backup column in meat_poultry_egg_inspect you created in Listing 9-9, run an UPDATE query ❶ that sets st to the values in st_copy. Both columns should again have the identical original values. Alternatively, you can create an UPDATE ❷ that sets st to values in the st column from the meat_poultry_egg_inspect_backup table you made in Listing 9-8.

Updating Values for Consistency

In Listing 9-5 we discovered several cases where a single company's name was entered inconsistently. If we want to aggregate data by company name, such inconsistencies will hinder us from doing so.

Here are the spelling variations of Armour-Eckrich Meats in Listing 9-5:

```
--snip--
Armour - Eckrich Meats, LLC
Armour-Eckrich Meats LLC
Armour-Eckrich Meats, Inc.
Armour-Eckrich Meats, LLC
--snip--
```

We can standardize the spelling of this company's name by using an UPDATE statement. To protect our data, we'll create a new column for the standardized spellings, copy the names in company into the new column, and work in the new column to avoid tampering with the original data. Listing 9-13 has the code for both actions:

```
ALTER TABLE meat_poultry_egg_inspect ADD COLUMN company_standard varchar(100);

UPDATE meat_poultry_egg_inspect
SET company_standard = company;
```

Listing 9-13: Creating and filling the company_standard column

Now, let's say we want any name in company that contains the string Armour to appear in company_standard as Armour-Eckrich Meats. (This assumes we've checked all entries containing Armour and want to standardize them.) We can update all the rows matching the string Armour by using a WHERE clause. Run the two statements in Listing 9-14:

```
UPDATE meat_poultry_egg_inspect
SET company_standard = 'Armour-Eckrich Meats'
❶ WHERE company LIKE 'Armour%';

SELECT company, company_standard
FROM meat_poultry_egg_inspect
WHERE company LIKE 'Armour%';
```

Listing 9-14: Using an UPDATE statement to modify field values that match a string

The important piece of this query is the WHERE clause that uses the LIKE keyword ❶ that was introduced with filtering in Chapter 2. Including the wildcard syntax % at the end of the string Armour updates all rows that start with those characters regardless of what comes after them. The clause lets us target all the varied spellings used for the company's name. The SELECT statement in Listing 9-14 returns the results of the updated company_standard column next to the original company column:

```
company                        company_standard
---------------------------    --------------------
Armour-Eckrich Meats LLC       Armour-Eckrich Meats
Armour - Eckrich Meats, LLC    Armour-Eckrich Meats
Armour-Eckrich Meats LLC       Armour-Eckrich Meats
Armour-Eckrich Meats LLC       Armour-Eckrich Meats
Armour-Eckrich Meats, Inc.     Armour-Eckrich Meats
Armour-Eckrich Meats, LLC      Armour-Eckrich Meats
Armour-Eckrich Meats, LLC      Armour-Eckrich Meats
```

The values for Armour-Eckrich in company_standard are now standardized with consistent spelling. If we want to standardize other company names in the table, we would create an UPDATE statement for each case. We would also keep the original company column for reference.

Repairing ZIP Codes Using Concatenation

Our final fix repairs values in the zip column that lost leading zeros as the result of my deliberate data faux pas. For companies in Puerto Rico and the U.S. Virgin Islands, we need to restore two leading zeros to the values in zip because (aside from an IRS processing facility in Holtsville, NY) they're the only locations in the United States where ZIP Codes start with two zeros. Then, for the other states, located mostly in New England, we'll restore a single leading zero.

We'll use UPDATE again but this time in conjunction with the double-pipe *string operator* (||), which performs *concatenation*. Concatenation combines two or more string or non-string values into one. For example, inserting || between the strings abc and 123 results in abc123. The double-pipe operator is a SQL standard for concatenation supported by PostgreSQL. You can use it in many contexts, such as UPDATE queries and SELECT, to provide custom output from existing as well as new data.

First, Listing 9-15 makes a backup copy of the zip column in the same way we made a backup of the st column earlier:

```
ALTER TABLE meat_poultry_egg_inspect ADD COLUMN zip_copy varchar(5);

UPDATE meat_poultry_egg_inspect
SET zip_copy = zip;
```

Listing 9-15: Creating and filling the zip_copy column

Next, we use the code in Listing 9-16 to perform the first update:

```
  UPDATE meat_poultry_egg_inspect
❶ SET zip = '00' || zip
❷ WHERE st IN('PR','VI') AND length(zip) = 3;
```

Listing 9-16: Modifying codes in the zip column missing two leading zeros

We use SET to set the zip column ❶ to a value that is the result of the concatenation of the string 00 and the existing content of the zip column. We limit the UPDATE to only those rows where the st column has the state codes PR and VI ❷ using the IN comparison operator from Chapter 2 and add a test for rows where the length of zip is 3. This entire statement will then only update the zip values for Puerto Rico and the Virgin Islands. Run the query; PostgreSQL should return the message UPDATE 86, which is the number of rows we expect to change based on our earlier count in Listing 9-6.

Let's repair the remaining ZIP Codes using a similar query in Listing 9-17:

```
UPDATE meat_poultry_egg_inspect
SET zip = '0' || zip
WHERE st IN('CT','MA','ME','NH','NJ','RI','VT') AND length(zip) = 4;
```

Listing 9-17: Modifying codes in the zip column missing one leading zero

PostgreSQL should return the message UPDATE 496. Now, let's check our progress. Earlier in the chapter, when we aggregated rows in the zip column by length, we found 86 rows with three characters and 496 with four:

length	count
3	86
4	496
5	5705

Using the same query in Listing 9-6 now returns a more desirable result: all the rows have a five-digit ZIP Code.

length	count
5	6287

In this example we used concatenation, but you can employ additional SQL string functions to modify data with UPDATE by changing words from uppercase to lowercase, trimming unwanted spaces, replacing characters in a string, and more. I'll discuss additional string functions in Chapter 13 when we consider advanced techniques for working with text.

Updating Values Across Tables

In "Modifying Values with UPDATE" on page 138, I showed the standard ANSI SQL and PostgreSQL-specific syntax for updating values in one table based on values in another. This syntax is particularly valuable in a relational database where primary keys and foreign keys establish table relationships. It's also useful when data in one table may be necessary context for updating values in another.

For example, let's say we're setting an inspection date for each of the companies in our table. We want to do this by U.S. regions, such as Northeast, Pacific, and so on, but those regional designations don't exist in our table. However, they *do* exist in a data set we can add to our database that also contains matching st state codes. This means we can use that other data as part of our UPDATE statement to provide the necessary information. Let's begin with the New England region to see how this works.

Enter the code in Listing 9-18, which contains the SQL statements to create a state_regions table and fill the table with data:

```
CREATE TABLE state_regions (
    st varchar(2) CONSTRAINT st_key PRIMARY KEY,
    region varchar(20) NOT NULL
);

COPY state_regions
FROM 'C:\YourDirectory\state_regions.csv'
WITH (FORMAT CSV, HEADER, DELIMITER ',');
```

Listing 9-18: Creating and filling a state_regions table

We'll create two columns in a state_regions table: one containing the two-character state code st and the other containing the region name. We set the primary key constraint to the st column, which holds a unique st_key value to identify each state. In the data you're importing, each state is present and assigned to a U.S. Census region, and territories outside the United States are labeled as outlying areas. We'll update the table one region at a time.

Next, let's return to the `meat_poultry_egg_inspect` table, add a column for inspection dates, and then fill in that column with the New England states. Listing 9-19 shows the code:

```
ALTER TABLE meat_poultry_egg_inspect ADD COLUMN inspection_date date;
```

```
❶ UPDATE meat_poultry_egg_inspect inspect
❷ SET inspection_date = '2019-12-01'
❸ WHERE EXISTS (SELECT state_regions.region
                FROM state_regions
                WHERE inspect.st = state_regions.st
                    AND state_regions.region = 'New England');
```

Listing 9-19: Adding and updating an inspection_date *column*

The `ALTER TABLE` statement creates the `inspection_date` column in the `meat_poultry_egg_inspect` table. In the `UPDATE` statement, we start by naming the table using an alias of inspect to make the code easier to read ❶. Next, the `SET` clause assigns a date value of 2019-12-01 to the new `inspection_date` column ❷. Finally, the `WHERE EXISTS` clause includes a subquery that connects the meat _poultry_egg_inspect table to the state_regions table we created in Listing 9-18 and specifies which rows to update ❸. The subquery (in parentheses, beginning with `SELECT`) looks for rows in the state_regions table where the region column matches the string New England. At the same time, it joins the meat _poultry_egg_inspect table with the state_regions table using the st column from both tables. In effect, the query is telling the database to find all the st codes that correspond to the New England region and use those codes to filter the update.

When you run the code, you should receive a message of UPDATE 252, which is the number of companies in New England. You can use the code in Listing 9-20 to see the effect of the change:

```
SELECT st, inspection_date
FROM meat_poultry_egg_inspect
GROUP BY st, inspection_date
ORDER BY st;
```

Listing 9-20: Viewing updated inspection_date *values*

The results should show the updated inspection dates for all New England companies. The top of the output shows Connecticut has received a date, for example, but states outside New England remain NULL because we haven't updated them yet:

```
st    inspection_date
--    ---------------
--snip--
CA
CO
CT    2019-12-01
DC
--snip--
```

To fill in dates for additional regions, substitute a different region for New England in Listing 9-19 and rerun the query.

Deleting Unnecessary Data

The most irrevocable way to modify data is to remove it entirely. SQL includes options to remove rows and columns from a table along with options to delete an entire table or database. We want to perform these operations with caution, removing only data or tables we don't need. Without a backup, the data is gone for good.

NOTE   *It's easy to exclude unwanted data in queries using a WHERE clause, so decide whether you truly need to delete the data or can just filter it out. Cases where deleting may be the best solution include data with errors or data imported incorrectly.*

In this section, we'll use a variety of SQL statements to delete unnecessary data. For removing rows from a table, we'll use the DELETE FROM statement. To remove a column from a table, we'll use ALTER TABLE. And to remove a whole table from the database, we'll use the DROP TABLE statement.

Writing and executing these statements is fairly simple, but doing so comes with a caveat. If deleting rows, a column, or a table would cause a violation of a constraint, such as the foreign key constraint covered in Chapter 7, you need to deal with that constraint first. That might involve removing the constraint, deleting data in another table, or deleting another table. Each case is unique and will require a different way to work around the constraint.

Deleting Rows from a Table

Using a DELETE FROM statement, we can remove all rows from a table, or we can use a WHERE clause to delete only the portion that matches an expression we supply. To delete all rows from a table, use the following syntax:

```
DELETE FROM table_name;
```

If your table has a large number of rows, it might be faster to erase the table and create a fresh version using the original CREATE TABLE statement. To erase the table, use the DROP TABLE command discussed in "Deleting a Table from a Database" on page 148.

To remove only selected rows, add a WHERE clause along with the matching value or pattern to specify which ones you want to delete:

```
DELETE FROM table_name WHERE expression;
```

For example, if we want our table of meat, poultry, and egg processors to include only establishments in the 50 U.S. states, we can remove the companies in Puerto Rico and the Virgin Islands from the table using the code in Listing 9-21:

```
DELETE FROM meat_poultry_egg_inspect
WHERE st IN('PR','VI');
```

Listing 9-21: Deleting rows matching an expression

Run the code; PostgreSQL should return the message DELETE 86. This means the 86 rows where the st column held either PR or VI have been removed from the table.

Deleting a Column from a Table

While working on the zip column in the meat_poultry_egg_inspect table earlier in this chapter, we created a backup column called zip_copy. Now that we've finished working on fixing the issues in zip, we no longer need zip_copy. We can remove the backup column, including all the data within the column, from the table by using the DROP keyword in the ALTER TABLE statement.

The syntax for removing a column is similar to other ALTER TABLE statements:

```
ALTER TABLE table_name DROP COLUMN column_name;
```

The code in Listing 9-22 removes the zip_copy column:

```
ALTER TABLE meat_poultry_egg_inspect DROP COLUMN zip_copy;
```

Listing 9-22: Removing a column from a table using DROP

PostgreSQL returns the message ALTER TABLE, and the zip_copy column should be deleted.

Deleting a Table from a Database

The DROP TABLE statement is a standard ANSI SQL feature that deletes a table from the database. This statement might come in handy if, for example, you have a collection of backups, or *working tables*, that have outlived their usefulness. It's also useful in other situations, such as when you need to change the structure of a table significantly; in that case, rather than using too many ALTER TABLE statements, you can just remove the table and create another one by running a new CREATE TABLE statement.

The syntax for the DROP TABLE command is simple:

```
DROP TABLE table_name;
```

For example, Listing 9-23 deletes the backup version of the meat_poultry _egg_inspect table:

```
DROP TABLE meat_poultry_egg_inspect_backup;
```

Listing 9-23: Removing a table from a database using DROP

Run the query; PostgreSQL should respond with the message DROP TABLE to indicate the table has been removed.

Using Transaction Blocks to Save or Revert Changes

The alterations you made on data using the techniques in this chapter so far are final. That is, after you run a DELETE or UPDATE query (or any other query that alters your data or database structure), the only way to undo the change is to restore from a backup. However, you can check your changes before finalizing them and cancel the change if it's not what you intended. You do this by wrapping the SQL statement within a *transaction block*, which is a group of statements you define using the following keywords at the beginning and end of the query:

START TRANSACTION signals the start of the transaction block. In PostgreSQL, you can also use the non-ANSI SQL BEGIN keyword.

COMMIT signals the end of the block and saves all changes.

ROLLBACK signals the end of the block and reverts all changes.

Usually, database programmers employ a transaction block to define the start and end of a sequence of operations that perform one unit of work in a database. An example is when you purchase tickets to a Broadway show. A successful transaction might involve two steps: charging your credit card and reserving your seats so someone else can't buy them. A database programmer would either want both steps in the transaction to happen (say, when your card charge goes through) or neither of them to happen (if your card is declined or you cancel at checkout). Defining both steps as one transaction keeps them as a unit; if one step fails, the other is canceled too. You can learn more details about transactions and PostgreSQL at *https://www.postgresql.org/docs/current/static/tutorial-transactions.html*.

We can apply this transaction block technique to review changes a query makes and then decide whether to keep or discard them. Using the meat_poultry_egg_inspect table, let's say we're cleaning dirty data related to the company AGRO Merchants Oakland LLC. The table has three rows listing the company, but one row has an extra comma in the name:

```
company
--------------------------
AGRO Merchants Oakland LLC
AGRO Merchants Oakland LLC
AGRO Merchants Oakland, LLC
```

We want the name to be consistent, so we'll remove the comma from the third row using an UPDATE query, as we did earlier. But this time we'll check the result of our update before we make it final (and we'll purposely make a mistake we want to discard). Listing 9-24 shows how to do this using a transaction block:

```
❶ START TRANSACTION;

  UPDATE meat_poultry_egg_inspect
❷ SET company = 'AGRO Merchantss Oakland LLC'
  WHERE company = 'AGRO Merchants Oakland, LLC';

❸ SELECT company
  FROM meat_poultry_egg_inspect
  WHERE company LIKE 'AGRO%'
  ORDER BY company;

❹ ROLLBACK;
```

Listing 9-24: Demonstrating a transaction block

We'll run each statement separately, beginning with START TRANSACTION; ❶. The database responds with the message START TRANSACTION, letting you know that any succeeding changes you make to data will not be made permanent unless you issue a COMMIT command. Next, we run the UPDATE statement, which changes the company name in the row where it has an extra comma. I intentionally added an extra s in the name used in the SET clause ❷ to introduce a mistake.

When we view the names of companies starting with the letters AGRO using the SELECT statement ❸, we see that, oops, one company name is misspelled now:

```
company
--------------------------
AGRO Merchants Oakland LLC
AGRO Merchants Oakland LLC
AGRO Merchantss Oakland LLC
```

Instead of rerunning the UPDATE statement to fix the typo, we can simply discard the change by running the ROLLBACK; ❹ command. When we rerun the SELECT statement to view the company names, we're back to where we started:

```
company
--------------------------
AGRO Merchants Oakland LLC
AGRO Merchants Oakland LLC
AGRO Merchants Oakland, LLC
```

From here, you could correct your UPDATE statement by removing the extra s and rerun it, beginning with the START TRANSACTION statement again. If you're happy with the changes, run COMMIT; to make them permanent.

NOTE *When you start a transaction, any changes you make to the data aren't visible to other database users until you execute COMMIT.*

Transaction blocks are often used in more complex database systems. Here you've used them to try a query and either accept or reject the changes, saving you time and headaches. Next, let's look at another way to save time when updating lots of data.

Improving Performance When Updating Large Tables

Because of how PostgreSQL works internally, adding a column to a table and filling it with values can quickly inflate the table's size. The reason is that the database creates a new version of the existing row each time a value is updated, but it doesn't delete the old row version. (You'll learn how to clean up these old rows when I discuss database maintenance in "Recovering Unused Space with VACUUM" on page 314.) For small data sets, the increase is negligible, but for tables with hundreds of thousands or millions of rows, the time required to update rows and the resulting extra disk usage can be substantial.

Instead of adding a column and filling it with values, we can save disk space by copying the entire table and adding a populated column during the operation. Then, we rename the tables so the copy replaces the original, and the original becomes a backup.

Listing 9-25 shows how to copy meat_poultry_egg_inspect into a new table while adding a populated column. To do this, first drop the meat_poultry_egg _inspect_backup table we made earlier. Then run the CREATE TABLE statement.

```
CREATE TABLE meat_poultry_egg_inspect_backup AS
❶ SELECT *,
        ❷ '2018-02-07'::date AS reviewed_date
FROM meat_poultry_egg_inspect;
```

Listing 9-25: Backing up a table while adding and filling a new column

The query is a modified version of the backup script in Listing 9-8. Here, in addition to selecting all the columns using the asterisk wildcard ❶, we also add a column called reviewed_date by providing a value cast as a date data type ❷ and the AS keyword. That syntax adds and fills reviewed_date, which we might use to track the last time we checked the status of each plant.

Then we use Listing 9-26 to swap the table names:

```
❶ ALTER TABLE meat_poultry_egg_inspect RENAME TO meat_poultry_egg_inspect_temp;
❷ ALTER TABLE meat_poultry_egg_inspect_backup
  RENAME TO meat_poultry_egg_inspect;
```

```
❸ ALTER TABLE meat_poultry_egg_inspect_temp
    RENAME TO meat_poultry_egg_inspect_backup;
```

Listing 9-26: Swapping table names using ALTER TABLE

Here we use ALTER TABLE with a RENAME TO clause to change a table name. Then we use the first statement to change the original table name to one that ends with _temp ❶. The second statement renames the copy we made with Listing 9-24 to the original name of the table ❷. Finally, we rename the table that ends with _temp to the ending _backup ❸. The original table is now called meat_poultry_egg_inspect_backup, and the copy with the added column is called meat_poultry_egg_inspect.

By using this process, we avoid updating rows and having the database inflate the size of the table. When we eventually drop the _backup table, the remaining data table is smaller and does not require cleanup.

Wrapping Up

Gleaning useful information from data sometimes requires modifying the data to remove inconsistencies, fix errors, and make it more suitable for supporting an accurate analysis. In this chapter you learned some useful tools to help you assess dirty data and clean it up. In a perfect world, all data sets would arrive with everything clean and complete. But such a perfect world doesn't exist, so the ability to alter, update, and delete data is indispensable.

Let me restate the important tasks of working safely. Be sure to back up your tables before you start making changes. Make copies of your columns, too, for an extra level of protection. When I discuss database maintenance for PostgreSQL later in the book, you'll learn how to back up entire databases. These few steps of precaution will save you a world of pain.

In the next chapter, we'll return to math to explore some of SQL's advanced statistical functions and techniques for analysis.

TRY IT YOURSELF

In this exercise, you'll turn the meat_poultry_egg_inspect table into useful information. You need to answer two questions: how many of the plants in the table process meat, and how many process poultry?

The answers to these two questions lie in the activities column. Unfortunately, the column contains an assortment of text with inconsistent input. Here's an example of the kind of text you'll find in the activities column:

```
Poultry Processing, Poultry Slaughter
Meat Processing, Poultry Processing
Poultry Processing, Poultry Slaughter
```

The mishmash of text makes it impossible to perform a typical count that would allow you to group processing plants by activity. However, you can make some modifications to fix this data. Your tasks are as follows:

1. Create two new columns called meat_processing and poultry_processing in your table. Each can be of the type boolean.

2. Using UPDATE, set meat_processing = TRUE on any row where the activities column contains the text *Meat Processing*. Do the same update on the poultry_processing column, but this time look for the text *Poultry Processing* in activities.

3. Use the data from the new, updated columns to count how many plants perform each type of activity. For a bonus challenge, count how many plants perform both activities.

10

STATISTICAL FUNCTIONS IN SQL

A SQL database isn't usually the first tool a data analyst chooses when performing statistical analysis that requires more than just calculating sums and averages. Typically, the software of choice would be full-featured statistics packages, such as SPSS or SAS, the programming languages R or Python, or even Excel. However, standard ANSI SQL, including PostgreSQL's implementation, offers a handful of powerful stats functions that reveal a lot about your data without having to export your data set to another program.

In this chapter, we'll explore these SQL stats functions along with guidelines on when to use them. Statistics is a vast subject worthy of its own book, so we'll only skim the surface here. Nevertheless, you'll learn how to apply high-level statistical concepts to help you derive meaning from your data using a new data set from the U.S. Census Bureau. You'll also learn to use SQL to create comparisons using rankings and rates with FBI crime data as our subject.

Creating a Census Stats Table

Let's return to one of my favorite data sources, the U.S. Census Bureau. In Chapters 4 and 5, you used the 2010 Decennial Census to import data and perform basic math and stats. This time you'll use county data points compiled from the 2011–2015 American Community Survey (ACS) 5-Year Estimates, a separate survey administered by the Census Bureau.

Use the code in Listing 10-1 to create the table acs_2011_2015_stats and import the CSV file *acs_2011_2015_stats.csv*. The code and data are available with all the book's resources at *https://www.nostarch.com/practicalSQL/*. Remember to change *C:\YourDirectory* to the location of the CSV file.

```
CREATE TABLE acs_2011_2015_stats (
❶ geoid varchar(14) CONSTRAINT geoid_key PRIMARY KEY,
   county varchar(50) NOT NULL,
   st varchar(20) NOT NULL,
❷ pct_travel_60_min numeric(5,3) NOT NULL,
   pct_bachelors_higher numeric(5,3) NOT NULL,
   pct_masters_higher numeric(5,3) NOT NULL,
   median_hh_income integer,
❸ CHECK (pct_masters_higher <= pct_bachelors_higher)
);

COPY acs_2011_2015_stats
FROM 'C:\YourDirectory\acs_2011_2015_stats.csv'
WITH (FORMAT CSV, HEADER, DELIMITER ',');

❹ SELECT * FROM acs_2011_2015_stats;
```

Listing 10-1: Creating the Census 2011–2015 ACS 5-Year stats table and import data

The acs_2011_2015_stats table has seven columns. The first three columns ❶ include a unique geoid that serves as the primary key, the name of the county, and the state name st. The next four columns display the following three percentages ❷ I derived for each county from raw data in the ACS release, plus one more economic indicator:

pct_travel_60_min The percentage of workers ages 16 and older who commute more than 60 minutes to work.

pct_bachelors_higher The percentage of people ages 25 and older whose level of education is a bachelor's degree or higher. (In the United States, a bachelor's degree is usually awarded upon completing a four-year college education.)

pct_masters_higher The percentage of people ages 25 and older whose level of education is a master's degree or higher. (In the United States, a master's degree is the first advanced degree earned after completing a bachelor's degree.)

median_hh_income The county's median household income in 2015 inflation-adjusted dollars. As you learned in Chapter 5, a median value is the midpoint in an ordered set of numbers, where half the values are larger than the midpoint and half are smaller. Because averages can be skewed by a few very large or very small values, government reporting on economic data, such as income, tends to use medians. In this column, we omit the NOT NULL constraint because one county had no data reported.

We include the CHECK constraint ❸ you learned in Chapter 7 to check that the figures for the bachelor's degree are equal to or higher than those for the master's degree, because in the United States, a bachelor's degree is earned before or concurrently with a master's degree. A county showing the opposite could indicate data imported incorrectly or a column mislabeled. Our data checks out: upon import, there are no errors showing a violation of the CHECK constraint.

We use the SELECT statement ❹ to view all 3,142 rows imported, each corresponding to a county surveyed in this Census release.

Next, we'll use statistics functions in SQL to better understand the relationships among the percentages.

THE DECENNIAL U.S. CENSUS VS. THE AMERICAN COMMUNITY SURVEY

Each U.S. Census data product has its own methodology. The Decennial Census is a full count of the U.S. population, conducted every 10 years via a form mailed to every household in the country. One of its primary purposes is to determine the number of seats each state holds in the U.S. House of Representatives. In contrast, the ACS is an ongoing annual survey of about 3.5 million U.S. households. It enquires into details about income, education, employment, ancestry, and housing. Private-sector and public-sector organizations alike use ACS data to track trends and make various decisions.

Currently, the Census Bureau packages ACS data into two releases: a 1-year data set that provides estimates for geographies with populations of 20,000 or more, and a 5-year data set that includes all geographies. Because it's a survey, ACS results are estimates and have a margin of error, which I've omitted for brevity but which you'll see included in a full ACS data set.

Measuring Correlation with corr(Y, X)

Researchers often want to understand the relationships between variables, and one such measure of relationships is *correlation*. In this section, we'll use the corr(Y, X) function to measure correlation and investigate what relationship exists, if any, between the percentage of people in a county who've attained a bachelor's degree and the median household income in that county. We'll also determine whether, according to our data, a better-educated population typically equates to higher income and how strong the relationship between education level and income is if it does.

First, some background. The *Pearson correlation coefficient* (generally denoted as *r*) is a measure for quantifying the strength of a *linear relationship* between two variables. It shows the extent to which an increase or decrease in one variable correlates to a change in another variable. The *r* values fall between −1 and 1. Either end of the range indicates a perfect correlation, whereas values near zero indicate a random distribution with no correlation. A positive *r* value indicates a *direct relationship*: as one variable increases, the other does too. When graphed on a scatterplot, the data points representing each pair of values in a direct relationship would slope upward from left to right. A negative *r* value indicates an *inverse relationship*: as one variable increases, the other decreases. Dots representing an inverse relationship would slope downward from left to right on a scatterplot.

Table 10-1 provides general guidelines for interpreting positive and negative *r* values, although as always with statistics, different statisticians may offer different interpretations.

Table 10-1: Interpreting Correlation Coefficients

Correlation coefficient (+/−)	What it could mean
0	No relationship
.01 to .29	Weak relationship
.3 to .59	Moderate relationship
.6 to .99	Strong to nearly perfect relationship
1	Perfect relationship

In standard ANSI SQL and PostgreSQL, we calculate the Pearson correlation coefficient using corr(Y, X). It's one of several *binary aggregate functions* in SQL and is so named because these functions accept two inputs. In binary aggregate functions, the input Y is the *dependent variable* whose variation depends on the value of another variable, and X is the *independent variable* whose value doesn't depend on another variable.

NOTE *Even though SQL specifies the Y and X inputs for the corr() function, correlation calculations don't distinguish between dependent and independent variables. Switching the order of inputs in corr() produces the same result. However, for convenience and readability, these examples order the input variables according to dependent and independent.*

We'll use the corr(Y, X) function to discover the relationship between education level and income. Enter the code in Listing 10-2 to use corr(Y, X) with the median_hh_income and pct_bachelors_higher variables as inputs:

```
SELECT corr(median_hh_income, pct_bachelors_higher)
    AS bachelors_income_r
FROM acs_2011_2015_stats;
```

Listing 10-2: Using corr(Y, X) to measure the relationship between education and income

Run the query; your result should be an *r* value of just above .68 given as the floating-point double precision data type:

```
bachelors_income_r
------------------
0.682185675451399
```

This positive *r* value indicates that as a county's educational attainment increases, household income tends to increase. The relationship isn't perfect, but the *r* value shows the relationship is fairly strong. We can visualize this pattern by plotting the variables on a scatterplot using Excel, as shown in Figure 10-1. Each data point represents one U.S. county; the data point's position on the x-axis shows the percentage of the population ages 25 and older that have a bachelor's degree or higher. The data point's position on the y-axis represents the county's median household income.

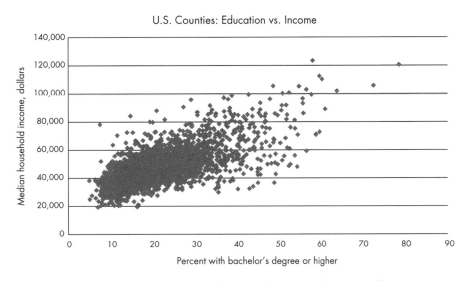

Figure 10-1: A scatterplot showing the relationship between education and income

Notice that although most of the data points are grouped together in the bottom-left corner of the graph, they do generally slope upward from left to right. Also, the points spread out rather than strictly follow a straight line. If they were in a straight line sloping up from left to right, the *r* value would be 1, indicating a perfect positive linear relationship.

Checking Additional Correlations

Now let's calculate the correlation coefficients for the remaining variable pairs using the code in Listing 10-3:

```
SELECT
❶ round(
    corr(median_hh_income, pct_bachelors_higher)::numeric, 2
    ) AS bachelors_income_r,
```

```
    round(
      corr(pct_travel_60_min, median_hh_income)::numeric, 2
      ) AS income_travel_r,
    round(
      corr(pct_travel_60_min, pct_bachelors_higher)::numeric, 2
      ) AS bachelors_travel_r
FROM acs_2011_2015_stats;
```

Listing 10-3: Using corr(Y, X) on additional variables

This time we'll make the output more readable by rounding off the decimal values. We'll do this by wrapping the corr(Y, X) function inside SQL's round() function ❶, which takes two inputs: the numeric value to be rounded and an integer value indicating the number of decimal places to round the first value. If the second parameter is omitted, the value is rounded to the nearest whole integer. Because corr(Y, X) returns a floating-point value by default, we'll change it to the numeric type using the :: notation you learned in Chapter 3. Here's the output:

bachelors_income_r	income_travel_r	bachelors_travel_r
0.68	0.05	-0.14

The bachelors_income_r value is 0.68, which is the same as our first run but rounded to two decimal places. Compared to bachelors_income_r, the other two correlations are weak.

The income_travel_r value shows that the correlation between income and the percentage of those who commute more than an hour to work is practically zero. This indicates that a county's median household income bears little connection to how long it takes people to get to work.

The bachelors_travel_r value shows that the correlation of bachelor's degrees and commuting is also low at -0.14. The negative value indicates an inverse relationship: as education increases, the percentage of the population that travels more than an hour to work decreases. Although this is interesting, a correlation coefficient that is this close to zero indicates a weak relationship.

When testing for correlation, we need to note some caveats. The first is that even a strong correlation does not imply causality. We can't say that a change in one variable causes a change in the other, only that the changes move together. The second is that correlations should be subject to testing to determine whether they're statistically significant. Those tests are beyond the scope of this book but worth studying on your own.

Nevertheless, the SQL corr(Y, X) function is a handy tool for quickly checking correlations between variables.

Predicting Values with Regression Analysis

Researchers not only want to understand relationships between variables; they also want to predict values using available data. For example, let's say 30 percent of a county's population has a bachelor's degree or higher. Given the trend in our data, what would we expect that county's median household income to be? Likewise, for each percent increase in education, how much increase, on average, would we expect in income?

We can answer both questions using *linear regression*. Simply put, the regression method finds the best linear equation, or straight line, that describes the relationship between an independent variable (such as education) and a dependent variable (such as income). Standard ANSI SQL and PostgreSQL include functions that perform linear regression.

Figure 10-2 shows our previous scatterplot with a regression line added.

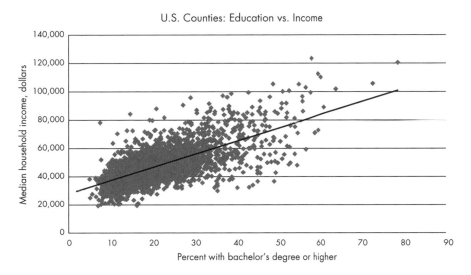

Figure 10-2: Scatterplot with least squares regression line showing the relationship between education and income

The straight line running through the middle of all the data points is called the *least squares regression line*, which approximates the "best fit" for a straight line that best describes the relationship between the variables. The equation for the regression line is like the *slope-intercept* formula you might remember from high school math but written using differently named variables: $Y = bX + a$. Here are the formula's components:

Y is the predicted value, which is also the value on the y-axis, or dependent variable.

b is the slope of the line, which can be positive or negative. It measures how many units the y-axis value will increase or decrease for each unit of the x-axis value.

X represents a value on the x-axis, or independent variable.

a is the y-intercept, the value at which the line crosses the y-axis when the *X* value is zero.

Let's apply this formula using SQL. Earlier, we questioned what the expected median household income in a county would be if the percentage of people with a bachelor's degree or higher in that county was 30 percent.

In our scatterplot, the percentage with bachelor's degrees falls along the x-axis, represented by X in the calculation. Let's plug that value into the regression line formula in place of X:

$$Y = b(30) + a$$

To calculate Y, which represents the predicted median household income, we need the line's slope, b, and the y-intercept, a. To get these values, we'll use the SQL functions `regr_slope(Y, X)` and `regr_intercept(Y, X)`, as shown in Listing 10-4:

```
SELECT
    round(
        regr_slope(median_hh_income, pct_bachelors_higher)::numeric, 2
        ) AS slope,
    round(
        regr_intercept(median_hh_income, pct_bachelors_higher)::numeric, 2
        ) AS y_intercept
FROM acs_2011_2015_stats;
```

Listing 10-4: Regression slope and intercept functions

Using the `median_hh_income` and `pct_bachelors_higher` variables as inputs for both functions, we'll set the resulting value of the `regr_slope(Y, X)` function as slope and the output for the `regr_intercept(Y, X)` function as y_intercept.

Run the query; the result should show the following:

```
slope      y_intercept
------     -----------
926.95       27901.15
```

The `slope` value shows that for every one-unit increase in bachelor's degree percentage, we can expect a county's median household income will increase by 926.95. Slope always refers to change per one unit of X. The y_intercept value shows that when the regression line crosses the y-axis, where the percentage with bachelor's degrees is at 0, the y-axis value is 27901.15. Now let's plug both values into the equation to get the Y value:

$$Y = 926.95(30) + 27901.15$$

$$Y = 55709.65$$

Based on our calculation, in a county in which 30 percent of people age 25 and older have a bachelor's degree or higher, we can expect a median household income in that county to be about $55,710. Of course, our data includes counties whose median income falls above and below that predicted value, but we expect this to be the case because our data points in the scatterplot don't line up perfectly along the regression line. Recall that the correlation coefficient we calculated was 0.68, indicating a strong but not perfect relationship between education and income. Other factors probably contributed to variations in income as well.

Finding the Effect of an Independent Variable with r-squared

Earlier in the chapter, we calculated the correlation coefficient, *r*, to determine the direction and strength of the relationship between two variables. We can also calculate the extent that the variation in the *x* (independent) variable explains the variation in the *y* (dependent) variable by squaring the *r* value to find the *coefficient of determination*, better known as *r-squared*. An *r*-squared value is between zero and one and indicates the percentage of the variation that is explained by the independent variable. For example, if *r*-squared equals .1, we would say that the independent variable explains 10 percent of the variation in the dependent variable, or not much at all.

To find *r*-squared, we use the regr_r2(*Y*, *X*) function in SQL. Let's apply it to our education and income variables using the code in Listing 10-5:

```
SELECT round(
        regr_r2(median_hh_income, pct_bachelors_higher)::numeric, 3
        ) AS r_squared
FROM acs_2011_2015_stats;
```

Listing 10-5: Calculating the coefficient of determination, or r-squared

This time we'll round off the output to the nearest thousandth place and set the result to r_squared. The query should return the following result:

```
r_squared
---------
    0.465
```

The *r*-squared value of 0.465 indicates that about 47 percent of the variation in median household income in a county can be explained by the percentage of people with a bachelor's degree or higher in that county. What explains the other 53 percent of the variation in household income? Any number of factors could explain the rest of the variation, and statisticians will typically test numerous combinations of variables to determine what they are.

But before you use these numbers in a headline or presentation, it's worth revisiting the following points:

1. Correlation doesn't prove causality. For verification, do a Google search on "correlation and causality." Many variables correlate well but have no meaning. (See *http://www.tylervigen.com/spurious-correlations* for examples of correlations that don't prove causality, including the correlation between divorce rate in Maine and margarine consumption.) Statisticians usually perform *significance testing* on the results to make sure values are not simply the result of randomness.

2. Statisticians also apply additional tests to data before accepting the results of a regression analysis, including whether the variables follow the standard bell curve distribution and meet other criteria for a valid result.

Given these factors, SQL's statistics functions are useful as a preliminary survey of your data before doing more rigorous analysis. If your work involves statistics, a full study on performing regression is worthwhile.

Creating Rankings with SQL

Rankings make the news often. You'll see them used anywhere from weekend box office charts to a sports team's league standings. You've already learned how to order query results based on values in a column, but SQL lets you go further and create numbered rankings. Rankings are useful for data analysis in several ways, such as tracking changes over time if you have several years' worth of data. You can also simply use a ranking as a fact on its own in a report. Let's explore how to create rankings using SQL.

Ranking with rank() and dense_rank()

Standard ANSI SQL includes several ranking functions, but we'll just focus on two: rank() and dense_rank(). Both are *window functions*, which perform calculations across sets of rows we specify using the OVER clause. Unlike aggregate functions, which group rows while calculating results, window functions present results for each row in the table.

The difference between rank() and dense_rank() is the way they handle the next rank value after a tie: rank() includes a gap in the rank order, but dense_rank() does not. This concept is easier to understand in action, so let's look at an example. Consider a Wall Street analyst who covers the highly competitive widget manufacturing market. The analyst wants to rank companies by their annual output. The SQL statements in Listing 10-6 create and fill a table with this data and then rank the companies by widget output:

```
CREATE TABLE widget_companies (
    id bigserial,
    company varchar(30) NOT NULL,
    widget_output integer NOT NULL
);

INSERT INTO widget_companies (company, widget_output)
VALUES
    ('Morse Widgets', 125000),
    ('Springfield Widget Masters', 143000),
    ('Best Widgets', 196000),
    ('Acme Inc.', 133000),
    ('District Widget Inc.', 201000),
    ('Clarke Amalgamated', 620000),
    ('Stavesacre Industries', 244000),
    ('Bowers Widget Emporium', 201000);

SELECT
    company,
    widget_output,
❶ rank() OVER (ORDER BY widget_output DESC),
```

❷ dense_rank() OVER (ORDER BY widget_output DESC)
FROM widget_companies;

Listing 10-6: Using the rank() and dense_rank() window functions

Notice the syntax in the SELECT statement that includes rank() **❶** and dense_rank() **❷**. After the function names, we use the OVER clause and in parentheses place an expression that specifies the "window" of rows the function should operate on. In this case, we want both functions to work on all rows of the widget_output column, sorted in descending order. Here's the output:

company	widget_output	rank	dense_rank
Clarke Amalgamated	620000	1	1
Stavesacre Industries	244000	2	2
Bowers Widget Emporium	201000	3	3
District Widget Inc.	201000	3	3
Best Widgets	196000	5	4
Springfield Widget Masters	143000	6	5
Acme Inc.	133000	7	6
Morse Widgets	125000	8	7

The columns produced by the rank() and dense_rank() functions show each company's ranking based on the widget_output value from highest to lowest, with Clarke Amalgamated at number one. To see how rank() and dense_rank() differ, check the fifth row listing, Best Widgets.

With rank(), Best Widgets is the fifth highest ranking company, showing there are four companies with more output and there is no company ranking in fourth place, because rank() allows a gap in the order when a tie occurs. In contrast, dense_rank(), which doesn't allow a gap in the rank order, reflects the fact that Best Widgets has the fourth highest output number regardless of how many companies produced more. Therefore, Best Widgets ranks in fourth place using dense_rank().

Both ways of handling ties have merit, but in practice rank() is used most often. It's also what I recommend using, because it more accurately reflects the total number of companies ranked, shown by the fact that Best Widgets has four companies ahead of it in total output, not three.

Let's look at a more complex ranking example.

Ranking Within Subgroups with PARTITION BY

The ranking we just did was a simple overall ranking based on widget output. But sometimes you'll want to produce ranks within groups of rows in a table. For example, you might want to rank government employees by salary within each department or rank movies by box office earnings within each genre.

To use window functions in this way, we'll add PARTITION BY to the OVER clause. A PARTITION BY clause divides table rows according to values in a column we specify.

Here's an example using made-up data about grocery stores. Enter the code in Listing 10-7 to fill a table called store_sales:

```
CREATE TABLE store_sales (
    store varchar(30),
    category varchar(30) NOT NULL,
    unit_sales bigint NOT NULL,
    CONSTRAINT store_category_key PRIMARY KEY (store, category)
);

INSERT INTO store_sales (store, category, unit_sales)
VALUES
    ('Broders', 'Cereal', 1104),
    ('Wallace', 'Ice Cream', 1863),
    ('Broders', 'Ice Cream', 2517),
    ('Cramers', 'Ice Cream', 2112),
    ('Broders', 'Beer', 641),
    ('Cramers', 'Cereal', 1003),
    ('Cramers', 'Beer', 640),
    ('Wallace', 'Cereal', 980),
    ('Wallace', 'Beer', 988);

SELECT
    category,
    store,
    unit_sales,
  ❶ rank() OVER (PARTITION BY category ORDER BY unit_sales DESC)
FROM store_sales;
```

Listing 10-7: Applying rank() within groups using PARTITION BY

In the table, each row includes a store's product category and sales for that category. The final SELECT statement creates a result set showing how each store's sales ranks within each category. The new element is the addition of PARTITION BY in the OVER clause ❶. In effect, the clause tells the program to create rankings one category at a time, using the store's unit sales in descending order. Here's the output:

category	store	unit_sales	rank
Beer	Wallace	988	1
Beer	Broders	641	2
Beer	Cramers	640	3
Cereal	Broders	1104	1
Cereal	Cramers	1003	2
Cereal	Wallace	980	3
Ice Cream	Broders	2517	1
Ice Cream	Cramers	2112	2
Ice Cream	Wallace	1863	3

Notice that category names are ordered and grouped in the category column as a result of PARTITION BY in the OVER clause. Rows for each category are ordered by category unit sales with the rank column displaying the ranking.

Using this table, we can see at a glance how each store ranks in a food category. For instance, Broders tops sales for cereal and ice cream, but Wallace wins in the beer category. You can apply this concept to many other scenarios: for example, for each auto manufacturer, finding the vehicle with the most consumer complaints; figuring out which month had the most rainfall in each of the last 20 years; finding the team with the most wins against left-handed pitchers; and so on.

SQL offers additional window functions. Check the official PostgreSQL documentation at *https://www.postgresql.org/docs/current/static/tutorial-window .html* for an overview of window functions, and check *https://www.postgresql .org/docs/current/static/functions-window.html* for a listing of window functions.

Calculating Rates for Meaningful Comparisons

As helpful and interesting as they are, rankings based on raw counts aren't always meaningful; in fact, they can actually be misleading. Consider this example of crime statistics: according to the U.S. Federal Bureau of Investigation (FBI), in 2015, New York City reported about 130,000 property crimes, which included burglary, larceny, motor vehicle thefts, and arson. Meanwhile, Chicago reported about 80,000 property crimes the same year.

So, you're more likely to find trouble in New York City, right? Not necessarily. In 2015, New York City had more than 8 million residents, whereas Chicago had 2.7 million. Given that context, just comparing the total numbers of property crimes in the two cities isn't very meaningful.

A more accurate way to compare these numbers is to turn them into rates. Analysts often calculate a rate per 1,000 people, or some multiple of that number, for apples-to-apples comparisons. For the property crimes in this example, the math is simple: divide the number of offenses by the population and then multiply that quotient by 1,000. For example, if a city has 80 vehicle thefts and a population of 15,000, you can calculate the rate of vehicle thefts per 1,000 people as follows:

$$(80 \ / \ 15{,}000) \times 1{,}000 = 5.3 \text{ vehicle thefts per thousand residents}$$

This is easy math with SQL, so let's try it using select city-level data I compiled from the FBI's *2015 Crime in the United States* report available at *https://ucr.fbi.gov/crime-in-the-u.s/2015/crime-in-the-u.s.-2015/home*. Listing 10-8 contains the code to create and fill a table. Remember to point the script to the location in which you've saved the CSV file, which you can download at *https://www.nostarch.com/practicalSQL/*.

```
CREATE TABLE fbi_crime_data_2015 (
    st varchar(20),
    city varchar(50),
    population integer,
    violent_crime integer,
    property_crime integer,
    burglary integer,
```

```
    larceny_theft integer,
    motor_vehicle_theft integer,
    CONSTRAINT st_city_key PRIMARY KEY (st, city)
);

COPY fbi_crime_data_2015
FROM 'C:\YourDirectory\fbi_crime_data_2015.csv'
WITH (FORMAT CSV, HEADER, DELIMITER ',');

SELECT * FROM fbi_crime_data_2015
ORDER BY population DESC;
```

Listing 10-8: Creating and filling a 2015 FBI crime data table

The fbi_crime_data_2015 table includes the state, city name, and population for that city. Next is the number of crimes reported by police in categories, including violent crime, vehicle thefts, and property crime. To calculate property crimes per 1,000 people in cities with more than 500,000 people and order them, we'll use the code in Listing 10-9:

```
SELECT
    city,
    st,
    population,
    property_crime,
    round(
      ❶ (property_crime::numeric / population) * 1000, 1
        ) AS pc_per_1000
FROM fbi_crime_data_2015
WHERE population >= 500000
ORDER BY (property_crime::numeric / population) DESC;
```

Listing 10-9: Finding property crime rates per thousand in cities with 500,000 or more people

In Chapter 5, you learned that when dividing an integer by an integer, one of the values must be a numeric or decimal for the result to include decimal places. We do that in the rate calculation ❶ with PostgreSQL's double-colon shorthand. Because we don't need to see many decimal places, we wrap the statement in the round() function to round off the output to the nearest tenth. Then we give the calculated column an alias of pc_per_1000 for easy reference. Here's a portion of the result set:

city	st	population	property_crime	pc_per_1000
Tucson	Arizona	529675	35185	66.4
San Francisco	California	863782	53019	61.4
Albuquerque	New Mexico	559721	33993	60.7
Memphis	Tennessee	657936	37047	56.3
Seattle	Washington	683700	37754	55.2
--snip--				
El Paso	Texas	686077	13133	19.1
New York	New York	8550861	129860	15.2

Tucson, Arizona, has the highest rate of property crimes, followed by San Francisco, California. At the bottom is New York City, with a rate that's one-fourth of Tucson's. If we had compared the cities based solely on the raw numbers of property crimes, we'd have a far different result than the one we derived by calculating the rate per thousand.

I'd be remiss not to point out that the FBI website at *https://ucr.fbi.gov/ ucr-statistics-their-proper-use/* discourages creating rankings from its crime data, stating that doing so creates "misleading perceptions which adversely affect geographic entities and their residents." They point out that variations in crimes and crime rates across the country are often due to a number of factors ranging from population density to economic conditions and even the climate. Also, the FBI's crime data has well-documented shortcomings, including incomplete reporting by police agencies.

That said, asking why a locality has higher or lower crime rates than others is still worth pursuing, and rates do provide some measure of comparison despite certain limitations.

Wrapping Up

That wraps up our exploration of statistical functions in SQL, rankings, and rates. Now your SQL analysis toolkit includes ways to find relationships among variables using statistics functions, create rankings from ordered data, and properly compare raw numbers by turning them into rates. That toolkit is starting to look impressive!

Next, we'll dive deeper into date and time data, using SQL functions to extract the information we need.

TRY IT YOURSELF

Test your new skills with the following questions:

1. In Listing 10-2, the correlation coefficient, or *r* value, of the variables pct_bachelors_higher and median_hh_income was about .68. Write a query using the same data set to show the correlation between pct_masters_higher and median_hh_income. Is the *r* value higher or lower? What might explain the difference?

2. In the FBI crime data, which cities with a population of 500,000 or more have the highest rates of motor vehicle thefts (column motor_vehicle_theft)? Which have the highest violent crime rates (column violent_crime)?

3. As a bonus challenge, revisit the libraries data in the table pls_fy2014 _pupld14a in Chapter 8. Rank library agencies based on the rate of visits per 1,000 population (column popu_lsa), and limit the query to agencies serving 250,000 people or more.

11

WORKING WITH DATES AND TIMES

Columns filled with dates and times can indicate *when* events happened or *how long* they took, and that can lead to interesting lines of inquiry. What patterns exist in the moments on a timeline? Which events were shortest or longest? What relationships exist between a particular activity and the time of day or season in which it occurred?

In this chapter, we'll explore these kinds of questions using SQL data types for dates and times and their related functions. We'll start with a closer look at data types and functions related to dates and times. Then we'll explore a data set that contains information on trips by New York City taxicabs to look for patterns and try to discover what, if any, story the data tells. We'll also explore time zones using Amtrak data to calculate the duration of train trips across the United States.

Data Types and Functions for Dates and Times

Chapter 3 explored primary SQL data types, but to review, here are the four data types related to dates and times:

date Records only the date. PostgreSQL accepts several date formats. For example, valid formats for adding the 21st day of September 2018 are September 21, 2018 or 9/21/2018. I recommend using YYYY-MM-DD (or 2018-09-21), which is the ISO 8601 international standard format and also the default PostgreSQL date output. Using the ISO format helps avoid confusion when sharing data internationally.

time Records only the time. Adding with time zone makes the column time zone aware. The ISO 8601 format is HH:MM:SS, where HH represents the hour, MM the minutes, and SS the seconds. You can add an optional time zone designator. For example, 2:24 PM in San Francisco during standard time in fall and winter would be 14:24 PST.

timestamp Records the date and time. You can add with time zone to make the column time zone aware. The format timestamp with time zone is part of the SQL standard, but with PostgreSQL, you can use the shorthand timestamptz, which combines the date and time formats plus a time zone designator at the end: YYYY-MM-DD HH:MM:SS TZ. You can specify time zones in three different formats: its UTC offset, an area/ location designator, or a standard abbreviation.

interval Holds a value that represents a unit of time expressed in the format *quantity unit*. It doesn't record the start or end of a period, only its duration. Examples include 12 days or 8 hours.

The first three data types, date, time, and timestamp, are known as *datetime types* whose values are called *datetimes*. The interval value is an *interval type* whose values are *intervals*. All four data types can track the system clock and the nuances of the calendar. For example, date and timestamp recognize that June has 30 days. Therefore, June 31 is an invalid datetime value that causes the database to throw an error. Likewise, the date February 29 is valid only in a leap year, such as 2020.

Manipulating Dates and Times

We can use SQL functions to perform calculations on dates and times or extract components from them. For example, we can retrieve the day of the week from a timestamp or extract just the month from a date. ANSI SQL outlines a handful of functions to do this, but many database managers (including MySQL and Microsoft SQL Server) deviate from the standard to implement their own date and time data types, syntax, and function names. If you're using a database other than PostgreSQL, check its documentation.

Let's review how to manipulate dates and times using PostgreSQL functions.

Extracting the Components of a timestamp Value

It's not unusual to need just one piece of a date or time value for analysis, particularly when you're aggregating results by month, year, or even minute. We can extract these components using the PostgreSQL date_part() function. Its format looks like this:

```
date_part(text, value)
```

The function takes two inputs. The first is a string in text format that represents the part of the date or time to extract, such as hour, minute, or week. The second is the date, time, or timestamp value. To see the date_part() function in action, we'll execute it multiple times on the same value using the code in Listing 11-1. In the listing, we format the string as a timestamp with time zone using the PostgreSQL-specific shorthand timestamptz. We also assign a column name to each with AS.

```
SELECT
    date_part('year', '2019-12-01 18:37:12 EST'::timestamptz) AS "year",
    date_part('month', '2019-12-01 18:37:12 EST'::timestamptz) AS "month",
    date_part('day', '2019-12-01 18:37:12 EST'::timestamptz) AS "day",
    date_part('hour', '2019-12-01 18:37:12 EST'::timestamptz) AS "hour",
    date_part('minute', '2019-12-01 18:37:12 EST'::timestamptz) AS "minute",
    date_part('seconds', '2019-12-01 18:37:12 EST'::timestamptz) AS "seconds",
    date_part('timezone_hour', '2019-12-01 18:37:12 EST'::timestamptz) AS "tz",
    date_part('week', '2019-12-01 18:37:12 EST'::timestamptz) AS "week",
    date_part('quarter', '2019-12-01 18:37:12 EST'::timestamptz) AS "quarter",
    date_part('epoch', '2019-12-01 18:37:12 EST'::timestamptz) AS "epoch";
```

Listing 11-1: Extracting components of a timestamp value using date_part()

Each column statement in this SELECT query first uses a string to name the component we want to extract: year, month, day, and so on. The second input uses the string 2019-12-01 18:37:12 EST cast as a timestamp with time zone with the PostgreSQL double-colon syntax and the timestamptz shorthand. In December, the United States is observing standard time, which is why we can designate the Eastern time zone using the Eastern Standard Time (EST) designation.

Here's the output as shown on my computer, which is located in the U.S. Eastern time zone. (The database converts the values to reflect your PostgreSQL time zone setting, so your output might be different; for example, if it's set to the U.S. Pacific time zone, the hour will show as 15):

year	month	day	hour	minute	seconds	tz	week	quarter	epoch
2019	12	1	18	37	12	-5	48	4	1575243432

Each column contains a single value that represents 6:37:12 PM on December 1, 2019, in the U.S. Eastern time zone. Even though you designated the time zone using EST in the string, PostgreSQL reports back the *UTC offset* of that time zone, which is the number of hours plus or minus from UTC. UTC refers to Coordinated Universal Time, a world time standard, as well as the value of UTC +/−00:00, the time zone that covers the United Kingdom and Western Africa. Here, the UTC offset is -5 (because EST is five hours behind UTC).

<blockquote>
NOTE *You can derive the UTC offset from the time zone but not vice versa. Each UTC offset can refer to multiple named time zones plus standard and daylight saving time variants.*
</blockquote>

The first seven values are easy to recognize from the original timestamp, but the last three are calculated values that deserve an explanation.

The week column shows that December 1, 2019, falls in the 48th week of the year. This number is determined by ISO 8601 standards, which start each week on a Monday. That means a week at the end of a year can extend from December into January of the following year.

The quarter column shows that our test date is part of the fourth quarter of the year. The epoch column shows a measurement, which is used in computer systems and programming languages, that represents the number of seconds elapsed before or after 12 AM, January 1, 1970, at UTC 0. A positive value designates a time since that point; a negative value designates a time before it. In this example, 1,575,243,432 seconds elapsed between January 1, 1970, and the timestamp. Epoch is useful if you need to compare two timestamps mathematically on an absolute scale.

PostgreSQL also supports the SQL-standard extract() function, which parses datetimes in the same way as the date_part() function. I've featured date_part() here instead for two reasons. First, its name helpfully reminds us what it does. Second, extract() isn't widely supported by database managers. Most notably, it's absent in Microsoft's SQL Server. Nevertheless, if you need to use extract(), the syntax takes this form:

```
extract(text from value)
```

To replicate the first date_part() example in Listing 11-1 where we pull the year from the timestamp, we'd set up the function like this:

```
extract('year' from '2019-12-01 18:37:12 EST'::timestamptz)
```

PostgreSQL provides additional components you can extract or calculate from dates and times. For the full list of functions, see the documentation at *https://www.postgresql.org/docs/current/static/functions-datetime.html*.

Creating Datetime Values from timestamp Components

It's not unusual to come across a data set in which the year, month, and day exist in separate columns, and you might want to create a datetime value from these components. To perform calculations on a date, it's helpful to combine and format those pieces correctly into one column.

You can use the following PostgreSQL functions to make datetime objects:

make_date(*year, month, day*)   Returns a value of type date

make_time(*hour, minute, seconds*)   Returns a value of type time without time zone

make_timestamptz(*year, month, day, hour, minute, second, time zone*) Returns a timestamp with time zone

The variables for these three functions take integer types as input, with two exceptions: seconds are of the type double precision because you can supply fractions of seconds, and time zones must be specified with a text string that names the time zone.

Listing 11-2 shows examples of the three functions in action using components of February 22, 2018, for the date, and 6:04:30.3 PM in Lisbon, Portugal for the time:

```
SELECT make_date(2018, 2, 22);
SELECT make_time(18, 4, 30.3);
SELECT make_timestamptz(2018, 2, 22, 18, 4, 30.3, 'Europe/Lisbon');
```

Listing 11-2: Three functions for making datetimes from components

When I run each query in order, the output on my computer in the U.S. Eastern time zone is as follows. Again, yours may differ depending on your time zone setting:

```
2018-02-22
18:04:30.3
2018-02-22 13:04:30.3-05
```

Notice that the timestamp in the third line shows 13:04:30.3, which is Eastern Standard Time and is five hours behind (-05) the time input to the function: 18:04:30.3. In our discussion on time zone–enabled columns in "Dates and Times" on page 32, I noted that PostgreSQL displays times relative to the client's time zone or the time zone set in the database session. This output reflects the appropriate time because my location is five hours behind Lisbon. We'll explore working with time zones in more detail, and you'll learn to adjust its display in "Working with Time Zones" on page 177.

Retrieving the Current Date and Time

If you need to record the current date or time as part of a query—when updating a row, for example—standard SQL provides functions for that too. The following functions record the time as of the start of the query:

current_date   Returns the date.

current_time   Returns the current time with time zone.

current_timestamp   Returns the current timestamp with time zone. A shorthand PostgreSQL-specific version is now().

localtime   Returns the current time without time zone.

localtimestamp   Returns the current timestamp without time zone.

Because these functions record the time at the start of the query (or a collection of queries grouped under a *transaction*, which I covered in Chapter 9), they'll provide that same time throughout the execution of a query regardless of how long the query runs. So, if your query updates 100,000 rows and takes 15 seconds to run, any timestamp recorded at the start of the query will be applied to each row, and so each row will receive the same timestamp.

If, instead, you want the date and time to reflect how the clock changes during the execution of the query, you can use the PostgreSQL-specific clock_timestamp() function to record the current time as it elapses. That way, if you're updating 100,000 rows and inserting a timestamp each time, each row gets the time the row updated rather than the time at the start of the query. Note that clock_timestamp() can slow large queries and may be subject to system limitations.

Listing 11-3 shows current_timestamp and clock_timestamp() in action when inserting a row in a table:

```
CREATE TABLE current_time_example (
    time_id bigserial,
 ❶  current_timestamp_col timestamp with time zone,
 ❷  clock_timestamp_col timestamp with time zone
);

INSERT INTO current_time_example (current_timestamp_col, clock_timestamp_col)
 ❸  (SELECT current_timestamp,
           clock_timestamp()
     FROM generate_series(1,1000));

SELECT * FROM current_time_example;
```

Listing 11-3: Comparing current_timestamp and clock_timestamp() during row insert

The code creates a table that includes two timestamp columns with a time zone. The first holds the result of the current_timestamp function ❶, which records the time at the start of the INSERT statement that adds 1,000 rows to the table. To do that, we use the generate_series() function, which returns a set of integers starting with 1 and ending with 1,000. The second column holds the result of the clock_timestamp() function ❷, which records the time of insertion of each row. You call both functions as part of the INSERT statement ❸. Run the query, and the result from the final SELECT statement should show that the time in the current_timestamp_col is the same for all rows, whereas the time in clock_timestamp_col increases with each row inserted.

Working with Time Zones

Time zone data lets the dates and times in your database reflect the location around the globe where those dates and times apply and their UTC offset. A timestamp of 1 PM is only useful, for example, if you know whether the value refers to local time in Asia, Eastern Europe, one of the 12 time zones of Antarctica, or anywhere else on the globe.

Of course, very often you'll receive data sets that contain no time zone data in their datetime columns. This isn't always a deal breaker in terms of whether or not you should continue to use the data. If you know that every event in the data happened in the same location, having the time zone in the timestamp is less critical, and it's relatively easy to modify all the time-stamps of your data to reflect that single time zone.

Let's look at some strategies for working with time zones in your data.

Finding Your Time Zone Setting

When working with time zones in SQL, you first need know the time zone setting for your database server. If you installed PostgreSQL on your own computer, the default will be your local time zone. If you're connecting to a PostgreSQL database elsewhere, perhaps on a network or a cloud provider such as Amazon Web Services, the time zone setting may be different than your own. To help avoid confusion, database administrators often set a shared server's time zone to UTC.

To find out the default time zone of your PostgreSQL server, use the SHOW command with timezone, as shown in Listing 11-4:

```
SHOW timezone;
```

Listing 11-4: Showing your PostgreSQL server's default time zone

Entering Listing 11-4 into pgAdmin and running it on my computer returns US/Eastern, one of several location names that falls into the Eastern time zone, which encompasses eastern Canada and the United States, the Caribbean, and parts of Mexico.

NOTE   *You can use SHOW ALL; to see the settings of every parameter on your PostgreSQL server.*

You can also use the two commands in Listing 11-5 to list all time zone names, abbreviations, and their UTC offsets:

```
SELECT * FROM pg_timezone_abbrevs;
SELECT * FROM pg_timezone_names;
```

Listing 11-5: Showing time zone abbreviations and names

You can easily filter either of these SELECT statements with a WHERE clause to look up specific location names or time zones:

```
SELECT * FROM pg_timezone_names
WHERE name LIKE 'Europe%';
```

This code should return a table listing that includes the time zone name, abbreviation, UTC offset, and a `boolean` column is_dst that notes whether the time zone is currently observing daylight saving time:

```
name                abbrev  utc_offset  is_dst
----------------    ------  ----------  ------
Europe/Amsterdam    CEST    02:00:00    t
Europe/Andorra      CEST    02:00:00    t
Europe/Astrakhan    +04     04:00:00    f
Europe/Athens       EEST    03:00:00    t
Europe/Belfast      BST     01:00:00    t
--snip--
```

This is a faster way of looking up time zones than using Wikipedia. Now let's look at how to set the time zone to a particular value.

Setting the Time Zone

When you installed PostgreSQL, the server's default time zone was set as a parameter in *postgresql.conf*, a file that contains dozens of values read by PostgreSQL each time it starts. The location of *postgresql.conf* in your file system varies depending on your operating system and sometimes on the way you installed PostgreSQL. To make permanent changes to *postgresql.conf*, you need to edit the file and restart the server, which might be impossible if you're not the owner of the machine. Changes to configurations might also have unintended consequences for other users or applications.

I'll cover working with *postgresql.conf* in more depth in Chapter 17. However, for now you can easily set the pgAdmin client's time zone on a per-session basis, and the change should last as long as you're connected to the server. This solution is handy when you want to specify how you view a particular table or handle timestamps in a query.

To set and change the pgAdmin client's time zone, we use the command SET timezone TO, as shown in Listing 11-6:

```
❶ SET timezone TO 'US/Pacific';

❷ CREATE TABLE time_zone_test (
      test_date timestamp with time zone
  );
❸ INSERT INTO time_zone_test VALUES ('2020-01-01 4:00');

❹ SELECT test_date
  FROM time_zone_test;

❺ SET timezone TO 'US/Eastern';

❻ SELECT test_date
  FROM time_zone_test;
```

```
❼ SELECT test_date AT TIME ZONE 'Asia/Seoul'
  FROM time_zone_test;
```

Listing 11-6: Setting the time zone for a client session

First, we set the time zone to US/Pacific ❶, which designates the Pacific time zone that covers western Canada and the United States along with Baja California in Mexico. Second, we create a one-column table ❷ with a data type of timestamp with time zone and insert a single row to display a test result. Notice that the value inserted, 2020-01-01 4:00, is a timestamp with no time zone ❸. You'll encounter timestamps with no time zone quite often, particularly when you acquire data sets restricted to a specific location.

When executed, the first SELECT statement ❹ returns 2020-01-01 4:00 as a timestamp that now contains time zone data:

```
test_date
----------------------
2020-01-01 04:00:00-08
```

Recall from our discussion on data types in Chapter 3 that the -08 at the end of this timestamp is the UTC offset. In this case, the -08 shows that the Pacific time zone is eight hours behind UTC. Because we initially set the pgAdmin client's time zone to US/Pacific for this session, any value we now enter into a column that is time zone aware will be in Pacific time and coded accordingly. However, it's worth noting that on the server, the timestamp with time zone data type always stores data as UTC internally; the time zone setting governs how it's displayed.

Now comes some fun. We change the time zone for this session to the Eastern time zone using the SET command ❺ and the US/Eastern designation. Then, when we execute the SELECT statement ❻ again, the result should be as follows:

```
test_date
----------------------
2020-01-01 07:00:00-05
```

In this example, two components of the timestamp have changed: the time is now 07:00, and the UTC offset is -05 because we're viewing the timestamp from the perspective of the Eastern time zone: 4 AM Pacific is 7 AM Eastern. The original Pacific time value remains unaltered in the table, and the database converts it to show the time in whatever time zone we set at ❺.

Even more convenient is that we can view a timestamp through the lens of any time zone without changing the session setting. The final SELECT statement uses the AT TIME ZONE keywords ❼ to display the timestamp in our session as Korea standard time (KST) by specifying Asia/Seoul:

```
timezone
-------------------
2020-01-01 21:00:00
```

Now we know that the database value of 4 AM in US/Pacific on January 1, 2020, is equivalent to 9 PM that same day in Asia/Seoul. Again, this syntax changes the output data type, but the data on the server remains unchanged. If the original value is a timestamp with time zone, the output removes the time zone. If the original value has no time zone, the output is timestamp with time zone.

The ability of databases to track time zones is extremely important for accurate calculations of intervals, as you'll see next.

Calculations with Dates and Times

We can perform simple arithmetic on datetime and interval types the same way we can on numbers. Addition, subtraction, multiplication, and division are all possible in PostgreSQL using the math operators +, -, *, and /. For example, you can subtract one date from another date to get an integer that represents the difference in days between the two dates. The following code returns an integer of 3:

```
SELECT '9/30/1929'::date - '9/27/1929'::date;
```

The result indicates that these two dates are exactly three days apart.

Likewise, you can use the following code to add a time interval to a date to return a new date:

```
SELECT '9/30/1929'::date + '5 years'::interval;
```

This code adds five years to the date 9/30/1929 to return a timestamp value of 9/30/1934.

You can find more examples of math functions you can use with dates and times in the PostgreSQL documentation at *https://www.postgresql.org/docs/current/static/functions-datetime.html*. Let's explore some more practical examples using actual transportation data.

Finding Patterns in New York City Taxi Data

When I visit New York City, I usually take at least one ride in one of the 13,500 iconic yellow cars that ferry hundreds of thousands of people across the city's five boroughs each day. The New York City Taxi and Limousine Commission releases data on monthly yellow taxi trips plus other for-hire vehicles. We'll use this large, rich data set to put date functions to practical use.

The *yellow_tripdata_2016_06_01.csv* file available from the book's resources (at *https://www.nostarch.com/practicalSQL/*) holds one day of yellow taxi trip records from June 1, 2016. Save the file to your computer and execute the code in Listing 11-7 to build the nyc_yellow _taxi_trips_2016_06_01 table. Remember to change the file path in the COPY command to the location where you've saved the file and adjust the path format to reflect whether you're using Windows, macOS, or Linux.

```
❶ CREATE TABLE nyc_yellow_taxi_trips_2016_06_01 (
       trip_id bigserial PRIMARY KEY,
       vendor_id varchar(1) NOT NULL,
       tpep_pickup_datetime timestamp with time zone NOT NULL,
       tpep_dropoff_datetime timestamp with time zone NOT NULL,
       passenger_count integer NOT NULL,
       trip_distance numeric(8,2) NOT NULL,
       pickup_longitude numeric(18,15) NOT NULL,
       pickup_latitude numeric(18,15) NOT NULL,
       rate_code_id varchar(2) NOT NULL,
       store_and_fwd_flag varchar(1) NOT NULL,
       dropoff_longitude numeric(18,15) NOT NULL,
       dropoff_latitude numeric(18,15) NOT NULL,
       payment_type varchar(1) NOT NULL,
       fare_amount numeric(9,2) NOT NULL,
       extra numeric(9,2) NOT NULL,
       mta_tax numeric(5,2) NOT NULL,
       tip_amount numeric(9,2) NOT NULL,
       tolls_amount numeric(9,2) NOT NULL,
       improvement_surcharge numeric(9,2) NOT NULL,
       total_amount numeric(9,2) NOT NULL
   );

❷ COPY nyc_yellow_taxi_trips_2016_06_01 (
       vendor_id,
       tpep_pickup_datetime,
       tpep_dropoff_datetime,
       passenger_count,
       trip_distance,
       pickup_longitude,
       pickup_latitude,
       rate_code_id,
       store_and_fwd_flag,
       dropoff_longitude,
       dropoff_latitude,
       payment_type,
       fare_amount,
       extra,
       mta_tax,
       tip_amount,
       tolls_amount,
       improvement_surcharge,
       total_amount
       )
   FROM 'C:\YourDirectory\yellow_tripdata_2016_06_01.csv'
   WITH (FORMAT CSV, HEADER, DELIMITER ',');

❸ CREATE INDEX tpep_pickup_idx
   ON nyc_yellow_taxi_trips_2016_06_01 (tpep_pickup_datetime);
```

Listing 11-7: Creating a table and importing NYC yellow taxi data

The code in Listing 11-7 builds the table ❶, imports the rows ❷, and creates an index ❸. In the COPY statement, we provide the names of columns because the input CSV file doesn't include the `trip_id` column that exists in the target table. That column is of type `bigserial`, which you've learned is an auto-incrementing integer and will fill automatically. After your import is complete, you should have 368,774 rows, one for each yellow cab ride on June 1, 2016. You can check the number of rows in your table with a count using the following code:

```
SELECT count(*) FROM nyc_yellow_taxi_trips_2016_06_01;
```

Each row includes data on the number of passengers, the location of pickup and drop-off in latitude and longitude, and the fare and tips in U.S. dollars. The data dictionary that describes all columns and codes is available at *http://www.nyc.gov/html/tlc/downloads/pdf/data_dictionary_trip_records_yellow.pdf*. For these exercises, we're most interested in the time-stamp columns `tpep_pickup_datetime` and `tpep_dropoff_datetime`, which represent the start and end times of the ride. (The Technology Passenger Enhancements Project [TPEP] is a program that in part includes automated collection of data about taxi rides.)

The values in both timestamp columns include the time zone provided by the Taxi and Limousine Commission. In all rows of the CSV file, the time zone included with the timestamp is shown as -4, which is the summertime UTC offset for the Eastern time zone when New York City and the rest of the U.S. East Coast observe daylight saving time. If you're not or your PostgreSQL server isn't located in Eastern time, I suggest setting your time zone using the following code so your results will match mine:

```
SET timezone TO 'US/Eastern';
```

Now let's explore the patterns we can identify in the data related to these times.

The Busiest Time of Day

One question you might ask after viewing this data set is when taxis provide the most rides. Is it morning or evening rush hour, or is there another time—at least, on this day—when rides spiked? You can determine the answer with a simple aggregation query that uses `date_part()`.

Listing 11-8 contains the query to count rides by hour using the pickup time as the input:

```
SELECT
❶ date_part('hour', tpep_pickup_datetime) AS trip_hour,
❷ count(*)
FROM nyc_yellow_taxi_trips_2016_06_01
GROUP BY trip_hour
ORDER BY trip_hour;
```

Listing 11-8: Counting taxi trips by hour

In the query's first column ❶, date_part() extracts the hour from tpep_pickup_datetime so we can group the number of rides by hour. Then we aggregate the number of rides in the second column via the count() function ❷. The rest of the query follows the standard patterns for grouping and ordering the results, which should return 24 rows, one for each hour of the day:

trip_hour	count
0	8182
1	5003
2	3070
3	2275
4	2229
5	3925
6	10825
7	18287
8	21062
9	18975
10	17367
11	17383
12	18031
13	17998
14	19125
15	18053
16	15069
17	18513
18	22689
19	23190
20	23098
21	24106
22	22554
23	17765

Eyeballing the numbers, it's apparent that on June 1, 2016, New York City taxis had the most passengers between 6 PM and 10 PM, possibly reflecting commutes home plus the plethora of city activities on a summer evening. But to see the overall pattern, it's best to visualize the data. Let's do this next.

Exporting to CSV for Visualization in Excel

Charting data with a tool such as Microsoft Excel makes it easier to understand patterns, so I often export query results to a CSV file and work up a quick chart. Listing 11-9 uses the query from the preceding example within a COPY ... TO statement, similar to Listing 4-9 on page 52:

```
COPY
    (SELECT
        date_part('hour', tpep_pickup_datetime) AS trip_hour,
        count(*)
    FROM nyc_yellow_taxi_trips_2016_06_01
```

```
    GROUP BY trip_hour
    ORDER BY trip_hour
    )
TO 'C:\YourDirectory\hourly_pickups_2016_06_01.csv'
WITH (FORMAT CSV, HEADER, DELIMITER ',');
```

Listing 11-9: Exporting taxi pickups per hour to a CSV file

When I load the data into Excel and build a line graph, the day's pattern becomes more obvious and thought-provoking, as shown in Figure 11-1.

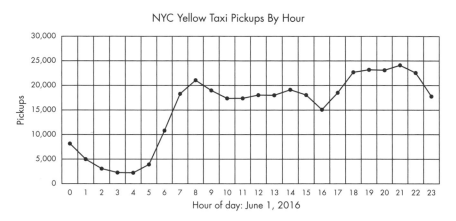

Figure 11-1: NYC yellow taxi pickups by hour

Rides bottomed out in the wee hours of the morning before rising sharply between 5 AM and 8 AM. Volume remained relatively steady throughout the day and increased again for evening rush hour after 5 PM. But there was a dip between 3 PM and 4 PM—why?

To answer that question, we would need to dig deeper to analyze data that spanned several days or even several months to see whether our data from June 1, 2016, is typical. We could use the date_part() function to compare trip volume on weekdays versus weekends by extracting the day of the week. To be even more ambitious, we could check weather reports and compare trips on rainy days versus sunny days. There are many different ways to slice a data set to derive conclusions.

When Do Trips Take the Longest?

Let's investigate another interesting question: at which hour did taxi trips take the longest? One way to find an answer is to calculate the median trip time for each hour. The median is the middle value in an ordered set of values; it's often more accurate than an average for making comparisons because a few very small or very large values in the set won't skew the results as they would with the average.

In Chapter 5, we used the percentile_cont() function to find medians. We use it again in Listing 11-10 to calculate median trip times:

```
SELECT
❶ date_part('hour', tpep_pickup_datetime) AS trip_hour,
❷ percentile_cont(.5)
    ❸ WITHIN GROUP (ORDER BY
            tpep_dropoff_datetime - tpep_pickup_datetime) AS median_trip
FROM nyc_yellow_taxi_trips_2016_06_01
GROUP BY trip_hour
ORDER BY trip_hour;
```

Listing 11-10: Calculating median trip time by hour

We're aggregating data by the hour portion of the timestamp column tpep_pickup_datetime again, which we extract using date_part() ❶. For the input to the percentile_cont() function ❷, we subtract the pickup time from the drop-off time in the WITHIN GROUP clause ❸. The results show that the 1 PM hour has the highest median trip time of 15 minutes:

```
date_part    median_trip
---------    -----------
        0    00:10:04
        1    00:09:27
        2    00:08:59
        3    00:09:57
        4    00:10:06
        5    00:07:37
        6    00:07:54
        7    00:10:23
        8    00:12:28
        9    00:13:11
       10    00:13:46
       11    00:14:20
       12    00:14:49
       13    00:15:00
       14    00:14:35
       15    00:14:43
       16    00:14:42
       17    00:14:15
       18    00:13:19
       19    00:12:25
       20    00:11:46
       21    00:11:54
       22    00:11:37
       23    00:11:14
```

As we would expect, trip times are shortest in the early morning hours. This result makes sense because less traffic in the early morning means passengers are more likely to get to their destinations faster.

Now that we've explored ways to extract portions of the timestamp for analysis, let's dig deeper into analysis that involves intervals.

Finding Patterns in Amtrak Data

Amtrak, the nationwide rail service in America, offers several packaged trips across the United States. The All American, for example, is a train that departs from Chicago and stops in New York, New Orleans, Los Angeles, San Francisco, and Denver before returning to Chicago. Using data from the Amtrak website (*http://www.amtrak.com/*), we'll build a table that shows information for each segment of the trip. The trip spans four time zones, so we'll need to track the time zones each time we enter an arrival or departure time. Then we'll calculate the duration of the journey at each segment and figure out the length of the entire trip.

Calculating the Duration of Train Trips

Let's create a table that divides The All American train route into six segments. Listing 11-11 contains SQL to create and fill a table with the departure and arrival time for each leg of the journey:

```
SET timezone TO 'US/Central'; ❶

CREATE TABLE train_rides (
    trip_id bigserial PRIMARY KEY,
    segment varchar(50) NOT NULL,
    departure timestamp with time zone NOT NULL, ❷
    arrival timestamp with time zone NOT NULL
);

INSERT INTO train_rides (segment, departure, arrival) ❸
VALUES
    ('Chicago to New York', '2017-11-13 21:30 CST', '2017-11-14 18:23 EST'),
    ('New York to New Orleans', '2017-11-15 14:15 EST', '2017-11-16 19:32 CST'),
    ('New Orleans to Los Angeles', '2017-11-17 13:45 CST', '2017-11-18 9:00 PST'),
    ('Los Angeles to San Francisco', '2017-11-19 10:10 PST', '2017-11-19 21:24 PST'),
    ('San Francisco to Denver', '2017-11-20 9:10 PST', '2017-11-21 18:38 MST'),
    ('Denver to Chicago', '2017-11-22 19:10 MST', '2017-11-23 14:50 CST');

SELECT * FROM train_rides;
```

Listing 11-11: Creating a table to hold train trip data

First, we set the session to the Central time zone, the value for Chicago, using the US/Central designator ❶. We'll use Central time as our reference when viewing the timestamps of the data we enter so that regardless of your and my machine's default time zones, we'll share the same view of the data.

Next, we use the standard CREATE TABLE statement. Note that columns for departures and arrival times are set to timestamp with time zone ❷. Finally, we insert rows that represent the six legs of the trip ❸. Each timestamp input reflects the time zone of the departure and arrival city. Specifying the city's time zone is the key to getting an accurate calculation of trip duration and accounting for time zone changes. It also accounts for annual changes to and from daylight saving time if they were to occur during the time span you're examining.

The final SELECT statement should return the contents of the table like this:

trip_id	segment	departure	arrival
1	Chicago to New York	2017-11-13 21:30:00-06	2017-11-14 17:23:00-06
2	New York to New Orleans	2017-11-15 13:15:00-06	2017-11-16 19:32:00-06
3	New Orleans to Los Angeles	2017-11-17 13:45:00-06	2017-11-18 11:00:00-06
4	Los Angeles to San Francisco	2017-11-19 12:10:00-06	2017-11-19 23:24:00-06
5	San Francisco to Denver	2017-11-20 11:10:00-06	2017-11-21 19:38:00-06
6	Denver to Chicago	2017-11-22 20:10:00-06	2017-11-23 14:50:00-06

All timestamps should now carry a UTC offset of -06, which is equivalent to the Central time zone in the United States during the month of November, after the nation had switched to standard time. Regardless of the time zone we supplied on insert, our view of the data is now in Central time, and the times are adjusted accordingly if they're in another time zone.

Now that we've created segments corresponding to each leg of the trip, we'll use Listing 11-12 to calculate the duration of each segment:

```
SELECT segment,
    ❶ to_char(departure, 'YYYY-MM-DD HH12:MI a.m. TZ') AS departure,
    ❷ arrival - departure AS segment_time
FROM train_rides;
```

Listing 11-12: Calculating the length of each trip segment

This query lists the trip segment, the departure time, and the duration of the segment journey. Before we look at the calculation, notice the additional code around the departure column ❶. These are PostgreSQL-specific formatting functions that specify how to format different components of the timestamp. In this case, the to_char() function turns the departure timestamp column into a string of characters formatted as YYYY-MM-DD HH12:MI a.m. TZ. The YYYY-MM-DD portion specifies the ISO format for the date, and the HH12:MI a.m. portion presents the time in hours and minutes. The HH12 portion specifies the use of a 12-hour clock rather than 24-hour military time. The a.m. portion specifies that we want to show morning or night times using lowercase characters separated by periods, and the TZ portion denotes the time zone.

For a complete list of formatting functions, check out the PostgreSQL documentation at *https://www.postgresql.org/docs/current/static/functions -formatting.html*.

Last, we subtract departure from arrival to determine the segment _time ❷. When you run the query, the output should look like this:

segment	departure	segment_time
Chicago to New York	2017-11-13 09:30 p.m. CST	19:53:00
New York to New Orleans	2017-11-15 01:15 p.m. CST	1 day 06:17:00
New Orleans to Los Angeles	2017-11-17 01:45 p.m. CST	21:15:00
Los Angeles to San Francisco	2017-11-19 12:10 p.m. CST	11:14:00

San Francisco to Denver	2017-11-20 11:10 a.m. CST	1 day 08:28:00
Denver to Chicago	2017-11-22 08:10 p.m. CST	18:40:00

Subtracting one timestamp from another produces an `interval` data type, which was introduced in Chapter 3. As long as the value is less than 24 hours, PostgreSQL presents the interval in the `HH:MM:SS` format. For values greater than 24 hours, it returns the format `1 day 08:28:00`, as shown in the San Francisco to Denver segment.

In each calculation, PostgreSQL accounts for the changes in time zones so we don't inadvertently add or lose hours when subtracting. If we used a `timestamp without time zone` data type, we would end up with an incorrect trip length if a segment spanned multiple time zones.

Calculating Cumulative Trip Time

As it turns out, San Francisco to Denver is the longest leg of the All American train trip. But how long does the entire trip take? To answer this question, we'll revisit window functions, which you learned about in "Ranking with `rank()` and `dense_rank()`" on page 164.

Our prior query produced an interval, which we labeled `segment_time`. It would seem like the natural next step would be to write a query to add those values, creating a cumulative interval after each segment. And indeed, we can use `sum()` as a window function, combined with the `OVER` clause mentioned in Chapter 10, to create running totals. But when we do, the resulting values are odd. To see what I mean, run the code in Listing 11-13:

```
SELECT segment,
       arrival - departure AS segment_time,
       sum(arrival - departure) OVER (ORDER BY trip_id) AS cume_time
FROM train_rides;
```

Listing 11-13: Calculating cumulative intervals using OVER

In the third column, we sum the intervals generated when we subtract `departure` from `arrival`. The resulting running total in the `cume_time` column is accurate but formatted in an unhelpful way:

segment	segment_time	cume_time
Chicago to New York	19:53:00	19:53:00
New York to New Orleans	1 day 06:17:00	1 day 26:10:00
New Orleans to Los Angeles	21:15:00	1 day 47:25:00
Los Angeles to San Francisco	11:14:00	1 day 58:39:00
San Francisco to Denver	1 day 08:28:00	2 days 67:07:00
Denver to Chicago	18:40:00	2 days 85:47:00

PostgreSQL creates one sum for the day portion of the interval and another for the hours and minutes. So, instead of a more understandable cumulative time of 5 days 13:47:00, the database reports 2 days 85:47:00. Both results amount to the same length of time, but 2 days 85:47:00 is harder to decipher. This is an unfortunate limitation of summing the database intervals using this syntax.

As a workaround, we'll use the code in Listing 11-14:

```
SELECT segment,
       arrival - departure AS segment_time,
       sum(date_part❶('epoch', (arrival - departure)))
           OVER (ORDER BY trip_id) * interval '1 second'❷ AS cume_time
FROM train_rides;
```

Listing 11-14: Better formatting for cumulative trip time

Recall from earlier in this chapter that epoch is the number of seconds that have elapsed since midnight on January 1, 1970, which makes it useful for calculating duration. In Listing 11-14, we use date_part() ❶ with the epoch setting to extract the number of seconds elapsed between the arrival and departure intervals. Then we multiply each sum with an interval of 1 second ❷ to convert those seconds to an interval value. The output is clearer using this method:

```
segment                       segment_time      cume_time
---------------------------   --------------    ---------
Chicago to New York           19:53:00          19:53:00
New York to New Orleans       1 day 06:17:00    50:10:00
New Orleans to Los Angeles    21:15:00          71:25:00
Los Angeles to San Francisco  11:14:00          82:39:00
San Francisco to Denver       1 day 08:28:00    115:07:00
Denver to Chicago             18:40:00          133:47:00
```

The final cume_time, now in *HH:MM:SS* format, adds all the segments to return the total trip length of 133 hours and 47 minutes. That's a long time to spend on a train, but I'm sure the scenery is well worth the ride.

Wrapping Up

Handling times and dates in SQL databases adds an intriguing dimension to your analysis, letting you answer questions about when an event occurred along with other temporal concerns in your data. With a solid grasp of time and date formats, time zones, and functions to dissect the components of a timestamp, you can analyze just about any data set you come across.

Next, we'll look at advanced query techniques that help answer more complex questions.

Try these exercises to test your skills on dates and times.

1. Using the New York City taxi data, calculate the length of each ride using the pickup and drop-off timestamps. Sort the query results from the longest ride to the shortest. Do you notice anything about the longest or shortest trips that you might want to ask city officials about?

2. Using the AT TIME ZONE keywords, write a query that displays the date and time for London, Johannesburg, Moscow, and Melbourne the moment January 1, 2100, arrives in New York City.

3. As a bonus challenge, use the statistics functions in Chapter 10 to calculate the correlation coefficient and r-squared values using trip time and the total_amount column in the New York City taxi data, which represents the total amount charged to passengers. Do the same with the trip_distance and total_amount columns. Limit the query to rides that last three hours or less.

12

ADVANCED QUERY TECHNIQUES

Sometimes data analysis requires advanced SQL techniques that go beyond a table join or basic SELECT query. For example, to find the story in your data, you might need to write a query that uses the results of other queries as inputs. Or you might need to reclassify numerical values into categories before counting them. Like other programming languages, SQL provides a collection of functions and options essential for solving more complex problems, and that is what we'll explore in this chapter.

For the exercises, I'll introduce a data set of temperatures recorded in select U.S. cities and we'll revisit data sets you've created in previous chapters. The code for the exercises is available, along with all the book's resources, at *https://www.nostarch.com/practicalSQL/*. You'll continue to use the analysis database you've already built. Let's get started.

Using Subqueries

A *subquery* is nested inside another query. Typically, it's used for a calculation or logical test that provides a value or set of data to be passed into the main portion of the query. Its syntax is not unusual: we just enclose the subquery in parentheses and use it where needed. For example, we can write a subquery that returns multiple rows and treat the results as a table in the FROM clause of the main query. Or we can create a *scalar subquery* that returns a single value and use it as part of an *expression* to filter rows via WHERE, IN, and HAVING clauses. These are the most common uses of subqueries.

You first encountered a subquery in Chapter 9 in the ANSI SQL standard syntax for a table UPDATE, which is shown again here. Both the data for the update and the condition that specifies which rows to update are generated by subqueries that look for values that match the columns in *table* and *table_b*:

```
UPDATE table
❶ SET column = (SELECT column
                FROM table_b
                WHERE table.column = table_b.column)
❷ WHERE EXISTS (SELECT column
                FROM table_b
                WHERE table.column = table_b.column);
```

This example query has two subqueries that use the same syntax. We use the SELECT statement inside parentheses ❶ as the first subquery in the SET clause, which generates values for the update. Similarly, we use a second subquery in the WHERE EXISTS clause, again with a SELECT statement ❷ to filter the rows we want to update. Both subqueries are *correlated subqueries* and are so named because they depend on a value or table name from the main query that surrounds them. In this case, both subqueries depend on *table* from the main UPDATE statement. An *uncorrelated subquery* has no reference to objects in the main query.

It's easier to understand these concepts by working with actual data, so let's look at some examples. We'll revisit two data sets from earlier chapters: the Decennial 2010 Census table us_counties_2010 you created in Chapter 4 and the meat_poultry_egg_inspect table in Chapter 9.

Filtering with Subqueries in a WHERE Clause

You know that a WHERE clause lets you filter query results based on criteria you provide, using an expression such as WHERE quantity > 1000. But this requires that you already know the value to use for comparison. What if you don't? That's one way a subquery comes in handy: it lets you write a query that generates one or more values to use as part of an expression in a WHERE clause.

Generating Values for a Query Expression

Say you wanted to write a query to show which U.S. counties are at or above the 90th percentile, or top 10 percent, for population. Rather than writing two separate queries—one to calculate the 90th percentile and the other to filter by counties—you can do both at once using a subquery in a WHERE clause, as shown in Listing 12-1:

```
SELECT geo_name,
       state_us_abbreviation,
       p0010001
FROM us_counties_2010
❶ WHERE p0010001 >= (
       SELECT percentile_cont(.9) WITHIN GROUP (ORDER BY p0010001)
       FROM us_counties_2010
       )
ORDER BY p0010001 DESC;
```

Listing 12-1: Using a subquery in a WHERE clause

This query is standard in terms of what we've done so far except that the WHERE clause ❶, which filters by the total population column p0010001, doesn't include a value like it normally would. Instead, after the >= comparison operators, we provide a second query in parentheses. This second query uses the percentile_cont() function in Chapter 5 to generate one value: the 90th percentile cut-off point in the p0010001 column, which will then be used in the main query.

NOTE *Using percentile_cont() to filter with a subquery works only if you pass in a single input, as shown. If you pass in an array, as in Listing 5-12 on page 68, percentile_cont() returns an array, and the query will fail to evaluate the >= against an array type.*

If you run the subquery separately by highlighting it in pgAdmin, you should see the results of the subquery, a value of 197444.6. But you won't see that number when you run the entire query in Listing 12-1, because the result of that subquery is passed directly to the WHERE clause to use in filtering the results.

The entire query should return 315 rows, or about 10 percent of the 3,143 rows in us_counties_2010.

geo_name	state_us_abbreviation	p0010001
Los Angeles County	CA	9818605
Cook County	IL	5194675
Harris County	TX	4092459
Maricopa County	AZ	3817117
San Diego County	CA	3095313
--snip--		
Elkhart County	IN	197559
Sangamon County	IL	197465

The result includes all counties with a population greater than or equal to 197444.6, the value the subquery generated.

Using a Subquery to Identify Rows to Delete

Adding a subquery to a WHERE clause can be useful in query statements other than SELECT. For example, we can use a similar subquery in a DELETE statement to specify what to remove from a table. Imagine you have a table with 100 million rows that, because of its size, takes a long time to query. If you just want to work on a subset of the data (such as a particular state), you can make a copy of the table and delete what you don't need from it.

Listing 12-2 shows an example of this approach. It makes a copy of the census table using the method you learned in Chapter 9 and then deletes everything from that backup except the 315 counties in the top 10 percent of population:

```
CREATE TABLE us_counties_2010_top10 AS
SELECT * FROM us_counties_2010;

DELETE FROM us_counties_2010_top10
WHERE p0010001 < (
    SELECT percentile_cont(.9) WITHIN GROUP (ORDER BY p0010001)
    FROM us_counties_2010_top10
    );
```

Listing 12-2: Using a subquery in a WHERE clause with DELETE

Run the code in Listing 12-2, and then execute SELECT count(*) FROM us_counties_2010_top10; to count the remaining rows in the table. The result should be 315 rows, which is the original 3,143 minus the 2,828 the subquery deleted.

Creating Derived Tables with Subqueries

If your subquery returns rows and columns of data, you can convert that data to a table by placing it in a FROM clause, the result of which is known as a *derived table*. A derived table behaves just like any other table, so you can query it or join it to other tables, even other derived tables. This approach is helpful when a single query can't perform all the operations you need.

Let's look at a simple example. In Chapter 5, you learned the difference between average and median values. I explained that a median can often better indicate a data set's central value because a few very large or small values (or outliers) can skew an average. For that reason, I often recommend comparing the average and median. If they're close, the data probably falls in a *normal distribution* (the familiar bell curve), and the average is a good representation of the central value. If the average and median are far apart, some outliers might be having an effect or the distribution is skewed, not normal.

Finding the average and median population of U.S. counties as well as the difference between them is a two-step process. We need to calculate the average and the median, and then we need to subtract the two. We can do both operations in one fell swoop with a subquery in the FROM clause, as shown in Listing 12-3.

```
SELECT round(calcs.average, 0) AS average,
       calcs.median,
       round(calcs.average - calcs.median, 0) AS median_average_diff
FROM (
   ❶ SELECT avg(p0010001) AS average,
             percentile_cont(.5)
                 WITHIN GROUP (ORDER BY p0010001)::numeric(10,1) AS median
       FROM us_counties_2010
       )
❷ AS calcs;
```

Listing 12-3: Subquery as a derived table in a FROM clause

The subquery ❶ is straightforward. We use the avg() and percentile
_cont() functions to find the average and median of the census table's
p0010001 total population column and name each column with an alias.
Then we name the subquery with an alias ❷ of calcs so we can reference it
as a table in the main query.

Subtracting the median from the average, both of which are returned by
the subquery, is done in the main query; then the main query rounds the
result and labels it with the alias median_average_diff. Run the query, and
the result should be the following:

average	median	median_average_diff
98233	25857.0	72376

The difference between the median and average, 72,736, is nearly three
times the size of the median. That helps show that a relatively small number of high-population counties push the average county size over 98,000,
whereas the median of all counties is much less at 25,857.

Joining Derived Tables

Because derived tables behave like regular tables, you can join them. Joining
derived tables lets you perform multiple preprocessing steps before arriving
at the result. For example, say we wanted to determine which states have the
most meat, egg, and poultry processing plants per million population; before
we can calculate that rate, we need to know the number of plants in each
state and the population of each state.

We start by counting producers by state using the meat_poultry_egg
_inspect table in Chapter 9. Then we can use the us_counties_2010 table
to count population by state by summing and grouping county values.
Listing 12-4 shows how to write subqueries for both tasks and join them
to calculate the overall rate.

```
SELECT census.state_us_abbreviation AS st,
       census.st_population,
       plants.plant_count,
    ❶ round((plants.plant_count/census.st_population::numeric(10,1))*1000000, 1)
           AS plants_per_million
```

```
FROM
    (
      ❷ SELECT st,
                count(*) AS plant_count
        FROM meat_poultry_egg_inspect
        GROUP BY st
    )
    AS plants
JOIN
    (
      ❸ SELECT state_us_abbreviation,
                sum(p0010001) AS st_population
        FROM us_counties_2010
        GROUP BY state_us_abbreviation
    )
    AS census
❹ ON plants.st = census.state_us_abbreviation
  ORDER BY plants_per_million DESC;
```

Listing 12-4: Joining two derived tables

You learned how to calculate rates in Chapter 10, so the math and syntax in the main query for finding `plants_per_million` ❶ should be familiar. We divide the number of plants by the population, and then multiply that quotient by 1 million. For the inputs, we use the values generated from derived tables using subqueries.

The first subquery ❷ finds the number of plants in each state using the `count()` aggregate function and then groups them by state. We label this subquery with the `plants` alias for reference in the main part of the query. The second subquery ❸ finds the total population by state by using `sum()` on the `p0010001` total population column and then groups those by `state_us_abbreviation`. We alias this derived table as `census`.

Next, we join the derived tables ❹ by linking the `st` column in `plants` to the `state_us_abbreviation` column in `census`. We then list the results in descending order based on the calculated rates. Here's a sample output of 51 rows showing the highest and lowest rates:

```
st    st_population    plant_count    plants_per_million
--    -------------    -----------    ------------------
NE         1826341            110                    60.2
IA         3046355            149                    48.9
VT          625741             27                    43.1
HI         1360301             47                    34.6
ND          672591             22                    32.7
--snip--
SC         4625364             55                    11.9
LA         4533372             49                    10.8
AZ         6392017             37                     5.8
DC          601723              2                     3.3
WY          563626              1                     1.8
```

The results line up with what we might expect. The top states are well-known meat producers. For example, Nebraska is one of the nation's top cattle exporters, and Iowa leads the United States in pork production. Washington, D.C., and Wyoming at the bottom of the list are among those states with the fewest plants per million.

NOTE *Your results will differ slightly if you didn't add missing state values to the meat _poultry_egg_inspect table as noted in "Updating Rows Where Values Are Missing" on page 141.*

Generating Columns with Subqueries

You can also generate new columns of data with subqueries by placing a subquery in the column list after SELECT. Typically, you would use a single value from an aggregate. For example, the query in Listing 12-5 selects the geo_name and total population column p0010001 from us_counties_2010, and then adds a subquery to add the median of all counties to each row in the new column us_median:

```
SELECT geo_name,
       state_us_abbreviation AS st,
       p0010001 AS total_pop,
       (SELECT percentile_cont(.5) WITHIN GROUP (ORDER BY p0010001)
        FROM us_counties_2010) AS us_median
FROM us_counties_2010;
```

Listing 12-5: Adding a subquery to a column list

The first rows of the result set should look like this:

geo_name	st	total_pop	us_median
Autauga County	AL	54571	25857
Baldwin County	AL	182265	25857
Barbour County	AL	27457	25857
Bibb County	AL	22915	25857
Blount County	AL	57322	25857
--snip--			

On its own, that repeating us_median value isn't very helpful because it's the same each time. It would be more interesting and useful to generate values that indicate how much each county's population deviates from the median value. Let's look at how we can use the same subquery technique to do that. Listing 12-6 builds on Listing 12-5 by adding a subquery expression after SELECT that calculates the difference between the population and the median for each county:

```
SELECT geo_name,
       state_us_abbreviation AS st,
       p0010001 AS total_pop,
       (SELECT percentile_cont(.5) WITHIN GROUP (ORDER BY p0010001)
```

```
        FROM us_counties_2010) AS us_median,
   ❶ p0010001 - (SELECT percentile_cont(.5) WITHIN GROUP (ORDER BY p0010001)
                FROM us_counties_2010) AS diff_from_median
FROM us_counties_2010
❷ WHERE (p0010001 - (SELECT percentile_cont(.5) WITHIN GROUP (ORDER BY p0010001)
                FROM us_counties_2010))
      BETWEEN -1000 AND 1000;
```

Listing 12-6: Using a subquery expression in a calculation

The added subquery ❶ is part of a column definition that subtracts the subquery's result from p0010001, the total population. It puts that new data in a column with an alias of diff_from_median. To make this query even more useful, we can narrow the results further to show only counties whose population falls within 1,000 of the median. This would help us identify which counties in America have close to the median county population. To do this, we repeat the subquery expression in the WHERE clause ❷ and filter results using the BETWEEN -1000 AND 1000 expression.

The outcome should reveal 71 counties with a population relatively close to the U.S. median. Here are the first five rows of the results:

```
geo_name           st    total_pop    us_median    diff_from_median
---------------    --    ---------    ---------    ----------------
Cherokee County    AL        25989        25857                 132
Clarke County      AL        25833        25857                 -24
Geneva County      AL        26790        25857                 933
Cleburne County    AR        25970        25857                 113
Johnson County     AR        25540        25857                -317
--snip--
```

Bear in mind that subqueries add to overall query execution time; therefore, if we were working with millions of rows, we could simplify Listing 12-6 by eliminating the subquery that displays the column us_median. I've left it in this example for your reference.

Subquery Expressions

You can also use subqueries to filter rows by evaluating whether a condition evaluates as true or false. For this, we can use several standard ANSI SQL *subquery expressions*, which are a combination of a keyword with a subquery and are generally used in WHERE clauses to filter rows based on the existence of values in another table.

The PostgreSQL documentation at *https://www.postgresql.org/docs/current/static/functions-subquery.html* lists available subquery expressions, but here we'll examine the syntax for just two of them.

Generating Values for the IN Operator

The subquery expression IN (*subquery*) is like the IN comparison operator in Chapter 2 except we use a subquery to provide the list of values to check against rather than having to manually provide one. In the following example, we use a subquery to generate id values from a retirees table, and then use that list for the IN operator in the WHERE clause. The NOT IN expression does the opposite to find employees whose id value does *not* appear in retirees.

```
SELECT first_name, last_name
FROM employees
WHERE id IN (
    SELECT id
    FROM retirees);
```

We would expect the output to show the names of employees who have id values that match those in retirees.

NOTE *The presence of NULL values in a subquery result set will cause a query with a NOT IN expression to return no rows. If your data contains NULL values, use the WHERE NOT EXISTS expression described in the next section.*

Checking Whether Values Exist

Another subquery expression, EXISTS (*subquery*), is a true/false test. It returns a value of true if the subquery in parentheses returns at least one row. If it returns no rows, EXISTS evaluates to false. In the following example, the query returns all names from an employees table as long as the subquery finds at least one value in id in a retirees table.

```
SELECT first_name, last_name
FROM employees
WHERE EXISTS (
    SELECT id
    FROM retirees);
```

Rather than return all names from employees, we instead could mimic the behavior of IN and limit names to where the subquery after EXISTS finds at least one corresponding id value in retirees. The following is a correlated subquery because the table named in the main query is referenced in the subquery.

```
SELECT first_name, last_name
FROM employees
WHERE EXISTS (
    SELECT id
    FROM retirees
    WHERE id = employees.id);
```

This approach is particularly helpful if you need to join on more than one column, which you can't do with the IN expression.

You can also use the NOT keyword with EXISTS. For example, to find employees with no corresponding record in retirees, you would run this query:

```
SELECT first_name, last_name
FROM employees
WHERE NOT EXISTS (
    SELECT id
    FROM retirees
    WHERE id = employees.id);
```

The technique of using NOT with EXISTS is helpful for assessing whether a data set is complete.

Common Table Expressions

Earlier in this chapter, you learned how to create derived tables by placing subqueries in a FROM clause. A second approach to creating temporary tables for querying uses the *Common Table Expression (CTE)*, a relatively recent addition to standard SQL that's informally called a "WITH clause." Using a CTE, you can define one or more tables up front with subqueries. Then you can query the table results as often as needed in a main query that follows.

Listing 12-7 shows a simple CTE called large_counties based on our census data, followed by a query of that table. The code determines how many counties in each state have 100,000 people or more. Let's walk through the example.

```
❶ WITH
    large_counties (geo_name, st, p0010001)
    AS
    (
    ❷ SELECT geo_name, state_us_abbreviation, p0010001
        FROM us_counties_2010
        WHERE p0010001 >= 100000
    )
❸ SELECT st, count(*)
  FROM large_counties
  GROUP BY st
  ORDER BY count(*) DESC;
```

Listing 12-7: Using a simple CTE to find large counties

The WITH ... AS block ❶ defines the CTE's temporary table large_counties. After WITH, we name the table and list its column names in parentheses. Unlike column definitions in a CREATE TABLE statement, we don't need to provide data types, because the temporary table inherits those from the subquery ❷, which is enclosed in parentheses after AS. The subquery must return the same number of columns as defined in the temporary table, but the column names don't need to match. Also, the column list is optional if you're not renaming columns, although including the list is still a good idea for clarity even if you don't rename columns.

The main query ❸ counts and groups the rows in large_counties by st, and then orders by the count in descending order. The top five rows of the results should look like this:

```
st    count
--    -----
TX       39
CA       35
FL       33
PA       31
OH       28
--snip--
```

As you can see, Texas, California, and Florida are among the states with the highest number of counties with a population of 100,000 or more.

You could find the same results using a SELECT query instead of a CTE, as shown here:

```
SELECT state_us_abbreviation, count(*)
FROM us_counties_2010
WHERE p0010001 >= 100000
GROUP BY state_us_abbreviation
ORDER BY count(*) DESC;
```

So why use a CTE? One reason is that by using a CTE, you can pre-stage subsets of data to feed into a larger query for more complex analysis. Also, you can reuse each table defined in a CTE in multiple places in the main query, which means you don't have to repeat the SELECT query each time. Another commonly cited advantage is that the code is more readable than if you performed the same operation with subqueries.

Listing 12-8 uses a CTE to rewrite the join of derived tables in Listing 12-4 (finding the states that have the most meat, egg, and poultry processing plants per million population) into a more readable format:

```
WITH
  ❶ counties (st, population) AS
     (SELECT state_us_abbreviation, sum(population_count_100_percent)
      FROM us_counties_2010
      GROUP BY state_us_abbreviation),

  ❷ plants (st, plants) AS
     (SELECT st, count(*) AS plants
      FROM meat_poultry_egg_inspect
      GROUP BY st)
```

```
    SELECT counties.st,
           population,
           plants,
           round((plants/population::numeric(10,1)) * 1000000, 1) AS per_million
❸ FROM counties JOIN plants
    ON counties.st = plants.st
    ORDER BY per_million DESC;
```

Listing 12-8: Using CTEs in a table join

Following the WITH keyword, we define two tables using subqueries. The first subquery, counties ❶, returns the population of each state. The second, plants ❷, returns the number of plants per state. With those tables defined, we join them ❸ on the st column in each table and calculate the rate per million. The results are identical to the joined derived tables in Listing 12-4, but Listing 12-8 is easier to read.

As another example, you can use a CTE to simplify queries with redundant code. For example, in Listing 12-6, we used a subquery with the percentile_cont() function in three different locations to find median county population. In Listing 12-9, we can write that subquery just once as a CTE:

```
❶ WITH us_median AS
        (SELECT percentile_cont(.5)
         WITHIN GROUP (ORDER BY p0010001) AS us_median_pop
         FROM us_counties_2010)

    SELECT geo_name,
           state_us_abbreviation AS st,
           p0010001 AS total_pop,
        ❷ us_median_pop,
        ❸ p0010001 - us_median_pop AS diff_from_median
❹ FROM us_counties_2010 CROSS JOIN us_median
❺ WHERE (p0010001 - us_median_pop)
           BETWEEN -1000 AND 1000;
```

Listing 12-9: Using CTEs to minimize redundant code

After the WITH keyword, we define us_median ❶ as the result of the same subquery used in Listing 12-6, which finds the median population using percentile_cont(). Then we reference the us_median_pop column on its own ❷, as part of a calculated column ❸, and in a WHERE clause ❺. To make the value available to every row in the us_counties_2010 table during SELECT, we use the CROSS JOIN query ❹ you learned in Chapter 6.

This query provides identical results to those in Listing 12-6, but we only had to write the subquery once to find the median. Not only does this save time, but it also lets you revise the query more easily. For example, to find counties whose population is close to the 90th percentile, you can substitute .9 for .5 as input to percentile_cont() in just one place.

Cross Tabulations

Cross tabulations provide a simple way to summarize and compare variables by displaying them in a table layout, or matrix. In a matrix, rows represent one variable, columns represent another variable, and each cell where a row and column intersects holds a value, such as a count or percentage.

You'll often see cross tabulations, also called *pivot tables* or *crosstabs*, used to report summaries of survey results or to compare sets of variables. A frequent example happens during every election when candidates' votes are tallied by geography:

```
candidate     ward 1    ward 2    ward 3
---------     ------    ------    ------
Dirk             602     1,799     2,112
Pratt            599     1,398     1,616
Lerxst           911       902     1,114
```

In this case, the candidates' names are one variable, the wards (or city districts) are another variable, and the cells at the intersection of the two hold the vote totals for that candidate in that ward. Let's look at how to generate cross tabulations.

Installing the crosstab() Function

Standard ANSI SQL doesn't have a crosstab function, but PostgreSQL does as part of a *module* you can install easily. Modules include PostgreSQL extras that aren't part of the core application; they include functions related to security, text search, and more. You can find a list of PostgreSQL modules at *https://www.postgresql.org/docs/current/static/contrib.html*.

PostgreSQL's crosstab() function is part of the tablefunc module. To install tablefunc in the pgAdmin Query Tool, execute this command:

```
CREATE EXTENSION tablefunc;
```

PostgreSQL should return the message CREATE EXTENSION when it's done installing. (If you're working with another database management system, check the documentation to see whether it offers a similar functionality. For example, Microsoft SQL Server has the PIVOT command.)

Next, we'll create a basic crosstab so you can learn the syntax, and then we'll handle a more complex case.

Tabulating Survey Results

Let's say your company needs a fun employee activity, so you coordinate an ice cream social at your three offices in the city. The trouble is, people are particular about ice cream flavors. To choose flavors people will like, you decide to conduct a survey.

The CSV file *ice_cream_survey.csv* contains 200 responses to your survey. You can download this file, along with all the book's resources, at *https://www.nostarch.com/practicalSQL/*. Each row includes a `response_id`, office, and flavor. You'll need to count how many people chose each flavor at each office and present the results in a readable way to your colleagues.

In your analysis database, use the code in Listing 12-10 to create a table and load the data. Make sure you change the file path to the location on your computer where you saved the CSV file.

```
CREATE TABLE ice_cream_survey (
    response_id integer PRIMARY KEY,
    office varchar(20),
    flavor varchar(20)
);

COPY ice_cream_survey
FROM 'C:\YourDirectory\ice_cream_survey.csv'
WITH (FORMAT CSV, HEADER);
```

Listing 12-10: Creating and filling the `ice_cream_survey` table

If you want to inspect the data, run the following to view the first five rows:

```
SELECT *
FROM ice_cream_survey
LIMIT 5;
```

The data should look like this:

response_id	office	flavor
1	Uptown	Chocolate
2	Midtown	Chocolate
3	Downtown	Strawberry
4	Uptown	Chocolate
5	Midtown	Chocolate

It looks like chocolate is in the lead! But let's confirm this choice by using the code in Listing 12-11 to generate a crosstab from the table:

```
SELECT *
❶ FROM crosstab('SELECT ❷office,
                        ❸flavor,
                        ❹count(*)
              FROM ice_cream_survey
              GROUP BY office, flavor
              ORDER BY office',

            ❺ 'SELECT flavor
              FROM ice_cream_survey
              GROUP BY flavor
              ORDER BY flavor')
```

```
❻ AS (office varchar(20),
    chocolate bigint,
    strawberry bigint,
    vanilla bigint);
```

Listing 12-11: Generating the ice cream survey crosstab

The query begins with a SELECT * statement that selects everything from the contents of the crosstab() function ❶. We place two subqueries inside the crosstab() function. The first subquery generates the data for the crosstab and has three required columns. The first column, office ❷, supplies the row names for the crosstab, and the second column, flavor ❸, supplies the category columns. The third column supplies the values for each cell where row and column intersect in the table. In this case, we want the intersecting cells to show a count() ❹ of each flavor selected at each office. This first subquery on its own creates a simple aggregated list.

The second subquery ❺ produces the set of category names for the columns. The crosstab() function requires that the second subquery return only one column, so here we use SELECT to retrieve the flavor column, and we use GROUP BY to return that column's unique values.

Then we specify the names and data types of the crosstab's output columns following the AS keyword ❻. The list must match the row and column names in the order the subqueries generate them. For example, because the second subquery that supplies the category columns orders the flavors alphabetically, the output column list does as well.

When we run the code, our data displays in a clean, readable crosstab:

```
office      chocolate   strawberry   vanilla
--------    ---------   ----------   -------
Downtown        23          32         19
Midtown         41                     23
Uptown          22          17         23
```

It's easy to see at a glance that the Midtown office favors chocolate but has no interest in strawberry, which is represented by a NULL value showing that strawberry received no votes. But strawberry is the top choice Downtown, and the Uptown office is more evenly split among the three flavors.

Tabulating City Temperature Readings

Let's create another crosstab, but this time we'll use real data. The *temperature _readings.csv* file, also available with all the book's resources at *https://www.no starch.com/practicalSQL/*, contains a year's worth of daily temperature readings from three observation stations around the United States: Chicago, Seattle, and Waikiki, a neighborhood on the south shore of the city of Honolulu. The data come from the U.S. National Oceanic and Atmospheric Administration (NOAA) at *https://www.ncdc.noaa.gov/cdo-web/datatools/findstation/*.

Each row in the CSV file contains four values: the station name, the date, the day's maximum temperature, and the day's minimum temperature. All temperatures are in Fahrenheit. For each month in each city, we want to calculate the median high temperature so we can compare climates. Listing 12-12 contains the code to create the temperature_readings table and import the CSV file:

```
CREATE TABLE temperature_readings (
    reading_id bigserial,
    station_name varchar(50),
    observation_date date,
    max_temp integer,
    min_temp integer
);

COPY temperature_readings
    (station_name, observation_date, max_temp, min_temp)
FROM 'C:\YourDirectory\temperature_readings.csv'
WITH (FORMAT CSV, HEADER);
```

Listing 12-12: Creating and filling a temperature_readings table

The table contains the four columns from the CSV file along with an added reading_id of type bigserial that we use as a surrogate primary key. If you perform a quick count on the table, you should have 1,077 rows. Now, let's see what cross tabulating the data does using Listing 12-13:

```
SELECT *
FROM crosstab('SELECT
            ❶ station_name,
            ❷ date_part(''month'', observation_date),
            ❸ percentile_cont(.5)
                WITHIN GROUP (ORDER BY max_temp)
            FROM temperature_readings
            GROUP BY station_name,
                    date_part(''month'', observation_date)
            ORDER BY station_name',

            'SELECT month
            FROM ❹generate_series(1,12) month')

AS (station varchar(50),
    jan numeric(3,0),
    feb numeric(3,0),
    mar numeric(3,0),
    apr numeric(3,0),
    may numeric(3,0),
    jun numeric(3,0),
    jul numeric(3,0),
    aug numeric(3,0),
    sep numeric(3,0),
    oct numeric(3,0),
    nov numeric(3,0),
    dec numeric(3,0)
);
```

Listing 12-13: Generating the temperature readings crosstab

The structure of the crosstab is the same as in Listing 12-11. The first subquery inside the crosstab() function generates the data for the crosstab, calculating the median maximum temperature for each month. It supplies the three required columns. The first column, station_name ❶, names the rows. The second column uses the date_part() function ❷ you learned in Chapter 11 to extract the month from observation_date, which provides the crosstab columns. Then we use percentile_cont(.5) ❸ to find the 50th percentile, or the median, of the max_temp. We group by station name and month so we have a median max_temp for each month at each station.

As in Listing 12-11, the second subquery produces the set of category names for the columns. I'm using a function called generate_series() ❹ in a manner noted in the official PostgreSQL documentation to create a list of numbers from 1 to 12 that match the month numbers date_part() extracts from observation_date.

Following AS, we provide the names and data types for the crosstab's output columns. Each is a numeric type, matching the output of the percentile function. The following output is practically poetry:

station	jan	feb	mar	apr	may	jun	jul	aug	sep	oct	nov	dec
CHICAGO NORTHERLY ISLAND IL US	34	36	46	50	66	77	81	80	77	65	57	35
SEATTLE BOEING FIELD WA US	50	54	56	64	66	71	76	77	69	62	55	42
WAIKIKI 717.2 HI US	83	84	84	86	87	87	88	87	87	86	84	82

We've transformed a raw set of daily readings into a compact table showing the median maximum temperature each month for each station. You can see at a glance that the temperature in Waikiki is consistently balmy, whereas Chicago's median high temperatures vary from just above freezing to downright pleasant. Seattle falls between the two.

Crosstabs do take time to set up, but viewing data sets in a matrix often makes comparisons easier than viewing the same data in a vertical list. Keep in mind that the crosstab() function is CPU-intensive, so tread carefully when querying sets that have millions or billions of rows.

Reclassifying Values with CASE

The ANSI Standard SQL CASE statement is a *conditional expression*, meaning it lets you add some "if this, then . . ." logic to a query. You can use CASE in multiple ways, but for data analysis, it's handy for reclassifying values into categories. You can create categories based on ranges in your data and classify values according to those categories.

The CASE syntax follows this pattern:

```
❶ CASE WHEN condition THEN result
   ❷ WHEN another_condition THEN result
   ❸ ELSE result
❹ END
```

We give the CASE keyword ❶, and then provide at least one WHEN *condition* THEN *result* clause, where *condition* is any expression the database can evaluate as true or false, such as county = 'Dutchess County' or date > '1995-08-09'. If the condition is true, the CASE statement returns the *result* and stops checking any further conditions. The result can be any valid data type. If the condition is false, the database moves on to evaluate the next condition.

To evaluate more conditions, we can add optional WHEN ... THEN clauses ❷. We can also provide an optional ELSE clause ❸ to return a result in case no condition evaluates as true. Without an ELSE clause, the statement would return a NULL when no conditions are true. The statement finishes with an END keyword ❹.

Listing 12-14 shows how to use the CASE statement to reclassify the temperature readings data into descriptive groups (named according to my own bias against cold weather):

```
SELECT max_temp,
       CASE WHEN max_temp >= 90 THEN 'Hot'
            WHEN max_temp BETWEEN 70 AND 89 THEN 'Warm'
            WHEN max_temp BETWEEN 50 AND 69 THEN 'Pleasant'
            WHEN max_temp BETWEEN 33 AND 49 THEN 'Cold'
            WHEN max_temp BETWEEN 20 AND 32 THEN 'Freezing'
            ELSE 'Inhumane'
       END AS temperature_group
FROM temperature_readings;
```

Listing 12-14: Reclassifying temperature data with CASE

We create five ranges for the max_temp column in temperature_readings, which we define using comparison operators. The CASE statement evaluates each value to find whether any of the five expressions are true. If so, the statement outputs the appropriate text. Note that the ranges account for all possible values in the column, leaving no gaps. If none of the statements is true, then the ELSE clause assigns the value to the category Inhumane. The way I've structured the ranges, this happens only when max_temp is below 20 degrees. Alternatively, we could replace ELSE with a WHEN clause that looks for temperatures less than or equal to 19 degrees by using max_temp <= 19.

Run the code; the first five rows of output should look like this:

```
max_temp   temperature_group
--------   -----------------
      31   Freezing
      34   Cold
      32   Freezing
      32   Freezing
      34   Cold
--snip--
```

Now that we've collapsed the data set into six categories, let's use those categories to compare climate among the three cities in the table.

Using CASE in a Common Table Expression

The operation we performed with CASE on the temperature data in the previous section is a good example of a preprocessing step you would use in a CTE. Now that we've grouped the temperatures in categories, let's count the groups by city in a CTE to see how many days of the year fall into each temperature category.

Listing 12-15 shows the code for reclassifying the daily maximum temperatures recast to generate a temps_collapsed CTE and then use it for an analysis:

```
❶ WITH temps_collapsed (station_name, max_temperature_group) AS
      (SELECT station_name,
             CASE WHEN max_temp >= 90 THEN 'Hot'
                  WHEN max_temp BETWEEN 70 AND 89 THEN 'Warm'
                  WHEN max_temp BETWEEN 50 AND 69 THEN 'Pleasant'
                  WHEN max_temp BETWEEN 33 AND 49 THEN 'Cold'
                  WHEN max_temp BETWEEN 20 AND 32 THEN 'Freezing'
                  ELSE 'Inhumane'
             END
       FROM temperature_readings)

❷ SELECT station_name, max_temperature_group, count(*)
   FROM temps_collapsed
   GROUP BY station_name, max_temperature_group
   ORDER BY station_name, count(*) DESC;
```

Listing 12-15: Using CASE in a CTE

This code reclassifies the temperatures, and then counts and groups by station name to find general climate classifications of each city. The WITH keyword defines the CTE of temps_collapsed ❶, which has two columns: station_name and max_temperature_group. We then run a SELECT query on the CTE ❷, performing straightforward count(*) and GROUP BY operations on both columns. The results should look like this:

```
station_name                    max_temperature_group    count
---------------------------     ---------------------    -----
CHICAGO NORTHERLY ISLAND IL US  Warm                       133
CHICAGO NORTHERLY ISLAND IL US  Cold                        92
CHICAGO NORTHERLY ISLAND IL US  Pleasant                    91
CHICAGO NORTHERLY ISLAND IL US  Freezing                    30
CHICAGO NORTHERLY ISLAND IL US  Inhumane                     8
CHICAGO NORTHERLY ISLAND IL US  Hot                          8
SEATTLE BOEING FIELD WA US      Pleasant                   198
SEATTLE BOEING FIELD WA US      Warm                        98
SEATTLE BOEING FIELD WA US      Cold                        50
SEATTLE BOEING FIELD WA US      Hot                          3
WAIKIKI 717.2 HI US             Warm                       361
WAIKIKI 717.2 HI US             Hot                          5
```

Using this classification scheme, the amazingly consistent Waikiki weather, with Warm maximum temperatures 361 days of the year, confirms its appeal as a vacation destination. From a temperature standpoint, Seattle looks good too, with nearly 300 days of high temps categorized as Pleasant or Warm (although this belies Seattle's legendary rainfall). Chicago, with 30 days of Freezing max temps and 8 days Inhumane, probably isn't for me.

Wrapping Up

In this chapter, you learned to make queries work harder for you. You can now add subqueries in multiple locations to provide finer control over filtering or preprocessing data before analyzing it in a main query. You also can visualize data in a matrix using cross tabulations and reclassify data into groups; both techniques give you more ways to find and tell stories using your data. Great work!

Throughout the next chapters, we'll dive into SQL techniques that are more specific to PostgreSQL. We'll begin by working with and searching text and strings.

TRY IT YOURSELF

Here are two tasks to help you become more familiar with the concepts introduced in the chapter:

1. Revise the code in Listing 12-15 to dig deeper into the nuances of Waikiki's high temperatures. Limit the temps_collapsed table to the Waikiki maximum daily temperature observations. Then use the WHEN clauses in the CASE statement to reclassify the temperatures into seven groups that would result in the following text output:

    ```
    '90 or more'
    '88-89'
    '86-87'
    '84-85'
    '82-83'
    '80-81'
    '79 or less'
    ```

    In which of those groups does Waikiki's daily maximum temperature fall most often?

2. Revise the ice cream survey crosstab in Listing 12-11 to flip the table. In other words, make flavor the rows and office the columns. Which elements of the query do you need to change? Are the counts different?

13

MINING TEXT TO FIND MEANINGFUL DATA

Although it might not be obvious at first glance, you can extract data and even quantify data from text in speeches, reports, press releases, and other documents. Even though most text exists as *unstructured* or *semi-structured data*, which is not organized in rows and columns, as in a table, you can use SQL to derive meaning from it.

One way to do this is to transform the text into *structured data*. You search for and extract elements such as dates or codes from the text, load them into a table, and analyze them. Another way to find meaning from textual data is to use advanced text analysis features, such as PostgreSQL's full text search. Using these techniques, ordinary text can reveal facts or trends that might otherwise remain hidden.

In this chapter, you'll learn how to use SQL to analyze and transform text. You'll start with simple text wrangling using string formatting and pattern matching before moving on to more advanced analysis functions. We'll use two data sets as examples: a small collection of crime reports from a sheriff's department near Washington, D.C., and a set of State of the Union addresses delivered by former U.S. presidents.

Formatting Text Using String Functions

Whether you're looking for data in text or simply want to change how it looks in a report, you first need to transform it into a format you can use. PostgreSQL has more than 50 built-in string functions that handle routine but necessary tasks, such as capitalizing letters, combining strings, and removing unwanted spaces. Some are part of the ANSI SQL standard, and others are specific to PostgreSQL. You'll find a complete list of string functions at *https://www.postgresql.org/docs/current/static/functions-string.html*, but in this section we'll examine several that you'll likely use most often.

You can use these functions inside a variety of queries. Let's try one now using a simple query that places a function after SELECT and runs it in the pgAdmin Query Tool, like this: SELECT upper('hello');. Examples of each function plus code for all the listings in this chapter are available at *https://www.nostarch.com/practicalSQL/*.

Case Formatting

The capitalization functions format the text's case. The upper(*string*) function capitalizes all alphabetical characters of a string passed to it. Nonalphabet characters, such as numbers, remain unchanged. For example, upper('Neal7') returns NEAL7. The lower(*string*) function lowercases all alphabetical characters while keeping nonalphabet characters unchanged. For example, lower('Randy') returns randy.

The initcap(*string*) function capitalizes the first letter of each word. For example, initcap('at the end of the day') returns At The End Of The Day. This function is handy for formatting titles of books or movies, but because it doesn't recognize acronyms, it's not always the perfect solution. For example, initcap('Practical SQL') would return Practical Sql, because it doesn't recognize SQL as an acronym.

The upper() and lower() functions are ANSI SQL standard commands, but initcap() is PostgreSQL-specific. These three functions give you enough options to rework a column of text into the case you prefer. Note that capitalization does not work with all locales or languages.

Character Information

Several functions return data about the string rather than transforming it. These functions are helpful on their own or combined with other functions. For example, the char_length(*string*) function returns the number of characters in a string, including any spaces. For example, char_length(' Pat ') returns a value of 5, because the three letters in Pat and the spaces on either end total five characters. You can also use the non-ANSI SQL function length(*string*) to count strings, which has a variant that lets you count the length of binary strings.

NOTE *The* length() *function can return a different value than* char_length() *when used with multibyte encodings, such as character sets covering the Chinese, Japanese, or Korean languages.*

The position(*substring* in *string*) function returns the location of the substring characters in the string. For example, position(', ' in 'Tan, Bella') returns 4, because the comma and space characters (,) specified in the substring passed as the first parameter start at the fourth index position in the main string Tan, Bella.

Both char_length() and position() are in the ANSI SQL standard.

Removing Characters

The trim(*characters* from *string*) function removes unwanted characters from strings. To declare one or more characters to remove, add them to the function followed by the keyword from and the main string you want to change. Options to remove leading characters (at the front of the string), trailing characters (at the end of the string), or both make this function super flexible.

For example, trim('s' from 'socks') removes all s characters and returns ock. To remove only the s at the end of the string, add the trailing keyword before the character to trim: trim(trailing 's' from 'socks') returns sock.

If you don't specify any characters to remove, trim() removes any spaces in the string by default. For example, trim(' Pat ') returns Pat without the leading or trailing spaces. To confirm the length of the trimmed string, we can nest trim() inside char_length() like this:

```
SELECT char_length(trim(' Pat '));
```

This query should return 3, the number of letters in Pat, which is the result of trim(' Pat ').

The ltrim(*string*, *characters*) and rtrim(*string*, *characters*) functions are PostgreSQL-specific variations of the trim() function. They remove characters from the left or right ends of a string. For example, rtrim('socks', 's') returns sock by removing only the s on the right end of the string.

Extracting and Replacing Characters

The left(*string*, *number*) and right(*string*, *number*) functions, both ANSI SQL standard, extract and return selected characters from a string. For example, to get just the 703 area code from the phone number 703-555-1212, use left('703-555-1212', 3) to specify that you want the first three characters of the string starting from the left. Likewise, right('703-555-1212', 8) returns eight characters from the right: 555-1212.

To substitute characters in a string, use the replace(*string, from, to*) function. To change bat to cat, for example, you would use replace('bat', 'b', 'c') to specify that you want to replace the b in bat with a c.

Now that you know basic functions for manipulating strings, let's look at how to match more complex patterns in text and turn those patterns into data we can analyze.

Matching Text Patterns with Regular Expressions

Regular expressions (or *regex*) are a type of notational language that describes text patterns. If you have a string with a noticeable pattern (say, four digits followed by a hyphen and then two more digits), you can write a regular expression that describes the pattern. You can then use the notation in a WHERE clause to filter rows by the pattern or use regular expression functions to extract and wrangle text that contains the same pattern.

Regular expressions can seem inscrutable to beginning programmers; they take practice to comprehend because they use single-character symbols that aren't intuitive. Getting an expression to match a pattern can involve trial and error, and each programming language has subtle differences in the way it handles regular expressions. Still, learning regular expressions is a good investment because you gain superpower-like abilities to search text using many programming languages, text editors, and other applications.

In this section, I'll provide enough regular expression basics to work through the exercises. To learn more, I recommend interactive online code testers, such as *https://regexr.com/* or *http://www.regexpal.com/*, which have notation references.

Regular Expression Notation

Matching letters and numbers using regular expression notation is straightforward because letters and numbers (and certain symbols) are literals that indicate the same characters. For example, Al matches the first two characters in Alicia.

For more complex patterns, you'll use combinations of the regular expression elements in Table 13-1.

Table 13-1: Regular Expression Notation Basics

Expression	Description
.	A dot is a wildcard that finds any character except a newline.
[FGz]	Any character in the square brackets. Here, F, G, or z.
[a-z]	A range of characters. Here, lowercase a to z.
[^a-z]	The caret negates the match. Here, not lowercase a to z.
\w	Any word character or underscore. Same as [A-Za-z0-9_].
\d	Any digit.

Expression	Description
\s	A space.
\t	Tab character.
\n	Newline character.
\r	Carriage return character.
^	Match at the start of a string.
$	Match at the end of a string.
?	Get the preceding match zero or one time.
*	Get the preceding match zero or more times.
+	Get the preceding match one or more times.
{m}	Get the preceding match exactly *m* times.
{m,n}	Get the preceding match between *m* and *n* times.
a|b	The pipe denotes alternation. Find either *a* or *b*.
( )	Create and report a capture group or set precedence.
(?:)	Negate the reporting of a capture group.

Using these basic regular expressions, you can match various kinds of characters and also indicate how many times and where to match them. For example, placing characters inside square brackets ([]) lets you match any single character or a range. So, [FGz] matches a single F, G, or z, whereas [A-Za-z] will match any uppercase or lowercase letter.

The backslash (\) precedes a designator for special characters, such as a tab (\t), digit (\d), or newline (\n), which is a line ending character in text files.

There are several ways to indicate how many times to match a character. Placing a number inside curly brackets indicates you want to match it that many times. For example, \d{4} matches four digits in a row, and \d{1,4} matches a digit between one and four times.

The ?, *, and + characters provide a useful shorthand notation for the number of matches. For example, the plus sign (+) after a character indicates to match it one or more times. So, the expression a+ would find the aa characters in the string aardvark.

Additionally, parentheses indicate a *capture group*, which you can use to specify just a portion of the matched text to display in the query results. This is useful for reporting back just a part of a matched expression. For example, if you were hunting for an HH:MM:SS time format in text and wanted to report only the hour, you could use an expression such as (\d{2}):\d{2}:\d{2}. This looks for two digits (\d{2}) of the hour followed by a colon, another two digits for the minutes and a colon, and then the two-digit seconds. By placing the first \d{2} inside parentheses, you can extract only those two digits, even though the entire expression matches the full time.

Table 13-2 shows examples of combining regular expressions to capture different portions of the sentence "The game starts at 7 p.m. on May 2, 2019."

Table 13-2: Regular Expression Matching Examples

Expression	What it matches	Result
.+	Any character one or more times	The game starts at 7 p.m. on May 2, 2019.
\d{1,2} (?:a.m.|p.m.)	One or two digits followed by a space and *a.m.* or *p.m.* in a noncapture group	7 p.m.
^\w+	One or more word characters at the start	The
\w+.$	One or more word characters followed by any character at the end	2019.
May|June	Either of the words *May* or *June*	May
\d{4}	Four digits	2019
May \d, \d{4}	*May* followed by a space, digit, comma, space, and four digits	May 2, 2019

These results show the usefulness of regular expressions for selecting only the parts of the string that interest us. For example, to find the time, we use the expression \d{1,2} (?:a.m.|p.m.) to look for either one or two digits because the time could be a single or double digit followed by a space. Then we look for either a.m. or p.m.; the pipe symbol separating the terms indicates the either-or condition, and placing them in parentheses separates the logic from the rest of the expression. We need the ?: symbol to indicate that we don't want to treat the terms inside the parentheses as a capture group, which would report a.m. or p.m. only. The ?: ensures that the full match will be returned.

You can use any of these regular expressions in pgAdmin by placing the text and regular expression inside the substring(*string* from *pattern*) function to return the matched text. For example, to find the four-digit year, use the following query:

```
SELECT substring('The game starts at 7 p.m. on May 2, 2019.' from '\d{4}');
```

This query should return 2019, because we specified that the pattern should look for any digit that is four characters long, and 2019 is the only digit in this string that matches these criteria. You can check out sample substring() queries for all the examples in Table 13-2 in the book's code resources at *https://www.nostarch.com/practicalSQL/*.

The lesson here is that if you can identify a pattern in the text, you can use a combination of regular expression symbols to locate it. This technique is particularly useful when you have repeating patterns in text that you want to turn into a set of data to analyze. Let's practice how to use regular expression functions using a real-world example.

Turning Text to Data with Regular Expression Functions

A sheriff's department in one of the Washington, D.C., suburbs publishes daily reports that detail the date, time, location, and description of incidents the department investigates. These reports would be great to analyze, except they post the information in Microsoft Word documents saved as PDF files, which is not the friendliest format for importing into a database.

If I copy and paste incidents from the PDF into a text editor, the result is blocks of text that look something like Listing 13-1:

❶ 4/16/17-4/17/17
❷ 2100-0900 hrs.
❸ 46000 Block Ashmere Sq.
❹ Sterling
❺ Larceny: ❻The victim reported that a
  bicycle was stolen from their opened
  garage door during the overnight hours.
❼ C0170006614

  04/10/17
  1605 hrs.
  21800 block Newlin Mill Rd.
  Middleburg
  Larceny: A license plate was reported
  stolen from a vehicle.
  S0170006250

Listing 13-1: Crime reports text

Each block of text includes dates ❶, times ❷, a street address ❸, city or town ❹, the type of crime ❺, and a description of the incident ❻. The last piece of information is a code ❼ that might be a unique ID for the incident, although we'd have to check with the sheriff's department to be sure. There are slight inconsistencies. For example, the first block of text has two dates (4/16/17-4/17/17) and two times (2100-0900 hrs.), meaning the exact time of the incident is unknown and likely occurred within that time span. The second block has one date and time.

If you compile these reports regularly, you can expect to find some good insights that could answer important questions: Where do crimes tend to occur? Which crime types occur most frequently? Do they happen more often on weekends or weekdays? Before you can start answering these questions, you'll need to extract the text into table columns using regular expressions.

Creating a Table for Crime Reports

I've collected five of the crime incidents into a file named *crime_reports.csv* that you can download at *https://www.nostarch.com/practicalSQL/*. Download the file and save it on your computer. Then use the code in Listing 13-2 to build a table that has a column for each data element you can parse from the text using a regular expression.

```
CREATE TABLE crime_reports (
    crime_id bigserial PRIMARY KEY,
    date_1 timestamp with time zone,
    date_2 timestamp with time zone,
    street varchar(250),
    city varchar(100),
    crime_type varchar(100),
    description text,
    case_number varchar(50),
    original_text text NOT NULL
);

COPY crime_reports (original_text)
FROM 'C:\YourDirectory\crime_reports.csv'
WITH (FORMAT CSV, HEADER OFF, QUOTE '"');
```

Listing 13-2: Creating and loading the crime_reports table

Run the CREATE TABLE statement in Listing 13-2, and then use COPY to load the text into the column original_text. The rest of the columns will be NULL until we fill them.

When you run SELECT original_text FROM crime_reports; in pgAdmin, the results grid should display five rows and the first several words of each report. When you hover your cursor over any cell, pgAdmin shows all the text in that row, as shown in Figure 13-1.

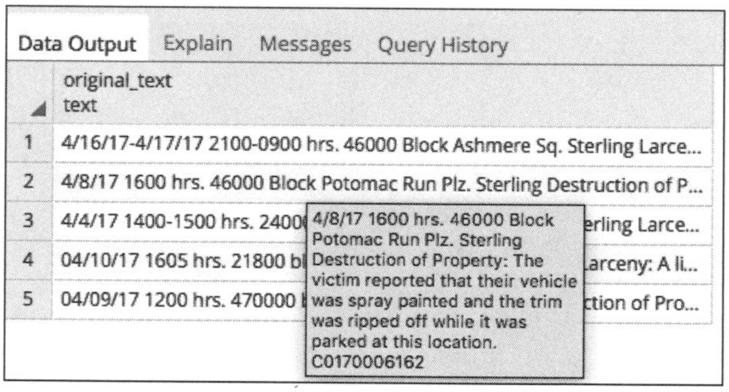

Figure 13-1: Displaying additional text in the pgAdmin results grid

Now that you've loaded the text you'll be parsing, let's explore this data using PostgreSQL regular expression functions.

Matching Crime Report Date Patterns

The first piece of data we want to extract from the report original_text is the date or dates of the crime. Most of the reports have one date, although one has two. The reports also have associated times, and we'll combine the extracted date and time into a timestamp. We'll fill date_1 with the first (or only) date and time in each report. In cases where a second date or second time exists, we'll create a timestamp and add it to date_2.

For extracting data, we'll use the regexp_match(*string*, *pattern*) function, which is similar to substring() with a few exceptions. One is that it returns each match as text in an array. Also, if there are no matches, it returns NULL. As you might recall from Chapter 5, arrays are a list of elements; in one exercise, you used an array to pass a list of values into the percentile_cont() function to calculate quartiles. I'll show you how to work with results that come back as an array when we parse the crime reports.

NOTE *The* regexp_match() *function was introduced in PostgreSQL 10 and is not available in earlier versions.*

To start, let's use regexp_match() to find dates in each of the five incidents in crime_reports. The general pattern to match is *MM/DD/YY*, although there may be one or two digits for both the month and date. Here's a regular expression that matches the pattern:

```
\d{1,2}\/\d{1,2}\/\d{2}
```

In this expression, \d{1,2} indicates the month. The numbers inside the curly brackets specify that you want at least one digit and at most two digits. Next, you want to look for a forward slash (/), but because a forward slash can have special meaning in regular expressions, you must *escape* that character by placing a backslash (\) in front of it, like this \/. Escaping a character in this context simply means we want to treat it as a literal rather than letting it take on special meaning. So, the combination of the backslash and forward slash (\/) indicates you want a forward slash.

Another \d{1,2} follows for a single- or double-digit day of the month. The expression ends with a second escaped forward slash and \d{2} to indicate the two-digit year. Let's pass the expression \d{1,2}\/\d{1,2}\/\d{2} to regexp_match(), as shown in Listing 13-3:

```
SELECT crime_id,
       regexp_match(original_text, '\d{1,2}\/\d{1,2}\/\d{2}')
FROM crime_reports;
```

Listing 13-3: Using regexp_match() to find the first date

Run that code in pgAdmin, and the results should look like this:

```
crime_id    regexp_match
--------    ------------
       1    {4/16/17}
       2    {4/8/17}
       3    {4/4/17}
       4    {04/10/17}
       5    {04/09/17}
```

Note that each row shows the first date listed for the incident, because regexp_match() returns the first match it finds by default. Also note that each date is enclosed in curly brackets. That's PostgreSQL indicating that regexp_match() returns each result in an array, or list of elements. In "Extracting Text from the regexp_match() Result" on page 224, I'll show you how to access those elements from the array. You can also read more about using arrays in PostgreSQL at *https://www.postgresql.org/docs/current/static/arrays.html*.

Matching the Second Date When Present

We've successfully extracted the first date from each report. But recall that one of the five incidents has a second date. To find and display all the dates in the text, you must use the related regexp_matches() function and pass in an option in the form of the flag g, as shown in Listing 13-4.

```
SELECT crime_id,
       regexp_matches(original_text, '\d{1,2}\/\d{1,2}\/\d{2}', 'g'❶)
FROM crime_reports;
```

Listing 13-4: Using the regexp_matches() function with the 'g' flag

The regexp_matches() function, when supplied the g flag ❶, differs from regexp_match() by returning each match the expression finds as a row in the results rather than returning just the first match.

Run the code again with this revision; you should now see two dates for the incident that has a crime_id of 1, like this:

```
crime_id    regexp_matches
--------    --------------
       1    {4/16/17}
       1    {4/17/17}
       2    {4/8/17}
       3    {4/4/17}
       4    {04/10/17}
       5    {04/09/17}
```

Any time a crime report has a second date, we want to load it and the associated time into the date_2 column. Although adding the g flag shows us all the dates, to extract just the second date in a report, we can use the pattern we always see when two dates exist. In Listing 13-1, the first block of text showed the two dates separated by a hyphen, like this:

```
4/16/17-4/17/17
```

This means you can switch back to regexp_match() and write a regular expression to look for a hyphen followed by a date, as shown in Listing 13-5.

```
SELECT crime_id,
       regexp_match(original_text, '-\d{1,2}\/\d{1,2}\/\d{2}')
FROM crime_reports;
```

Listing 13-5: Using `regexp_match()` to find the second date

Although this query finds the second date in the first item (and returns a NULL for the rest), there's an unintended consequence: it displays the hyphen along with it.

```
crime_id    regexp_match
--------    ------------
       1    {-4/17/17}
       2
       3
       4
       5
```

You don't want to include the hyphen, because it's an invalid format for the `timestamp` data type. Fortunately, you can specify the exact part of the regular expression you want to return by placing parentheses around it to create a capture group, like this:

```
-(\d{1,2}/\d{1,2}/\d{1,2})
```

This notation returns only the part of the regular expression you want. Run the modified query in Listing 13-6 to report only the data in parentheses.

```
SELECT crime_id,
       regexp_match(original_text, '-(\d{1,2}\/\d{1,2}\/\d{1,2})')
FROM crime_reports;
```

Listing 13-6: Using a capture group to return only the date

The query in Listing 13-6 should return just the second date without the leading hyphen, as shown here:

```
crime_id    regexp_match
--------    ------------
       1    {4/17/17}
       2
       3
       4
       5
```

The process you've just completed is typical. You start with text to analyze, and then write and refine the regular expression until it finds the data you want. So far, we've created regular expressions to match the first date and a second date, if it exists. Now, let's use regular expressions to extract additional data elements.

Matching Additional Crime Report Elements

In this section, we'll capture times, addresses, crime type, description, and case number from the crime reports. Here are the expressions for capturing this information:

First hour \/\d{2}\n(\d{4})

The first hour, which is the hour the crime was committed or the start of the time range, always follows the date in each crime report, like this:

```
4/16/17-4/17/17
2100-0900 hrs.
```

To find the first hour, we start with an escaped forward slash and \d{2}, which represents the two-digit year preceding the first date (17). The \n character indicates the newline because the hour always starts on a new line, and \d{4} represents the four-digit hour (2100). Because we just want to return the four digits, we put \d{4} inside parentheses as a capture group.

Second hour \/\d{2}\n\d{4}-(\d{4})

If the second hour exists, it will follow a hyphen, so we add a hyphen and another \d{4} to the expression we just created for the first hour. Again, the second \d{4} goes inside a capture group, because 0900 is the only hour we want to return.

Street hrs.\n(\d+ .+(?:Sq.|Plz.|Dr.|Ter.|Rd.))

In this data, the street always follows the time's hrs. designation and a newline (\n), like this:

```
04/10/17
1605 hrs.
21800 block Newlin Mill Rd.
```

The street address always starts with some number that varies in length and ends with an abbreviated suffix of some kind. To describe this pattern, we use \d+ to match any digit that appears one or more times. Then we specify a space and look for any character one or more times using the dot wildcard and plus sign (.+) notation. The expression ends with a series of terms separated by the alternation pipe symbol that looks like this: (?:Sq.|Plz.|Dr.|Ter.|Rd.). The terms are inside parentheses, so the expression will match one or another of those terms. When we group terms like this, if we don't want the parentheses to act as a capture group, we need to add ?: to negate that effect.

NOTE   *In a large data set, it's likely roadway names would end with suffixes beyond the five in our regular expression. After making an initial pass at extracting the street, you can run a query to check for unmatched rows to find additional suffixes to match.*

City `(?:Sq.|Plz.|Dr.|Ter.|Rd.)\n(\w+ \w+|\w+)\n`

Because the city always follows the street suffix, we reuse the terms separated by the alternation symbol we just created for the street. We follow that with a newline (\n) and then use a capture group to look for two words or one word (\w+ \w+|\w+) before a final newline, because a town or city name can be more than a single word.

Crime type `\n(?:\w+ \w+|\w+)\n(.*):`

The type of crime always precedes a colon (the only time a colon is used in each report) and might consist of one or more words, like this:

```
--snip--
Middleburg
Larceny: A license plate was reported
stolen from a vehicle.
SO170006250
--snip--
```

To create an expression that matches this pattern, we follow a new-line with a nonreporting capture group that looks for the one- or two-word city. Then we add another newline and match any character that occurs zero or more times before a colon using (.*):.

Description `:\s(.+)(?:C0|SO)`

The crime description always comes between the colon after the crime type and the case number. The expression starts with the colon, a space character (\s), and then a capture group to find any character that appears one or more times using the .+ notation. The nonreporting capture group (?:C0|SO) tells the program to stop looking when it encounters either C0 or SO, the two character pairs that start each case number (a C followed by a zero, and an S followed by a capital O). We have to do this because the description might have one or more line breaks.

Case number `(?:C0|SO)[0-9]+`

The case number starts with either C0 or SO, followed by a set of digits. To match this pattern, the expression looks for either C0 or SO in a non-reporting capture group followed by any digit from 0 to 9 that occurs one or more times using the [0-9] range notation.

Now let's pass these regular expressions to `regexp_match()` to see them in action. Listing 13-7 shows a sample `regexp_match()` query that retrieves the case number, first date, crime type, and city:

```
SELECT
    regexp_match(original_text, '(?:C0|SO)[0-9]+') AS case_number,
    regexp_match(original_text, '\d{1,2}\/\d{1,2}\/\d{2}') AS date_1,
    regexp_match(original_text, '\n(?:\w+ \w+|\w+)\n(.*):') AS crime_type,
    regexp_match(original_text, '(?:Sq.|Plz.|Dr.|Ter.|Rd.)\n(\w+ \w+|\w+)\n')
        AS city
FROM crime_reports;
```

Listing 13-7: Matching case number, date, crime type, and city

Run the code, and the results should look like this:

case_number	date_1	crime_type	city
{C0170006614}	{4/16/17}	{Larceny}	{Sterling}
{C0170006162}	{4/8/17}	{Destruction of Property}	{Sterling}
{C0170006079}	{4/4/17}	{Larceny}	{Sterling}
{S0170006250}	{04/10/17}	{Larceny}	{Middleburg}
{S0170006211}	{04/09/17}	{Destruction of Property}	{Sterling}

After all that wrangling, we've transformed the text into a structure that is more suitable for analysis. Of course, you would have to include many more incidents to count the frequency of crime type by city or the number of crimes per month to identify any trends.

To load each parsed element into the table's columns, we'll create an UPDATE query. But before you can insert the text into a column, you'll need to learn how to extract the text from the array that regexp_match() returns.

Extracting Text from the regexp_match() Result

In "Matching Crime Report Date Patterns" on page 218, I mentioned that regexp_match() returns an array containing text values. Two clues reveal that these are text values. The first is that the data type designation in the column header shows text[] instead of text. The second is that each result is surrounded by curly brackets. Figure 13-2 shows how pgAdmin displays the results of the query in Listing 13-7.

	case_number text[]	date_1 text[]	crime_type text[]	city text[]
1	{C0170006614}	{4/16/17}	{Larceny}	{Sterling}
2	{C0170006162}	{4/8/17}	{Destruction of Property}	{Sterling}
3	{C0170006079}	{4/4/17}	{Larceny}	{Sterling}
4	{S0170006250}	{04/10/17}	{Larceny}	{Middleburg}
5	{S0170006211}	{04/09/17}	{Destruction of Property}	{Sterling}

Figure 13-2: Array values in the pgAdmin results grid

The crime_reports columns we want to update are not array types, so rather than passing in the array values returned by regexp_match(), we need to extract the values from the array first. We do this by using array notation, as shown in Listing 13-8.

```
SELECT
    crime_id,
 ❶ (regexp_match(original_text, '(?:CO|SO)[0-9]+'))[1]❷
        AS case_number
FROM crime_reports;
```

Listing 13-8: Retrieving a value from within an array

First, we wrap the regexp_match() function ❶ in parentheses. Then, at the end, we provide a value of 1, which represents the first element in the array, enclosed in square brackets ❷. The query should produce the following results:

```
crime_id    case_number
--------    -----------
       1    C0170006614
       2    C0170006162
       3    C0170006079
       4    S0170006250
       5    S0170006211
```

Now the data type designation in the pgAdmin column header should show text instead of text[], and the values are no longer enclosed in curly brackets. We can now insert these values into crime_reports using an UPDATE query.

Updating the crime_reports Table with Extracted Data

With each element currently available as text, we can update columns in the crime_reports table with the appropriate data from the original crime report. To start, Listing 13-9 combines the extracted first date and time into a single timestamp value for the column date_1.

```
  UPDATE crime_reports
❶ SET date_1 =
  (
    ❷ (regexp_match(original_text, '\d{1,2}\/\d{1,2}\/\d{2}'))[1]
      ❸ || ' ' ||
    ❹ (regexp_match(original_text, '\/\d{2}\n(\d{4})'))[1]
      ❺ ||' US/Eastern'
❻ )::timestamptz;

  SELECT crime_id,
         date_1,
         original_text
  FROM crime_reports;
```

Listing 13-9: Updating the crime_reports date_1 column

Because the date_1 column is of type timestamp, we must provide an input in that data type. To do that, we'll use the PostgreSQL double-pipe (||) concatenation operator to combine the extracted date and time in a format that's acceptable for timestamp with time zone input. In the SET clause ❶, we start with the regex pattern that matches the first date ❷. Next, we concatenate the date with a space using two single quotes ❸ and repeat the concatenation operator. This step combines the date with a space before connecting it to the regex pattern that matches the time ❹. Then we include the time zone for the Washington, D.C., area by concatenating that at the end of the string ❺ using the US/Eastern designation.

Concatenating these elements creates a string in the pattern of *MM/DD/YY HHMM TIMEZONE*, which is acceptable as a timestamp input. We cast the string to a timestamp with time zone data type ❻ using the PostgreSQL double-colon shorthand and the timestamptz abbreviation.

When you run the UPDATE portion of the code, PostgreSQL should return the message UPDATE 5. Running the SELECT statement in pgAdmin should show the now-filled date_1 column alongside a portion of the original_text column, like this:

```
crime_id    date_1                   original_text
--------    ---------------------    -------------------------------------
       1    2017-04-16 21:00:00-04   4/16/17-4/17/17 2100-0900 hrs. 460 ...
       2    2017-04-08 16:00:00-04   4/8/17 1600 hrs. 46000 Block Potom ...
       3    2017-04-04 14:00:00-04   4/4/17 1400-1500 hrs. 24000 Block   ...
       4    2017-04-10 16:05:00-04   04/10/17 1605 hrs. 21800 block New  ...
       5    2017-04-09 12:00:00-04   04/09/17 1200 hrs. 470000 block Fa  ...
```

At a glance, you can see that date_1 accurately captures the first date and time that appears in the original text and puts it into a useable format that we can analyze. Note that if you're not in the Eastern time zone, the time-stamps will instead reflect your pgAdmin client's time zone. As you learned in "Setting the Time Zone" on page 178, you can use the command SET timezone TO 'US/Eastern'; to change the client to reflect Eastern time.

Using CASE to Handle Special Instances

You could write an UPDATE statement for each remaining data element, but combining those statements into one would be more efficient. Listing 13-10 updates all the crime_reports columns using a single statement while handling inconsistent values in the data.

```
UPDATE crime_reports
SET date_1❶ =
    (
      (regexp_match(original_text, '\d{1,2}\/\d{1,2}\/\d{2}'))[1]
          || ' ' ||
      (regexp_match(original_text, '\/\d{2}\n(\d{4})'))[1]
          ||' US/Eastern'
    )::timestamptz,

    date_2❷ =
    CASE❸
        WHEN❹ (SELECT regexp_match(original_text, '-(\d{1,2}\/\d{1,2}\/\d{1,2})') IS NULL❺)
              AND (SELECT regexp_match(original_text, '\/\d{2}\n\d{4}-(\d{4})') IS NOT NULL❻)
        THEN❼
          ((regexp_match(original_text, '\d{1,2}\/\d{1,2}\/\d{2}'))[1]
              || ' ' ||
          (regexp_match(original_text, '\/\d{2}\n\d{4}-(\d{4})'))[1]
              ||' US/Eastern'
          )::timestamptz
```

```
WHEN❽ (SELECT regexp_match(original_text, '-(\d{1,2}\/\d{1,2}\/\d{1,2})') IS NOT NULL)
          AND (SELECT regexp_match(original_text, '\/\d{2}\n\d{4}-(\d{4})') IS NOT NULL)
    THEN
      ((regexp_match(original_text, '-(\d{1,2}\/\d{1,2}\/\d{1,2})'))[1]
          || ' ' ||
      (regexp_match(original_text, '\/\d{2}\n\d{4}-(\d{4})'))[1]
          ||' US/Eastern'
      )::timestamptz

      ELSE NULL❾
END,
street = (regexp_match(original_text, 'hrs.\n(\d+ .+(?:Sq.|Plz.|Dr.|Ter.|Rd.))'))[1],
city = (regexp_match(original_text,
                        '(?:Sq.|Plz.|Dr.|Ter.|Rd.)\n(\w+ \w+|\w+)\n'))[1],
crime_type = (regexp_match(original_text, '\n(?:\w+ \w+|\w+)\n(.*):'))[1],
description = (regexp_match(original_text, ':\s(.+)(?:CO|SO)'))[1],
case_number = (regexp_match(original_text, '(?:CO|SO)[0-9]+'))[1];
```

Listing 13-10: Updating all crime_reports columns

This UPDATE statement might look intimidating, but it's not if we break
it down by column. First, we use the same code from Listing 13-9 to update
the date_1 column ❶. But to update date_2 ❷, we need to account for the
inconsistent presence of a second date and time. In our limited data set,
there are three possibilities:

1. A second hour exists but not a second date. This occurs when a report
   covers a range of hours on one date.

2. A second date and second hour exist. This occurs when a report covers
   more than one date.

3. Neither a second date nor a second hour exists.

To insert the correct value in date_2 for each scenario, we use the
CASE statement syntax you learned in "Reclassifying Values with CASE" on
page 207 to test for each possibility. After the CASE keyword ❸, we use a
series of WHEN ... THEN statements to check for the first two conditions and
provide the value to insert; if neither condition exists, we use an ELSE keyword to provide a NULL.

The first WHEN statement ❹ checks whether regexp_match() returns a NULL ❺
for the second date and a value for the second hour (using IS NOT NULL ❻). If
that condition evaluates as true, the THEN statement ❼ concatenates the first
date with the second hour to create a timestamp for the update.

The second WHEN statement ❽ checks that regexp_match() returns a value
for the second hour and second date. If true, the THEN statement concatenates the second date with the second hour to create a timestamp.

If neither of the two WHEN statements returns true, the ELSE statement ❾
provides a NULL for the update because there is only a first date and first time.

NOTE   *The WHEN statements handle the possibilities that exist in our small sample data set.*
If you are working with more data, you might need to handle additional variations,
such as a second date but not a second time.

When we run the full query in Listing 13-10, PostgreSQL should report UPDATE 5. Success! Now that we've updated all the columns with the appropriate data while accounting for elements that have additional data, we can examine all the columns of the table and find the parsed elements from original_text. Listing 13-11 queries four of the columns:

```
SELECT date_1,
       street,
       city,
       crime_type
FROM crime_reports;
```

Listing 13-11: Viewing selected crime data

The results of the query should show a nicely organized set of data that looks something like this:

date_1	street	city	crime_type
2017-04-16 21:00:00-04	46000 Block Ashmere Sq.	Sterling	Larceny
2017-04-08 16:00:00-04	46000 Block Potomac Run Plz.	Sterling	Destruction of ...
2017-04-04 14:00:00-04	24000 Block Hawthorn Thicket Ter.	Sterling	Larceny
2017-04-10 16:05:00-04	21800 block Newlin Mill Rd.	Middleburg	Larceny
2017-04-09 12:00:00-04	470000 block Fairway Dr.	Sterling	Destruction of ...

You've successfully transformed raw text into a table that can answer questions and reveal storylines about crime in this area.

The Value of the Process

Writing regular expressions and coding a query to update a table can take time, but there is value to identifying and collecting data this way. In fact, some of the best data sets you'll encounter are those you build yourself. Everyone can download the same data sets, but the ones you build are yours alone. You get to be first person to find and tell the story behind the data.

Also, after you set up your database and queries, you can use them again and again. In this example, you could collect crime reports every day (either by hand or by automating downloads using a programming language such as Python) for an ongoing data set that you can mine continually for trends.

In the next section, we'll finish our exploration of regular expressions using additional PostgreSQL functions.

Using Regular Expressions with WHERE

You've filtered queries using LIKE and ILIKE in WHERE clauses. In this section, you'll learn to use regular expressions in WHERE clauses so you can perform more complex matches.

We use a tilde (~) to make a case-sensitive match on a regular expression and a tilde-asterisk (~*) to perform a case-insensitive match. You can negate either expression by adding an exclamation point in front.

For example, !~* indicates to *not* match a regular expression that is case-insensitive. Listing 13-12 shows how this works using the 2010 Census table us_counties_2010 from previous exercises:

```
  SELECT geo_name
  FROM us_counties_2010
❶ WHERE geo_name ~* '(.+lade.+|.+lare.+)'
  ORDER BY geo_name;

  SELECT geo_name
  FROM us_counties_2010
❷ WHERE geo_name ~* '.+ash.+' AND geo_name !~ 'Wash.+'
  ORDER BY geo_name;
```

Listing 13-12: Using regular expressions in a WHERE clause

The first WHERE clause ❶ uses the tilde-asterisk (~*) to perform a case-insensitive match on the regular expression (.+lade.+|.+lare.+) to find any county names that contain either the letters lade or lare between other characters. The results should show eight rows:

```
geo_name
-------------------
Bladen County
Clare County
Clarendon County
Glades County
Langlade County
Philadelphia County
Talladega County
Tulare County
```

As you can see, the county names include the letters lade or lare between other characters.

The second WHERE clause ❷ uses the tilde-asterisk (~*) as well as a negated tilde (!~) to find county names containing the letters ash but excluding those starting with Wash. This query should return the following:

```
geo_name
--------------
Nash County
Wabash County
Wabash County
Wabasha County
```

All four counties in this output have names that contain the letters ash but don't start with Wash.

These are fairly simple examples, but you can do more complex matches using regular expressions that you wouldn't be able to perform with the wildcards available with just LIKE and ILIKE.

Additional Regular Expression Functions

Let's look at three more regular expression functions you might find useful when working with text. Listing 13-13 shows several regular expression functions that replace and split text:

❶ `SELECT regexp_replace('05/12/2018', '\d{4}', '2017');`

❷ `SELECT regexp_split_to_table('Four,score,and,seven,years,ago', ',');`

❸ `SELECT regexp_split_to_array('Phil Mike Tony Steve', ',');`

Listing 13-13: Regular expression functions to replace and split text

The `regexp_replace(`*string, pattern, replacement text*`)` function lets you substitute a matched pattern with replacement text. In the example at ❶, we're searching the date string `05/12/2018` for any set of four digits in a row using `\d{4}`. When found, we replace them with the replacement text `2017`. The result of that query is `05/12/2017` returned as text.

The `regexp_split_to_table(`*string, pattern*`)` function splits delimited text into rows. Listing 13-13 uses this function to split the string `'Four,score,and,seven,years,ago'` on commas ❷, resulting in a set of rows that has one word in each row:

```
regexp_split_to_table
---------------------
Four
score
and
seven
years
ago
```

Keep this function in mind as you tackle the "Try It Yourself" exercises at the end of the chapter.

The `regexp_split_to_array(`*string, pattern*`)` function splits delimited text into an array. The example splits the string `Phil Mike Tony Steve` on spaces ❸, returning a text array that should look like this in pgAdmin:

```
regexp_split_to_array
---------------------
{Phil,Mike,Tony,Steve}
```

The `text[]` notation in pgAdmin's column header along with curly brackets around the results confirms that this is indeed an array type, which provides another means of analysis. For example, you could then use a function such as `array_length()` to count the number of words, as shown in Listing 13-14.

```
SELECT array_length(regexp_split_to_array('Phil Mike Tony Steve', ' '), 1);
```

Listing 13-14: Finding an array length

The query should return 4 because four elements are in this array. You can read more about array_length() and other array functions at *https://www .postgresql.org/docs/current/static/functions-array.html.*

Full Text Search in PostgreSQL

PostgreSQL comes with a powerful full text search engine that gives you more options when searching for information in large amounts of text. You're familiar with Google or other web search engines and similar technology that powers search on news websites or research databases, such as LexisNexis. Although the implementation and capability of full text search demands several chapters, here I'll walk you through a simple example of setting up a table for text search and functions for searching using PostgreSQL.

For this example, I assembled 35 speeches by former U.S. presidents who served after World War II through the Gerald R. Ford administration. Consisting mostly of State of the Union addresses, these public texts are available through the Internet Archive at *https://archive.org/* and the University of California's American Presidency Project at *http://www.presidency.ucsb.edu/ws/ index.php/.* You can find the data in the *sotu-1946-1977.csv* file along with the book's resources at *https://www.nostarch.com/practicalSQL/.*

Let's start with the data types unique to full text search.

Text Search Data Types

PostgreSQL's implementation of text search includes two data types. The tsvector data type represents the text to be searched and to be stored in an optimized form. The tsquery data type represents the search query terms and operators. Let's look at the details of both.

Storing Text as Lexemes with tsvector

The tsvector data type reduces text to a sorted list of *lexemes*, which are units of meaning in language. Think of lexemes as words without the variations created by suffixes. For example, the tsvector format would store the words *washes, washed,* and *washing* as the lexeme *wash* while noting each word's position in the original text. Converting text to tsvector also removes small *stop words* that usually don't play a role in search, such as *the* or *it.*

To see how this data type works, let's convert a string to tsvector format. Listing 13-15 uses the PostgreSQL search function to_tsvector(), which normalizes the text "I am walking across the sitting room to sit with you" to lexemes:

```
SELECT to_tsvector('I am walking across the sitting room to sit with you.');
```

Listing 13-15: Converting text to tsvector data

Execute the code, and it should return the following output in tsvector format:

```
'across':4 'room':7 'sit':6,9 'walk':3
```

The to_tsvector() function reduces the number of words from eleven to four, eliminating words such as *I*, *am*, and *the*, which are not helpful search terms. The function removes suffixes, changing *walking* to *walk* and *sitting* to *sit*. It also orders the words alphabetically, and the number following each colon indicates its position in the original string, taking stop words into account. Note that *sit* is recognized as being in two positions, one for *sitting* and one for *sit*.

Creating the Search Terms with tsquery

The tsquery data type represents the full text search query, again optimized as lexemes. It also provides operators for controlling the search. Examples of operators include the ampersand (&) for AND, the pipe symbol (|) for OR, and the exclamation point (!) for NOT. A special <-> operator lets you search for adjacent words or words a certain distance apart.

Listing 13-16 shows how the to_tsquery() function converts search terms to the tsquery data type.

```
SELECT to_tsquery('walking & sitting');
```

Listing 13-16: Converting search terms to tsquery data

After running the code, you should see that the resulting tsquery data type has normalized the terms into lexemes, which match the format of the data to search:

```
'walk' & 'sit'
```

Now you can use terms stored as tsquery to search text optimized as tsvector.

Using the @@ Match Operator for Searching

With the text and search terms converted to the full text search data types, you can use the double at sign (@@) match operator to check whether a query matches text. The first query in Listing 13-17 uses to_tsquery() to search for the words *walking* and *sitting*, which we combine with the & operator. It returns a Boolean value of true because both *walking* and *sitting* are present in the text converted by to_tsvector().

```
SELECT to_tsvector('I am walking across the sitting room') @@ to_tsquery('walking & sitting');
SELECT to_tsvector('I am walking across the sitting room') @@ to_tsquery('walking & running');
```

Listing 13-17: Querying a tsvector type with a tsquery

However, the second query returns false because both *walking* and *running* are not present in the text. Now let's build a table for searching the speeches.

Creating a Table for Full Text Search

Let's start by creating a table to hold the speech text. The code in Listing 13-18 creates and fills president_speeches so it contains a column for the original speech text as well as a column of type tsvector. The reason is that we need to convert the original speech text into that tsvector column to optimize it for searching. We can't easily do that conversion during import, so let's handle that as a separate step. Be sure to change the file path to match the location of your saved CSV file:

```
CREATE TABLE president_speeches (
    sotu_id serial PRIMARY KEY,
    president varchar(100) NOT NULL,
    title varchar(250) NOT NULL,
    speech_date date NOT NULL,
    speech_text text NOT NULL,
    search_speech_text tsvector
);

COPY president_speeches (president, title, speech_date, speech_text)
FROM 'C:\YourDirectory\sotu-1946-1977.csv'
WTTH (FORMAT CSV, DELIMITER '|', HEADER OFF, QUOTE '@');
```

Listing 13-18: Creating and filling the president_speeches table

After executing the query, run SELECT * FROM president_speeches; to see the data. In pgAdmin, hover your mouse over any cell to see extra words not visible in the results grid. You should see a sizeable amount of text in each row of the speech_text column.

Next, we copy the contents of speech_text to the tsvector column search_speech_text and transform it to that data type at the same time. The UPDATE query in Listing 13-19 handles the task:

```
UPDATE president_speeches
❶ SET search_speech_text = to_tsvector('english', speech_text);
```

Listing 13-19: Converting speeches to tsvector in the search_speech_text column

The SET clause ❶ fills search_speech_text with the output of to_tsvector(). The first argument in the function specifies the language for parsing the lexemes. We're using the default of english here, but you can substitute spanish, german, french, or whatever language you want to use (some languages may require you to find and install additional dictionaries). The second argument is the name of the input column. Run the code to fill the column.

Finally, we want to index the search_speech_text column to speed up searches. You learned about indexing in Chapter 7, which focused on PostgreSQL's default index type, B-Tree. For full text search, the PostgreSQL documentation recommends using the *Generalized Inverted Index* (*GIN*; see *https://www.postgresql.org/docs/current/static/textsearch-indexes .html*). You can add a GIN index using CREATE INDEX in Listing 13-20:

```
CREATE INDEX search_idx ON president_speeches USING gin(search_speech_text);
```

Listing 13-20: Creating a GIN index for text search

The GIN index contains an entry for each lexeme and its location, allowing the database to find matches more quickly.

NOTE *Another way to set up a column for search is to create an index on a text column using the to_tsvector() function. See* https://www.postgresql.org/docs/current/static/textsearch-tables.html *for details.*

Now you're ready to use search functions.

Searching Speech Text

Thirty-two years' worth of presidential speeches is fertile ground for exploring history. For example, the query in Listing 13-21 lists the speeches in which the president mentioned Vietnam:

```
  SELECT president, speech_date
  FROM president_speeches
❶ WHERE search_speech_text @@ to_tsquery('Vietnam')
  ORDER BY speech_date;
```

Listing 13-21: Finding speeches containing the word Vietnam

In the WHERE clause, the query uses the double at sign (@@) match operator ❶ between the search_speech_text column (of data type tsvector) and the query term *Vietnam*, which to_tsquery() transforms into tsquery data. The results should list 10 speeches, showing that the first mention of Vietnam came up in a 1961 special message to Congress by John F. Kennedy and became a recurring topic starting in 1966 as America's involvement in the Vietnam War escalated.

```
president            speech_date
-----------------    ----------
John F. Kennedy      1961-05-25
Lyndon B. Johnson    1966-01-12
Lyndon B. Johnson    1967-01-10
Lyndon B. Johnson    1968-01-17
Lyndon B. Johnson    1969-01-14
Richard M. Nixon     1970-01-22
Richard M. Nixon     1972-01-20
Richard M. Nixon     1973-02-02
Gerald R. Ford       1975-01-15
Gerald R. Ford       1977-01-12
```

Before we try more searches, let's add a method for showing the location of our search term in the text.

Showing Search Result Locations

To see where our search terms appear in text, we can use the ts_headline() function. It displays one or more highlighted search terms surrounded by adjacent words. Options for this function give you flexibility in how to format the display. Listing 13-22 highlights how to display a search for a specific instance of *Vietnam* using ts_headline():

```
SELECT president,
       speech_date,
❶ ts_headline(speech_text, to_tsquery('Vietnam'),
❷         'StartSel = <,
           StopSel = >,
           MinWords=5,
           MaxWords=7,
           MaxFragments=1')
FROM president_speeches
WHERE search_speech_text @@ to_tsquery('Vietnam');
```

Listing 13-22: Displaying search results with ts_headline()

To declare ts_headline() ❶, we pass the original speech_text column rather than the tsvector column we used in the search and relevance functions as the first argument. Then, as the second argument, we pass a to_tsquery() function that specifies the word to highlight. We follow this with a third argument that lists optional formatting parameters ❷ separated by commas. Here, we specify the characters to identify the start and end of the highlighted word (StartSel and StopSel). We also set the minimum and maximum number of words to display (MinWords and MaxWords), plus the maximum number of fragments to show using MaxFragments. These settings are optional, and you can adjust them according to your needs.

The results of this query should show at most seven words per speech, highlighting the word *Vietnam*:

president	speech_date	ts_headline
John F. Kennedy	1961-05-25	twelve months in <Vietnam> alone--by subversives
Lyndon B. Johnson	1966-01-12	bitter conflict in <Vietnam>. Later
Lyndon B. Johnson	1967-01-10	<Vietnam>--is not a simple one. There
Lyndon B. Johnson	1968-01-17	been held in <Vietnam>--in the midst
Lyndon B. Johnson	1969-01-14	conflict in <Vietnam>, the dangers of nuclear
Richard M. Nixon	1970-01-22	<Vietnam> in a way that our generation
--snip--		

Using this technique, we can quickly see the context of the term we searched. You might also use this function to provide flexible display options for a search feature on a web application. Let's continue trying forms of searches.

Using Multiple Search Terms

As another example, we could look for speeches in which a president mentioned the word *transportation* but didn't discuss *roads*. We might want to do this to find speeches that focused on broader policy rather than a specific roads program. To do this, we use the syntax in Listing 13-23:

```
SELECT president,
       speech_date,
    ❶ ts_headline(speech_text, to_tsquery('transportation & !roads'),
                  'StartSel = <,
                   StopSel = >,
                   MinWords=5,
                   MaxWords=7,
                   MaxFragments=1')
FROM president_speeches
❷ WHERE search_speech_text @@ to_tsquery('transportation & !roads');
```

Listing 13-23: Finding speeches with the word transportation *but not* roads

Again, we use `ts_headline()` ❶ to highlight the terms our search finds. In the `to_tsquery()` function in the `WHERE` clause ❷, we pass transportation and roads, combining them with the ampersand (&) operator. We use the exclamation point (!) in front of roads to indicate that we want speeches that do not contain this word. This query should find eight speeches that fit the criteria. Here are the first four rows:

```
president           speech_date   ts_headline
------------------  -----------   -------------------------------------------------------------
Harry S. Truman     1947-01-06    such industries as <transportation>, coal, oil, steel
Harry S. Truman     1949-01-05    field of <transportation>.
John F. Kennedy     1961-01-30    Obtaining additional air <transport> mobility--and obtaining
Lyndon B. Johnson   1964-01-08    reformed our tangled <transportation> and transit policies
--snip--
```

Notice that the highlighted words in the `ts_headline` column include transportation and transport. The reason is that the `to_tsquery()` function converted transportation to the lexeme transport for the search term. This database behavior is extremely useful in helping to find relevant related words.

Searching for Adjacent Words

Finally, we'll use the distance (<->) operator, which consists of a hyphen between the less than and greater than signs, to find adjacent words. Alternatively, you can place a number between the signs to find terms that many words apart. For example, Listing 13-24 searches for any speeches that include the word *military* immediately followed by *defense*:

```
SELECT president,
       speech_date,
```

```
        ts_headline(speech_text, to_tsquery('military <-> defense'),
                    'StartSel = <,
                    StopSel = >,
                    MinWords=5,
                    MaxWords=7,
                    MaxFragments=1')
FROM president_speeches
WHERE search_speech_text @@ to_tsquery('military <-> defense');
```

Listing 13-24: Finding speeches where defense follows military

This query should find four speeches, and because to_tsquery() converts the search terms to lexemes, the words identified in the speeches should include plurals, such as *military defenses*. The following shows the four speeches that have the adjacent terms:

```
president               speech_date   ts_headline
--------------------    -----------   ----------------------------------------------------
Dwight D. Eisenhower    1956-01-05    system our <military> <defenses> are designed
Dwight D. Eisenhower    1958-01-09    direct <military> <defense> efforts, but likewise
Dwight D. Eisenhower    1959-01-09    survival--the <military> <defense> of national life
Richard M. Nixon        1972-01-20    spending. Strong <military> <defenses>
```

If you changed the query terms to military <2> defense, the database would return matches where the terms are exactly two words apart, as in the phrase "our military and defense commitments."

Ranking Query Matches by Relevance

You can also rank search results by relevance using two of PostgreSQL's full text search functions. These functions are helpful when you're trying to understand which piece of text, or speech in this case, is most relevant to your particular search terms.

One function, ts_rank(), generates a rank value (returned as a variable-precision real data type) based on how often the lexemes you're searching for appear in the text. The other function, ts_rank_cd(), considers how close the lexemes searched are to each other. Both functions can take optional arguments to take into account document length and other factors. The rank value they generate is an arbitrary decimal that's useful for sorting but doesn't have any inherent meaning. For example, a value of 0.375 generated during one query isn't directly comparable to the same value generated during a different query.

As an example, Listing 13-25 uses ts_rank() to rank speeches containing all the words *war, security, threat,* and *enemy*:

```
SELECT president,
       speech_date,
❶ ts_rank(search_speech_text,
           to_tsquery('war & security & threat & enemy')) AS score
```

```
  FROM president_speeches
❷ WHERE search_speech_text @@ to_tsquery('war & security & threat & enemy')
  ORDER BY score DESC
  LIMIT 5
```

Listing 13-25: Scoring relevance with ts_rank()

In this query, the ts_rank() function ❶ takes two arguments: the search_speech_text column and the output of a to_tsquery() function containing the search terms. The output of the function receives the alias score. In the WHERE clause ❷ we filter the results to only those speeches that contain the search terms specified. Then we order the results in score in descending order and return just five of the highest-ranking speeches. The results should be as follows:

```
president              speech_date    score
--------------------   -----------    ---------
Harry S. Truman        1946-01-21      0.257522
Lyndon B. Johnson      1968-01-17      0.186296
Dwight D. Eisenhower   1957-01-10      0.140851
Harry S. Truman        1952-01-09      0.0982469
Richard M. Nixon       1972-01-20      0.0973585
```

Harry S. Truman's 1946 State of the Union message, just four months after the end of World War II, contains the words *war, security, threat,* and *enemy* more often than the other speeches. However, it also happens to be the longest speech in the table (which you can determine by using char_length(), as you learned earlier in the chapter). The length of the speeches influences these rankings because ts_rank() factors in the number of matching terms in a given text. Lyndon B. Johnson's 1968 State of the Union address, delivered at the height of the Vietnam War, comes in second.

It would be ideal to compare frequencies between speeches of identical lengths to get a more accurate ranking, but this isn't always possible. However, we can factor in the length of each speech by adding a normalization code as a third parameter of the ts_rank() function, as shown in Listing 13-26:

```
SELECT president,
       speech_date,
       ts_rank(search_speech_text,
               to_tsquery('war & security & threat & enemy'), 2❶)::numeric
               AS score
FROM president_speeches
WHERE search_speech_text @@ to_tsquery('war & security & threat & enemy')
ORDER BY score DESC
LIMIT 5;
```

Listing 13-26: Normalizing ts_rank() by speech length

Adding the optional code 2 ❶ instructs the function to divide the score by the length of the data in the search_speech_text column. This quotient then represents a score normalized by the document length, giving an apples-to-apples comparison among the speeches. The PostgreSQL documentation at *https://www.postgresql.org/docs/current/static/textsearch-controls.html* lists all the options available for text search, including using the document length and dividing by the number of unique words.

After running the code in Listing 13-26, the rankings should change:

```
president              speech_date   score
--------------------   -----------   -----------
Lyndon B. Johnson      1968-01-17    0.0000728288
Dwight D. Eisenhower   1957-01-10    0.0000633609
Richard M. Nixon       1972-01-20    0.0000497998
Harry S. Truman        1952-01-09    0.0000365366
Dwight D. Eisenhower   1958-01-09    0.0000355315
```

In contrast to the ranking results in Listing 13-25, Johnson's 1968 speech now tops the rankings, and Truman's 1946 message falls out of the top five. This might be a more meaningful ranking than the first sample output, because we normalized it by length. But four of the five top-ranked speeches are the same between the two sets, and you can be reasonably certain that each of these four is worthy of closer examination to understand more about wartime presidential speeches.

Wrapping Up

Far from being boring, text offers abundant opportunities for data analysis. In this chapter, you've learned valuable techniques for turning ordinary text into data you can extract, quantify, search, and rank. In your work or studies, keep an eye out for routine reports that have facts buried inside chunks of text. You can use regular expressions to dig them out, turn them into structured data, and analyze them to find trends. You can also use search functions to analyze the text.

In the next chapter, you'll learn how PostgreSQL can help you analyze geographic information.

TRY IT YOURSELF

Use your new text-wrangling skills to tackle these tasks:

1. The style guide of a publishing company you're writing for wants you to avoid commas before suffixes in names. But there are several names like Alvarez, Jr. and Williams, Sr. in your database. Which functions can you use to remove the comma? Would a regular expression function help? How would you capture just the suffixes to place them into a separate column?

(continued)

---

2. Using any one of the State of the Union addresses, count the number of unique words that are five characters or more. (Hint: You can use regexp_split_to_table() in a subquery to create a table of words to count.) Bonus: Remove commas and periods at the end of each word.

3. Rewrite the query in Listing 13-25 using the ts_rank_cd() function instead of ts_rank(). According to the PostgreSQL documentation, ts_rank_cd() computes cover density, which takes into account how close the lexeme search terms are to each other. Does using the ts_rank_cd() function significantly change the results?

14

ANALYZING SPATIAL DATA WITH POSTGIS

These days, mobile apps can provide a list of coffee shops near you within seconds. They can do that because they're powered by a *geographic information system (GIS)*, which is any system that allows for storing, editing, analyzing, and displaying spatial data. As you can imagine, GIS has many practical applications today, from helping city planners decide where to build schools based on population patterns to finding the best detour around a traffic jam.

Spatial data refers to information about the location and shape of objects, which can be two and three dimensional. For example, the spatial data we'll use in this chapter contains coordinates describing geometric shapes, such as points, lines, and polygons. These shapes in turn represent features you would find on a map, such as roads, lakes, or countries.

Conveniently, you can use PostgreSQL to store and analyze spatial data, which allows you to calculate the distance between points, compute the size of areas, and identify whether two objects intersect. However, to enable spatial analysis and store spatial data types in PostgreSQL, you need to install an open source extension called PostGIS. The PostGIS extension also provides additional functions and operators that work specifically with spatial data.

In this chapter, you'll learn to use PostGIS to analyze roadways in Santa Fe, New Mexico as well as the location of farmers' markets across the United States. You'll learn how to construct and query spatial data types and how to work with different geographic data formats you might encounter when you obtain data from public and private data sources. You'll also learn about map projections and grid systems. The goal is to give you tools to glean information from spatial data, similar to how you've analyzed numbers and text.

We'll begin by setting up PostGIS so we can explore different types of spatial data. All code and data for the exercises are available with the book's resources at *https://www.nostarch.com/practicalSQL/*.

Installing PostGIS and Creating a Spatial Database

PostGIS is a free, open source project created by the Canadian geospatial company Refractions Research and maintained by an international team of developers under the Open Source Geospatial Foundation. You'll find documentation and updates at *http://postgis.net/*. If you're using Windows or macOS and have installed PostgreSQL following the steps in the book's Introduction, PostGIS should be on your machine. It's also often installed on PostgreSQL on cloud providers, such as Amazon Web Services. But if you're using Linux or if you installed PostgreSQL some other way on Windows or macOS, follow the installation instructions at *http://postgis.net/install/*.

Let's create a database and enable PostGIS. The process is similar to the one you used to create your first database in Chapter 1 but with a few extra steps. Follow these steps in pgAdmin to make a database called gis_analysis:

1. In the pgAdmin object browser (left pane), connect to your server and expand the **Databases** node by clicking the plus sign.
2. Click once on the analysis database you've used for past exercises.
3. Choose **Tools ▸ Query Tool**.
4. In the Query Tool, run the code in Listing 14-1.

```
CREATE DATABASE gis_analysis;
```

Listing 14-1: Creating a gis_analysis database

PostgreSQL will create the gis_analysis database, which is no different than others you've made. To enable PostGIS extensions on it, follow these steps:

1. Close the Query Tool tab.
2. In the object browser, right-click **Databases** and select **Refresh**.
3. Click the new gis_analysis database in the list to highlight it.

4. Open a new Query Tool tab by selecting **Tools ▸ Query Tool**. The gis_analysis database should be listed at the top of the editing pane.

5. In the Query Tool, run the code in Listing 14-2.

```
CREATE EXTENSION postgis;
```

Listing 14-2: Loading the PostGIS extension

You'll see the message CREATE EXTENSION. Your database has now been updated to include spatial data types and dozens of spatial analysis functions. Run **SELECT postgis_full_version();** to display the version number of PostGIS along with its installed components. The version won't match the PostgreSQL version installed, but that's okay.

The Building Blocks of Spatial Data

Before you learn to query spatial data, let's look at how it's described in GIS and related data formats (although if you want to dive straight into queries, you can skip to "Analyzing Farmers' Markets Data" on page 250 and return here later).

A point on a grid is the smallest building block of spatial data. The grid might be marked with x- and y-axes, or longitude and latitude if we're using a map. A grid could be flat, with two dimensions, or it could describe a three-dimensional space such as a cube. In some data formats, such as the JavaScript-based *GeoJSON*, a point might have a location on the grid as well as attributes providing additional information. For example, a grocery store could be described by a point containing its longitude and latitude as well as attributes showing the store's name and hours of operation.

Two-Dimensional Geometries

To create more complex spatial data, you connect multiple points using lines. The International Organization for Standardization (ISO) and the Open Geospatial Consortium (OGC) have created a *simple feature* standard for building and accessing two- and three-dimensional shapes, sometimes referred to as *geometries*. PostGIS supports the standard.

The most commonly used simple features you'll encounter when querying or creating spatial data with PostGIS include the following:

Point   A single location in a two- or three-dimensional plane. On maps, a Point is usually represented by a dot marking a longitude and latitude.

LineString   Two or more points connected by a straight line. With LineStrings, you can represent features such as a road, hiking trail, or stream.

Polygon   A two-dimensional shape, like a triangle or a square, that has three or more straight sides, each constructed from a LineString. In geographic analysis, Polygons represent objects such as nations, states, buildings, and bodies of water. A Polygon also can have one or more interior Polygons that act as holes inside the larger Polygon.

MultiPoint   A set of Points. For example, you can represent multiple locations of a retailer with a single MultiPoint object that contains each store's latitude and longitude.

MultiLineString   A set of LineStrings. You can represent, for example, an object such as a road with several noncontinuous segments.

MultiPolygon   A set of Polygons. For example, you can represent a parcel of land that is divided into two parts by a road: you can group them in one MultiPolygon object rather than using separate polygons.

Figure 14-1 shows an example of each feature.

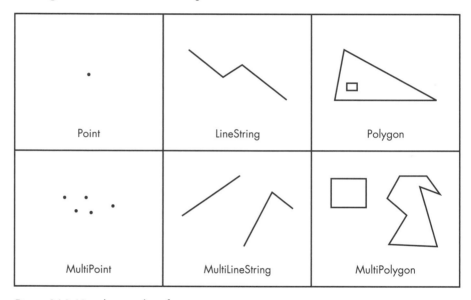

Figure 14-1: Visual examples of geometries

Using PostGIS functions, you can create your own spatial data by constructing these objects using points or other geometries. Or, you can use PostGIS functions to perform calculations on existing spatial data. Generally, to create a spatial object, the functions require input of a *well-known text (WKT)* string, which is text that represents a geometry, plus an optional *Spatial Reference System Identifier (SRID)* that specifies the grid on which to place the objects. I'll explain the SRID shortly, but first, let's look at examples of WKT strings and then build some geometries using them.

Well-Known Text Formats

The OGC standard's WKT format includes the geometry type and its coordinates inside one or more sets of parentheses. The number of coordinates and parentheses varies depending on the geometry you want to create. Table 14-1 shows examples of the more frequently used geometry types and their WKT formats. Here, I show longitude/latitude pairs for the coordinates, but you might encounter grid systems that use other measures.

NOTE   *WKT accepts coordinates in the order of longitude, latitude, which is backward from Google Maps and some other software. Tom MacWright, formerly of the Mapbox software company, notes at* https://macwright.org/lonlat/ *that neither order is "right" and catalogs the "frustrating inconsistency" in which mapping-related code handles the order of coordinates.*

Table 14-1: Well-Known Text Formats for Geometries

Geometry	Format	Notes
Point	POINT (-74.9 42.7)	A coordinate pair marking a point at –74.9 longitude and 42.7 latitude.
LineString	LINESTRING (-74.9 42.7, -75.1 42.7)	A straight line with endpoints marked by two coordinate pairs.
Polygon	POLYGON ((-74.9 42.7, -75.1 42.7, -75.1 42.6, -74.9 42.7))	A triangle outlined by three different pairs of coordinates. Although listed twice, the first and last pair are the same coordinates, closing the shape.
MultiPoint	MULTIPOINT (-74.9 42.7, -75.1 42.7)	Two Points, one for each pair of coordinates.
MultiLineString	MULTILINESTRING ((-76.27 43.1, -76.06 43.08), (-76.2 43.3, -76.2 43.4, -76.4 43.1))	Two LineStrings. The first has two points; the second has three.
MultiPolygon	MULTIPOLYGON (((-74.92 42.7, -75.06 42.71, -75.07 42.64, -74.92 42.7), (-75.0 42.66, -75.0 42.64, -74.98 42.64, -74.98 42.66, -75.0 42.66)))	Two Polygons. The first is a triangle, and the second is a rectangle.

Although these examples create simple shapes, in practice, complex geometries could comprise thousands of coordinates.

A Note on Coordinate Systems

Representing the Earth's spherical surface on a two-dimensional map is not easy. Imagine peeling the outer layer of the Earth from the globe and trying to spread it on a table while keeping all pieces of the continents and oceans connected. Inevitably, some areas of the map would stretch. This is what occurs when cartographers create a map *projection* with its own *projected coordinate system* that flattens the Earth's round surface to a two-dimensional plane.

Some projections represent the entire world; others are specific to regions or purposes. For example, the *Mercator projection* is commonly used for navigation in apps, such as Google Maps. The math behind its transformation distorts land areas close to the North and South Poles, making them appear much larger than reality. The *Albers projection* is the one you would most likely see displayed on TV screens in the United States as votes are tallied on election night. It's also used by the U.S. Census Bureau.

Projections are derived from *geographic coordinate systems*, which define the grid of latitude, longitude, and height of any point on the globe along with factors including the Earth's shape. Whenever you obtain geographic data, it's critical to know the coordinate systems it references to check whether your calculations are accurate. Often, the coordinate system or projection is named in user documentation.

Spatial Reference System Identifier

When using PostGIS (and many GIS applications), you need to specify the coordinate system you're using via its SRID. When you enabled the PostGIS extension at the beginning of this chapter, the process created the table spatial_ref_sys, which contains SRIDs as its primary key. The table also contains the column srtext, which includes a WKT representation of the spatial reference system as well as other metadata.

In this chapter, we'll frequently use SRID 4326, the ID for the geographic coordinate system WGS 84. It's the most recent World Geodetic System (WGS) standard used by GPS, and you'll encounter it often if you acquire spatial data. You can see the WKT representation for WGS 84 by running the code in Listing 14-3 that looks for its SRID, 4326:

```
SELECT srtext
FROM spatial_ref_sys
WHERE srid = 4326;
```

Listing 14-3: Retrieving the WKT for SRID 4326

Run the query and you should get the following result, which I've indented for readability:

```
GEOGCS["WGS 84",
    DATUM["WGS_1984",
        SPHEROID["WGS 84",6378137,298.257223563,
            AUTHORITY["EPSG","7030"]],
        AUTHORITY["EPSG","6326"]],
    PRIMEM["Greenwich",0,
        AUTHORITY["EPSG","8901"]],
    UNIT["degree",0.0174532925199433,
        AUTHORITY["EPSG","9122"]],
    AUTHORITY["EPSG","4326"]]
```

You don't need to use this information for any of this chapter's exercises, but it's helpful to know some of the variables and how they define the projection. The GEOGCS keyword provides the geographic coordinate system in use. Keyword PRIMEM specifies the location of the *Prime Meridian,* or longitude 0. To see definitions of all the variables, check the reference at *http://docs.geotools.org/stable/javadocs/org/opengis/referencing/doc-files/WKT.html.*

Conversely, if you ever need to find the SRID associated with a coordinate system, you can query the srtext column in spatial_ref_sys to find it.

PostGIS Data Types

Installing PostGIS adds five data types to your database. The two data types we'll use in the exercises are geography and geometry. Both types can store spatial data, such as the points, lines, polygons, SRIDs, and so on you just learned about, but they have important distinctions:

geography A data type based on a sphere, using the round-earth coordinate system (longitude and latitude). All calculations occur on the globe, taking its curvature into account. That makes the math complicated and limits the number of functions available to work with the geography type. But because the Earth's curvature is factored in, calculations for distance are more precise; you should use the geography data type when handling data that spans large areas. Also, the results from calculations on the geography type will be expressed in meters.

geometry A data type based on a plane, using the Euclidean coordinate system. Calculations occur on straight lines as opposed to along the curvature of a sphere, making calculations for geographical distance less precise than with the geography data type; the results of calculations are expressed in units of whichever coordinate system you've designated.

The PostGIS documentation at *https://postgis.net/docs/using_postgis _dbmanagement.html* offers guidance on when to use one or the other type. In short, if you're working strictly with longitude/latitude data or if your data covers a large area, such as a continent or the globe, use the geography type, even though it limits the functions you can use. If your data covers a smaller area, the geometry type provides more functions and better performance. You can also change one type to the other using CAST.

With the background you have now, we can start working with spatial objects.

Creating Spatial Objects with PostGIS Functions

PostGIS has more than three dozen constructor functions that build spatial objects using WKT or coordinates. You can find a list at *https://postgis.net/ docs/reference.html#Geometry_Constructors*, but the following sections explain several that you'll use in the exercises. Most PostGIS functions begin with the letters ST, which is an ISO naming standard that means *spatial type*.

Creating a Geometry Type from Well-Known Text

The ST_GeomFromText(*WKT*, *SRID*) function creates a geometry data type from an input of a WKT string and an optional SRID. Listing 14-4 shows simple SELECT statements that generate geometry data types for each of the simple features described in Table 14-1. Running these SELECT statements is optional, but it's important to know how to construct each simple feature.

```
SELECT ST_GeomFromText(❶'POINT(-74.9233606 42.699992)', ❷4326);

SELECT ST_GeomFromText('LINESTRING(-74.9 42.7, -75.1 42.7)', 4326);

SELECT ST_GeomFromText('POLYGON((-74.9 42.7, -75.1 42.7,
                                 -75.1 42.6, -74.9 42.7))', 4326);

SELECT ST_GeomFromText('MULTIPOINT (-74.9 42.7, -75.1 42.7)', 4326);

SELECT ST_GeomFromText('MULTILINESTRING((-76.27 43.1, -76.06 43.08),
                                        (-76.2 43.3, -76.2 43.4,
                                         -76.4 43.1))', 4326);

SELECT ST_GeomFromText('MULTIPOLYGON❸((
                                (-74.92 42.7, -75.06 42.71,
                                 -75.07 42.64, -74.92 42.7)❹,
                                (-75.0 42.66, -75.0 42.64,
                                 -74.98 42.64, -74.98 42.66,
                                 -75.0 42.66)))', 4326);
```

Listing 14-4: Using ST_GeomFromText() to create spatial objects

For each example, we give coordinates as the first input and the SRID 4326 as the second. In the first example, we create a point by inserting the WKT POINT string ❶ as the first argument to ST_GeomFromText() with the SRID ❷ as the optional second argument. We use the same format in the rest of the examples. Note that we don't have to indent the coordinates. I only do so here to make the coordinate pairs more readable.

Be sure to keep track of the number of parentheses that segregate objects, particularly in complex structures, such as the MultiPolygon. For example, we need to use two opening parentheses ❸ and enclose each polygon's coordinates within another set of parentheses ❹.

Executing each statement should return the geometry data type encoded in a string of characters that looks something like this truncated example:

```
0101000020E61000008EDA0E5718BB52C017BB7D5699594540 ...
```

This result shows how the data is stored in a table. Typically, you won't be reading that string of code. Instead, you'll use geometry (or geography) columns as inputs to functions.

Creating a Geography Type from Well-Known Text

To create a geography data type, you can use ST_GeogFromText(*WKT*) to convert a WKT or ST_GeogFromText(*EWKT*) to convert a PostGIS-specific variation called *extended WKT* that includes the SRID. Listing 14-5 shows how to pass in the SRID as part of the extended WKT string to create a MultiPoint geography object with three points:

```
SELECT
ST_GeogFromText('SRID=4326;MULTIPOINT(-74.9 42.7, -75.1 42.7, -74.924 42.6)')
```

Listing 14-5: Using ST_GeogFromText() to create spatial objects

Along with the all-purpose `ST_GeomFromText()` and `ST_GeogFromText()` functions, PostGIS includes several that are specific to creating certain spatial objects. I'll cover those briefly next.

Point Functions

The `ST_PointFromText()` and `ST_MakePoint()` functions will turn a WKT `POINT` into a geometry data type. Points mark coordinates, such as longitude and latitude, which you would use to identify locations or use as building blocks of other objects, such as LineStrings.

Listing 14-6 shows how these functions work:

```
SELECT ❶ST_PointFromText('POINT(-74.9233606 42.699992)', 4326);

SELECT ❷ST_MakePoint(-74.9233606, 42.699992);
SELECT ❸ST_SetSRID(ST_MakePoint(-74.9233606, 42.699992), 4326);
```

Listing 14-6: Functions specific to making Points

The `ST_PointFromText(WKT, SRID)` ❶ function creates a point geometry type from a WKT `POINT` and an optional SRID as the second input. The PostGIS docs note that the function includes validation of coordinates that makes it slower than the `ST_GeomFromText()` function.

The `ST_MakePoint(x, y, z, m)` ❷ function creates a point geometry type on a two-, three-, and four-dimensional grid. The first two parameters, *x* and *y* in the example, represent longitude and latitude coordinates. You can use the optional *z* to represent altitude and *m* to represent a fourth-dimensional measure, such as time. That would allow you to mark a location at a certain time, for example. The `ST_MakePoint()` function is faster than `ST_GeomFromText()` and `ST_PointFromText()`, but if you want to specify an SRID, you'll need to designate one by wrapping it inside the `ST_SetSRID()` ❸ function.

LineString Functions

Now let's examine some functions we use specifically for creating LineString geometry data types. Listing 14-7 shows how they work:

```
SELECT ❶ST_LineFromText('LINESTRING(-105.90 35.67,-105.91 35.67)', 4326);
SELECT ❷ST_MakeLine(ST_MakePoint(-74.9, 42.7), ST_MakePoint(-74.1, 42.4));
```

Listing 14-7: Functions specific to making LineStrings

The ST_LineFromText(*WKT, SRID*) ❶ function creates a LineString from a WKT LINESTRING and an optional SRID as its second input. Like ST_PointFromText() earlier, this function includes validation of coordinates that makes it slower than ST_GeomFromText().

The ST_MakeLine(*geom, geom*) ❷ function creates a LineString from inputs that must be of the geometry data type. In Listing 14-7, the example uses two ST_MakePoint() functions as inputs to create the start and endpoint of the line. You can also pass in an ARRAY object with multiple points, perhaps generated by a subquery, to generate a more complex line.

Polygon Functions

Let's look at three Polygon functions: ST_PolygonFromText(), ST_MakePolygon(), and ST_MPolyFromText(). All create geometry data types. Listing 14-8 shows how you can create Polygons with each:

```
SELECT ❶ST_PolygonFromText('POLYGON((-74.9 42.7, -75.1 42.7,
                                      -75.1 42.6, -74.9 42.7))', 4326);

SELECT ❷ST_MakePolygon(
            ST_GeomFromText('LINESTRING(-74.92 42.7, -75.06 42.71,
                                        -75.07 42.64, -74.92 42.7)', 4326));

SELECT ❸ST_MPolyFromText('MULTIPOLYGON((
                              (-74.92 42.7, -75.06 42.71,
                               -75.07 42.64, -74.92 42.7),
                              (-75.0 42.66, -75.0 42.64,
                               -74.98 42.64, -74.98 42.66,
                               -75.0 42.66)
                          ))', 4326);
```

Listing 14-8: Functions specific to making Polygons

The ST_PolygonFromText(*WKT, SRID*) ❶ function creates a Polygon from a WKT POLYGON and an optional SRID. As with the similarly named functions for creating points and lines, it includes a validation step that makes it slower than ST_GeomFromText().

The ST_MakePolygon(*linestring*) ❷ function creates a Polygon from a LineString that must open and close with the same coordinates, ensuring the object is closed. This example uses ST_GeomFromText() to create the LineString geometry using a WKT LINESTRING.

The ST_MPolyFromText(*WKT, SRID*) ❸ function creates a MultiPolygon from a WKT and an optional SRID.

Now you have the building blocks to analyze spatial data. Next, we'll use them to explore a set of data.

Analyzing Farmers' Markets Data

The National Farmers' Market Directory from the U.S. Department of Agriculture catalogs the location and offerings of more than

8,600 "markets that feature two or more farm vendors selling agricultural products directly to customers at a common, recurrent physical location," according to *https://www.ams.usda.gov/local-food-directories/farmersmarkets/*. Attending these markets makes for an enjoyable weekend activity, so it would help to find those within a reasonable traveling distance. We can use SQL spatial queries to find the closest markets.

The *farmers_markets.csv* file contains a portion of the USDA data on each market, and it's available along with the book's resources at *https://www.nostarch.com/practicalSQL/*. Save the file to your computer and run the code in Listing 14-9 to create and load a farmers_markets table. Make sure you're connected to the gis_analysis database you made earlier in this chapter, and change the COPY statement file path to match your file's location.

```
CREATE TABLE farmers_markets (
    fmid bigint PRIMARY KEY,
    market_name varchar(100) NOT NULL,
    street varchar(180),
    city varchar(60),
    county varchar(25),
    st varchar(20) NOT NULL,
    zip varchar(10),
    longitude numeric(10,7),
    latitude numeric(10,7),
    organic varchar(1) NOT NULL
);

COPY farmers_markets
FROM 'C:\YourDirectory\farmers_markets.csv'
WITH (FORMAT CSV, HEADER);
```

Listing 14-9: Creating and loading the farmers_markets table

The table contains routine address data plus the longitude and latitude for most markets. Twenty-nine of the markets were missing those values when I downloaded the file from the USDA. An organic column indicates whether the market offers organic products; a hyphen (-) in that column indicates an unknown value. After you import the data, count the rows using SELECT count(*) FROM farmers_markets;. If everything imported correctly, you should have 8,681 rows.

Creating and Filling a Geography Column

To perform spatial queries on the markets' longitude and latitude, we need to convert those coordinates into a single column of a spatial data type. Because we're working with locations spanning the entire United States and an accurate measurement of a large spherical distance is important, we'll use the geography type. After creating the column, we can update it using Points derived from the coordinates, and then apply an index to speed up queries. Listing 14-10 contains the statements for doing these tasks:

```
❶ ALTER TABLE farmers_markets ADD COLUMN geog_point geography(POINT,4326);

UPDATE farmers_markets
SET geog_point =
    ❷ST_SetSRID(
            ❸ST_MakePoint(longitude,latitude),4326
            )❹::geography;

❺ CREATE INDEX market_pts_idx ON farmers_markets USING GIST (geog_point);

SELECT longitude,
       latitude,
       geog_point,
     ❻ ST_AsText(geog_point)
FROM farmers_markets
WHERE longitude IS NOT NULL
LIMIT 5;
```

Listing 14-10: Creating and indexing a geography column

The ALTER TABLE statement ❶ you learned in Chapter 9 with the ADD COLUMN option creates a column of the geography type called geog_point that will hold points and reference the WSG 84 coordinate system, which we denote using SRID 4326.

Next, we run a standard UPDATE statement to fill the geog_point column. Nested inside a ST_SetSRID() ❷ function, the ST_MakePoint() ❸ function takes as input the longitude and latitude columns from the table. The output, which is the geometry type by default, must be cast to geography to match the geog_point column type. To do this, we use the PostgreSQL-specific double-colon syntax (::) ❹ for casting data types.

Adding a GiST Index

Before you start analysis, it's wise to add an index to the new column to speed up calculations. In Chapter 7, you learned about PostgreSQL's default index, the B-Tree. A B-Tree index is useful for data that you can order and search using equality and range operators, but it's less useful for spatial objects. The reason is that you cannot easily sort GIS data along one axis. For example, the application has no way to determine which of these coordinate pairs is greatest: (0,0), (0,1), or (1,0).

Instead, for spatial data, the makers of PostGIS recommend using the Generalized Search Tree (GiST) index. PostgreSQL core team member Bruce Momjian describes GiST as "a general indexing framework designed to allow indexing of complex data types," including geometries.

The CREATE INDEX statement ❺ in Listing 14-10 adds a GiST index to geog_point. We can then use the SELECT statement to view the geography data to show the newly encoded geog_points column. To view the WKT version of geog_point, we wrap it in a ST_AsText() function ❻. The results should look similar to this, with geog_point truncated for brevity:

longitude	latitude	geog_point	st_astext
-121.9982460	37.5253970	010100002 ...	POINT(-121.998246 37.525397)
-100.5288290	39.8204690	010100002 ...	POINT(-100.528829 39.820469)
-92.6256000	44.8560000	010100002 ...	POINT(-92.6256 44.856)
-104.8997430	39.7580430	010100002 ...	POINT(-104.899743 39.758043)
-101.9175330	33.5480160	010100002 ...	POINT(-101.917533 33.548016)

Now we're ready to perform calculations on the points.

Finding Geographies Within a Given Distance

While in Iowa in 2014 to report a story on farming, I visited the massive Downtown Farmers' Market in Des Moines. With hundreds of vendors, the market spans several city blocks in the Iowa capital. Farming is big business in Iowa, and even though the downtown market is huge, it's not the only one in the area. Let's use PostGIS to find more farmers' markets within a short distance from the downtown Des Moines market.

The PostGIS function ST_DWithin() returns a Boolean value of true if one spatial object is within a specified distance of another object. If you're working with the geography data type, as we are here, you need to use meters as the distance unit. If you're using the geometry type, use the distance unit specified by the SRID.

NOTE *PostGIS distance measurements are on a straight line for geometry data, whereas for geography data, they're on a sphere. Be careful not to confuse either with driving distance along roadways, which is usually farther from point to point. To perform calculations related to driving distances, check out the extension pgRouting at http:// pgrouting.org/.*

Listing 14-11 uses the ST_DWithin() function to filter farmers_markets to show markets within 10 kilometers of the Downtown Farmers' Market in Des Moines:

```
SELECT market_name,
       city,
       st
FROM farmers_markets
WHERE ST_DWithin(❶geog_point,
                 ❷ST_GeogFromText('POINT(-93.6204386 41.5853202)'),
                 ❸10000)
ORDER BY market_name;
```

Listing 14-11: Using ST_DWithin() to locate farmers' markets within 10 kilometers of a point

The first input for ST_DWithin() is geog_point ❶, which holds the location of each row's market in the geography data type. The second input is the

ST_GeogFromText() function ❷ that returns a point geography from WKT. The coordinates -93.6204386 and 41.5853202 represent the longitude and latitude of the Downtown Farmers' Market in Des Moines. The final input is 10000 ❸, which is the number of meters in 10 kilometers. The database calculates the distance between each market in the table and the downtown market. If a market is within 10 kilometers, it is included in the results.

We're using points here, but this function works with any geography or geometry type. If you're working with objects such as polygons, you can use the related ST_DFullyWithin() function to find objects that are completely within a specified distance.

Run the query; it should return nine rows:

market_name	city	st
Beaverdale Farmers Market	Des Moines	Iowa
Capitol Hill Farmers Market	Des Moines	Iowa
Downtown Farmers' Market - Des Moines	Des Moines	Iowa
Drake Neighborhood Farmers Market	Des Moines	Iowa
Eastside Farmers Market	Des Moines	Iowa
Highland Park Farmers Market	Des Moines	Iowa
Historic Valley Junction Farmers Market	West Des Moines	Iowa
LSI Global Greens Farmers' Market	Des Moines	Iowa
Valley Junction Farmers Market	West Des Moines	Iowa

One of these nine markets is the Downtown Farmers' Market in Des Moines, which makes sense because its location is at the point used for comparison. The rest are other markets in Des Moines or in nearby West Des Moines. This operation should be familiar because it's a standard feature on many online maps and product apps that let you locate stores or points of interest near you.

Although this list of nearby markets is helpful, it would be even more helpful to know the exact distance of markets from downtown. We'll use another function to report that.

Finding the Distance Between Geographies

The ST_Distance() function returns the minimum distance between two spatial objects. It also returns meters for geographies and SRID units for geometries. For example, Listing 14-12 calculates the distance in miles from Yankee Stadium in New York City's Bronx borough to Citi Field in Queens, home of the New York Mets:

```
SELECT ST_Distance(
            ST_GeogFromText('POINT(-73.9283685 40.8296466)'),
            ST_GeogFromText('POINT(-73.8480153 40.7570917)')
            ) / 1609.344 AS mets_to_yanks;
```

Listing 14-12: Using ST_Distance() to calculate the miles between Yankee Stadium and Citi Field (Mets)

In this example, to see the result in miles, we divide the result of the ST_Distance() function by 1609.344 (the number of meters in a mile) to convert the unit of distance from meters to miles. The result is about 6.5 miles:

```
mets_to_yanks
---------------
6.54386182787521
```

Let's apply this technique for finding distance between points to the farmers' market data using the code in Listing 14-13. We'll display all farmers' markets within 10 kilometers of the Downtown Farmers' Market in Des Moines and show the distance in miles:

```
SELECT market_name,
       city,
     ❶round(
         (ST_Distance(geog_point,
                     ST_GeogFromText('POINT(-93.6204386 41.5853202)')
                 ) / 1609.344)❷::numeric(8,5), 2
         ) AS miles_from_dt
FROM farmers_markets
❸ WHERE ST_DWithin(geog_point,
                 ST_GeogFromText('POINT(-93.6204386 41.5853202)'),
                 10000)
ORDER BY miles_from_dt ASC;
```

Listing 14-13: Using ST_Distance() for each row in farmers_markets

The query is similar to Listing 14-11, which used ST_DWithin() to find markets 10 kilometers or closer to downtown, but adds the ST_Distance() function as a column to calculate and display the distance from downtown. I've wrapped the function inside round() ❶ to trim the output.

We provide ST_Distance() with the same two inputs we gave ST_DWithin() in Listing 14-11: geog_point and the ST_GeogFromText() function. The ST_Distance() function then calculates the distance between the points specified by both inputs, returning the result in meters. To convert to miles, we divide by 1609.344 ❷, which is the approximate number of meters in a mile. Then, to provide the round() function with the correct input data type, we cast the column result to type numeric.

The WHERE clause ❸ uses the same ST_DWithin() function and inputs as in Listing 14-11. You should see the following results, ordered by distance in ascending order:

market_name	city	miles_from_dt
Downtown Farmers' Market - Des Moines	Des Moines	0.00
Capitol Hill Farmers Market	Des Moines	1.15
Drake Neighborhood Farmers Market	Des Moines	1.70
LSI Global Greens Farmers' Market	Des Moines	2.30
Highland Park Farmers Market	Des Moines	2.93

Eastside Farmers Market	Des Moines	3.40
Beaverdale Farmers Market	Des Moines	3.74
Historic Valley Junction Farmers Market	West Des Moines	4.68
Valley Junction Farmers Market	West Des Moines	4.70

Again, this is the type of list you see every day on your phone or computer when you're searching online for a nearby store or address. You might also find it helpful for many other analysis scenarios, such as finding all the schools within a certain distance of a known source of pollution or all the houses within five miles of an airport.

NOTE *Another type of distance measurement supported by PostGIS,* K-Nearest Neighbor, *provides the ability to quickly find the closest point or shape to one you specify. For a lengthy overview of how it works, see* http://workshops.boundlessgeo.com/postgis-intro/knn.html.

So far, you've learned how to build spatial objects from WKT. Next, I'll show you a common data format used in GIS called the *shapefile* and how to bring it into PostGIS for analysis.

Working with Census Shapefiles

A *shapefile* is a GIS data format developed by Esri, a U.S. company known for its ArcGIS mapping visualization and analysis platform. In addition to serving as the standard file format for GIS platforms—such as ArcGIS and the open source QGIS—governments, corporations, nonprofits, and technical organizations use shapefiles to display, analyze, and distribute data that includes a variety of geographic features, such as buildings, roads, and territorial boundaries.

Shapefiles contain the information describing the shape of a feature (such as a county, a road, or a lake) as well as a database containing attributes about them. Those attributes might include their name and other descriptors. A single shapefile can contain only one type of shape, such as polygons or points, and when you load a shapefile into a GIS platform that supports visualization, you can view the shapes and query their attributes. PostgreSQL, with the PostGIS extension, doesn't visualize the shapefile data, but it does allow you to run complex queries on the spatial data in the shapefile, which we'll do in "Exploring the Census 2010 Counties Shapefile" on page 259 and "Performing Spatial Joins" on page 262.

First, let's examine the structure and contents of shapefiles.

Contents of a Shapefile

A shapefile refers to a collection of files with different extensions, and each serves a different purpose. Usually, when you download a shapefile from a source, it comes in a compressed archive, such as *.zip*. You'll need to unzip it to access the individual files.

Per ArcGIS documentation, these are the most common extensions you'll encounter:

.shp   Main file that stores the feature geometry.

.shx   Index file that stores the index of the feature geometry.

.dbf   Database table (in dBASE format) that stores the attribute information of features.

.xml   XML-format file that stores metadata about the shapefile.

.prj   Projection file that stores the coordinate system information. You can open this file with a text editor to view the geographic coordinate system and projection.

According to the documentation, files with the first three extensions include necessary data required for working with a shapefile. The other file types are optional. You can load a shapefile into PostGIS to access its spatial objects and the attributes for each. Let's do that next and explore some additional analysis functions.

Loading Shapefiles via the GUI Tool

There are two ways to load shapefiles into your database. The PostGIS suite includes a Shapefile Import/Export Manager with a simple *graphical user interface (GUI)*, which users may prefer. Alternately, you can use the command line application shp2pgsql, which is described in "Loading Shapefiles with shp2pgsql" on page 311.

Let's start with a look at how to work with the GUI tool.

Windows Shapefile Importer/Exporter

On Windows, if you followed the installation steps in the book's Introduction, you should find the Shapefile Import/Export Manager by selecting **Start ▸ PostGIS Bundle *x.y* for PostgreSQL x64 *x.y* ▸ PostGIS 2.0 Shapefile and DBF Loader Exporter**.

Whatever you see in place of *x.y* should match the version of the software you downloaded. You can skip ahead to "Connecting to the Database and Loading a Shapefile" on page 258.

macOS and Linux Shapefile Importer/Exporter

On macOS, the *postgres.app* installation outlined in the book's Introduction doesn't include the GUI tool, and as of this writing the only macOS version of the tool available (from the geospatial firm Boundless) doesn't work with macOS High Sierra. I'll update the status at the book's resources at *https://www.nostarch.com/practicalSQL/* if that changes. In the meantime, follow the instructions found in "Loading Shapefiles with shp2pgsql" on page 311. Then move on to "Exploring the Census 2010 Counties Shapefile" on page 259.

For Linux users, pgShapeLoader is available as the application *shp2p-gsql-gui*. Visit *http://postgis.net/install/* and follow the instructions for your Linux distribution.

Now, you can connect to the database and load a shapefile.

Connecting to the Database and Loading a Shapefile

Let's connect the Shapefile Import/Export Manager to your database and then load a shapefile. I've included several shapefiles with the resources for this chapter at *https://www.nostarch.com/practicalSQL/*. We'll start with TIGER/Line Shapefiles from the U.S. Census that contain the boundaries for each county or county equivalent, such as parish or borough, as of the 2010 Decennial Census. You can learn more about this series of shapefiles at *https://www.census.gov/geo/maps-data/data/tiger-line.html*.

NOTE *Many organizations provide data in shapefile format. Start with your national or local government agencies or check the Wikipedia entry "List of GIS data sources."*

Save *tl_2010_us_county10.zip* to your computer and unzip it; the archive should contain five files with the extensions I listed earlier on page 257. Then open the Shapefile and DBF Loader Exporter app.

First, you need to establish a connection between the app and your gis_analysis database. To do that, follow these steps:

1. Click **View connection details**.

2. In the dialog that opens, enter postgres for the **Username**, and enter a password if you added one for the server during initial setup.

3. Ensure that **Server Host** has localhost and 5432 by default. Leave those as is unless you're on a different server or port.

4. Enter gis_analysis for the **Database** name. Figure 14-2 shows a screenshot of what the connection should look like.

Figure 14-2: Establishing the PostGIS connection in the shapefile loader

5. Click **OK**. You should see the message Connection Succeeded in the log window.

Now that you've successfully established the PostGIS connection, you can load your shapefile:

1. Under **Options**, change **DBF file character encoding** to Latin1—we do this because the shapefile attributes include county names with characters that require this encoding. Keep the default checked boxes, including the one to create an index on the spatial column. Click **OK**.

2. Click **Add File** and select *tl_2010_us_county10.shp* from the location you saved it. Click **Open**. The file should appear in the Shapefile list in the loader, as shown in Figure 14-3.

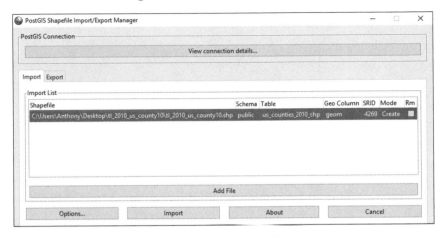

Figure 14-3: Specifying upload details in the shapefile loader

3. In the **Table** column, double-click to select the table name. Replace it with us_counties_2010_shp.

4. In the **SRID** column, double-click and enter **4269**. That's the ID for the North American Datum 1983 coordinate system, which is often used by U.S. federal agencies including the Census Bureau.

5. Click **Import**.

In the log window, you should see a message that ends with the following message:

```
Shapefile type: Polygon
PostGIS type: MULTIPOLYGON[2]
Shapefile import completed.
```

Switch to pgAdmin, and in the object browser, expand the gis_analysis node and continue expanding by selecting **Schemas ▶ public ▶ Tables**. Refresh your tables by right-clicking **Tables** and selecting **Refresh** from the pop-up menu. You should see us_counties_2010_shp listed. Congrats! You've loaded your shapefile into a table. As part of the import, the shapefile loader also indexed the geom column.

Exploring the Census 2010 Counties Shapefile

The us_counties_2010_shp table contains columns including each county's name as well as the *Federal Information Processing Standards (FIPS)* codes uniquely assigned to each state and county. The geom column contains the spatial data on each county's boundary. To start, let's check what kind of spatial object geom contains using the ST_AsText() function. Use the code in Listing 14-14 to show the WKT representation of the first geom value in the table.

```
SELECT ST_AsText(geom)
FROM us_counties_2010_shp
LIMIT 1;
```

Listing 14-14: Checking the geom column's WKT representation

The result is a MultiPolygon with hundreds of coordinate pairs that outline the boundary of the county. Here's a portion of the output:

```
MULTIPOLYGON(((-162.637688 54.801121,-162.641178 54.795317,-162.644046
54.789099,-162.653751 54.780339,-162.666629 54.770215,-162.677799 54.762716,-
162.692356 54.758771,-162.70676 54.754987,-162.722965 54.753155,-162.740178
54.753102,-162.76206 54.757968,-162.783454 54.765285,-162.797004 54.772181,-
162.802591 54.775817,-162.807411 54.779871,-162.811898 54.786852, --snip-- )))
```

Each coordinate pair marks a point on the boundary of the county. Now, you're ready to analyze the data.

Finding the Largest Counties in Square Miles

The census data leads us to a natural question: which county has the largest area? To calculate the county area, Listing 14-15 uses the ST_Area() function, which returns the area of a Polygon or MultiPolygon object. If you're working with a geography data type, ST_Area() returns the result in square meters. With a geometry data type, the function returns the area in SRID units. Typically, the units are not useful for practical analysis, but you can cast the geometry data to geography to obtain square meters. That's what we'll do here. This is a more intensive calculation than others we've done so far, so if you're using an older computer, expect extra time for the query to complete.

```
SELECT name10,
       statefp10 AS st,
       round(
             ( ST_Area(❶geom::geography) / ❷2589988.110336 )::numeric, 2
           ) AS ❸square_miles
FROM us_counties_2010_shp
ORDER BY square_miles ❹DESC
LIMIT 5;
```

Listing 14-15: Finding the largest counties by area using ST_Area()

The geom column is data type geometry, so to find the area in square meters, we cast the geom column as a geography data type using the double-colon syntax ❶. Then, to get square miles, we divide the area by 2589988.110336, which is the number of square meters in a square mile ❷. To make the result easier to read, I've wrapped it in a round()

function and named the resulting column `square_miles` ❸. Finally, we list the results in descending order from the largest area to the smallest ❹ and use `LIMIT 5` to show only the first five results, which should look like this:

```
name10              st    square_miles
----------------    --    ------------
Yukon-Koyukuk       02       147805.08
North Slope         02        94796.21
Bethel              02        45504.36
Northwest Arctic    02        40748.95
Valdez-Cordova      02        40340.08
```

The five counties with the largest areas are all in Alaska, denoted by the state FIPS code 02. Yukon-Koyukuk, located in the heart of Alaska, is more than 147,800 square miles. (Keep that information in mind for the "Try It Yourself" exercise at the end of the chapter.)

Finding a County by Longitude and Latitude

If you've ever wondered how website ads seem to know where you live ("You won't believe what this Boston man did with his old shoes!"), it's thanks to *geolocation services* that use various means, such as your phone's GPS, to find your longitude and latitude. Once your coordinates are known, they can be used in a spatial query to find which geography contains that point.

You can do the same using your census shapefile and the `ST_Within()` function, which returns true if one geometry is inside another. Listing 14-16 shows an example using the longitude and latitude of downtown Hollywood:

```
SELECT name10,
       statefp10
FROM us_counties_2010_shp
WHERE ST_Within('SRID=4269;POINT(-118.3419063 34.0977076)'::geometry, geom);
```

Listing 14-16: Using `ST_Within()` to find the county belonging to a pair of coordinates

The `ST_Within()` function inside the `WHERE` clause requires two geometry inputs and checks whether the first is inside the second. For the function to work properly, both geometry inputs must have the same SRID. In this example, the first input is an extended WKT representation of a Point that includes the SRID 4269 (same as the census data), which is then cast as a geometry type. The `ST_Within()` function doesn't accept a separate SRID input, so to set it for the supplied WKT, you must prefix it to the string like this: `'SRID=4269;POINT(-118.3419063 34.0977076)'`. The second input is the `geom` column from the table. Run the query; you should see the following result:

```
name10         statefp10
-----------    ---------
Los Angeles    06
```

The query shows that the Point you supplied is within Los Angeles county in California (state FIPS 06). This information is very handy, because by joining additional data to this table you can tell a person about demographics or points of interest near them. Try supplying other longitude and latitude pairs to see which U.S. county they fall in. If you provide coordinates outside the United States, the query should return no results because the shapefile only contains U.S. areas.

Performing Spatial Joins

In Chapter 6, you learned about SQL joins, which involved linking related tables via columns where values match or where an expression is true. You can perform joins using spatial data columns too, which opens up interesting opportunities for analysis. For example, you could join a table of coffee shops (which includes their longitude and latitude) to the counties table to find out how many shops exist in each county based on their location. Or, you can use a spatial join to append data from one table to another for analysis, again based on location. In this section, we'll explore spatial joins with a detailed look at roads and waterways using census data.

Exploring Roads and Waterways Data

Much of the year, the Santa Fe River, which cuts through the New Mexico state capital, is a dry riverbed better described as an *intermittent stream*. According to the Santa Fe city website, the river is susceptible to flash flooding and was named the nation's most endangered river in 2007. If you were an urban planner, it would help to know where the river crosses roadways so you could plan for emergency response when it floods.

You can determine these locations using another set of U.S. Census TIGER/Line shapefiles, which has details on roads and waterways in Santa Fe County. These shapefiles are also included with the book's resources. Download and unzip *tl_2016_35049_linearwater.zip* and *tl_2016_35049_roads.zip*, and then launch the Shapefile and DBF Loader Exporter. Following the same steps in "Loading Shapefiles via the GUI Tool" on page 257, import both shapefiles to gis_analysis. Name the water table santafe_linearwater_2016 and the roads table santafe_roads_2016.

Next, refresh your database and run a quick SELECT * FROM query on both tables to view the data. You should have 12,926 rows in the roads table and 1,198 in the linear water table.

As with the counties shapefile you imported via the loader GUI, both tables have an indexed geom column of type geometry. It's helpful to check the type of spatial object in the column so you know the type of spatial feature you're querying. You can do that using the ST_AsText() function you learned in Listing 14-14 or using ST_GeometryType(), as shown in Listing 14-17:

```
SELECT ST_GeometryType(geom)
FROM santafe_linearwater_2016
LIMIT 1;
```

```
SELECT ST_GeometryType(geom)
FROM santafe_roads_2016
LIMIT 1;
```

Listing 14-17: Using ST_GeometryType() to determine geometry

Both queries should return one row with the same value:
ST_MultiLineString. That value indicates that waterways and roads
are stored as MultiLineString objects, which are a series of points
connected by straight lines.

Joining the Census Roads and Water Tables

To find all the roads in Santa Fe that cross the Santa Fe River, we'll join
the tables using the JOIN ... ON syntax you learned in Chapter 6. Rather
than looking for values that match in columns in both tables as usual,
we'll write a query that tells us where objects overlap. We'll do this using
the ST_Intersects() function, which returns a Boolean true if two spatial
objects contact each other. Inputs can be either geometry or geography types.
Listing 14-18 joins the tables:

```
❶ SELECT water.fullname AS waterway,
         roads.rttyp,
         roads.fullname AS road
❷ FROM santafe_linearwater_2016 water JOIN santafe_roads_2016 roads
    ❸ ON ST_Intersects(water.geom, roads.geom)
  WHERE water.fullname = ❹'Santa Fe Riv'
  ORDER BY roads.fullname;
```

Listing 14-18: Spatial join with ST_Intersects() to find roads crossing the Santa Fe River

The SELECT column list ❶ includes the fullname column from the
santafe_linearwater_2016 table, which gets water as its alias in the FROM ❷
clause. The column list includes the rttyp code, which represents the
route type, and fullname columns from the santafe_roads_2016 table,
aliased as roads.

In the ON portion ❸ of the JOIN clause, we use the ST_Intersects() function with the geom columns from both tables as inputs. This is an example
of using the ON clause with an expression that evaluates to a Boolean result,
as noted in "Linking Tables Using JOIN" on page 74. Then we use fullname
to filter the results to show only those that have the full string 'Santa Fe
Riv' ❹, which is how the Santa Fe River is listed in the water table. The
query should return 54 rows; here are the first five:

```
waterway        rttyp    road
-----------     -----    ----------------
Santa Fe Riv    M        Baca Ranch Ln
Santa Fe Riv    M        Cam Alire
Santa Fe Riv    M        Cam Carlos Rael
Santa Fe Riv    M        Cam Dos Antonios
Santa Fe Riv    M        Cerro Gordo Rd
--snip--
```

Each road in the results intersects with a portion of the Santa Fe River. The route type code for each of the first results is M, which indicates that the road name shown is its *common* name as opposed to a county or state recognized name, for example. Other road names in the complete results carry route types of C, S, or U (for unknown). The full route type code list is available at *https://www.census.gov/geo/reference/rttyp.html*.

Finding the Location Where Objects Intersect

We successfully identified all the roads that intersect the Santa Fe River. This is a good start, but it would help our survey of flood-danger areas more to know precisely where each intersection occurs. We can modify the query to include the ST_Intersection() function, which returns the location of the place where objects cross. I've added it as a column in Listing 14-19:

```
SELECT water.fullname AS waterway,
       roads.rttyp,
       roads.fullname AS road,
    ❶ST_AsText(ST_Intersection(❷water.geom, roads.geom))
FROM santafe_linearwater_2016 water JOIN santafe_roads_2016 roads
    ON ST_Intersects(water.geom, roads.geom)
WHERE water.fullname = 'Santa Fe Riv'
ORDER BY roads.fullname;
```

Listing 14-19: Using ST_Intersection() to show where roads cross the river

The function returns a geometry object, so to get its WKT representation, we must wrap it in ST_AsText() ❶. The ST_Intersection() function takes two inputs: the geom columns ❷ from both the water and roads tables. Run the query, and the results should now include the exact coordinate location, or locations, where the river crosses the roads:

```
waterway      rttyp   road              st_astext
-----------   -----   ---------------   --------------------------
Santa Fe Riv  M       Baca Ranch Ln     POINT(-106.049782 35.642805)
Santa Fe Riv  M       Cam Alire         POINT(-105.967111 35.68479)
Santa Fe Riv  M       Cam Carlos Rael   POINT(-105.986712 35.672483)
Santa Fe Riv  M       Cam Dos Antonios  POINT(-106.007913 35.661576)
Santa Fe Riv  M       Cerro Gordo Rd    POINT(-105.895799 35.686198)
--snip--
```

You can probably think of more ideas for analyzing spatial data. For example, if you obtained a shapefile showing buildings, you could find those close to the river and in danger of flooding during heavy rains. Governments and private organizations regularly use these techniques as part of their planning process.

Wrapping Up

Mapping features is a powerful analysis tool, and the techniques you learned in this chapter provide you with a strong start toward exploring more with PostGIS. You might also want to look at the open source mapping application QGIS (*http://www.qgis.org/*), which provides tools for visualizing geographic data and working in depth with shapefiles. QGIS also works quite well with PostGIS, letting you add data from your tables directly onto a map.

You've now added working with geographic data to your analysis skills. In the remaining chapters, I'll give you additional tools and tips for working with PostgreSQL and related tools to continue to increase your skills.

TRY IT YOURSELF

Use the spatial data you've imported in this chapter to try additional analysis:

1. Earlier, you found which U.S. county has the largest area. Now, aggregate the county data to find the area of each state in square miles. (Use the statefp10 column in the us_counties_2010_shp table.) How many states are bigger than the Yukon-Koyukuk area?

2. Using ST_Distance(), determine how many miles separate these two farmers' markets: the Oakleaf Greenmarket (9700 Argyle Forest Blvd, Jacksonville, Florida) and Columbia Farmers Market (1701 West Ash Street, Columbia, Missouri). You'll need to first find the coordinates for both in the farmers_markets table. (Hint: You can also write this query using the Common Table Expression syntax you learned in Chapter 12.)

3. More than 500 rows in the farmers_markets table are missing a value in the county column, which is an example of dirty government data. Using the us_counties_2010_shp table and the ST_Intersects() function, perform a spatial join to find the missing county names based on the longitude and latitude of each market. Because geog_point in farmers_markets is of the geography type and its SRID is 4326, you'll need to cast geom in the census table to the geography type and change its SRID using ST_SetSRID().

15

SAVING TIME WITH VIEWS, FUNCTIONS, AND TRIGGERS

One of the advantages of using a programming language is that it allows us to automate repetitive, boring tasks. For example, if you have to run the same query every month to update the same table, sooner or later you'll search for a shortcut to accomplish the task. The good news is that shortcuts exist! In this chapter, you'll learn techniques to encapsulate queries and logic into reusable PostgreSQL database objects that will speed up your workflow. As you read through this chapter, keep in mind the DRY programming principle: Don't Repeat Yourself. Avoiding repetition saves time and prevents unnecessary mistakes.

You'll begin by learning to save queries as reusable database *views*. Next, you'll explore how to create your own functions to perform operations on your data. You've already used functions, such as round() and upper(), to transform data; now, you'll make functions to perform operations you specify. Then you'll set up *triggers* to run functions automatically when certain events occur on a table. Using these techniques, you can reduce repetitive work and help maintain the integrity of your data.

We'll use tables created from examples in earlier chapters to practice these techniques. If you connected to the gis_analysis database in pgAdmin while working through Chapter 14, follow the instructions in that chapter to return to the analysis database. All the code for this chapter is available for download along with the book's resources at *https://www.nostarch.com/ practicalSQL/*. Let's get started.

Using Views to Simplify Queries

A *view* is a virtual table you can create dynamically using a saved query. For example, every time you access the view, the saved query runs automatically and displays the results. Similar to a regular table, you can query a view, join a view to regular tables (or other views), and use the view to update or insert data into the table it's based on, albeit with some caveats.

In this section, we'll look at regular views with a PostgreSQL syntax that is largely in line with the ANSI SQL standard. These views execute their underlying query each time you access the view, but they don't store data the way a table does. A *materialized view*, which is specific to PostgreSQL, Oracle, and a limited number of other database systems, caches data created by the view, and you can later update that cached data. We won't explore materialized views here, but you can browse to *https://www.postgresql.org/docs/current/static/sql-creatematerializedview.html* to learn more.

Views are especially useful because they allow you to:

- **Avoid duplicate effort** by letting you write a query once and access the results when needed

- **Reduce complexity** for yourself or other database users by showing only columns relevant to your needs

- **Provide security** by limiting access to only certain columns in a table

NOTE *To ensure data security and fully prevent users from seeing sensitive information, such as the underlying salary data in the* employees *table, you must restrict access by setting account permissions in PostgreSQL. Typically, a database administrator handles this function for an organization, but if you want to explore this issue further, read the PostgreSQL documentation on user roles at* https://www.postgresql.org/ docs/current/static/sql-createrole.html *and the* GRANT *command at* https:// www.postgresql.org/docs/current/static/sql-grant.html.

Views are easy to create and maintain. Let's work through several examples to see how they work.

Creating and Querying Views

In this section, we'll use data in the Decennial U.S. Census us_counties_2010 table you imported in Chapter 4. Listing 15-1 uses this data to create a view called nevada_counties_pop_2010 that displays only four out of the original 16 columns, showing data on just Nevada counties:

```
❶ CREATE OR REPLACE VIEW nevada_counties_pop_2010 AS
    ❷ SELECT geo_name,
             state_fips,
             county_fips,
             p0010001 AS pop_2010
      FROM us_counties_2010
      WHERE state_us_abbreviation = 'NV'
    ❸ ORDER BY county_fips;
```

Listing 15-1: Creating a view that displays Nevada 2010 counties

Here, we define the view using the keywords CREATE OR REPLACE VIEW ❶, followed by the view's name and AS. Next is a standard SQL query SELECT ❷ that fetches the total population (the p0010001 column) for each Nevada county from the us_counties_2010 table. Then we order the data by the county's FIPS (Federal Information Processing Standards) code ❸, which is a standard designator the Census Bureau and other federal agencies use to specify each county and state.

Notice the OR REPLACE keywords after CREATE, which tell the database that if a view with this name already exists, replace it with the definition here. But here's a caveat according to the PostgreSQL documentation: the query that generates the view ❷ must have the columns with the same names and same data types in the same order as the view it's replacing. However, you can add columns at the end of the column list.

Run the code in Listing 15-1 using pgAdmin. The database should respond with the message CREATE VIEW. To find the view you created, in pgAdmin's object browser, right-click the analysis database and choose **Refresh**. Choose **Schemas ▶ public ▶ Views** to see the new view. When you right-click the view and choose **Properties**, you should see the query under the **Definition** tab in the dialog that opens.

NOTE *As with other database objects, you can delete a view using the DROP command. In this example, the syntax would be DROP VIEW nevada_counties_pop_2010;.*

After creating the view, you can use the view in the FROM clause of a SELECT query the same way you would use an ordinary table. Enter the code in Listing 15-2, which retrieves the first five rows from the view:

```
SELECT *
FROM nevada_counties_pop_2010
LIMIT 5;
```

Listing 15-2: Querying the nevada_counties_pop_2010 view

Aside from the five-row limit, the result should be the same as if you had run the SELECT query used to create the view in Listing 15-1:

geo_name	state_fips	county_fips	pop_2010
Churchill County	32	001	24877
Clark County	32	003	1951269
Douglas County	32	005	46997
Elko County	32	007	48818
Esmeralda County	32	009	783

This simple example isn't very useful unless quickly listing Nevada county population is a task you'll perform frequently. So, let's imagine a question data-minded analysts in a political research organization might ask often: what was the percent change in population for each county in Nevada (or any other state) from 2000 to 2010?

We wrote a query to answer this question in Listing 6-13 (see "Performing Math on Joined Table Columns" on page 88). It wasn't onerous to create, but it did require joining tables on two columns and using a percent change formula that involved rounding and type casting. To avoid repeating that work, we can save a query similar to the one in Listing 6-13 as a view. Listing 15-3 does this using a modified version of the earlier code in Listing 15-1:

```
❶ CREATE OR REPLACE VIEW county_pop_change_2010_2000 AS
    ❷ SELECT c2010.geo_name,
            c2010.state_us_abbreviation AS st,
            c2010.state_fips,
            c2010.county_fips,
            c2010.p0010001 AS pop_2010,
            c2000.p0010001 AS pop_2000,
        ❸ round( (CAST(c2010.p0010001 AS numeric(8,1)) - c2000.p0010001)
                / c2000.p0010001 * 100, 1 ) AS pct_change_2010_2000
    ❹ FROM us_counties_2010 c2010 INNER JOIN us_counties_2000 c2000
        ON c2010.state_fips = c2000.state_fips
            AND c2010.county_fips = c2000.county_fips
        ORDER BY c2010.state_fips, c2010.county_fips;
```

Listing 15-3: Creating a view showing population change for U.S. counties

We start the view definition with CREATE OR REPLACE VIEW ❶, followed by the name of the view and AS. The SELECT query ❷ names columns from the census tables and includes a column definition with a percent change calculation ❸ that you learned about in Chapter 5. Then we join the Census 2010 and 2000 tables ❹ using the state and county FIPS codes. Run the code, and the database should again respond with CREATE VIEW.

Now that we've created the view, we can use the code in Listing 15-4 to run a simple query against the new view that retrieves data for Nevada counties:

```
SELECT geo_name,
        st,
```

```
        pop_2010,
   ❶ pct_change_2010_2000
FROM county_pop_change_2010_2000
❷ WHERE st = 'NV'
LIMIT 5;
```

Listing 15-4: Selecting columns from the county_pop_change_2010_2000 view

In Listing 15-2, in the query against the first view we created, we retrieved every column in the view by using the asterisk wildcard after the SELECT keyword. Listing 15-4 shows that, as with a query on a table, we can name specific columns when querying a view. Here, we specify four of the county_pop _change_2010_2000 view's seven columns. One is pct_change_2010_2000 ❶, which returns the result of the percent change calculation we're looking for. As you can see, it's much simpler to write the column name like this than the whole formula! We're also filtering the results using a WHERE clause ❷, similar to how we would filter any query instead of returning all rows.

After querying the four columns from the view, the results should look like this:

```
geo_name            st    pop_2010    pct_change_2010_2000
----------------    --    --------    --------------------
Churchill County    NV       24877                     3.7
Clark County        NV     1951269                    41.8
Douglas County      NV       46997                    13.9
Elko County         NV       48818                     7.8
Esmeralda County    NV         783                   -19.4
```

Now we can revisit this view as often as we like to pull data for presentations or to answer questions about the percent change in population for each county in Nevada (or any other state) from 2000 to 2010.

Looking at just these five rows, you can see that a couple of interesting stories emerge: the effect of the 2000s' housing boom on Clark County, which includes the city of Las Vegas, as well as a sharp drop in population in Esmeralda County, which has one of the lowest population densities in the United States.

Inserting, Updating, and Deleting Data Using a View

You can update or insert data in the underlying table that a view queries as long as the view meets certain conditions. One requirement is that the view must reference a single table. If the view's query joins tables, as with the population change view we just built in the previous section, then you can't perform inserts or updates directly. Also, the view's query can't contain DISTINCT, GROUP BY, or other clauses. (See a complete list of restrictions at *https://www.postgresql.org/docs/current/static/sql-createview.html*.)

You already know how to directly insert and update data on a table, so why do it through a view? One reason is that with a view you can exercise more control over which data a user can update. Let's work through an example to see how this works.

Creating a View of Employees

In the Chapter 6 lesson on joins, we created and filled departments and employees tables with four rows about people and where they work (if you skipped that section, you can revisit Listing 6-1 on page 75). Running a quick SELECT * FROM employees; query shows the table's contents, as you can see here:

```
emp_id    first_name    last_name    salary    dept_id
------    ----------    ---------    ------    -------
     1    Nancy         Jones         62500          1
     2    Lee           Smith         59300          1
     3    Soo           Nguyen        83000          2
     4    Janet         King          95000          2
```

Let's say we want to give users in the Tax Department (its dept_id is 1) the ability to add, remove, or update their employees' names without letting them change salary information or data of employees in another department. To do this, we can set up a view using Listing 15-5:

```
CREATE OR REPLACE VIEW employees_tax_dept AS
    SELECT emp_id,
           first_name,
           last_name,
           dept_id
    FROM employees
❶ WHERE dept_id = 1
    ORDER BY emp_id
❷ WITH LOCAL CHECK OPTION;
```

Listing 15-5: Creating a view on the employees table

Similar to the views we've created so far, we're selecting only the columns we want to show from the employees table and using WHERE to filter the results on dept_id = 1 ❶ to list only Tax Department staff. To restrict inserts or updates to Tax Department employees only, we add the WITH LOCAL CHECK OPTION ❷, which rejects any insert or update that does not meet the criteria of the WHERE clause. For example, the option won't allow anyone to insert or update a row in the underlying table where the employee's dept_id is 3.

Create the employees_tax_dept view by running the code in Listing 15-5. Then run SELECT * FROM employees_tax_dept;, which should provide these two rows:

```
emp_id    first_name    last_name    dept_id
------    ----------    ---------    -------
     1    Nancy         Jones              1
     2    Lee           Smith              1
```

The result shows the employees who work in the Tax Department; they're two of the four rows in the entire employees table.

Now, let's look at how inserts and updates work via this view.

Inserting Rows Using the employees_tax_dept View

We can also use a view to insert or update data, but instead of using the table name in the INSERT or UPDATE statement, we substitute the view name. After we add or change data using a view, the change is applied to the underlying table, which in this case is employees. The view then reflects the change via the query it runs.

Listing 15-6 shows two examples that attempt to add new employee records via the employees_tax_dept view. The first succeeds, but the second fails.

```
❶ INSERT INTO employees_tax_dept (first_name, last_name, dept_id)
   VALUES ('Suzanne', 'Legere', 1);

❷ INSERT INTO employees_tax_dept (first_name, last_name, dept_id)
   VALUES ('Jamil', 'White', 2);

❸ SELECT * FROM employees_tax_dept;

❹ SELECT * FROM employees;
```

Listing 15-6: Successful and rejected inserts via the employees_tax_dept view

In the first INSERT ❶, which follows the insert format you learned in Chapter 1, we supply the first and last names of Suzanne Legere plus her dept_id. Because the dept_id is 1, the value satisfies the LOCAL CHECK in the view, and the insert succeeds when it executes.

But when we run the second INSERT ❷ to add an employee named Jamil White using a dept_id of 2, the operation fails with the error message new row violates check option for view "employees_tax_dept". The reason is that when we created the view in Listing 15-5, we used the WHERE clause to show only rows with dept_id = 1. The dept_id of 2 does not pass the LOCAL CHECK in the view, and it's prevented from being inserted.

Run the SELECT statement ❸ on the view to check that Suzanne Legere was successfully added:

emp_id	first_name	last_name	dept_id
1	Nancy	Jones	1
2	Lee	Smith	1
5	Suzanne	Legere	1

We can also query the employees table ❹ to see that, in fact, Suzanne Legere was added to the full table. The view queries the employees table each time we access it.

emp_id	first_name	last_name	salary	dept_id
1	Nancy	Jones	62500	1
2	Lee	Smith	59300	1

3	Soo	Nguyen	83000	2
4	Janet	King	95000	2
5	Suzanne	Legere		1

As you can see from the addition of "Suzanne Legere," the data we add using a view is also added to the underlying table. However, because the view doesn't include the salary column, its value in her row is NULL. If you attempt to insert a salary value using this view, you would receive the error message column "salary" of relation "employees_tax_dept" does not exist. The reason is that even though the salary column exists in the underlying employees table, it's not referenced in the view. Again, this is one way to limit access to sensitive data. Check the links I provided in the note on page 268 to learn more about granting permissions to users if you plan to take on database administrator responsibilities.

Updating Rows Using the employees_tax_dept View

The same restrictions on accessing data in an underlying table apply when we make updates on data in the employees_tax_dept view. Listing 15-7 shows a standard query to update the spelling of Suzanne's last name using UPDATE (as a person with more than one uppercase letter in his last name, I can confirm misspelling names isn't unusual).

```
UPDATE employees_tax_dept
SET last_name = 'Le Gere'
WHERE emp_id = 5;

SELECT * FROM employees_tax_dept;
```

Listing 15-7: Updating a row via the employees_tax_dept view

Run the code, and the result from the SELECT query should show the updated last name, which occurs in the underlying employees table:

emp_id	first_name	last_name	dept_id
1	Nancy	Jones	1
2	Lee	Smith	1
5	Suzanne	Le Gere	1

Suzanne's last name is now correctly spelled as "Le Gere," not "Legere."
However, if we try to update the name of an employee who is not in the Tax Department, the query fails just as it did when we tried to insert Jamil White in Listing 15-6. In addition, trying to use this view to update the salary of an employee—even one in the Tax Department—will fail with the same error I noted in the previous section. If the view doesn't reference a

column in the underlying table, you cannot access that column through the view. Again, the fact that updates on views are restricted in this way offers ways to ensure privacy and security for certain pieces of data.

Deleting Rows Using the employees_tax_dept View

Now, let's explore how to delete rows using a view. The restrictions on which data you can affect apply here as well. For example, if Suzanne Le Gere in the Tax Department gets a better offer from another firm and decides to join the other company, you could remove her from the employees table through the employees_tax_dept view. Listing 15-8 shows the query in the standard DELETE syntax:

```
DELETE FROM employees_tax_dept
WHERE emp_id = 5;
```

Listing 15-8: Deleting a row via the employees_tax_dept view

Run the query, and PostgreSQL should respond with DELETE 1. However, when you try to delete a row for an employee in a department other than the Tax Department, PostgreSQL won't allow it and will report DELETE 0.

In summary, views not only give you control over access to data, but also shortcuts for working with data. Next, let's explore how to use functions to save more time.

Programming Your Own Functions

You've used plenty of functions throughout the book, whether to capitalize letters with upper() or add numbers with sum(). Behind these functions is a significant amount of (sometimes complex) programming that takes an input, transforms it or initiates an action, and returns a response. You saw that extent of code in Listing 5-14 on page 69 when you created a median() function, which uses 30 lines of code to find the middle value in a group of numbers. PostgreSQL's built-in functions and other functions database programmers develop to automate processes can use even more lines of code, including links to external code written in another language, such as C.

We won't write complicated code here, but we'll work through some examples of building functions that you can use as a launching pad for your own ideas. Even simple, user-created functions can help you avoid repeating code when you're analyzing data.

The code in this section is specific to PostgreSQL and is not part of the ANSI SQL standard. In some databases, notably Microsoft SQL Server and MySQL, implementing reusable code happens in a *stored procedure*. If you're using another database management system, check its documentation for specifics.

Creating the percent_change() Function

To learn the syntax for creating a function, let's write a function to simplify calculating the percent change of two values, which is a staple of data analysis. In Chapter 5, you learned that the percent change formula can be expressed this way:

```
percent change = (New Number – Old Number) / Old Number
```

Rather than writing that formula each time we need it, we can create a function called percent_change() that takes the new and old numbers as inputs and returns the result rounded to a user-specified number of decimal places. Let's walk through the code in Listing 15-9 to see how to declare a simple SQL function:

```
❶ CREATE OR REPLACE FUNCTION
❷ percent_change(new_value numeric,
                  old_value numeric,
                  decimal_places integer ❸DEFAULT 1)
❹ RETURNS numeric AS
❺ 'SELECT round(
          ((new_value - old_value) / old_value) * 100, decimal_places
   );'
❻ LANGUAGE SQL
❼ IMMUTABLE
❽ RETURNS NULL ON NULL INPUT;
```

Listing 15-9: Creating a percent_change() function

A lot is happening in this code, but it's not as complicated as it looks. We start with the command CREATE OR REPLACE FUNCTION ❶, followed by the name of the function ❷ and, in parentheses, a list of *arguments* that are the function's inputs. Each argument has a name and data type. For example, we specify that new_value and old_value are numeric, whereas decimal_places (which specifies the number of places to round results) is integer. For decimal_places, we specify 1 as the DEFAULT ❸ value to indicate that we want the results to display only one decimal place. Because we set a default value, the argument will be optional when we call the function later.

We then use the keywords RETURNS numeric AS ❹ to tell the function to return its calculation as type numeric. If this were a function to concatenate strings, we might return text.

Next, we write the meat of the function that performs the calculation. Inside single quotes, we place a SELECT query ❺ that includes the percent change calculation nested inside a round() function. In the formula, we use the function's argument names instead of numbers.

We then supply a series of keywords that define the function's attributes and behavior. The LANGUAGE ❻ keyword specifies that we've written this function using plain SQL, which is one of several languages PostgreSQL supports in functions. Another common option is a PostgreSQL-specific *procedural language* called PL/pgSQL that, in addition to providing the means to create functions, adds features not found in standard SQL, such as logical control structures (IF ... THEN ... ELSE). PL/pgSQL is the default procedural language installed with PostgreSQL, but you can install others, such as PL/Perl and PL/Python, to use the Perl and Python programming languages in your database. Later in this chapter, I'll show examples of PL/pgSQL and Python.

Next, the IMMUTABLE keyword ❼ indicates that the function won't be making any changes to the database, which can improve performance. The line RETURNS NULL ON NULL INPUT ❽ guarantees that the function will supply a NULL response if any input that is not supplied by default is a NULL.

Run the code using pgAdmin to create the percent_change() function. The server should respond with the message CREATE FUNCTION.

Using the percent_change() Function

To test the new percent_change() function, run it by itself using SELECT, as shown in Listing 15-10:

```
SELECT percent_change(110, 108, 2);
```

Listing 15-10: Testing the percent_change() function

This example uses a value of 110 for the new number, 108 for the old number, and 2 as the desired number of decimal places to round the result.

Run the code; the result should look like this:

```
percent_change
--------------
          1.85
```

The result indicates that there is a 1.85 percent increase between 108 and 110. You can experiment with other numbers to see how the results change. Also, try changing the decimal_places argument to values including 0, or omit it, to see how that affects the output. You should see results that have more or fewer numbers after the decimal point, based on your input.

Of course, we created this function to avoid having to write the full percent change formula in queries. Now let's use it to calculate the percent change using a version of the Decennial Census population change query we wrote in Chapter 6, as shown in Listing 15-11:

```
SELECT c2010.geo_name,
       c2010.state_us_abbreviation AS st,
       c2010.p0010001 AS pop_2010,
     ❶ percent_change(c2010.p0010001, c2000.p0010001) AS pct_chg_func,
     ❷ round( (CAST(c2010.p0010001 AS numeric(8,1)) - c2000.p0010001)
           / c2000.p0010001 * 100, 1 ) AS pct_chg_formula
FROM us_counties_2010 c2010 INNER JOIN us_counties_2000 c2000
ON c2010.state_fips = c2000.state_fips
   AND c2010.county_fips = c2000.county_fips
```

```
ORDER BY pct_chg_func DESC
LIMIT 5;
```

Listing 15-11: Testing percent_change() on census data

Listing 15-11 uses the original query in Listing 6-13 and adds the percent_change() function ❶ as a column before the formula ❷ so we can compare results. As inputs, we use the 2010 total population column (c2010.p0010001) as the new number and the 2000 total population as the old (c2000.p0010001).

When you run the query, the results should display the five counties with the greatest percent change in population, and the results from the function should match the results from the formula entered directly into the query ❷.

geo_name	st	pop_2010	pct_chg_func	pct_chg_formula
Kendall County	IL	114736	110.4	110.4
Pinal County	AZ	375770	109.1	109.1
Flagler County	FL	95696	92.0	92.0
Lincoln County	SD	44828	85.8	85.8
Loudoun County	VA	312311	84.1	84.1

Each result displays one decimal place, the function's default value, because we didn't provide the optional third argument when we called the function. Now that we know the function works as intended, we can use percent_change() any time we need to solve that calculation. Using a function is much faster than having to write a formula each time we need to use it!

Updating Data with a Function

We can also use a function to simplify routine updates to data. In this section, we'll write a function that assigns the correct number of personal days available to a teacher (in addition to vacation) based on their hire date. We'll use the teachers table from the first lesson in Chapter 1, "Creating a Table" on page 5. If you skipped that section, you can return to it to create the table and insert the data using the example code in Listing 1-2 on page 6 and Listing 1-3 on page 8.

Let's start by adding a column to teachers to hold the personal days using the code in Listing 15-12:

```
ALTER TABLE teachers ADD COLUMN personal_days integer;

SELECT first_name,
       last_name,
       hire_date,
       personal_days
FROM teachers;
```

Listing 15-12: Adding a column to the teachers table and seeing the data

Listing 15-12 updates the teachers table using ALTER and adds the personal_days column using the keywords ADD COLUMN. Run the SELECT statement to view the data. When both queries finish, you should see the following six rows:

first_name	last_name	hire_date	personal_days
Janet	Smith	2011-10-30	
Lee	Reynolds	1993-05-22	
Samuel	Cole	2005-08-01	
Samantha	Bush	2011-10-30	
Betty	Diaz	2005-08-30	
Kathleen	Roush	2010-10-22	

The personal_days column holds NULL values because we haven't provided any values yet.

Now, let's create a function called update_personal_days() that updates the personal_days column with the correct personal days based on the teacher's hire date. We'll use the following rules to update the data in the personal_days column:

- Less than five years since hire: 3 personal days
- Between five and 10 years since hire: 4 personal days
- More than 10 years since hire: 5 personal days

The code in Listing 15-13 is similar to the code we used to create the percent_change() function, but this time we'll use the PL/pgSQL language instead of plain SQL. Let's walk through some differences.

```
CREATE OR REPLACE FUNCTION update_personal_days()
❶ RETURNS void AS ❷$$
❸ BEGIN
    UPDATE teachers
    SET personal_days =
        ❹ CASE WHEN (now() - hire_date) BETWEEN '5 years'::interval
                                        AND '10 years'::interval THEN 4
             WHEN (now() - hire_date) > '10 years'::interval THEN 5
             ELSE 3
        END;
    ❺ RAISE NOTICE 'personal_days updated!';
END;
❻ $$ LANGUAGE plpgsql;
```

Listing 15-13: Creating an update_personal_days() function

We begin with CREATE OR REPLACE FUNCTION, followed by the function's name. This time, we provide no arguments because no user input is required. The function operates on predetermined columns with set rules for calculating intervals. Also, we use RETURNS void ❶ to note that the function returns no data; it simply updates the personal_days column.

Often, when writing PL/pgSQL-based functions, the PostgreSQL convention is to use the non-ANSI SQL standard dollar-quote ($$) ❷ to mark the start and end of the string that contains all the function's commands. (As with the percent_change() function earlier, you could use single quote marks to enclose the string, but then any single quotes in the string would need to be doubled, and that looks messy.) So, everything between the pairs of $$ is the code that does the work. You can also add some text between the dollar signs, like $namestring$, to create a unique pair of beginning and ending quotes. This is useful, for example, if you need to quote a query inside the function.

Right after the first $$ we start a BEGIN ... END; ❸ block to denote the function; inside it we place an UPDATE statement that uses a CASE statement ❹ to determine the number of days each teacher gets. We subtract the hire_date from the current date, which is retrieved from the server by the now() function. Depending on which range now() - hire_date falls into, the CASE statement returns the correct number of days off corresponding to the range. We use RAISE NOTICE ❺ to display a message in pgAdmin that the function is done. At the end, we use the LANGUAGE ❻ keyword to specify that we've written this function using PL/pgSQL.

Run the code in Listing 15-13 to create the update_personal_days() function. Then use the following line to run it in pgAdmin:

```
SELECT update_personal_days();
```

Now when you rerun the SELECT statement in Listing 15-12, you should see that each row of the personal_days column is filled with the appropriate values. Note that your results may vary depending on when you run this function, because the result of now() is constantly updated with the passage of time.

first_name	last_name	hire_date	personal_days
Janet	Smith	2011-10-30	4
Lee	Reynolds	1993-05-22	5
Samuel	Cole	2005-08-01	5
Samantha	Bush	2011-10-30	4
Betty	Diaz	2005-08-30	5
Kathleen	Roush	2010-10-22	4

You could use the update_personal_days() function to regularly update data manually after performing certain tasks, or you could use a task scheduler such as pgAgent (a separate open source tool) to run it automatically. You can learn about pgAgent and other tools in "PostgreSQL Utilities, Tools, and Extensions" on page 334.

Using the Python Language in a Function

Previously, I mentioned that PL/pgSQL is the default procedural language within PostgreSQL, but the database also supports creating functions using open source languages, such as Perl and Python. This support allows you to take advantage of those languages' features as well as related modules within functions you create. For example, with Python, you can use the pandas library for data analysis. The documentation at *https://www.postgresql.org/docs/current/static/server-programming.html* provides a comprehensive review of the available languages, but here I'll show you a very simple function using Python.

To enable PL/Python, you must add the extension using the code in Listing 15-14. If you get an error, such as `could not access file "$libdir/plpython2"`, that means PL/Python wasn't included when you installed PostgreSQL. Refer back to the troubleshooting links for each operating system in "Installing PostgreSQL" on page xxviii.

```
CREATE EXTENSION plpythonu;
```

Listing 15-14: Enabling the PL/Python procedural language

NOTE *The extension* `plpythonu` *currently installs Python version 2.x. If you want to use Python 3.x, install the extension* `plpython3u` *instead. However, available versions might vary based on PostgreSQL distribution.*

After enabling the extension, create a function following the same syntax you just learned in Listing 15-9 and Listing 15-13, but use Python for the body of the function. Listing 15-15 shows how to use PL/Python to create a function called `trim_county()` that removes the word "County" from the end of a string. We'll use this function to clean up names of counties in the census data.

```
   CREATE OR REPLACE FUNCTION trim_county(input_string text)
❶ RETURNS text AS $$
      ❷ import re
      ❸ cleaned = re.sub(r' County', '', input_string)
         return cleaned
❹ $$ LANGUAGE plpythonu;
```

Listing 15-15: Using PL/Python to create the `trim_county()` *function*

The structure should look familiar with some exceptions. Unlike the example in Listing 15-13, we don't follow the $$ ❶ with a `BEGIN ... END;` block. That is a PL/pgSQL–specific requirement that we don't need in PL/Python. Instead, we get straight to the Python code by starting with a statement to import the Python regular expressions module, re ❷. Even if you don't know much about Python, you can probably deduce that the next two lines of code ❸ set a variable called cleaned to the results of a Python regular expression function called sub(). That function looks for a space followed by the word *County* in the input_string passed into the function and substitutes an empty string, which is denoted by two apostrophes. Then the function returns the content of the variable cleaned. To end, we specify LANGUAGE plpythonu ❹ to note we're writing the function with PL/Python.

Run the code to create the function, and then execute the SELECT statement in Listing 15-16 to see it in action.

```
SELECT geo_name,
       trim_county(geo_name)
FROM us_counties_2010
ORDER BY state_fips, county_fips
LIMIT 5;
```

Listing 15-16: Testing the trim_county() function

We use the geo_name column in the us_counties_2010 table as input to trim_county(). That should return these results:

```
geo_name          trim_county
--------------    -----------
Autauga County    Autauga
Baldwin County    Baldwin
Barbour County    Barbour
Bibb County       Bibb
Blount County     Blount
```

As you can see, the trim_county() function evaluated each value in the geo_name column and removed a space and the word *County* when present. Although this is a trivial example, it shows how easy it is to use Python—or one of the other supported procedural languages—inside a function.

Next, you'll learn how to use triggers to automate your database.

Automating Database Actions with Triggers

A database *trigger* executes a function whenever a specified event, such as an INSERT, UPDATE, or DELETE, occurs on a table or a view. You can set a trigger to fire before, after, or instead of the event, and you can also set it to fire once for each row affected by the event or just once per operation. For example, let's say you delete 20 rows from a table. You could set the trigger to fire once for each of the 20 rows deleted or just one time.

We'll work through two examples. The first example keeps a log of changes made to grades at a school. The second automatically classifies temperatures each time we collect a reading.

Logging Grade Updates to a Table

Let's say we want to automatically track changes made to a student grades table in our school's database. Every time a row is updated, we want to record the old and new grade plus the time the change occurred (search for "David Lightman and grades" and you'll see why this might be worth tracking). To handle this task automatically, we'll need three items:

- A grades_history table to record the changes to grades in a grades table
- A trigger to run a function every time a change occurs in the grades table, which we'll name grades_update
- The function the trigger will execute; we'll call this function record_if_grade_changed()

Creating Tables to Track Grades and Updates

Let's start by making the tables we need. Listing 15-17 includes the code to first create and fill grades and then create grades_history:

```
❶ CREATE TABLE grades (
      student_id bigint,
      course_id bigint,
      course varchar(30) NOT NULL,
      grade varchar(5) NOT NULL,
  PRIMARY KEY (student_id, course_id)
  );

❷ INSERT INTO grades
  VALUES
      (1, 1, 'Biology 2', 'F'),
      (1, 2, 'English 11B', 'D'),
      (1, 3, 'World History 11B', 'C'),
      (1, 4, 'Trig 2', 'B');

❸ CREATE TABLE grades_history (
      student_id bigint NOT NULL,
      course_id bigint NOT NULL,
      change_time timestamp with time zone NOT NULL,
      course varchar(30) NOT NULL,
      old_grade varchar(5) NOT NULL,
      new_grade varchar(5) NOT NULL,
  PRIMARY KEY (student_id, course_id, change_time)
  );
```

Listing 15-17: Creating the grades and grades_history tables

These commands are straightforward. We use CREATE to make a grades table ❶ and add four rows using INSERT ❷, where each row represents a student's grade in a class. Then we use CREATE TABLE to make the grades_history table ❸ to hold the data we log each time an existing grade is altered. The grades_history table has columns for the new grade, old grade, and the time of the change. Run the code to create the tables and fill the grades table. We insert no data into grades_history here because the trigger process will handle that task.

Creating the Function and Trigger

Next, let's write the record_if_grade_changed() function the trigger will execute. We must write the function before naming it in the trigger. Let's go through the code in Listing 15-18:

```
CREATE OR REPLACE FUNCTION record_if_grade_changed()
❶ RETURNS trigger AS
$$
BEGIN
  ❷ IF NEW.grade <> OLD.grade THEN
     INSERT INTO grades_history (
          student_id,
          course_id,
          change_time,
          course,
          old_grade,
          new_grade)
     VALUES
          (OLD.student_id,
           OLD.course_id,
           now(),
           OLD.course,
         ❸ OLD.grade,
         ❹ NEW.grade);
     END IF;
  ❺ RETURN NEW;
END;
$$ LANGUAGE plpgsql;
```

Listing 15-18: Creating the record_if_grade_changed() function

The record_if_grade_changed() function follows the pattern of earlier examples in the chapter but with exceptions specific to working with triggers. First, we specify RETURNS trigger ❶ instead of a data type or void. Because record_if_grade_changed() is a PL/pgSQL function, we place the procedure inside the BEGIN ... END; block. We start the procedure using an IF ... THEN statement ❷, which is one of the control structures PL/pgSQL provides. We use it here to run the INSERT statement only if the updated grade is different from the old grade, which we check using the <> operator.

When a change occurs to the grades table, the trigger (which we'll create next) will execute. For each row that is changed, the trigger will pass two collections of data into record_if_grade_changed(). The first is the row values *before* they were changed, noted with the prefix OLD. The second is the row values *after* they were changed, noted with the prefix NEW. The function can access the original row values and the updated row values, which it will use for a comparison. If the IF ... THEN statement evaluates as true, which means that the old and new grade values are different, we use INSERT to add a row to grades_history that contains both OLD.grade ❸ and NEW.grade ❹.

A trigger must have a RETURN statement ❺, although the PostgreSQL documentation at *https://www.postgresql.org/docs/current/static/plpgsql-trigger .html* details the scenarios in which a trigger return value actually matters (sometimes it is ignored). The documentation also explains that you can use statements to return a NULL or raise an exception in case of error.

Run the code in Listing 15-18 to create the function. Next, add the grades_update trigger to the grades table using Listing 15-19:

```
❶ CREATE TRIGGER grades_update
❷   AFTER UPDATE
      ON grades
❸   FOR EACH ROW
❹   EXECUTE PROCEDURE record_if_grade_changed();
```

Listing 15-19: Creating the grades_update trigger

In PostgreSQL, the syntax for creating a trigger follows the ANSI SQL standard (although the contents of the trigger function do not). The code begins with a CREATE TRIGGER ❶ statement, followed by clauses that control when the trigger runs and how it behaves. We use AFTER UPDATE ❷ to specify that we want the trigger to fire after the update occurs on the grades row. We could also use the keywords BEFORE or INSTEAD OF depending on the situation.

We write FOR EACH ROW ❸ to tell the trigger to execute the procedure once for each row updated in the table. For example, if someone ran an update that affected three rows, the procedure would run three times. The alternate (and default) is FOR EACH STATEMENT, which runs the procedure once. If we didn't care about capturing changes to each row and simply wanted to record that grades were changed at a certain time, we could use that option. Finally, we use EXECUTE PROCEDURE ❹ to name record_if_grade_changed() as the function the trigger should run.

Create the trigger by running the code in Listing 15-19 in pgAdmin. The database should respond with the message CREATE TRIGGER.

Testing the Trigger

Now that we've created the trigger and the function it should run, let's make sure they work. First, when you run SELECT * FROM grades_history;, you'll see that the table is empty because we haven't made any changes to the grades table yet and there's nothing to track. Next, when you run SELECT * FROM grades; you should see the grade data, as shown here:

student_id	course_id	course	grade
1	1	Biology 2	F
1	2	English 11B	D
1	3	World History 11B	C
1	4	Trig 2	B

That Biology 2 grade doesn't look very good. Let's update it using the code in Listing 15-20:

```
UPDATE grades
SET grade = 'C'
WHERE student_id = 1 AND course_id = 1;
```

Listing 15-20: Testing the grades_update trigger

When you run the UPDATE, pgAdmin doesn't display anything to let you know that the trigger executed in the background. It just reports UPDATE 1, meaning the row with grade F was updated. But our trigger did run, which we can confirm by examining columns in grades_history using this SELECT query:

```
SELECT student_id,
       change_time,
       course,
       old_grade,
       new_grade
FROM grades_history;
```

When you run this query, you should see that the grades_history table, which contains all changes to grades, now has one row:

student_id	change_time	course	old_grade	new_grade
1	2018-07-09 13:51:45.937-04	Biology 2	F	C

This row displays the old Biology 2 grade of F, the new value C, and change_time, showing the time of the change made (your result should reflect your date and time). Note that the addition of this row to grades_history happened in the background without the knowledge of the person making the update. But the UPDATE event on the table caused the trigger to fire, which executed the record_if_grade_changed() function.

If you've used a content management system, such as WordPress or Drupal, this sort of revision tracking might be familiar. It provides a helpful record of changes made to content for reference and auditing purposes, and, unfortunately, can lead to occasional finger-pointing. Regardless, the ability to trigger actions on a database automatically gives you more control over your data.

Automatically Classifying Temperatures

In Chapter 12, we used the SQL CASE statement to reclassify temperature readings into descriptive categories. The CASE statement (with a slightly different syntax) is also part of the PL/pgSQL procedural language, and we can use its capability to assign values to variables to automatically store those category names in a table each time we add a temperature reading.

If we're routinely collecting temperature readings, using this technique to automate the classification spares us from having to handle the task manually.

We'll follow the same steps we used for logging the grade changes: we first create a function to classify the temperatures, and then create a trigger to run the function each time the table is updated. Use Listing 15-21 to create a temperature_test table for the exercise:

```
CREATE TABLE temperature_test (
    station_name varchar(50),
    observation_date date,
    max_temp integer,
    min_temp integer,
    max_temp_group varchar(40),
PRIMARY KEY (station_name, observation_date)
);
```

Listing 15-21: Creating a temperature_test table

In Listing 15-21, the temperature_test table contains columns to hold the name of the station and date of the temperature observation. Let's imagine that we have some process to insert a row once a day that provides the maximum and minimum temperature for that location, and we need to fill the max_temp_group column with a descriptive classification of the day's high reading to provide text to a weather forecast we're distributing.

To do this, we first make a function called classify_max_temp(), as shown in Listing 15-22:

```
CREATE OR REPLACE FUNCTION classify_max_temp()
    RETURNS trigger AS
$$
BEGIN
  ❶ CASE
      WHEN NEW.max_temp >= 90 THEN
          NEW.max_temp_group := 'Hot';❷
      WHEN NEW.max_temp BETWEEN 70 AND 89 THEN
          NEW.max_temp_group := 'Warm';
      WHEN NEW.max_temp BETWEEN 50 AND 69 THEN
          NEW.max_temp_group := 'Pleasant';
      WHEN NEW.max_temp BETWEEN 33 AND 49 THEN
          NEW.max_temp_group :=  'Cold';
      WHEN NEW.max_temp BETWEEN 20 AND 32 THEN
          NEW.max_temp_group :=  'Freezing';
      ELSE NEW.max_temp_group :=  'Inhumane';
    END CASE;
    RETURN NEW;
END;
$$ LANGUAGE plpgsql;
```

Listing 15-22: Creating the classify_max_temp() function

By now, these functions should look familiar. What is new here is the PL/pgSQL version of the CASE syntax ❶, which differs slightly from the

SQL syntax in that the PL/pgSQL syntax includes a semicolon after each WHEN ... THEN clause ❷. Also new is the *assignment operator* (:=), which we use to assign the descriptive name to the NEW.max_temp_group column based on the outcome of the CASE function. For example, the statement NEW.max_temp_group := 'Cold' assigns the string 'Cold' to NEW.max_temp_group when the temperature value is between 33 and 49 degrees Fahrenheit, and when the function returns the NEW row to be inserted in the table, it will include the string value Cold. Run the code to create the function.

Next, using the code in Listing 15-23, create a trigger to execute the function each time a row is added to temperature_test:

```
CREATE TRIGGER temperature_insert
❶ BEFORE INSERT
  ON temperature_test
❷ FOR EACH ROW
❸ EXECUTE PROCEDURE classify_max_temp();
```

Listing 15-23: Creating the temperature_insert trigger

In this example, we classify max_temp and create a value for max_temp_group prior to inserting the row into the table. Doing so is more efficient than performing a separate update after the row is inserted. To specify that behavior, we set the temperature_insert trigger to fire BEFORE INSERT ❶.

We also want the trigger to fire FOR EACH ROW inserted ❷ because we want each max_temp recorded in the table to get a descriptive classification. The final EXECUTE PROCEDURE statement names the classify_max_temp() function ❸ we just created. Run the CREATE TRIGGER statement in pgAdmin, and then test the setup using Listing 15-24:

```
INSERT INTO temperature_test (station_name, observation_date, max_temp, min_temp)
VALUES
    ('North Station', '1/19/2019', 10, -3),
    ('North Station', '3/20/2019', 28, 19),
    ('North Station', '5/2/2019', 65, 42),
    ('North Station', '8/9/2019', 93, 74);

SELECT * FROM temperature_test;
```

Listing 15-24: Inserting rows to test the temperature_insert trigger

Here we insert four rows into temperature_test, and we expect the temperature_insert trigger to fire for each row—and it does! The SELECT statement in the listing should display these results:

station_name	observation_date	max_temp	min_temp	max_temp_group
North Station	2019-01-19	10	-3	Inhumane
North Station	2019-03-20	28	19	Freezing
North Station	2019-05-02	65	42	Pleasant
North Station	2019-08-09	93	74	Hot

Due to the trigger and function we created, each `max_temp` inserted automatically receives the appropriate classification in the `max_temp_group` column.

This temperature example and the earlier grade-change auditing example are rudimentary, but they give you a glimpse of how useful triggers and functions can be in simplifying data maintenance.

Wrapping Up

Although the techniques you learned in this chapter begin to merge with those of a database administrator, you can apply the concepts to reduce the amount of time you spend repeating certain tasks. I hope these approaches will help you free up more time to find interesting stories in your data.

This chapter concludes our discussion of analysis techniques and the SQL language. The next two chapters offer workflow tips to help you increase your command of PostgreSQL. They include how to connect to a database and run queries from your computer's command line, and how to maintain your database.

TRY IT YOURSELF

Review the concepts in the chapter with these exercises:

1. Create a view that displays the number of New York City taxi trips per hour. Use the taxi data in Chapter 11 and the query in Listing 11-8 on page 182.

2. In Chapter 10, you learned how to calculate rates per thousand. Turn that formula into a `rates_per_thousand()` function that takes three arguments to calculate the result: `observed_number`, `base_number`, and `decimal_places`.

3. In Chapter 9, you worked with the `meat_poultry_egg_inspect` table that listed food processing facilities. Write a trigger that automatically adds an inspection date each time you insert a new facility into the table. Use the `inspection_date` column added in Listing 9-19 on page 146, and set the date to be six months from the current date. You should be able to describe the steps needed to implement a trigger and how the steps relate to each other.

16

USING POSTGRESQL FROM THE COMMAND LINE

Before computers featured a graphical user interface (GUI), which lets you use menus, icons, and buttons to navigate applications, the main way to issue instructions to them was by entering commands on the *command line*. The command line—also called a command line interface, console, shell, or terminal—is a text-based interface where you enter names of programs or other commands to perform tasks, such as editing files or listing the contents of a file directory.

When I was in college, to edit a file, I had to enter commands into a terminal connected to an IBM mainframe computer. The reams of text that then scrolled onscreen were reminiscent of the green characters that define the virtual world portrayed in *The Matrix*. It felt mysterious and as though I had attained new powers. Even today, movies portray fictional hackers by showing them entering cryptic, text-only commands on a computer.

In this chapter, I'll show you how to access this text-only world. Here are some advantages of working from the command line instead of a GUI, such as pgAdmin:

- You can often work faster by entering short commands instead of clicking through layers of menu items.
- You gain access to some functions that only the command line provides.
- If command line access is all you have to work with (for example, when you've connected to a remote computer), you can still get work done.

We'll use psql, a command line tool in PostgreSQL that lets you run queries, manage database objects, and interact with the computer's operating system via text command. You'll first learn how to set up and access your computer's command line, and then launch psql.

It takes time to learn how to use the command line, and even experienced experts often resort to documentation to recall the available command line options. But learning to use the command line greatly enhances your work efficiency.

Setting Up the Command Line for psql

To start, we'll access the command line on your operating system and set an *environment variable* called PATH that tells your system where to find psql. Environment variables hold parameters that specify system or application configurations, such as where to store temporary files, or allow you to enable or disable options. Setting PATH, which stores the names of one or more directories containing executable programs, tells the command line interface the location of psql, avoiding the hassle of having to enter its full directory path each time you launch it.

Windows psql Setup

On Windows, you'll run psql within Command Prompt, the application that provides that system's command line interface. Let's start by using PATH to tell Command Prompt where to find *psql.exe*, which is the full name of the psql application on Windows, as well as other PostgreSQL command line utilities.

Adding psql and Utilities to the Windows PATH

The following steps assume that you installed PostgreSQL according to the instructions described in "Windows Installation" on page xxix. (If you installed PostgreSQL another way, use the Windows File Explorer to search your C: drive to find the directory that holds *psql.exe*, and then replace *C:\Program Files\PostgreSQL\x.y\bin* in steps 5 and 6 with your own path.)

1. Open the Windows Control Panel. Enter `Control Panel` in the search box on the Windows taskbar, and then click the **Control Panel** icon.

2. Inside the Control Panel app, enter `Environment` in the search box at the top right. In the list of search results displayed, click **Edit the System Environment Variables**. A System Properties dialog should appear.

3. In the System Properties dialog, on the Advanced tab, click **Environment Variables**. The dialog that opens should have two sections: User variables and System variables. In the User variables section, if you don't see a `PATH` variable, continue to step a to create a new one. If you do see an existing `PATH` variable, continue to step b to modify it.

   a. If you don't see `PATH` in the User variables section, click **New** to open a New User Variable dialog, shown in Figure 16-1.

Figure 16-1: Creating a new PATH environment variable in Windows 10

   In the Variable name box, enter `PATH`. In the Variable value box, enter `C:\Program Files\PostgreSQL\x.y\bin`, where *x.y* is the version of PostgreSQL you're using. Click **OK** to close all the dialogs.

   b. If you do see an existing `PATH` variable in the User variables section, highlight it and click **Edit**. In the list of variables that displays, click **New** and enter `C:\Program Files\PostgreSQL\x.y\bin`, where *x.y* is the version of PostgreSQL you're using. It should look like the highlighted line in Figure 16-2. When you're finished, click **OK** to close all the dialogs.

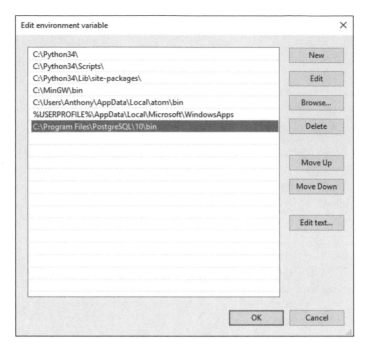

Figure 16-2: Editing existing PATH environment variables in Windows 10

Now when you launch Command Prompt, the PATH should include the directory. Note that any time you make changes to the PATH, you must close and reopen Command Prompt for the changes to take effect. Next, let's set up Command Prompt.

Launching and Configuring the Windows Command Prompt

Command Prompt is an executable file named *cmd.exe*. To launch it, select **Start ▸ Windows System ▸ Command Prompt**. When the application opens, you should see a window with a black background that displays version and copyright information along with a prompt showing your current directory. On my Windows 10 system, Command Prompt opens to my default user directory and displays C:\Users\Anthony>, as shown in Figure 16-3.

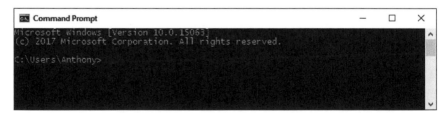

Figure 16-3: My Command Prompt in Windows 10

NOTE *For fast access to Command Prompt, you can add it to your Windows taskbar. When Command Prompt is running, right-click its icon on the taskbar and then select **Pin to taskbar**.*

The line `C:\Users\Anthony>` indicates that Command Prompt's current working directory is my C: drive, which is typically the main hard drive on a Windows system, and the *\Users\Anthony* directory on that drive. The right arrow (>) indicates the area where you type your commands.

You can customize the font and colors plus access other settings by clicking the Command Prompt icon at the left of its window bar and selecting **Properties** from the menu. To make Command Prompt more suited for query output, I recommend setting the window size (on the Layout tab) to a width of 80 and a height of 25. My preferred font is Lucida Console 14, but experiment to find one you like.

Entering Instructions on Windows Command Prompt

Now you're ready to enter instructions in Command Prompt. Enter `help` at the prompt, and press ENTER on your keyboard to see a list of available commands. You can view information about a particular command by typing its name after `help`. For example, enter `help time` to display information on using the `time` command to set or view the system time.

Exploring the full workings of Command Prompt is beyond the scope of this book; however, you should try some of the commands in Table 16-1, which contains frequently used commands you'll find immediately useful but are not necessary for the exercises in this chapter. Also, check out Command Prompt cheat sheets online for more information.

Table 16-1: Useful Windows Commands

Command	Function	Example	Action
cd	Change directory	`cd C:\my-stuff`	Change to the *my-stuff* directory on the C: drive
copy	Copy a file	`copy C:\my-stuff\` `song.mp3 C:\Music\` `song_favorite.mp3`	Copy the *song.mp3* file from *my-stuff* to a new file called *song_favorite.mp3* in the *Music* directory
del	Delete	`del *.jpg`	Delete all files with a *.jpg* extension in the current directory (asterisk wildcard)
dir	List directory contents	`dir /p`	Show directory contents one screen at a time (using the /p option)
findstr	Find strings in text files matching a regular expression	`findstr "peach" *.txt`	Search for the text "peach" in all *.txt* files in the current directory
mkdir	Make a new directory	`makedir C:\my-stuff\` `Salad`	Create a *Salad* directory inside the *my-stuff* directory
move	Move a file	`move C:\my-stuff\song` `.mp3 C:\Music\`	Move the file *song.mp3* to the *C:\Music* directory

With your Command Prompt open and configured, you're ready to roll. Skip ahead to "Working with psql" on page 299.

macOS psql Setup

On macOS, you'll run psql within Terminal, the application that provides access to that system's command line via a *shell* program called bash. Shell programs on Unix- or Linux-based systems, including macOS, provide not only the command prompt where users enter instructions, but also their own programming language for automating tasks. For example, you can use bash commands to write a program to log in to a remote computer, transfer files, and log out. Let's start by telling bash where to find psql and other PostgreSQL command line utilities by setting the PATH environment variable. Then we'll launch Terminal.

Adding psql and Utilities to the macOS PATH

Before Terminal loads the bash shell, it checks for the presence of several optional text files that can supply configuration information. We'll place our PATH information inside *.bash_profile*, which is one of these optional text files. Then, whenever we open Terminal, the startup process should read *.bash_profile* and obtain the PATH value.

NOTE *You can also use* .bash_profile *to set your command line's colors, automatically run programs, and create shortcuts, among other tasks. See* https://natelandau.com/my-mac-osx-bash_profile/ *for a great example of customizing the file.*

On Unix- or Linux-based systems, files that begin with a period are called *dot files* and are hidden by default. We'll need to edit *.bash_profile* to add PATH. Using the following steps, unhide *.bash_profile* so it appears in the macOS Finder:

1. Launch Terminal by navigating to **Applications ▸ Utilities ▸ Terminal**.
2. At the command prompt, which displays your username and computer name followed by a dollar sign (\$), enter the following text and then press RETURN:

```
defaults write com.apple.finder AppleShowAllFiles YES
```

3. Quit Terminal (⌘-Q). Then, while holding down the OPTION key, right-click the Finder icon on your Mac dock, and select **Relaunch**.

Follow these steps to edit or create *.bash_profile*:

1. Using the macOS Finder, navigate to your user directory by opening the Finder and clicking **Macintosh HD** then **Users**.
2. Open your user directory (it should have a house icon). Because you changed the setting to show hidden files, you should now see grayed-out files and directories, which are normally hidden, along with regular files and directories.

3. Check for an existing *.bash_profile* file. If one exists, right-click and open it with your preferred text editor or use the macOS TextEdit app. If *.bash_profile* doesn't exist, open TextEdit to create and save a file with that name to your user directory.

Next, we'll add a PATH statement to *.bash_profile*. These instructions assume you installed PostgreSQL using Postgres.app, as outlined in "macOS Installation" on page xxx. To add to the path, place the following line in *.bash_profile*:

```
export PATH="/Applications/Postgres.app/Contents/Versions/latest/bin:$PATH"
```

Save and close the file. If Terminal is open, close and relaunch it before moving on to the next section.

Launching and Configuring the macOS Terminal

Launch Terminal by navigating to **Applications ▸ Utilities ▸ Terminal**. When it opens, you should see a window that displays the date and time of your last login followed by a prompt that includes your computer name, current working directory, and username, ending with a dollar sign ($). On my Mac, the prompt displays ad:~ anthony$, as shown in Figure 16-4.

Figure 16-4: Terminal command line in macOS

The tilde (~) indicates that Terminal is currently working in my home directory, which is /Users/anthony. Terminal doesn't display the full directory path, but you can see that information at any time by entering the pwd command (short for "print working directory") and pressing RETURN on your keyboard. The area after the dollar sign is where you type commands.

NOTE *For fast access to Terminal, add it to your macOS Dock. While Terminal is running, right-click its icon and select **Options ▸ Keep in Dock**.*

If you've never used Terminal, its default black and white color scheme might seem boring. You can change fonts, colors, and other settings by selecting **Terminal ▸ Preferences**. To make Terminal bigger to better fit the query output display, I recommend setting the window size (on the Window tab) to a width of 80 columns and a height of 25 rows. My preferred font (on the Text tab) is Monaco 14, but experiment to find one you like.

Exploring the full workings of Terminal and related commands is beyond the scope of this book, but take some time to try several commands. Table 16-2 lists commonly used commands you'll find immediately useful but not necessary for the exercises in this chapter. Enter man (short for "manual") followed by a command name to get help on any command. For example, you can use man ls to find out how to use the ls command to list directory contents.

Table 16-2: Useful Terminal Commands

Command	Function	Example	Action
cd	Change directory	cd /Users/pparker/ my-stuff/	Change to the *my-stuff* directory
cp	Copy files	cp song.mp3 song_backup.mp3	Copy the file *song.mp3* to *song_backup .mp3* in the current directory
grep	Find strings in a text file matching a regular expression	grep 'us_counties _2010' *.sql	Find all lines in files with a *.sql* extension that have the text "us_counties_2010"
ls	List directory contents	ls -al	List all files and directories (including hidden) in "long" format
mkdir	Make a new directory	mkdir resumes	Make a directory named *resumes* under the current working directory
mv	Move a file	mv song.mp3 /Users/ pparker/songs	Move the file *song.mp3* from the current directory to a */songs* directory under a user directory
rm	Remove (delete) files	rm *.jpg	Delete all files with a *.jpg* extension in the current directory (asterisk wildcard)

With your Terminal open and configured, you're ready to roll. Skip ahead to "Working with psql" on page 299.

Linux psql Setup

Recall from "Linux Installation" on page xxxi that methods for installing PostgreSQL vary according to your Linux distribution. Nevertheless, psql is part of the standard PostgreSQL install, and you probably already ran psql commands as part of the installation process via your distribution's command line terminal application. Even if you didn't, standard Linux installations of PostgreSQL will automatically add psql to your PATH, so you should be able to access it.

Launch a terminal application. On some distributions, such as Ubuntu, you can open a terminal by pressing CTRL-ALT-T. Also note that the macOS Terminal commands in Table 16-2 apply to Linux as well and may be useful to you.

With your terminal open, you're ready to roll. Proceed to the next section, "Working with psql."

Working with psql

Now that you've identified your command line interface and set it up to recognize the location of psql, let's launch psql and connect to a database on your local installation of PostgreSQL. Then we'll explore executing queries and special commands for retrieving database information.

Launching psql and Connecting to a Database

Regardless of the operating system you're using, you start psql in the same way. Open your command line interface (Command Prompt on Windows, Terminal on macOS or Linux). To launch psql, we use the following pattern at the command prompt:

```
psql -d database_name -U user_name
```

Following the psql application name, we provide the database name after a -d argument and a username after -U.

For the database name, we'll use analysis, which is where we created the majority of our tables for the book's exercises. For username, we'll use postgres, which is the default user created during installation. For example, to connect your local machine to the analysis database, you would enter this:

```
psql -d analysis -U postgres
```

You can connect to a database on a remote server by specifying the -h argument followed by the host name. For example, you would use the following line if you were connecting to a computer on a server called example.com:

```
psql -d analysis -U postgres -h example.com
```

If you set a password during installation, you should receive a password prompt when psql launches. If so, enter your password and press ENTER. You should then see a prompt that looks like this:

```
psql (10.1)
Type "help" for help.

analysis=#
```

Here, the first line lists the version number of psql and the server you're connected to. Your version will vary depending on when you installed PostgreSQL. The prompt where you'll enter commands is analysis=#, which refers to the name of the database, followed by an equal sign (=) and a hash mark (#). The hash mark indicates that you're logged in with *superuser* privileges, which give you unlimited ability to access and create objects and set up accounts and security. If you're logged in as a user without superuser privileges, the last character of the prompt will be a greater-than sign (>). As you can see, the user account you logged in with here (postgres) is a superuser.

NOTE   *PostgreSQL installations create a default superuser account called* postgres. *If you're running postgres.app on macOS, that installation created an additional superuser account that has your system username and no password.*

Getting Help

At the psql prompt, you can easily get help with psql commands and SQL commands. Table 16-3 lists commands you can type at the psql prompt and shows the information they'll display.

Table 16-3: Help Commands Within psql

Command	Displays
\?	Commands available within psql, such as \dt to list tables.
\? options	Options for use with the psql command, such as -U to specify a username.
\? variables	Variables for use with psql, such as VERSION for the current psql version.
\h	List of SQL commands. Add a command name to see detailed help for it (for example, \h INSERT).

Even experienced users often need a refresher on commands and options, and having the details in the psql application is handy. Let's move on and explore some commands.

Changing the User and Database Connection

You can use a series of *meta-commands*, which are preceded by a backslash, to issue instructions to psql rather than the database. For example, to connect to a different database or switch the user account you're connected to, you can use the \c meta-command. To switch to the gis_analysis database we created in Chapter 14, enter \c followed by the name of the database at the psql prompt:

```
analysis=# \c gis_analysis
```

The application should respond with the following message:

```
You are now connected to database "gis_analysis" as user "postgres".
gis_analysis=#
```

To log in as a different user, for example, using a username the macOS installation created for me, I could add that username after the database name. On my Mac, the syntax looks like this:

```
analysis-# \c gis_analysis anthony
```

The response should be as follows:

```
You are now connected to database "gis_analysis" as user "anthony".
gis_analysis=#
```

You might have various reasons to use multiple user accounts like this. For example, you might want to create a user account with limited permissions for colleagues or for a database application. You can learn more about creating and managing user roles by reading the PostgreSQL documentation at *https://www.postgresql.org/docs/current/static/sql-createrole.html*.

Let's switch back to the analysis database using the \c command. Next, we'll enter SQL commands at the psql prompt.

Running SQL Queries on psql

We've configured psql and connected to a database, so now let's run some SQL queries, starting with a single-line query and then a multiline query.

To enter SQL into psql, you can type it directly at the prompt. For example, to see a few rows from the 2010 Census table we've used throughout the book, enter a query at the prompt, as shown in Listing 16-1:

```
analysis=# SELECT geo_name FROM us_counties_2010 LIMIT 3;
```

Listing 16-1: Entering a single-line query in psql

Press ENTER to execute the query, and psql should display the following results in text including the number of rows returned:

```
    geo_name
----------------
 Autauga County
 Baldwin County
```

```
Barbour County
(3 rows)

analysis=#
```

Below the result, you can see the analysis=# prompt again, ready for further input from the user. Press the up and down arrows on your keyboard to you scroll through recent queries to avoid having to retype them. Or you can simply enter a new query.

Entering a Multiline Query

You're not limited to single-line queries. For example, you can press ENTER each time you want to enter a new line. Note that psql won't execute the query until you provide a line that ends with a semicolon. To see an example, re-enter the query in Listing 16-1 using the format shown in Listing 16-2:

```
analysis=# SELECT geo_name
analysis-# FROM us_counties_2010
analysis-# LIMIT 3;
```

Listing 16-2: Entering a multiline query in psql

Note that when your query extends past one line, the symbol between the database name and the hash mark changes from an equal sign (=) to a hyphen (-). This multiline query executes only when you press ENTER after the final line, which ends with a semicolon.

Checking for Open Parentheses in the psql Prompt

Another helpful feature of psql is that it shows when you haven't closed a pair of parentheses. Listing 16-3 shows this in action:

```
analysis=# CREATE TABLE wineries (
analysis(# id bigint,
analysis(# winery_name varchar(100)
analysis(# );
CREATE TABLE
```

Listing 16-3: Showing open parentheses in the psql prompt

Here, you create a simple table called wineries that has two columns. After entering the first line of the CREATE TABLE statement and an open parenthesis, the prompt then changes from analysis=# to analysis(# to include an open parenthesis that reminds you an open parenthesis needs closing. The prompt maintains that configuration until you add the closing parenthesis.

NOTE   *If you have a lengthy query saved in a text file, such as one from this book's resources, you can copy it to your computer clipboard and paste it into psql (CTRL-V on Windows, ⌘-V on macOS, and SHIFT-CTRL-V on Linux). That saves you from typing the whole query. After you paste the query text into psql, press ENTER to execute it.*

Editing Queries

If you're working with a query in psql and want to modify it, you can edit it using the \e or \edit meta-command. Enter \e to open the last-executed query in a text editor. Which editor psql uses by default depends on your operating system.

On Windows, psql defaults to Notepad, a simple GUI text editor. On macOS and Linux, psql uses a command line application called vim, which is a favorite among programmers but can seem inscrutable for beginners. Check out a helpful vim cheat sheet at *https://vim.rtorr.com/*. For now, you can use the following steps to make simple edits:

- When vim opens the query in an editing window, press **I** to activate insert mode.

- Make your edits to the query.

- Press ESC and then SHIFT+: to display a colon command prompt at the bottom left of the vim screen, which is where you enter commands to control vim.

- Enter **wq** (for "write, quit") and press ENTER to save your changes.

Now when you exit to the psql prompt, it should execute your revised query. Press the up arrow key to see the revised text.

Navigating and Formatting Results

The query you ran in Listings 16-1 and 16-2 returned only one column and a handful of rows, so its output was contained nicely in your command line interface. But for queries with more columns or rows, the output can take up more than one screen, making it difficult to navigate. Fortunately, you can use formatting options using the \pset meta-command to tailor the output into a format you prefer.

Setting Paging of Results

You can adjust the output format by specifying how psql displays lengthy query results. For example, Listing 16-4 shows the change in output format when we remove the LIMIT clause from the query in Listing 16-1 and execute it at the psql prompt:

```
analysis=# SELECT geo_name FROM us_counties_2010;
          geo_name
----------------------------------
 Autauga County
 Baldwin County
 Barbour County
 Bibb County
 Blount County
 Bullock County
 Butler County
 Calhoun County
 Chambers County
```

```
Cherokee County
Chilton County
Choctaw County
Clarke County
Clay County
Cleburne County
Coffee County
Colbert County
:
```

Listing 16-4: A query with scrolling results

Recall that this table has 3,143 rows. Listing 16-4 shows only the first 17 on the screen with a colon at the bottom (the number of visible rows depends on your terminal configuration). The colon indicates that there are more results than shown; press the down arrow key to scroll through them. Scrolling through this many rows can take a while. Press Q at any time to exit the scrolling results and return to the psql prompt.

You can have your results immediately scroll to the end by changing the pager setting using the \pset pager meta-command. Run that command at your psql prompt, and it should return the message Pager usage is off. Now when you rerun the query in Listing 16-3 with the pager setting turned off, you should see something like this:

```
--snip--
Niobrara County
Park County
Platte County
Sheridan County
Sublette County
Sweetwater County
Teton County
Uinta County
Washakie County
Weston County
(3143 rows)

analysis=#
```

You're immediately taken to the end of the results without having to scroll. To turn paging back on, run \pset pager again.

Formatting the Results Grid

You can also use the \pset meta-command with the following options to format how the results look:

border *int*   Use this option to specify whether the results grid has no border (0), internal lines dividing columns (1), or lines around all cells (2). For example, \pset border 2 sets lines around all cells.

format unaligned   Use the option \pset format unaligned to display the results in lines separated by a delimiter rather than in columns, similar to what you would see in a CSV file. The separator defaults to a pipe symbol (|). You can set a different separator using the fieldsep command. For example, to set a comma as the separator, run \pset fieldsep ','. To revert to a column view, run \pset format aligned. You can use the psql meta-command \a to toggle between aligned and unaligned views.

footer   Use this option to toggle the results footer, which displays the result row count, on or off.

null   Use this option to set how null values are displayed. By default, they show as blanks. You can run \pset null 'NULL' to replace blanks with all-caps NULL when the column value is NULL.

You can explore additional options in the PostgreSQL documentation at *https://www.postgresql.org/docs/current/static/app-psql.html*. In addition, it's possible to set up a *.psqlrc* file on macOS or Linux or a *psqlrc.conf* file on Windows to hold your configuration preferences and load them each time psql starts. A good example is provided at *https://www.citusdata.com/blog/2017/07/16/customizing-my-postgres-shell-using-psqlrc/*.

Viewing Expanded Results

Sometimes, it's helpful to view results as a vertical block listing rather than in rows and columns, particularly when data is too big to fit onscreen in the normal horizontal results grid. Also, I often employ this format when I want an easy-to-scan way to review the values in columns on a row-by-row basis. In psql, you can switch to this view using the \x (for expanded) meta-command. The best way to understand the difference between normal and expanded view is by looking at an example. Listing 16-5 shows the normal display you see when querying the grades table in Chapter 15 using psql:

```
analysis=# SELECT * FROM grades;
 student_id | course_id |        course       | grade
------------+-----------+---------------------+-------
          1 |         2 | English 11B         | D
          1 |         3 | World History 11B   | C
          1 |         4 | Trig 2              | B
          1 |         1 | Biology 2           | C
(4 rows)
```

Listing 16-5: Normal display of the grades table query

To change to the expanded view, enter \x at the psql prompt, which should display the Expanded display is on message. Then, when you run the same query again, you should see the expanded results, as shown in Listing 16-6:

```
analysis=# SELECT * FROM grades;
-[ RECORD 1 ]----------------
student_id | 1
course_id  | 2
course     | English 11B
grade      | D
```

```
-[ RECORD 2 ]-----------------
student_id | 1
course_id  | 3
course     | World History 11B
grade      | C
-[ RECORD 3 ]-----------------
student_id | 1
course_id  | 4
course     | Trig 2
grade      | B
-[ RECORD 4 ]-----------------
student_id | 1
course_id  | 1
course     | Biology 2
grade      | C
```

Listing 16-6: Expanded display of the grades table query

The results appear in vertical blocks separated by record numbers. Depending on your needs and the type of data you're working with, this format might be easier to read. You can revert to column display by entering \x again at the psql prompt. In addition, setting \x auto will make PostgreSQL automatically display the results in a table or expanded view based on the size of the output.

Next, let's explore how to use psql to dig into database information.

Meta-Commands for Database Information

In addition to writing queries from the command line, you can also use psql to display details about tables and other objects and functions in your database. To do this, you use a series of meta-commands that start with \d and append a plus sign (+) to expand the output. You can also supply an optional pattern to filter the output.

For example, you can enter \dt+ to list all tables in the database and their size. Here's a snippet of the output on my system:

```
                              List of relations
 Schema |         Name         | Type  |  Owner   |    Size    | Description
--------+----------------------+-------+----------+------------+------------
 public | acs_2011_2015_stats  | table | postgres | 320 kB     |
 public | crime_reports        | table | postgres | 16 kB      |
 public | date_time_types      | table | postgres | 8192 bytes |
 public | departments          | table | postgres | 8192 bytes |
 public | employees            | table | postgres | 8192 bytes |
 --snip--
```

This result lists all tables in the current database alphabetically.

You can filter the output by adding a pattern to match using a regular expression. For example, use \dt+ us* to show only tables whose names begin with us (the asterisk acts as a wildcard). The results should look like this:

```
                           List of relations
 Schema |       Name        | Type  |  Owner   |  Size   | Description
--------+-------------------+-------+----------+---------+-------------
 public | us_counties_2000  | table | postgres | 336 kB  |
 public | us_counties_2010  | table | postgres | 1352 kB |
```

Table 16-4 shows several additional \d commands you might find helpful.

Table 16-4: Examples of psql \d Commands

Command	Displays
\d [pattern]	Columns, data types, plus other information on objects
\di [pattern]	Indexes and their associated tables
\dt [pattern]	Tables and the account that owns them
\du [pattern]	User accounts and their attributes
\dv [pattern]	Views and the account that owns them
\dx [pattern]	Installed extensions

The entire list of \d commands is available in the PostgreSQL documentation at *https://www.postgresql.org/docs/current/static/app-psql.html*, or you can see details by using the \? command noted earlier.

Importing, Exporting, and Using Files

Now let's explore how to get data in and out of tables or save information when you're working on a remote server. The psql command line tool offers one meta-command for importing and exporting data (\copy) and another for copying query output to a file (\o). We'll start with the \copy command.

Using \copy for Import and Export

In Chapter 4, you learned how to use the SQL COPY command to import and export data. It's a straightforward process, but there is one significant limitation: the file you're importing or exporting must be on the same machine as the PostgreSQL server. That's fine if you're working on your local machine, as you've been doing with these exercises. But if you're connecting to a database on a remote computer, you might not have access to the file system to provide a file to import or to fetch a file you've exported. You can get around this restriction by using the \copy meta-command in psql.

The \copy meta-command works just like the SQL COPY command except when you execute it at the psql prompt, it can route data from your local machine to a remote server if that's what you're connected to. We won't actually connect to a remote server to try this, but you can still learn the syntax.

In Listing 16-7, we use psql to DROP the small state_regions table you created in Chapter 9, and then re-create the table and import data using \copy. You'll need to change the file path to match the location of the file on your computer.

```
analysis=# DROP TABLE state_regions;
DROP TABLE

analysis=# CREATE TABLE state_regions (
analysis(#     st varchar(2) CONSTRAINT st_key PRIMARY KEY,
analysis(#     region varchar(20) NOT NULL
analysis(# );

CREATE TABLE

analysis=# \copy state_regions FROM 'C:\YourDirectory\state_regions.csv' WITH (FORMAT CSV, HEADER);
COPY 56
```

Listing 16-7: Importing data using \copy

The DROP TABLE and CREATE TABLE statements in Listing 16-7 are straightforward. We first delete the state_regions table if it exists, and then re-create it. Then, to load the table, we use \copy with the same syntax used with SQL COPY, naming a FROM clause that includes the file path on your machine, and a WITH clause that specifies the file is a CSV and has a header row. When you execute the statement, the server should respond with COPY 56, letting you know the rows have been successfully imported.

If you were connected via psql to a remote server, you would use the same \copy syntax, and the command would just route your local file to the remote server for importing. In this example, we used \copy FROM to import a file. We could also use \copy TO for exporting. Let's look at another way to export output to a file.

Saving Query Output to a File

It's sometimes helpful to save the query results and messages generated during a psql session to a file, whether to keep a history of your work or to use the output in a spreadsheet or other application. To send query output to a file, you can use the \o meta-command along with the full path and name of the output file.

NOTE *On Windows, file paths for the \o command must either use Linux-style forward slashes, such as* C:/my-stuff/my-file.txt, *or double backslashes, such as* C:\\my-stuff\\my-file.txt.

For example, one of my favorite tricks is to set the output format to unaligned with a comma as a field separator and no row count in the footer, similar but not identical to a CSV output. (It's not identical because a true CSV file, as you learned in Chapter 4, can include a character to quote values that contain a delimiter. Still, this trick works for simple CSV-like output.) Listing 16-8 shows the sequence of commands at the psql prompt:

```
❶ analysis=# \a \f , \pset footer
  Output format is unaligned.
  Field separator is ",".
  Default footer is off.

  analysis=# SELECT * FROM grades;
❷ student_id,course_id,course,grade
  1,2,English 11B,D
  1,3,World History 11B,C
  1,4,Trig 2,B
  1,1,Biology 2,C

❸ analysis=# \o 'C:/YourDirectory/query_output.csv'

  analysis=# SELECT * FROM grades;
❹ analysis=#
```

Listing 16-8: Saving query output to a file

First, set the output format ❶ using the meta-commands \a, \f, and \pset footer for unaligned, comma-separated data with no footer. When you run a simple SELECT query on the grades table, the output ❷ should return as values separated by commas. Next, to send that data to a file the next time you run the query, use the \o meta-command and then provide a complete path to a file called *query_output.csv* ❸. When you run the SELECT query again, there should be no output to the screen ❹. Instead, you'll find a file with the contents of the query in the directory specified at ❸.

Note that every time you run a query from this point, the output is appended to the same file specified after the \o command. To stop saving output to that file, you can either specify a new file or enter \o with no filename to resume having results output to the screen.

Reading and Executing SQL Stored in a File

You can run SQL stored in a text file by executing psql on the command line and supplying the file name after an -f argument. This syntax lets you quickly run a query or table update from the command line or in conjunction with a system scheduler to run a job at regular intervals.

Let's say you saved the SELECT * FROM grades; query in a file called *display-grades.sql*. To run the saved query, use the following psql syntax at your command line:

```
psql -d analysis -U postgres -f display-grades.sql
```

When you press ENTER, psql should launch, run the stored query in the file, display the results, and exit. For repetitive tasks, this workflow can save you considerable time because you avoid launching pgAdmin or rewriting a query. You also can stack multiple queries in the file so they run in succession, which, for example, you might do if you want to run multiple updates on your database.

Additional Command Line Utilities to Expedite Tasks

PostgreSQL includes additional command line utilities that come in handy if you're connected to a remote server or just want to save time by using the command line instead of launching pgAdmin or another GUI. You can enter these commands in your command line interface without launching psql. A listing is available at *https://www.postgresql.org/docs/current/static/reference-client .html*, and I'll explain several in Chapter 17 that are specific to database maintenance. But here I'll cover two that are particularly useful: creating a database at the command line with the createdb utility and loading shapefiles into a PostGIS database via the shp2pgsql utility.

Adding a Database with createdb

The first SQL statement you learned in Chapter 1 was CREATE DATABASE, which you used to add the database analysis to your PostgreSQL server. Rather than launching pgAdmin and writing a CREATE DATABASE statement, you can perform a similar action using the createdb command line utility. For example, to create a new database on your server named box_office, run the following at your command line:

```
createdb -U postgres -e box_office
```

The -U argument tells the command to connect to the PostgreSQL server using the postgres account. The -e argument (for "echo") tells the command to print the SQL statement to the screen. Running this command generates the response CREATE DATABASE box_office; in addition to creating the database. You can then connect to the new database via psql using the following line:

```
psql -d box_office -U postgres
```

The createdb command accepts arguments to connect to a remote server (just like psql does) and to set options for the new database. A full list of arguments is available at *https://www.postgresql.org/docs/current/static/ app-createdb.html*. Again, the createdb command is a time-saver that comes in handy when you don't have access to a GUI.

Loading Shapefiles with shp2pgsql

In Chapter 14, you learned to import a shapefile into a database with the Shapefile Import/Export Manager included in the PostGIS suite. That tool's GUI is easy to navigate, but importing a shapefile using the PostGIS command line tool shp2pgsql lets you accomplish the same thing using a single text command.

To import a shapefile into a new table from the command line, use the following syntax:

```
shp2pgsql -I -s SRID -W encoding shapefile_name table_name | psql -d database -U user
```

A lot is happening in this single line. Here's a breakdown of the arguments (if you skipped Chapter 14, you might need to review it now):

-I Adds a GiST index on the new table's geometry column.

-s Lets you specify an SRID for the geometric data.

-W Lets you specify encoding. (Recall that we used Latin1 for census shapefiles.)

shapefile_name The name (including full path) of the file ending with the *.shp* extension.

table_name The name of the table the shapefile is imported to.

Following these arguments, you place a pipe symbol (|) to direct the output of shp2pgsql to psql, which has the arguments for naming the database and user. For example, to load the *tl_2010_us_county10.shp* shapefile into a us_counties_2010_shp table in the gis_analysis database, as you did in Chapter 14, you can simply run the following command. Note that although this command wraps onto two lines here, it should be entered as one line in the command line:

```
shp2pgsql -I -s 4269 -W Latin1 tl_2010_us_county10.shp us_counties_2010_shp | psql -d
gis_analysis -U postgres
```

The server should respond with a number of SQL INSERT statements before creating the index and returning you to the command line. It might take some time to construct the entire set of arguments the first time around. But after you've done one, subsequent imports should take less time because you can simply substitute file and table names into the syntax you already wrote.

Wrapping Up

Are you feeling mysterious and powerful yet? Indeed, when you delve into a command line interface and make the computer do your bidding using text commands, you enter a world of computing that resembles a sci-fi movie sequence. Not only does working from the command line save you time, but it also helps you overcome barriers you encounter when you're working in environments that don't support graphical tools. In this chapter, you learned the basics of working with the command line plus PostgreSQL specifics. You discovered your operating system's command line application and set it up to work with psql. Then you connected psql to a database and learned how to run SQL queries via the command line. Many experienced computer users prefer to use the command line for its simplicity and speed once they become familiar with using it. You might, too.

In Chapter 17, we'll review common database maintenance tasks including backing up data, changing server settings, and managing the growth of your database. These tasks will give you more control over your working environment and help you better manage your data analysis projects.

TRY IT YOURSELF

To reinforce the techniques in this chapter, choose an example from an earlier chapter and try working through it using only the command line. Chapter 14 is a good choice because it gives you the opportunity to work with psql and the shapefile loader shp2pgsql. But choose any example that you think you would benefit from reviewing.

17

MAINTAINING YOUR DATABASE

To wrap up our exploration of SQL, we'll look at key database maintenance tasks and options for customizing PostgreSQL. In this chapter, you'll learn how to track and conserve space in your databases, how to change system settings, and how to back up and restore databases. How often you'll need to perform these tasks depends on your current role and interests. But if you want to be a *database administrator* or a *backend developer,* the topics covered here are vital to both jobs.

It's worth noting that database maintenance and performance tuning are often the subjects of entire books, and this chapter mainly serves as an introduction to a handful of essentials. If you want to learn more, a good place to begin is with the resources in the Appendix.

Let's start with the PostgreSQL VACUUM feature, which lets you shrink the size of tables by removing unused rows.

Recovering Unused Space with VACUUM

To prevent database files from growing out of control, you can use the PostgreSQL VACUUM command. In "Improving Performance When Updating Large Tables" on page 151, you learned that the size of PostgreSQL tables can grow as a result of routine operations. For example, when you update a value in a row, the database creates a new version of that row that includes the updated value, but it doesn't delete the old version of the row. (PostgreSQL documentation refers to these leftover rows that you can't see as "dead" rows.)

Similarly, when you delete a row, even though the row is no longer visible, it lives on as a dead row in the table. The database uses dead rows to provide certain features in environments where multiple transactions are occurring and old versions of rows might be needed by transactions other than the current one.

Running VACUUM designates the space occupied by dead rows as available for the database to use again. But VACUUM doesn't return the space to your system's disk. Instead, it just flags that space as available for the database to use for its next operation. To return unused space to your disk, you must use the VACUUM FULL option, which creates a new version of the table that doesn't include the freed-up dead row space.

Although you can run VACUUM on demand, by default PostgreSQL runs the *autovacuum* background process that monitors the database and runs VACUUM as needed. Later in this chapter I'll show you how to monitor autovacuum as well as run the VACUUM command manually.

But first, let's look at how a table grows as a result of updates and how you can track this growth.

Tracking Table Size

We'll create a small test table and monitor its growth in size as we fill it with data and perform an update. The code for this exercise, as with all resources for the book, is available at *https://www.nostarch.com/practicalSQL/*.

Creating a Table and Checking Its Size

Listing 17-1 creates a vacuum_test table with a single column to hold an integer. Run the code, and then we'll measure the table's size.

```
CREATE TABLE vacuum_test (
    integer_column integer
);
```

Listing 17-1: Creating a table to test vacuuming

Before we fill the table with test data, let's check how much space it occupies on disk to establish a reference point. We can do so in two ways: check the table properties via the pgAdmin interface, or run queries using

PostgreSQL administrative functions. In pgAdmin, click once on a table to highlight it, and then click the **Statistics** tab. Table size is one of about two dozen indicators in the list.

I'll focus on running queries here because knowing them is helpful if for some reason pgAdmin isn't available or you're using another GUI. For example, Listing 17-2 shows how to check the vacuum_test table size using PostgreSQL functions:

```
SELECT ❶pg_size_pretty(
        ❷pg_total_relation_size('vacuum_test')
    );
```

Listing 17-2: Determining the size of vacuum_test

The outermost function, pg_size_pretty() ❶, converts bytes to a more easily understandable format in kilobytes, megabytes, or gigabytes. Wrapped inside pg_size_pretty() is the pg_total_relation_size() function ❷, which reports how many bytes a table, its indexes, and offline compressed data takes up on disk. Because the table is empty at this point, running the code in pgAdmin should return a value of 0 bytes, like this:

```
pg_size_pretty
--------------
0 bytes
```

You can get the same information using the command line. Launch psql as you learned in Chapter 16. Then, at the prompt, enter the command **\dt+ vacuum_test**, which should display the following information including table size:

```
                    List of relations
Schema    Name         Type    Owner     Size      Description
------    -----------  -----   --------  -------   -----------
public    vacuum_test  table   postgres  0 bytes
```

Again, the current size of the vacuum_test table should display 0 bytes.

Checking Table Size After Adding New Data

Let's add some data to the table and then check its size again. We'll use the generate_series() function introduced in Chapter 11 to fill the table's integer_column with 500,000 rows. Run the code in Listing 17-3 to do this:

```
INSERT INTO vacuum_test
SELECT * FROM generate_series(1,500000);
```

Listing 17-3: Inserting 500,000 rows into vacuum_test

This standard INSERT INTO statement adds the results of generate_series(), which is a series of values from 1 to 500,000, as rows to the table. After the query completes, rerun the query in Listing 17-2 to check the table size. You should see the following output:

```
pg_size_pretty
--------------
17 MB
```

The query reports that the vacuum_test table, now with a single column of 500,000 integers, uses 17MB of disk space.

Checking Table Size After Updates

Now, let's update the data to see how that affects the table size. We'll use the code in Listing 17-4 to update every row in the vacuum_test table by adding 1 to the integer_column values, replacing the existing value with a number that's one greater.

```
UPDATE vacuum_test
SET integer_column = integer_column + 1;
```

Listing 17-4: Updating all rows in vacuum_test

Run the code, and then test the table size again.

```
pg_size_pretty
--------------
35 MB
```

The table size has doubled from 17MB to 35MB! The increase seems excessive, because the UPDATE simply replaced existing numbers with values of a similar size. But as you might have guessed, the reason for this increase in table size is that for every updated value, PostgreSQL creates a new row, and the old row (a "dead" row) remains in the table. So even though you only see 500,000 rows, the table has double that number of rows.

Consequently, if you're working with a database that is frequently updated, it will grow even if you're not adding rows. This can surprise database owners who don't monitor disk space because the drive eventually fills up and leads to server errors. You can use VACUUM to avoid this scenario. We'll look at how using VACUUM and VACUUM FULL affects the table's size on disk. But first, let's review the process that runs VACUUM automatically as well as how to check on statistics related to table vacuums.

Monitoring the autovacuum Process

PostgreSQL's autovacuum process monitors the database and launches VACUUM automatically when it detects a large number of dead rows in a table. Although autovacuum is enabled by default, you can turn it on or off and configure it using the settings I'll cover in "Changing Server Settings" on page 318. Because autovacuum runs in the background, you won't see any immediately visible indication that it's working, but you can check its activity by running a query.

PostgreSQL has its own *statistics collector* that tracks database activity and usage. You can look at the statistics by querying one of several views the system provides. (See a complete list of views for monitoring the state of the system at *https://www.postgresql.org/docs/current/static/monitoring-stats .html*). To check the activity of autovacuum, query a view called pg_stat _all_tables using the code in Listing 17-5:

```
SELECT ❶relname,
       ❷last_vacuum,
       ❸last_autovacuum,
       ❹vacuum_count,
       ❺autovacuum_count
FROM pg_stat_all_tables
WHERE relname = 'vacuum_test';
```

Listing 17-5: Viewing autovacuum statistics for vacuum_test

The pg_stat_all_tables view shows relname ❶, which is the name of the table, plus statistics related to index scans, rows inserted and deleted, and other data. For this query, we're interested in last_vacuum ❷ and last_autovacuum ❸, which contain the last time the table was vacuumed manually and automatically, respectively. We also ask for vacuum_count ❹ and autovacuum_count ❺, which show the number of times the vacuum was run manually and automatically.

By default, autovacuum checks tables every minute. So, if a minute has passed since you last updated vacuum_test, you should see details of vacuum activity when you run the query in Listing 17-5. Here's what my system shows (note that I've removed seconds from the time to save space here):

relname	last_vacuum	last_autovacuum	vacuum_count	autovacuum_count
vacuum_test		2018-02-08 13:28	0	1

The table shows the date and time of the last autovacuum, and the autovacuum_count column shows one occurrence. This result indicates that autovacuum executed a VACUUM command on the table once. However, because we've not vacuumed manually, the last_vacuum column is empty and the vacuum_count is 0.

NOTE *The autovacuum process also runs the ANALYZE command, which gathers data on the contents of tables. PostgreSQL stores this information and uses it to execute queries efficiently in the future. You can run ANALYZE manually if needed.*

Recall that VACUUM designates dead rows as available for the database to reuse but doesn't reduce the size of the table on disk. You can confirm this by rerunning the code in Listing 17-2, which shows the table remains at 35MB even after the automatic vacuum.

Running VACUUM Manually

Depending on the server you're using, you can turn off autovacuum. (I'll show you how to view that setting in "Locating and Editing *postgresql.conf*" on page 319.) If autovacuum is off or if you simply want to run VACUUM manually, you can do so using a single line of code, as shown in Listing 17-6:

```
VACUUM vacuum_test;
```

Listing 17-6: Running VACUUM manually

After you run this command, it should return the message VACUUM from the server. Now when you fetch statistics again using the query in Listing 17-5, you should see that the last_vacuum column reflects the date and time of the manual vacuum you just ran and the number in the vacuum_count column should increase by one.

In this example, we executed VACUUM on our test table. But you can also run VACUUM on the entire database by omitting the table name. In addition, you can add the VERBOSE keyword to provide more detailed information, such as the number of rows found in a table and the number of rows removed, among other information.

Reducing Table Size with VACUUM FULL

Next, we'll run VACUUM with the FULL option. Unlike the default VACUUM, which only marks the space held by dead rows as available for future use, the FULL option returns space back to disk. As mentioned, VACUUM FULL creates a new version of a table, discarding dead rows in the process. Although this frees space on your system's disk, there are a couple of caveats to keep in mind. First, VACUUM FULL takes more time to complete than VACUUM. Second, it must have exclusive access to the table while rewriting it, which means that no one can update data during the operation. The regular VACUUM command can run while updates and other operations are happening.

To see how VACUUM FULL works, run the command in Listing 17-7:

```
VACUUM FULL vacuum_test;
```

Listing 17-7: Using VACUUM FULL to reclaim disk space

After the command executes, test the table size again. It should be back down to 17MB, which is the size it was when we first inserted data.

It's never prudent or safe to run out of disk space, so minding the size of your database files as well as your overall system space is a worthwhile routine to establish. Using VACUUM to prevent database files from growing bigger than they have to is a good start.

Changing Server Settings

It's possible to alter dozens of settings for your PostgreSQL server by editing values in *postgresql.conf*, one of several configuration text files that control server settings. Other files include *pg_hba.conf*, which controls connections to the server, and *pg_ident.conf*, which database administrators can use to map usernames on a network to usernames in PostgreSQL. See the PostgreSQL documentation on these files for details.

For our purposes, we'll use the *postgresql.conf* file because it contains settings we're most interested in. Most of the values in the file are set to defaults you won't ever need to adjust, but it's worth exploring in case you want to change them to suit your needs. Let's start with the basics.

Locating and Editing postgresql.conf

Before you can edit *postgresql.conf*, you'll need to find its location, which varies depending on your operating system and install method. You can run the command in Listing 17-8 to locate the file:

```
SHOW config_file;
```

Listing 17-8: Showing the location of postgresql.conf

When I run the command on a Mac, it shows the path to the file as:

```
/Users/anthony/Library/Application Support/Postgres/var-10/postgresql.conf
```

To edit *postgresql.conf*, navigate to the directory displayed by SHOW config_file; in your system, and open the file using a plain text editor, not a rich text editor like Microsoft Word.

NOTE *It's a good idea to save a copy of* postgresql.conf *for reference in case you make a change that breaks the system and you need to revert to the original version.*

When you open the file, the first several lines should read as follows:

```
# ----------------------------
# PostgreSQL configuration file
# ----------------------------
#
# This file consists of lines of the form:
#
#   name = value
```

The *postgresql.conf* file is organized into sections that specify settings for file locations, security, logging of information, and other processes. Many lines begin with a hash mark (#), which indicates the line is commented out and the setting shown is the active default.

For example, in the *postgresql.conf* file section "Autovacuum Parameters," the default is for autovacuum to be turned on. The hash mark (#) in front of the line means that the line is commented out and the default is in effect:

```
#autovacuum = on                    # Enable autovacuum subprocess?  'on'
```

To turn off autovacuum, you remove the hash mark at the beginning of the line and change the value to off:

```
autovacuum = off                    # Enable autovacuum subprocess?  'on'
```

Listing 17-9 shows some other settings you might want to explore, which are excerpted from the *postgresql.conf* section "Client Connection Defaults." Use your text editor to search the file for the following settings.

❶ `datestyle = 'iso, mdy'`

❷ `timezone = 'US/Eastern'`

❸ `default_text_search_config = 'pg_catalog.english'`

Listing 17-9: Sample postgresql.conf *settings*

You can use the `datestyle` setting ❶ to specify how PostgreSQL displays dates in query results. This setting takes two parameters: the output format and the ordering of month, day, and year. The default for the output format is the ISO format (`YYYY-MM-DD`) we've used throughout this book, which I recommend you use for cross-national portability. However, you can also use the traditional SQL format (`MM/DD/YYYY`), the expanded Postgres format (`Mon Nov 12 22:30:00 2018 EST`), or the German format (`DD.MM.YYYY`) with dots between the date, month, and year. To specify the format using the second parameter, arrange `m`, `d`, and `y` in the order you prefer.

The `timezone` parameter ❷ sets the (you guessed it) server time zone. Listing 17-9 shows the value `US/Eastern`, which reflects the time zone on my machine when I installed PostgreSQL. Yours should vary based on your location. When setting up PostgreSQL for use as the backend to a database application or on a network, administrators often set this value to `UTC` and use that as a standard on machines across multiple locations.

The `default_text_search_config` value ❸ sets the language used by the full text search operations. Here, mine is set to `english`. Depending on your needs, you can set this to `spanish`, `german`, `russian`, or another language of your choice.

These three examples represent only a handful of settings available for adjustment. Unless you end up deep in system tuning, you probably won't have to tweak much else. Also, use caution when changing settings on a network server used by multiple people or applications; changes can have unintended consequences, so it's worth communicating with colleagues first.

After you make changes to *postgresql.conf*, you must save the file and then reload settings using the `pg_ctl` PostgreSQL command to apply the new settings. Let's look at how to do that next.

Reloading Settings with pg_ctl

The command line utility `pg_ctl` allows you to perform actions on a PostgreSQL server, such as starting and stopping it, and checking its status. Here, we'll use the utility to reload the settings files so changes we make will take effect. Running the command reloads all settings files at once.

You'll need to open and configure a command line prompt the same way you did in Chapter 16 when you learned how to set up and use `psql`. After you launch a command prompt, use one of the following commands to reload:

- On Windows, use:

```
pg_ctl reload -D "C:\path\to\data\directory\"
```

- On macOS or Linux, use:

```
pg_ctl reload -D '/path/to/data/directory/'
```

To find the location of your PostgreSQL data directory, run the query in Listing 17-10:

```
SHOW data_directory;
```

Listing 17-10: Showing the location of the data directory

You place the path between double quotes on Windows and single quotes on macOS or Linux after the `-D` argument. You run this command on your system's command prompt, not inside the `psql` application. Enter the command and press ENTER; it should respond with the message `server signaled`. The settings files will be reloaded and changes should take effect. Some settings, such as memory allocations, require a restart of the server. PostgreSQL will warn you if that's the case.

Backing Up and Restoring Your Database

When you cleaned up the "dirty" USDA food producer data in Chapter 9, you learned how to create a backup copy of a table. However, depending on your needs, you might want to back up your entire database regularly either for safekeeping or for transferring data to a new or upgraded server. PostgreSQL offers command line tools that make backup and restore operations easy. The next few sections show examples of how to create a backup of a database or a single table, as well as how to restore them.

Using pg_dump to Back Up a Database or Table

The PostgreSQL command line tool `pg_dump` creates an output file that contains all the data from your database, SQL commands for re-creating tables, and other database objects, as well as loading the data into tables. You can also use pg_dump to save only selected tables in your database. By default, pg_dump outputs a plain text file; I'll discuss a custom compressed format first and then discuss other options.

To back up the analysis database we've used for our exercises, run the command in Listing 17-11 at your system's command prompt (not in psql):

```
pg_dump -d analysis -U user_name -Fc > analysis_backup.sql
```

Listing 17-11: Backing up the analysis database with pg_dump

Here, we start the command with pg_dump, the -d argument, and name of the database to back up, followed by the -U argument and your username. Next, we use the -Fc argument to specify that we want to generate this backup in a custom PostgreSQL compressed format. Then we place a greater-than symbol (>) to redirect the output of pg_dump to a text file named *analysis_backup.sql*. To place the file in a directory other than the one your terminal prompt is currently open to, you can specify the complete directory path before the filename.

When you execute the command by pressing ENTER, depending on your installation, you might see a password prompt. Fill in that password, if prompted. Then, depending on the size of your database, the command could take a few minutes to complete. The operation doesn't output any messages to the screen while it's working, but when it's done, it should return you to a new command prompt and you should see a file named *analysis_backup.sql* in your current directory.

To limit the backup to one or more tables that match a particular name, use the -t argument followed by the name of the table in single quotes. For example, to back up just the train_rides table, use the following command:

```
pg_dump -t 'train_rides' -d analysis -U user_name -Fc > train_backup.sql
```

Now let's look at how to restore a backup, and then we'll explore additional pg_dump options.

Restoring a Database Backup with pg_restore

After you've backed up your database using pg_dump, it's very easy to restore it using the pg_restore utility. You might need to restore your database when migrating data to a new server or when upgrading to a new version of PostgreSQL. To restore the analysis database (assuming you're on a server where analysis doesn't exist), run the command in Listing 17-12 at the command prompt:

```
pg_restore -C -d postgres -U user_name analysis_backup.sql
```

Listing 17-12: Restoring the analysis database with pg_restore

After pg_restore, you add the -C argument, which tells the utility to create the analysis database on the server. (It gets the database name from the backup file.) Then, as you saw previously, the -d argument specifies the name of the database to connect to, followed by the -U argument and your username. Press ENTER and the restore will begin. When it's done, you should be able to view your restored database via psql or in pgAdmin.

Additional Backup and Restore Options

You can configure pg_dump with multiple options to include or exclude certain database objects, such as tables matching a name pattern, or to specify the output format.

Also, when we backed up the analysis database in "Using pg_dump to Back Up a Database or Table" on page 321, we specified the -Fc option with pg_dump to generate a custom PostgreSQL compressed format. The utility supports additional format options, including plain text. For details, check the full pg_dump documentation at *https://www.postgresql.org/docs/current/static/app-pgdump.html*. For corresponding restore options, check the pg_restore documentation at *https://www.postgresql.org/docs/current/static/app-pgrestore.html*.

Wrapping Up

In this chapter, you learned how to track and conserve space in your databases using the VACUUM feature in PostgreSQL. You also learned how to change system settings as well as back up and restore databases using other command line tools. You may not need to perform these tasks every day, but the maintenance tricks you learned here can help enhance the performance of your databases. Note that this is not a comprehensive overview of the topic; see the Appendix for more resources on database maintenance.

In the next and final chapter of this book, I'll share guidelines for identifying hidden trends and telling an effective story using your data.

TRY IT YOURSELF

Using the techniques you learned in this chapter, back up and restore the gis_analysis database you made in Chapter 14. After you back up the full database, you'll need to delete the original to be able to restore it. You might also try backing up and restoring individual tables.

In addition, use a text editor to explore the backup file created by pg_dump. Examine how it organizes the statements to create objects and insert data.

18

IDENTIFYING AND TELLING THE STORY BEHIND YOUR DATA

Although learning SQL can be fun in and of itself, it serves a greater purpose: it helps uncover the hidden stories in your data. As you learned in this book, SQL gives you the tools to find interesting trends, insights, or anomalies in your data and then make smart decisions based on what you've learned. But how do you identify these trends just from a collection of rows and columns? And how can you glean meaningful insights from these trends after identifying them?

Identifying trends in your data set and creating a narrative of your findings sometimes requires considerable experimentation and enough fortitude to weather the occasional dead end. In this chapter, I outline a process I've used as an investigative journalist to discover stories in data and communicate my findings. I start with how to generate ideas by asking good questions as well as gathering and exploring data. Then I explain the analysis process, which culminates in presenting your findings clearly. These tips are less of a checklist and more of a general guideline that can help you avoid certain mistakes.

Start with a Question

Curiosity, intuition, or sometimes just dumb luck can often spark ideas for data analysis. If you're a keen observer of your surroundings, you might notice changes in your community over time and wonder if you can measure that change. Consider your local real estate market as an example. If you see more "For Sale" signs popping up around town than usual, you might start asking questions. Is there a dramatic increase in home sales this year compared to last year? If so, by how much? Which neighborhoods are affected? These questions create a great opportunity for data analysis. If you're a journalist, you might find a story. If you run a business, you might discover a new marketing opportunity.

Likewise, if you surmise that a trend is occurring in your industry, confirming it might provide you with a business opportunity. For example, if you suspect that sales of a particular product have become sluggish, you can use data analysis to confirm the hunch and adjust inventory or marketing efforts appropriately.

Keep track of these ideas and prioritize them according to their potential value. Analyzing data to satisfy your curiosity is perfectly fine, but if the answers can make your institution more effective or your company more profitable, that's a sign they're worth pursuing.

Document Your Process

Before you delve into analysis, consider how to make your process transparent and reproducible. For the sake of credibility, others in your organization as well as those outside it should be able to reproduce your work. In addition, make sure you document enough information so that if you set the project aside for several weeks, you won't have a problem picking it up again.

There isn't one right way to document your work. Taking notes on research or creating step-by-step SQL queries that another person could use to replicate your data import, cleaning, and analysis can make it easier for others to verify your findings. Some analysts store notes and code in a text file. Others use version control systems, such as GitHub. The important factor is that you create your own system of documentation and use it consistently.

Gather Your Data

After you've hatched an idea for analysis, the next step is to find data that relates to the trend or question. If you're working in an organization that already has its own data on the topic, lucky you—you're set! In that case, you might be able to tap into internal marketing or sales databases, customer relationship management (CRM) systems, or subscriber or event registration data. But if your topic encompasses broader issues involving demographics, the economy, or industry-specific subjects, you'll need to do some digging.

A good place to start is to ask experts about the sources they use. Analysts, government decision-makers, and academics can often point you to available data and its usefulness. Federal, state, and local governments, as you've seen throughout the book, produce volumes of data on all kinds of topics. In the United States, check out the federal government's data catalog site at *https://www.data.gov/* or individual agency sites, such as the National Center for Education Statistics (NCES) at *https://nces.ed.gov/.*

You can also browse local government websites. Any time you see a form for users to fill out or a report formatted in rows and columns, those are signs that structured data might be available for analysis. But all is not lost if you only have access to unstructured data. As you learned in Chapter 13, you can even mine unstructured data, such as text files.

If the data you want to analyze was collected over multiple years, I recommend examining five or 10 years, or more, instead of just one or two, if possible. Although analyzing a snapshot of data collected over a month or a year can yield interesting results, many trends play out over a longer period of time and may not be evident if you look at a single year of data. I discuss this further in "Identify Key Indicators and Trends over Time" on page 329.

No Data? Build Your Own Database

Sometimes, no one has the data you need in a format you can use. But if you have time, patience, and a methodology, you might be able to build your own data set. That is what my *USA TODAY* colleague, Robert Davis, and I did when we wanted to study issues related to the deaths of college students on campuses in the United States. Not a single organization—not the schools or state or federal officials—could tell us how many college students were dying each year from accidents, overdoses, or illnesses on campus. We decided to collect our own data and structure the information into tables in a database.

We started by researching news articles, police reports, and lawsuits related to student deaths. After finding reports of more than 600 student deaths from 2000 to 2005, we followed up with interviews with education experts, police, school officials, and parents. From each report, we cataloged details such as each student's age, school, cause of death, year in school, and whether drugs or alcohol played a role. Our findings led to the publication of the article "In College, First Year Is by Far the Riskiest" in *USA TODAY* in 2006. The story featured the key finding from the analysis of our SQL database: freshmen were particularly vulnerable and accounted for the highest percentage of the student deaths we studied.

You too can create a database if you lack the data you need. The key is to identify the pieces of information that matter, and then systematically collect them.

Assess the Data's Origins

After you've identified a data set, find as much information about its origins and maintenance methods as you can. Governments and institutions gather data in all sorts of ways, and some methods produce data that is more credible and standardized than others.

For example, you've already seen that USDA food producer data includes the same company names spelled in multiple ways. It's worth knowing why. (Perhaps the data is manually copied from a written form to a computer.) Similarly, the New York City taxi data you analyzed in Chapter 11 records the start and end times of each trip. This begs the question, does the timer start when the passenger gets in and out of the vehicle, or is there some other trigger? You should know these details not only to draw better conclusions from analysis but also to pass them along to others who might be interpreting your analysis.

The origins of a data set might also affect how you analyze the data and report your findings. For example, with U.S. Census data, it's important to know that the Decennial Census conducted every 10 years is a complete count of the population, whereas the American Community Survey (ACS) is drawn from only a sample of households. As a result, ACS counts have a margin of error, but the Decennial Census doesn't. It would be irresponsible to report on the ACS without considering how the margin of error could make differences between numbers insignificant.

Interview the Data with Queries

Once you have your data, understand its origins, and have loaded it into your database, you can explore it with queries. Throughout the book, I call this step "interviewing data," which is what you should do to find out more about the contents of your data and whether they contain any red flags.

A good place to start is with aggregates. Counts, sums, sorting, and grouping by column values should reveal minimum and maximum values, potential issues with duplicate entries, and a sense of the general scope of your data. If your database contains multiple, related tables, try joins to make sure you understand how the tables relate. Using LEFT JOIN and RIGHT JOIN, as you learned in Chapter 6, should show whether key values from one table are missing in another. That may or may not be a concern, but at least you'll be able to identify potential problems you might want to address. Jot down a list of questions or concerns you have, and then move on to the next step.

Consult the Data's Owner

After exploring your database and forming early conclusions about the quality and trends you observed, take some time to bring any questions or concerns you have to a person who knows the data well. That person could work at the agency or firm that gave you the data, or the person might be an analyst who has worked with the data before. This step is your chance to clarify your understanding of the data, verify initial findings, and discover whether the data has any issues that make it unsuitable for your needs.

For example, if you're querying a table and notice values in columns that seem to be gross outliers (such as dates in the future for events that were supposed to have happened in the past), you should ask about that discrepancy. Or, if you expect to find someone's name in a table (perhaps even your own name), and it's not there, that should prompt another question. Is it possible you don't have the whole data set, or is there a problem with data collection?

The goal is to get expert help to do the following:

- **Understand the limits of the data.** Make sure you know what the data includes, what it excludes, and any caveats about content that might affect how you perform your analysis.

- **Make sure you have a complete data set.** Verify that you have all the records you should expect to see and that if any data is missing, you understand why.

- **Determine whether the data set suits your needs.** Consider looking elsewhere for more reliable data if your source acknowledges problems with the data's quality.

Every data set and situation is unique, but consulting another user or owner of the data can help you avoid unnecessary missteps.

Identify Key Indicators and Trends over Time

When you're satisfied that you understand the data and are confident in its trustworthiness, completeness, and appropriateness to your analysis, the next step is to run queries to identify key indicators and, if possible, trends over time.

Your goal is to unearth data that you can summarize in a sentence or present as a slide in a presentation. An example finding would be something like this: "After five years of declines, the number of people enrolling in Widget University has increased by 5 percent for two consecutive semesters."

To identify this type of trend, you'll follow a two-step process:

1. Choose an indicator to track. In U.S. Census data, it might be the percentage of the population that is over age 60. Or in the New York City taxi data, it could be the median number of weekday trips over the span of one year.

2. Track that indicator over multiple years to see how it has changed, if at all.

In fact, these are the steps we used in Chapter 6 to apply percent change calculations to multiple years of census data contained in joined tables. In that case, we looked at the change in population in counties between 2000 and 2010. The population count was the key indicator, and the percent change showed the trend over the 10-year span for each county.

One caveat about measuring change over time: even when you see a dramatic change between any two years, it's worth digging into as many years' worth of data as possible to understand the shorter-term change in the context of a long-term trend. Although a year-to-year change might seem dramatic, seeing it in context of multiyear activity can help you assess its true significance.

For example, the U.S. National Center for Health Statistics releases data on the number of babies born each year. As a data nerd, I like to keep tabs on indicators like these, because births often reflect broader trends in culture or the economy. Figure 18-1 shows the annual number of births from 1910 to 2016.

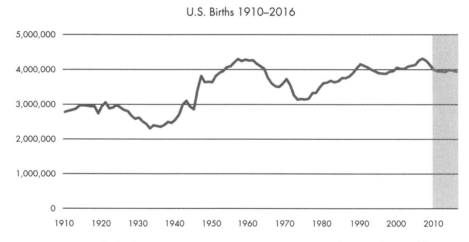

Figure 18-1: U.S. births from 1910 to 2016. Source: U.S. National Center for Health Statistics

Looking at only the last five years of this graph (shaded in gray), we see that the number of births hovered steadily at approximately 3.9 million with small decreases in the last two years. Although the recent drops seem noteworthy (likely reflecting continuing decreases in birth rates for teens and women in their 20s), in the long-term context, they're less interesting given that the number of births has remained near or over 4 million for the last 20 years. In fact, U.S. births have seen far more dramatic increases and decreases. One example you can see in Figure 18-1 is the major rise in the mid-1940s following World War II, which signaled the start of the Baby Boom generation.

By identifying key indicators and looking at change over time, both short term and long term, you might uncover one or more findings worth presenting to others or acting on.

NOTE
Any time you work with data from a survey, poll, or other sample, it's important to test for statistical significance. Are the results actually a trend or just the result of chance? Significance testing is a statistical concept beyond the scope of this book but one that data analysts should know. See the Appendix for PostgreSQL resources for advanced statistics.

Ask Why

Data analysis can tell you what happened, but it doesn't usually indicate why something happened. To learn why something happened, it's worth revisiting the data with experts in the topic or the owners of the data. In the U.S. births data, it's easy to calculate year-to-year percent change from those numbers. But the data doesn't tell us why births steadily increased from the early 1980s to 1990. For that information, you might need to consult a demographer who would most likely explain that the rise in births during those years coincided with more Baby Boomers entering their childbearing years.

When you share your findings and methodology with experts, ask them to note anything that seems unlikely or worthy of further examination. For the findings they can corroborate, ask them to help you understand the forces behind those findings. If they're willing to be cited, you can use their comments to supplement your report or presentation. This is a standard approach journalists often use to quote experts' reactions to data trends.

Communicate Your Findings

How you share the results of your analysis depends on your role. A student might present their results in a paper or dissertation. A person who works in a corporate setting might present their findings using PowerPoint, Keynote, or Google Slides. A journalist might write a story or produce a data visualization. Regardless of the end product, here are my tips for presenting the information well (using a fictional home sales analysis as an example):

- **Identify an overarching theme based on your findings.** Make the theme the title of your presentation, paper, or visualization. For example, for a presentation on real estate, you might use, "Home sales rise in suburban neighborhoods, fall in cities."

- **Present overall numbers to show the general trend.** Highlight the key findings from your analysis. For example, "All suburban neighborhoods saw sales up 5 percent each of the last two years, reversing three years of declines. Meanwhile, city neighborhoods saw a decline of 2 percent."

- **Highlight specific examples that support the trend.** Describe one or two relevant cases. For example, "In Smithtown, home sales increased 15 percent following the relocation of XYZ Corporation's headquarters last year."

- **Acknowledge examples counter to the overall trend.** Use one or two relevant cases here as well. For example, "Two city neighborhoods did show growth in home sales: Arvis (up 4.5 percent) and Zuma (up 3 percent)."

- **Stick to the facts.** Avoid distorting or exaggerating any findings.
- **Provide expert opinion.** Use quotes or citations.
- **Visualize numbers using bar charts or line charts.** Tables are helpful for giving your audience specific numbers, but it's easier to understand trends from a visualization.
- **Cite the source of the data and what your analysis includes or omits.** Provide dates covered, the name of the provider, and any distinctions that affect the analysis. For example, "Based on Walton County tax filings in 2015 and 2016. Excludes commercial properties."
- **Share your data.** Post data online for download, including the queries you used. Nothing says transparency more than sharing the data you analyzed with others so they can perform their own analysis and corroborate your findings.

Generally, a short presentation that communicates your findings clearly and succinctly, and then invites dialogue from your audience thereafter, works best. Of course, you can follow your own preferred pattern for working with data and presenting your conclusions. But over the years, these steps have helped me avoid bad data and mistaken assumptions.

Wrapping Up

At last, you've reached the end of our practical exploration of SQL! Thank you for reading this book, and I welcome your suggestions and feedback on my website at *https://www.anthonydebarros.com/contact/*. At the end of this book is an appendix that lists additional PostgreSQL-related tools you might want to try.

I hope you've come away with data analysis skills you can start using immediately on the data you encounter. More importantly, I hope you've seen that each data set has a story, or several stories, to tell. Identifying and telling these stories is what makes working with data worthwhile; it's more than just combing through a collection of rows and columns. I look forward to hearing about what you discover!

TRY IT YOURSELF

It's your turn to find and tell a story using the SQL techniques we've covered. Using the process outlined in this chapter, consider a local or national topic and search for available data. Assess its quality, the questions it might answer, and its timeliness. Consult with an expert who knows the data and the topic well. Load the data into PostgreSQL and interview it using aggregate queries and filters. What trends can you discover? Summarize your findings in a short presentation.

ADDITIONAL POSTGRESQL RESOURCES

This appendix contains some resources to help you stay informed about PostgreSQL developments, find additional software, and get help. Because software resources are likely to change, I'll maintain a copy of this appendix at the GitHub repository that contains all the book's resources. You can find a link via *https://www.nostarch .com/practicalSQL/*.

PostgreSQL Development Environments

Throughout the book, we've used the graphical user interface pgAdmin to connect to PostgreSQL, run queries, and view database objects. Although pgAdmin is free, open source, and popular, it's not your only choice for working with PostgreSQL. You can read the entry called "Community

Guide to PostgreSQL GUI Tools," which catalogs many alternatives, on the PostgreSQL wiki at *https://wiki.postgresql.org/wiki/Community_Guide _to_PostgreSQL_GUI_Tools.*

The following list contains information on several tools I've tried, including free and paid options. The free tools work well for general analysis work. But if you wade deeper into database development, you might want to upgrade to the paid options, which typically offer advanced features and support:

DataGrip   A SQL development environment that offers code completion, bug detection, and suggestions for streamlining code, among many other features. It's a paid product, but the company, JetBrains, offers discounts and free versions for students, educators, and non-profits (see *http://www.jetbrains.com/datagrip/*).

Navicat   A richly featured SQL development environment with versions that support PostgreSQL as well as other databases, including MySQL, Oracle, and Microsoft SQL Server. Navicat is a paid version only, but the company offers a 14-day free trial (see *https://www.navicat.com/*).

pgManage   A free, open source GUI client for Windows, macOS, and Linux, formerly known as Postage (see *https://github.com/pgManage/ pgManage/*).

Postico   A macOS-only client from the maker of Postgres.app that looks like it takes its cues from Apple design. The full version is paid, but a restricted-feature version is available with no time limit (see *https://eggerapps.at/postico/*).

PSequel   Also macOS-only, PSequel is a free PostgreSQL client that is decidedly minimalist (see *http://www.psequel.com/*).

A trial version can help you decide whether the product is right for you.

PostgreSQL Utilities, Tools, and Extensions

You can expand the capabilities of PostgreSQL via numerous third-party utilities, tools, and extensions. These range from additional backup and import/export options to improved formatting for the command line to powerful statistics packages. You'll find a curated list online at *https://github .com/dhamaniasad/awesome-postgres/*, but here are several to highlight:

Devart Excel Add-In for PostgreSQL   An add-in that lets you load and edit data from PostgreSQL directly in Excel workbooks (see *https://www .devart.com/excel-addins/postgresql.html*).

MADlib   A machine learning and analytics library for large data sets (see *http://madlib.apache.org/*).

pgAgent   A job manager that lets you run queries at scheduled times, among other tasks (see *https://www.pgadmin.org/docs/pgadmin4/dev/ pgagent.html*).

pgcli A replacement for `psql` that includes improved formatting when writing queries and viewing output (see *https://github.com/dbcli/pgcli/*).

PL/R A loadable procedural language that provides the ability to use the R statistical programming language within PostgreSQL functions and triggers (see *http://www.joeconway.com/plr.html*).

SciPy A collection of Python science and engineering libraries you can use with the PL/Python procedural language in PostgreSQL (see *https://www.scipy.org/*).

PostgreSQL News

Now that you're a bona fide PostgreSQL user, it's wise to stay on top of community news. The PostgreSQL development team releases new versions of the software on a regular basis, and its ecosystem spawns constant innovation and related products. Updates to PostgreSQL might impact code you've written or even offer new opportunities for analysis.

Here's a collection of online resources you can use to stay informed:

EDB Blog Posts from the team at EnterpriseDB, a PostgreSQL services company that provides the Windows installer referenced in this book (see *https://www.enterprisedb.com/blog/*).

Planet PostgreSQL A collection of blog posts and announcements from the database community (see *https://planet.postgresql.org/*).

Postgres Weekly An email newsletter that rounds up announcements, blog posts, and product announcements (see *https://postgresweekly.com/*).

PostgreSQL Mailing Lists These lists are useful for asking questions of community experts. The pgsql-novice and pgsql-general lists are particularly good for beginners, although note that email volume can be heavy (see *https://www.postgresql.org/list/*).

PostgreSQL News Archive Official news from the Postgres team (see *https://www.postgresql.org/about/newsarchive/*).

PostGIS Blog Announcements and updates on the PostGIS extension covered in Chapter 14 (see *http://postgis.net/blog/*).

Additionally, I recommend paying attention to developer notes for any of the PostgreSQL-related software you use, such as pgAdmin.

Documentation

Throughout this book, I've made frequent reference to pages in the official PostgreSQL documentation. You can find documentation for each version of the software along with an FAQ and wiki on the main page at *https://www.postgresql.org/docs/*. It's worth reading through various sections of the manual as you learn more about a particular topic, such as indexes, or search for all the options that come with functions. In particular, the Preface, Tutorial, and SQL Language sections cover much of the material presented in the book's chapters.

Other good resources for documentation are the Postgres Guide at *http://postgresguide.com/* and Stack Overflow, where you can find questions and answers posted by developers at *https://stackoverflow.com/questions/tagged/postgresql/*. You can also check out the Q&A site for PostGIS at *https://gis .stackexchange.com/questions/tagged/postgis/*.

INDEX

Symbols

+ (addition operator), 56, 57
& (ampersand operator), 232, 236
* (asterisk)
   as multiplication operator, 56, 57
   as wildcard in SELECT, 12
\ (backslash), 42–43, 215
   escaping characters with, 219
, (comma), 40
||/ (cube root operator), 56, 58
{} (curly brackets), 215
   denoting an array, 68
<-> (distance operator), 232, 236
@@ (double at sign match operator), 232
:: (double-colon CAST operator), 36
$$ (double-dollar quoting), 280
|| (double-pipe concatenation
      operator), 143, 225
" (double quote), 41, 94
= (equals comparison operator), 18
! (exclamation point)
   as factorial operator, 56, 59
   as negation, 228, 232, 236
^ (exponentiation operator), 56, 58
/ (forward slash)
   as division operator, 56, 57
   in macOS file paths, 42
> (greater than comparison
      operator), 18
>= (greater than or equals comparison
      operator), 18
- (hyphen subtraction operator), 56, 57
< (less than comparison operator), 18
<= (less than or equals comparison
      operator), 18
!= (not equal comparison operator), 18
<> (not equal comparison operator), 18
() (parentheses), 6, 8
   to designate order of operations, 20
   to specify columns for
      importing, 50

% (percent sign)
   as modulo operator, 56, 57
   wildcard for pattern matching, 19
| (pipe character)
   as delimiter, 26, 43
   to redirect output, 311
; (semicolon), 3
' (single quote), 8, 42
|/ (square root operator), 56, 58
~* (tilde-asterisk case-insensitive
      matching operator), 228
~ (tilde case-sensitive matching
      operator), 228
_ (underscore wildcard for pattern
      matching), 19

A

adding numbers, 57
   across columns, 60
addition operator (+), 56, 57
aggregate functions, 64, 117
   avg(), 64
   binary (two-input), 158
   count(), 117–119, 131
   filtering with HAVING, 127
   interviewing data, 131
   max(), 119–120
   min(), 119–120
   PostgreSQL documentation, 117
   sum(), 64, 124–125
   using GROUP BY clause, 120–123
aliases for table names, 86, 125
ALTER COLUMN statement, 107
ALTER TABLE statement, 137
   ADD COLUMN, 137, 252
   ADD CONSTRAINT, 107
   ALTER COLUMN, 137
   DROP COLUMN, 137, 148
   table constraints, adding and
      removing, 107

American National Standards Institute (ANSI), xxiv
ampersand operator (&), 232, 236
ANALYZE keyword
    with EXPLAIN command, 109
    with VACUUM command, 317
AND operator, 20
ANSI (American National Standards Institute), xxiv
antimeridian, 46
array, 68
    array_length() function, 230
    functions, 68
    notation in query, 224
    passing into ST_MakePoint(), 250
    returned from regexp_match(), 219, 224
    type indicated in results grid, 224
    unnest() function, 68
    with curly brackets, 68, 220
array_length() function, 230
AS keyword
    declaring table aliases with, 86, 90
    renaming columns in query results with, 60, 61, 205
ASC keyword, 15
asterisk (*)
    as multiplication operator, 56, 57
    as wildcard in SELECT statement, 12
attribute, 5
auto-incrementing integers, 27
    as surrogate primary key, 101
    gaps in sequence, 28
    identity column SQL standard, 27
autovacuum, 316
    editing server setting, 319
    time of last vacuum, 317
average, 64
    vs. median, 65, 194
avg() function, 64, 195

B

backslash (\), 42–43, 215
    escaping characters with, 219
backups
    column, 140
    improving performance when updating tables, 151–152
    restoring from copied table, 142
    tables, 139

BETWEEN comparison operator, 18, 198
    inclusive property, 19
bigint integer data type, 27
bigserial integer data type, 6, 27, 101
    as surrogate primary key, 102
binary aggregate functions, 158
BINARY file format, 42
birth data, U.S., 330
Boolean value, 74
B-Tree (balanced tree) index, 108

C

camel case, 10, 94
caret symbol (^) exponentiation operator, 58
carriage return, 43
Cartesian Product
    as result of CROSS JOIN, 82
CASCADE keyword, 104
case sensitivity
    with ILIKE operator, 19
    with LIKE operator, 19
CASE statement, 207
    ELSE clause, 208
    in Common Table Expression, 209–210
    in UPDATE statement, 226
    syntax, 207
    WHEN clause, 208, 288
    with trigger, 286
CAST() function, 35
    shortcut notation, 36
categorizing data, 207
char character string type, 24
character set, 16
character string types, 24–26
    char, 24
    functional difference from number types, 26
    performance in PostgreSQL, 25
    text, 25
    varchar, 24
character varying data type. See varchar data type
char_length() function, 212
CHECK constraint, 104–105
classify_max_temp() user function, 287
clock_timestamp() function, 176
Codd, Edgar F., xxiv, 73
coefficient of determination. See r-squared

collation setting, 16
column, 5
    adding numbers in, 64
    alias, 60
    alter data type, 137
    averaging values in, 64
    avoiding spaces in name, 95
    deleting, 148
    indexes, 110
    naming, 94
    populating new during backup, 151
    retrieving in queries, 13
    updating values, 138
comma (,), 40
comma-delimited files. *See* CSV
        (comma-separated values)
command line, 291
    advantages of using, 292
    createdb command, 310
    psql application, 299
    setup, 292
        macOS, 296
        PATH environment variable,
            292, 296
        Windows, 292
    shell programs, 296
comma-separated values (CSV).
        See CSV
comments in code, xxvii
COMMIT statement, 149
Common Table Expression (CTE), 200
    advantages, 201
    CASE statement example, 209
    definition, 200
comparison operators, 18
    combining with AND and OR, 20
concatenation, 143
conditional expression, 207
constraints, 6, 96–97
    adding and removing, 107
    CHECK, 104–105, 157
    column vs. table, 97
    CONSTRAINT keyword, 76
    foreign key, 102–103
    NOT NULL, 106–107
    PRIMARY KEY, 99
    primary keys, 75, 97
    UNIQUE, 76, 105–106
    violations when altering table, 138
constructor, 68
Coordinated Universal Time
        (UTC), 33

COPY statement
    DELIMITER option, 43
    description of, 39
    exporting data, 25, 51–52
    FORMAT option, 42
    FROM keyword, 42
    HEADER option, 43
    importing data, 42–43
    naming file paths, 25
    QUOTE option, 43
    specifying file formats, 42
    TO, 51, 183
    WITH keyword, 42
correlated subquery, 192, 199
corr() function, 157
    correlation vs. causation, 163
count() function, 117, 131, 196
    distinct values, 118
    on multiple columns, 123
    values present in a column, 118
    with GROUP BY, 122
counting
    distinct values, 118
    missing values displayed, 133
    rows, 117
    using pgAdmin, 118
CREATE DATABASE statement, 3
createdb utility, 310
CREATE EXTENSION statement, 203
CREATE FUNCTION statement, 276
CREATE INDEX statement, 108, 110
CREATE TABLE statement, 6
    backing up a table with, 139
    declaring data types, 24
    TEMPORARY TABLE, 50
CREATE TRIGGER statement, 285
CREATE VIEW statement, 269
CROSS JOIN keywords, 82, 202
crosstab() function, 203, 205, 207
    with tablefunc module, 203
cross tabulations, 203
CSV (comma-separated values), 40
    header row, 41
CTE. *See* Common Table
        Expression (CTE)
cube root operator (||/), 58
curly brackets ({}), 215
    denoting an array, 68
current_date function, 175
current_time function, 175
current_timestamp function, 176
cut points, 66

D

data
- identifying and telling stories in, 325
- spatial, 241
- structured and unstructured, 211

database
- backup and restore, 321
- connecting to, 4, 5
- create from command line, 310
- creation, 1, 3–5
- importing data with COPY, 42–43
- maintenance, 313
- server, 3
- using consistent names, 94

database management system, 3
data dictionary, 23
data types, 5, 23
- bigint, 27
- bigserial, 6, 101
- char, 24
- character string types, 24–26
- date, 5, 32, 172
- date and time types, 32–34
- decimal, 29
- declaring with CREATE TABLE, 24
- double precision, 29
- full text search, 231
- geography, 247
- geometry, 247
- importance of using appropriate type, 23, 46
- integer, 27
- interval, 32, 172
- modifying with ALTER COLUMN, 137
- number types, 26–31
- numeric, 6, 28
- real, 29
- returned by math operations, 56
- serial, 12, 101
- smallint, 27
- smallserial, 101
- text, 25
- time, 32, 172
- timestamp, 32, 172
- transforming values with CAST(), 35–36
- tsquery, 232
- tsvector, 231
- varchar, 6, 24

date data types
- date, 5, 32, 172
- interval, 32, 172
- matching with regular expression, 217

date_part() function, 173, 207
dates
- input format, 5, 8, 33, 173
- setting default style, 320

daylight saving time, 178
deciles, 67
decimal data types, 28
- decimal, 29
- double precision, 29
- numeric, 28
- real, 29

decimal degrees, 46
DELETE statement, 50
- removing rows matching criteria, 147
- with subquery, 194

DELETE CASCADE statement
- with foreign key constraint, 104

delimited text files, 39, 40–41
delimiter character, 40
DELIMITER keyword
- with COPY statement, 43

dense_rank() function, 164
derived table, 194
- joining, 195–197

DESC keyword, 15
direct relationship in correlation, 158
dirty data, 11, 129
- cleaning, 129
- foreign keys help to avoid, 103
- when to discard, 137

distance operator (<->), 232, 236
DISTINCT keyword, 14, 118
division, 57
- finding the remainder, 58
- integer vs. decimal, 57, 58

documenting code, 23
double at sign match operator (@@), 232
double-colon CAST operator (::), 36
double-dollar quoting ($$), 280
double-pipe concatenation operator (||), 143, 225
double quote ("), 41, 94
DROP statement
- COLUMN, 148
- INDEX, 111
- TABLE, 148

duplicate data
    created by spelling variations, 132
    guarding against with
        constraints, 76

E

Eastern Standard Time (EST), 33
ELSE clause, 208, 227
entity, 2
environment variable, 292
epoch, 174, 189
equals comparison operator (=), 18
error messages, 9
    CSV import failure, 47, 49
    foreign key violation, 103
    out of range value, 27
    primary key violation, 99, 101
    relation already exists, 95
    UNIQUE constraint violation, 106
    when using CAST(), 36
escaping characters, 219
EST (Eastern Standard Time), 33
exclamation point (!)
    as factorial operator, 56, 59
    as negation, 228, 232, 236
EXISTS operator
    in WHERE clause, 139
    with subquery, 199
EXPLAIN statement, 109
exponentiation operator (^), 56, 58
exporting data
    all data in table, 51–52
    from query results, 52
    including header row, 43
    limiting columns, 52
    to BINARY file format, 42
    to CSV file format, 42, 183–184
    to TEXT file format, 42
    using command line, 307
    using COPY statement, 51–52
    using pgAdmin wizard, 52–53
expressions, 34, 192
    conditional, 207
    subquery, 198
extract() function, 174

F

factorials, 58
false (Boolean value), 74
Federal Information Processing
    Standards (FIPS), 259, 269

field, 5
file paths
    import and export file locations, 42
    naming conventions for operating
        systems, 25, 42
filtering rows
    HAVING clause, 127
    WHERE clause, 17, 192
    with subquery, 192
findstr Windows command, 134
FIPS (Federal Information Processing
    Standards), 259, 269
fixed-point numbers, 28
floating-point numbers, 29
    inexact math calculations, 30
foreign key
    creating with REFERENCES
        keyword, 102
    definition, 76, 102
formatting SQL for readability, 10
forward slash (/)
    as division operator, 56, 57
    in macOS file paths, 42
FROM keyword, 12
    with COPY, 42
FULL OUTER JOIN keywords, 82
full text search, 231
    adjacent words, locating, 236–237
    data types, 231–233
    functions to rank results, 237–239
    highlighting terms, 235
    lexemes, 231–232
    multiple terms in query, 236
    querying, 234
    setting default language, 320
    table and column setup, 233
    to_tsquery() function, 232
    to_tsvector() function, 231
    ts_headline() function, 235
    ts_rank_cd() function, 237
    ts_rank() function, 237
    using GIN index, 234
functions, 267
    creating, 275, 276–277
    full text search, 231
    IMMUTABLE keyword, 277
    RAISE NOTICE keywords, 280
    RETURNS keyword, 277
    specifying language, 276
    string, 212
    structure of, 276
    updating data with, 278–280

G

generate_series() function, 176, 207, 315
geography data type, 247
GeoJSON, 243
geometry data type, 247
GIN (Generalized Inverted Index), 108
    with full text search, 234
GIS (Geographic Information System), 241
    decimal degrees, 46
GiST (Generalized Search Tree) index, 108, 252
greater than comparison operator (>), 18
greater than or equals comparison operator (>=), 18
grep Linux command, 134
GROUP BY clause
    eliminating duplicate values, 120
    on multiple columns, 121
    with aggregate functions, 120
GUI (graphical user interface), 257, 291
    list of tools, 333

H

HAVING clause, 127
    with aggregate functions, 127, 132
HEADER keyword
    with COPY statement, 43
header row
    found in CSV file, 41
    ignoring during import, 41
hyphen subtraction operator (-), 56, 57

I

identifiers
    avoiding reserved keywords, 95
    enabling mixed case, 94–95
    naming, 10, 94, 96
    quoting, 95
identifying and telling stories in data, 325
    asking why, 331
    assessing the data's origins, 328
    building your own database, 327
    communicating your findings, 331
    consulting the data's owner, 328

documenting your process, 326
gathering your data, 326
identifying trends over time, 329
interviewing the data with queries, 328
starting with a question, 326
ILIKE comparison operator, 18, 19–20
importing data, 39, 42–43
    adding default column value, 50
    choosing a subset of columns, 49
    from non-text sources, 40
    from TEXT file format, 42
    from CSV file format, 42
    ignoring header row in text files, 41, 43
    using command line, 307
    using COPY statement, 39
    using pgAdmin import wizard, 52–53
IN comparison operator, 18, 144, 198
    with subquery, 198
indexes, 108
    B-Tree, 108
    considerations before adding, 111
    creating on columns, 110
    dropping, 111
    GIN, 108
    GiST, 108, 252
    measuring effect on performance, 109
    not included with table backups, 140
    syntax for creating, 108
initcap() function, 212
INSERT statement, 8–9
inserting rows into a table, 9–10
Institute of Museum and Library Services (IMLS), 114
integer data types, 27
    auto-incrementing, 27
    basic math operations, 57
    bigint, 27
    bigserial, 27
    difference in integer type capacities, 27
    integer, 27
    serial, 27
    smallint, 27
    smallserial, 27
International Date Line, 46

International Organization for
  Standardization (ISO),
  xxiv, 33, 243
interval data type, 32, 172
  calculations with, 34, 187
  cumulative, 188
  value options, 34
interviewing data, 11, 131–132
  across joined tables, 124
  artificial values as indicators,
    120, 124
  checking for missing values, 13,
    132–134
  correlations, 157–159
  counting rows and values, 117–119
  determining correct format, 13
  finding inconsistent values, 134
  malformed values, 135–136
  maximum and minimum values,
    119–120
  rankings, 164–167
  rates calculations, 167–169
  statistics, 155
  summing grouped values, 124
  unique combinations of values, 15
inverse relationship, 158
ISO (International Organization for
  Standardization), xxiv,
  33, 243
  time format, 172

J

JOIN keyword, 74
  example of using, 80
  in FROM clause, 74
joining tables, 73
  derived tables, 195–197
  inequality condition, 90
  multiple-table joins, 87
  naming tables in column list,
    85, 125
  performing calculations across
    tables, 88
  spatial joins, 262, 263
  specifying columns to link
    tables, 77
  specifying columns to query, 85
  using JOIN keyword, 74, 77

join types
  CROSS JOIN, 82–83
  FULL OUTER JOIN, 82
  JOIN (INNER JOIN), 80, 125
  LEFT JOIN, 80–81
  list of, 78
  RIGHT JOIN, 80–81
JSON, 35

K

key columns
  foreign key, 76
  primary key, 75
  relating tables with, 74

L

latitude
  in U.S. Census data, 46
  in well-known text, 245
least squares regression line, 161
LEFT JOIN keyword, 80–81
left() string function, 213
length() string function, 135, 213
less than comparison operator (<), 18
less than or equals comparison
  operator (<=), 18
lexemes, 231
LIKE comparison operator, 18
  case-sensitive search, 19
  in UPDATE statement, 143
LIMIT clause, 48
limiting number of rows query
  returns, 48
linear regression, 161
linear relationship, 158
Linux
  file path declaration, 26, 42
  Terminal setup, 299
literals, 8
locale setting, 16
localhost, xxxii, 4
localtime function, 176
localtimestamp function, 176
longitude
  in U.S. Census data, 46
  in well-known text, 245
  positive and negative values, 49
lower() function, 212

M

macOS
 file path declaration, 25, 42
 Terminal, 296
  .bash_profile, 296
  bash shell, 296
  entering instructions, 297
  setup, 296, 297
  useful commands, 298
make_date() function, 175
make_time() function, 175
make_timestamptz() function, 175
many-to-many table relationship, 85
map
 projected coordinate system, 245
 projection, 245
math
 across joined table columns, 88
 across table columns, 60–64
 median, 65–70
 mode, 70
 order of operations, 59
 with aggregate functions, 64–65
math operators, 56–59
 addition (+), 57
 cube root (||/), 58
 division (/), 57
 exponentiation (^), 58
 factorial (!), 58
 modulo (%), 57
 multiplication (*), 57
 square root (|/), 58
 subtraction (-), 57
max() function, 119
median, 65
 definition, 65
 vs. average, 65, 194
 with percentile_cont() function, 66
median() user function
 creation, 69
 performance concerns, 70
 vs. percentile_cont(), 70
Microsoft Access, xxiv
Microsoft Excel, xxiv
Microsoft SQL Server, xxviii, 94, 203
Microsoft Windows
 Command Prompt
  entering instructions, 295
  setup, 292, 294
  useful commands, 295
 file path declaration, 25, 42
 folder permissions, xxvii

min() function, 119
mode, 70
mode() function, 70
modifying data, 136–137
 for consistency, 142
 updating column values, 141
modulo operator (%), 56, 57–58
multiplying numbers, 57
MySQL, xxviii

N

naming conventions
 camel case, 94
 Pascal case, 94
 snake case, 94, 96
National Center for Education
  Statistics, 327
National Center for Health
  Statistics, 330
natural primary key, 97, 131
New York City taxi data, 180
 calculating busiest hour of day, 182
 creating table for, 180
 exporting results, 183–184
 importing, 181
 longest trips, 184–185
normal distribution of data, 194
NOT comparison operator, 18
 with EXISTS, 200
not equal comparison operator
 != syntax, 18
 <> syntax, 18
NOT NULL keywords
 adding to column, 137
 definition, 106
 removing from column, 107, 138
now() function, 33, 176
NULL keyword
 definition, 83
 ordering with FIRST and LAST, 133
 using in table joins, 83
number data types, 26
 decimal types, 28
  double precision, 29
  fixed-point type, 28
  floating-point types, 29
  numeric data type, 6, 28
  real, 29

integer types, 27
    bigint, 27
    integer, 27
    serial types, 27
    smallint, 27
    usage considerations, 31

O

OGC (Open Geospatial
    Consortium), 243
ON keyword
    used with DELETE CASCADE, 104
    used with JOIN, 74
one-to-many table relationship, 84
one-to-one table relationship, 84
operators
    addition (+), 56, 57
    comparisons with, 17
    cube root (||/), 56, 58
    division (/), 56, 57
    exponentiation (^), 56, 58
    factorial (!), 56, 58
    modulo (%), 56, 57
    multiplication (*), 56, 57
    precedence, 59
    prefix, 58
    square root (|/), 56, 58
    subtraction (-), 56, 57
    suffix, 59
OR operator, 20
Oracle, xxiv
ORDER BY clause, 15
    ASC, DESC options, 15
    on multiple columns, 16
    specifying columns to sort, 15
    specifying NULLS FIRST or LAST, 133
OVER clause, 164

P

Pacific time zone, 33
padding character columns with
    spaces, 24, 26
parentheses (), 6, 8
    to designate order of operations, 20
    to specify columns for
        importing, 50
Pascal case, 94
pattern matching
    using LIKE and ILIKE, 19
    with regular expressions, 214
    with wildcards, 19

Pearson correlation coefficient (r), 157
percent sign (%)
    as modulo operator, 56, 57
    wildcard for pattern matching, 19
percentage
    of the whole, 62
    percent change, 63
        formula, 63, 89, 276
        function, 276
percent_change() user function, 276
    using with Census data, 277
percentile, 66, 192
    continuous vs. discrete values, 66
percentile_cont() function, 66
    finding median with, 185
    in subquery, 193
    using array to enter multiple
        values, 68
percentile_disc() function, 66
pgAdmin, xxxi
    connecting to database, 4, 5, 242
    connecting to server, xxxii, 4
    executing SQL, 3
    importing and exporting data,
        52–53
    installation
        Linux, xxxi
        macOS, xxxi, xxxii
        Windows, xxix, xxxi
    keyword highlighting, 95
    localhost, xxxii, 4
    object browser, xxxii, 5, 7
    Query Tool, xxxiii, 4, 243
    text display in results grid, 218
    viewing data, 9, 75, 118
    viewing tables, 45
    views, 269
pg_ctl utility, 321
pg_dump utility, 321
pg_restore utility, 322
pg_size_pretty() function, 315
pg_total_relation_size() function, 315
pipe character (|)
    as delimiter, 26, 43
    to redirect output, 311
pivot table. *See* cross tabulations
PL/pgSQL, 276, 279
    BEGIN ... END block, 280, 284
    IF ... THEN statement, 284
PL/Python, 281
point, 46
position() string function, 213

PostGIS, xxviii, 242
    creating spatial database, 242–243
    creating spatial objects, 247
    data types, 247
        geography, 247
        geometry, 247
    displaying version, 243
    functions
        ST_AsText(), 260
        ST_DFullyWithin(), 254
        ST_Distance(), 254
        ST_DWithin(), 253
        ST_GeogFromText(), 248, 254
        ST_GeometryType(), 262
        ST_GeomFromText(), 247
        ST_Intersection(), 264
        ST_Intersects(), 263
        ST_LineFromText(), 250
        ST_MakeLine(), 250
        ST_MakePoint(), 249
        ST_MakePolygon(), 250
        ST_MPolyFromText(), 250
        ST_PointFromText(), 249
        ST_PolygonFromText(), 250
    installation, 242–243
        Linux, xxxi
        macOS, xxx
        troubleshooting, xxx
        Windows, xxix–xxx
    loading extension, 243
    shapefile
        loading, 257, 258, 311
        querying, 259
    spatial joins, 262, 263
Postgres.app, xxx–xxxi, 4
PostgreSQL
    advantages of using, xxviii
    backup and restore, 321
        pg_dump, 321
        pg_restore, 322
    collation setting, 16
    command line usage, 291
    comparison operators, 18
    configuration, 313
    creating functions, 275
    default postgres database, 3
    description of, 3
    documentation, 335
    functions, 267
    GUI tools, 333
    importing from other database
        managers, 40

    installation, xxviii
        Linux, xxxi
        macOS, xxx–xxxi
        troubleshooting, xxx
        Windows, xxix–xxx
    locale setting, xxix, 16
    maintenance, 313
    news websites, 335
    postgresql.conf settings file, 319
    recovering unused space, 314
    settings, 318
    spatial data analysis, 241, 253, 254
    starting and stopping, 321
    statistics collector, 317
    table size, 314
    triggers, 267, 282
    utilities, tools, and extensions, 334
    views, 267
postgresql.conf settings file, 178, 319
    editing, 319
    reloading settings, 321
precision argument
    with numeric and decimal types, 28
primary key, 2, 12
    composite, 100–101
    definition of, 75, 97
    natural, 97, 131
    surrogate, 97, 98
        auto-incrementing, 101–102
        creating, 102
        data types for, 101
    syntax, 98–100
    uniqueness, 76
    using auto-incrementing serial
        type, 28
    using Universally Unique
        Identifier, 98
    violation, 99, 101
Prime Meridian, 46, 246
procedural language, 276
projection (map), 245
    Albers, 246
    Mercator, 245
psql command line application, 3, 292
    connecting to database, 299, 300
    displaying table info, 306
    editing queries, 303
    executing queries from a file, 309
    formatting results, 303, 304
    help commands, 300
    importing and exporting files, 307

meta-commands, 306
multiline queries, 302
paging results, 303
parentheses in queries, 302
running queries, 301
saving query output, 308
setup
Linux, 299
macOS, 296–298
Microsoft Windows, 293–295
superuser prompt, 300
Public Libraries Survey, 114
Python programming language,
xxv, 335
creating PL/Python extension, 281
in PostgreSQL function, 277, 281

Q

quantiles, 66
quartiles, 67
query
choosing order of columns, 13
definition, 1
eliminating duplicate values, 14
execution time, 109–110
exporting results of, 52
limiting number of rows
returned, 48
measuring performance with
EXPLAIN, 109
order of clauses, 21
retrieving a subset of columns, 13
selecting all rows and columns, 12
quintiles, 67
quotes, single vs. double, 8

R

rank() function, 164
ranking data, 164
by subgroup, 165–167
rank() and dense_rank() functions,
164–165
rates calculations, 167, 196
record_if_grade_changed() user
function, 284
REFERENCES keyword, 103
referential integrity, 97
cascading deletes, 104
foreign keys, 102
primary key, 99

regexp_match() function, 219
extracting text from result, 224
regexp_matches() function, 220
regexp_replace() function, 230
regexp_split_to_array() function, 230
regexp_split_to_table() function, 230
regr_intercept() function, 162
regr_r2() function, 163
regr_slope() function, 162
regular expressions, 214
capture group, 215, 221
escaping characters, 219
examples, 216
in WHERE clause, 228–229
notation, 214–216
parsing unstructured data, 216, 222
regexp_match() function, 219
regexp_matches() function, 220
regexp_replace() function, 230
regexp_split_to_array()
function, 230
regexp_split_to_table()
function, 230
with substring() function, 216
relational databases, 2, 73
join types
CROSS JOIN, 82–83
FULL OUTER JOIN, 82
JOIN (INNER JOIN), 80, 125
LEFT JOIN, 80–81
list of, 78
RIGHT JOIN, 80–81
querying, 77
relating tables, 74–77
relational model, 73, 84
reducing redundant data, 77
table relationships
many-to-many, 85
one-to-many, 84
one-to-one, 84
replace() string function, 214
reserved keywords, 95
RIGHT JOIN keywords, 80–81
right() string function, 213
ROLLBACK statement, 149
roots, square and cube, 58
round() function, 64, 160
row
counting, 117
definition, 73
deleting, 147–148

row *(continued)*
    in a CSV file, 40
    inserting, 8
    recovering unused, 314
    updating specific, 141
r (Pearson correlation coefficient), 157
r-squared, 163
R programming language, xxv

S

scalar subquery, 192
scale argument
    with `numeric` and `decimal` types, 29
scatterplot, 158, 159
search. *See* full text search
`SELECT` statement
    definition, 11
    order of clauses, 21
    syntax, 12
    with `DISTINCT` keyword, 14–15
    with `GROUP BY` clause, 120
    with `ORDER BY` clause, 15–17
    with `WHERE` clause, 17–20
selecting all rows and columns, 12
semicolon (;), 3
serial, 27, 101
server
    connecting, 4
    localhost, 4
    postgresql.conf file, 178
    setting time zone, 178
`SET` keyword
    clause in `UPDATE`, 138, 192
    `timezone`, 178
shapefile, 256
    contents of, 256–257
    loading into database, 257
    shp2pgsql command line utility, 311
    U.S. Census TIGER/Line, 258, 262
`SHOW` command
    `config_file`, 319
    `data_directory`, 321
    `timezone`, 177
shp2pgsql command line utility, 311
significance testing, 163
simple feature standard, 243
single quote ('), 8, 42
slope-intercept formula, 161
`smallint` data type, 27
`smallserial` data type, 27, 101

snake case, 10, 94, 96
sorting data, 15
    by multiple columns, 16
    dependent on locale setting, 16
    on aggregate results, 123
spatial data, 241
    area analysis, 260
    building blocks, 243
    distance analysis, 253, 254
    finding location, 261
    geographic coordinate system, 243, 245, 246
    geometries, 243
        constructing, 245, 247
        LineString, 243, 249–250
        MultiLineString, 244
        MultiPoint, 244
        MultiPolygon, 244
        Point, 243, 249
        Polygon, 243, 250
    intersection analysis, 264
    joins, 262, 263
    projected coordinate system, 245
    projection, 245
    shapefile, 256
    simple feature standard, 243
    Spatial Reference System Identifier (SRID), 244, 246
    well-known text (WKT), 244
    WGS 84 coordinate system, 246
Spatial Reference System Identifier (SRID), 244, 246
    setting with `ST_SetSRID()`, 252
SQL
    comments in code, xxvii
    history of, xxiv
    indenting code, 10
    math operators, 56
    relational model, 73
    reserved keywords, 95
    standards, xxiv
    statistical functions, 155
    style conventions, 6, 10, 36, 94
    using with external programming languages, xxv
    value of using, xxiv
square root operator (|/), 56, 58
SRID (Spatial Reference System Identifier), 244, 246
    setting with `ST_SetSRID()`, 252

statistical functions, 155
    correlation with corr(), 157–159
    dependent and independent
        variables, 158
    linear regression, 160
        regr_intercept() function, 162
        regr_r2() function, 163
        regr_slope() function, 162
    rates calculations, 167
string functions, 135, 212
    case formatting, 212
    character information, 212
    char_length(), 212
    extracting and replacing
        characters, 213
    initcap(), 212
    left(), 213
    length(), 135, 213
    lower(), 212
    position(), 213
    removing characters, 213
    replace(), 214
    right(), 213
    to_char(), 187
    trim(), 213
    upper(), 212
subquery
    correlated, 192, 199
    definition, 192
    expressions, 198
    generating column with, 197–198
    in DELETE statement, 194
    in FROM clause, 194
    IN operator expression, 198–199
    in UPDATE statement, 139, 192
    in WHERE clause, 192–194
    scalar, 192
    uncorrelated, 192
    with crosstab() function, 205
substring() function, 216
subtracting numbers, 57
    across columns, 60
sum() function, 64
    example on joined tables, 124
    grouping by column value, 125
summarizing data, 113
surrogate primary key, 98
    creating, 102

T
tab character
    as delimiter, 42–43
    as regular expression, 215
table
    add column, 137, 140
    aliases, 86, 195
    alter column, 137
    autovacuum, 316
    backup, 94
    constraints, 6
    creation, 5–7
    definition of, 1
    deleting columns, 137, 148
    deleting data, 147–149
    deleting from database, 148–149
    derived table, 194
    design best practices, 93
    dropping, 148
    holds data on one entity, 73
    indexes, 108
    inserting rows, 8–9
    key columns, 74
    modifying with ALTER statement,
        137–138
    naming, 94, 96
    querying multiple tables using
        joins, 77
    relationships, 1
    size, 314
    temporary tables, 50
    viewing data, 9
tablefunc module, 203
table relationships
    many-to-many, 85
    one-to-many, 84
    one-to-one, 84
temporary table
    declaring, 50
    removing with DROP TABLE, 51
text data types, 24–26
    char, 24
    text, 25
    varchar, 6, 24
text operations
    case formatting, 212
    concatenation, 143
    escaping characters, 219

text operations (*continued*)
    extracting and replacing
        characters, 213–214
    formatting as timestamp, 173
    formatting with functions, 212–214
    matching patterns with regular
        expressions, 214
    removing characters, 213
    sorting, 16
text files, delimited. *See* delimited
        text files
text qualifier
    ignoring delimiters with, 41
    specifying with QUOTE option in
        COPY, 43
tilde-asterisk case-insensitive matching
        operator (~*), 228
tilde case-sensitive matching
        operator (~), 228
time data types
    interval, 32, 172
    matching with regular
        expression, 215
    time, 32, 172
    timestamp, 32, 172
timestamp, 32, 172
    calculations with, 180
    creating from components,
        174–175, 225
    extracting components from,
        173–174
    finding current date and time,
        175–176
    formatting display, 187
    subtracting to find interval, 187
    timestamptz shorthand, 172
    with time zone, 32, 172
    within transactions, 176
time zones
    AT TIME ZONE keywords, 179
    automatic conversion of, 173, 175
    finding server setting, 177–178
    including in timestamp, 32,
        173, 226
    setting, 178–180
    setting server default, 320
    standard name database, 33
    viewing names of, 177
    working with, 177
to_char() function, 187
to_tsquery() function, 232
to_tsvector() function, 231

transaction blocks, 149–151
    COMMIT, 149
    definition, 149
    ROLLBACK, 149
    START TRANSACTION, 149
    visibility to other users, 151
transactions, 149
    with time functions, 176
triggers, 267, 282
    BEFORE INSERT statement, 288
    CREATE TRIGGER statement, 285
    FOR EACH ROW statement, 285
    FOR EACH STATEMENT statement, 285
    NEW and OLD variables, 284
    RETURN statement, 285
    testing, 285, 288
trim_county() user function, 281
trim() function, 213
true (Boolean value), 74
ts_headline() function, 235
tsquery data type, 232
ts_rank_cd() function, 237
ts_rank() function, 237
tsvector data type, 231

U

uncorrelated subquery, 192
underscore wildcard for pattern
        matching (_), 19
UNIQUE constraint, 76, 105–106
Universally Unique Identifier (UUID),
        35, 98
unnest() function, 68
unstructured data, 211
    parsing with regular expressions,
        216, 222
UPDATE statement
    definition, 138
    PostgreSQL syntax, 139
    SET clause, 138
    using across tables, 138, 145, 192
    with CASE statement, 226
update_personal_days() user
        function, 279
upper() function, 212
USA TODAY, xxiii
U.S. Census
    2010 Decennial Census data, 43
        calculating population
            change, 89
        county shapefile analysis, 259

description of columns, 45–47
finding total population, 64
importing data, 43–44
racial categories, 60
short form, 60
2011–2015 American Community
    Survey
    description of columns, 156
    estimates and margin of
        error, 157
    importing data, 156
apportionment of U.S. House of
    Representatives, 44
methodologies compared, 157, 328
U.S. Department of Agriculture, 130
    farmers' market data, 250
U.S. Federal Bureau of Investigation
    (FBI) crime report
    data, 167
UTC (Coordinated Universal Time),
    33, 174
    UTC offset, 33, 179, 187
UTF-8, 16
UUID (Universally Unique Identifier),
    35, 98

V

VACUUM command, 314
    ANALYZE option, 317
    autovacuum process, 316
    editing server setting, 319
    FULL option, 318
    monitoring table size, 314
    pg_stat_all_tables view, 317
    running manually, 318
    time of last vacuum, 317
    VERBOSE option, 318
VALUES clause with INSERT, 8
varchar data type, 6, 24
views, 267
    advantage of using, 268
    creating, 269–271
    deleting data with, 275
    dropping, 269
    inserting data with, 273–274
    inserting, updating, deleting
        data, 271
    LOCAL CHECK OPTION, 272, 273

materialized, 268
pg_stat_all_tables, 317
queries in, 269
retrieving specific columns, 271
updating data with, 274

W

well-known text (WKT), 244
    extended, 248
    order of coordinates, 245
WHEN clause, 208
    in CASE statement, 227
WHERE clause, 17
    in UPDATE statement, 138
    filtering rows with, 17–19
    with DELETE FROM statement, 147
    with EXISTS clause, 139, 192
    with ILIKE operator, 19–20
    with IS NULL keywords, 133
    with LIKE operator, 19–20, 143
    with regular expressions, 228
whole numbers, 27
wildcard
    asterisk (*) in SELECT statement, 12
    percent sign (%), 19
    underscore (_), 19
window functions
    definition of, 164
    OVER clause, 164
    PARTITION BY clause, 165
WITH
    as Common Table Expression, 200
    options with COPY, 42
WKT (well-known text), 244
    extended, 248
    order of coordinates, 245
working tables, 148

X

XML, 35

Z

ZIP Codes, 135
    loss of leading zeros, 135
    repairing botched, 143

Practical SQL is set in New Baskerville, Futura, Dogma, and TheSansMono Condensed. This book was printed and bound at Sheridan Books, Inc. in Chelsea, Michigan. The paper is 60# Finch Offset, which is certified by the Forest Stewardship Council (FSC).

The book uses a layflat binding, in which the pages are bound together with a cold-set, flexible glue and the first and last pages of the resulting book block are attached to the cover. The cover is not actually glued to the book's spine, and when open, the book lies flat and the spine doesn't crack.

RESOURCES

Visit *https://www.nostarch.com/practicalSQL/* for resources, errata, and more information.

More no-nonsense books from **NO STARCH PRESS**

THE BOOK OF R
A First Course in Programming and Statistics

by TILMAN M. DAVIES
JULY 2016, 832 PP., $49.95
ISBN 978-1-59327-651-5
color insert

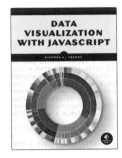

DATA VISUALIZATION WITH JAVASCRIPT

by STEPHEN A. THOMAS
MARCH 2015, 384 PP., $39.95
ISBN 978-1-59327-605-8
full color

PYTHON CRASH COURSE
A Hands-On, Project-Based Introduction to Programming

by ERIC MATTHES
NOVEMBER 2015, 560 PP., $39.95
ISBN 978-1-59327-603-4

STATISTICS DONE WRONG
The Woefully Complete Guide

by ALEX REINHART
MARCH 2015, 176 PP., $24.95
ISBN 978-1-59327-620-1

THE MANGA GUIDE TO DATABASES

by MANA TAKAHASHI, SHOKO AZUMA, *and* TREND-PRO CO., LTD
JANUARY 2009, 224 PP., $19.95
ISBN 978-1-59327-190-9

DOING MATH WITH PYTHON
Use Programming to Explore Algebra, Statistics, Calculus, and More!

by AMIT SAHA
AUGUST 2015, 264 PP., $29.95
ISBN 978-1-59327-640-9

PHONE:
1.800.420.7240 OR
1.415.863.9900

EMAIL:
SALES@NOSTARCH.COM

WEB:
WWW.NOSTARCH.COM

The Electronic Frontier Foundation (EFF) is the leading organization defending civil liberties in the digital world. We defend free speech on the Internet, fight illegal surveillance, promote the rights of innovators to develop new digital technologies, and work to ensure that the rights and freedoms we enjoy are enhanced — rather than eroded — as our use of technology grows.

EFF.ORG

ELECTRONIC FRONTIER FOUNDATION

Protecting Rights and Promoting Freedom on the Electronic Frontier